Evoking Story for Transformation

Evoking Story for Transformation

New Testament Quotation at the Reader-Author Intersection

LYN NIXON

Foreword by Jeannine K. Brown

◆PICKWICK Publications · Eugene, Oregon

EVOKING STORY FOR TRANSFORMATION
New Testament Quotation at the Reader-Author Intersection

Copyright © 2025 Lyn Nixon. All rights reserved. Except for brief quotations in critical publications or reviews, no part of this book may be reproduced in any manner without prior written permission from the publisher. Write: Permissions, Wipf and Stock Publishers, 199 W. 8th Ave., Suite 3, Eugene, OR 97401.

Pickwick Publications
An Imprint of Wipf and Stock Publishers
199 W. 8th Ave., Suite 3
Eugene, OR 97401

www.wipfandstock.com

PAPERBACK ISBN: 979-8-3852-3792-0
HARDCOVER ISBN: 979-8-3852-3793-7
EBOOK ISBN: 979-8-3852-3794-4

Cataloguing-in-Publication data:

Names: Nixon, Lyn, author. | Brown, Jeannine K., 1961–, foreword.

Title: Evoking story for transformation : New Testament quotation at the reader-author intersection / Lyn Nixon ; foreword by Jeannine K. Brown.

Description: Eugene, OR: Pickwick Publications, 2025. | Includes bibliographical references.

Identifiers: ISBN 979-8-3852-3792-0 (paperback). | ISBN 979-8-3852-3793-7 (hardcover). | ISBN 979-8-3852-3794-4 (ebook).

Subjects: LCSH: Bible.—New Testament—Relation to the Old Testament. | Bible.—Old Testament—Quotations in the New Testament. | Bible.—Reader response criticism. | Bible.—Hermeneutics. | Speech acts (Linguistics).

Classification: BS2387 N59 2025 (print). | BS2387 (ebook)

08/20/25

For Carver,
without whose support and encouragement this study might not have been attempted much less completed.

Contents

Permissions | xi
Foreword by Jeannine K. Brown | xiii
Preface | xvii
Acknowledgments | xix
List of Abbreviations | xxi

1 Introduction | 1

PART I | DEVELOPING A METHODOLOGY

2 Quotation | 11
   Quotation and Intertextuality | 11
   The Production of Meaning | 14
   The Function of Quotation | 15
   Linguistic Theories of Quotation | 18
   Literary Theories of Quotation | 22
   Conclusion | 34

3 Context and the Author/Reader Relationship | 35
   Empirical and Implied Author and Reader | 35
   Context | 41
   Mutual Context and Cooperative Communication | 46
   The Activation of Mutual Context by Quotation | 50
   Echoes of Scripture in the Letters of Paul by Richard B. Hays | 54

4 Tradition, Story, Lifeworld, and Theology | 60
   Tradition and Story | 60
   Four Works on "Tradition" | 61

Story and Lifeworld/Worldview | 75
"Story" | 78
Lifeworld/Worldview, Story, and Theology | 80
Evoking Story by Quotation | 82
Transformation | 83
Transformation and Power | 86

5 Communicative Interaction and Reader Roles | 88
The Communication of Meaning | 89
Speech Acts | 92
Speech Act Complexes | 123

PART II | CASE STUDIES

6 Introduction to the Case Studies | 129
The Organization of the Case Studies | 129
The Psalms within the Jewish Lifeworld | 131
The Psalms in the Praxis of the First-Century People of Yahweh | 133

7 Ps 115:1a LXX as Quoted in 2 Cor 4:13 | 138
Ps 115 LXX [116:10–19 MT] | 140
The Contribution of Ps 115:1–3 LXX to Story, Lifeworld, and Theology | 148
Intervening Interpretation | 148
The Quotation of Ps 115:1a LXX in 2 Cor 4:13 | 149
Conclusion | 167

8 Ps 110:1 as Quoted by Various NT Authors | 168
Ps 110 [109 LXX] | 169
A Summary of the Contribution of Ps 110:1 to Story, Lifeworld, and Theology | 184
Post-Exilic Interpretation of Ps 110 | 184
Messianic Expectations in the First Century | 186
Ps 110:1 as Quoted by Jesus and Reported in the Synoptic Gospels | 192
The "Son of Man" Seated at the Right Hand of God | 204
Ps 110:1 as Quoted by Peter and Reported in Acts 2:34–35 | 210
Ps 110:1 as Quoted in 1 Cor 15:25 | 221

Ps 110:1 as Quoted in Heb 1:13 | 226
Conclusion | 234

9   Conclusion | 236
    The Development and Use of This Methodology | 236
    Looking Ahead | 238

Appendix: The Speech Act Complexes of Pss 115:1–3 and 109:1 LXX and Their Quoting NT Texts | 241
Bibliography | 247

Permissions

All Scripture quotations, unless otherwise indicated, are from New Revised Standard Version Bible, copyright © 1989 National Council of the Churches of Christ in the United States of America. Used by permission. All rights reserved worldwide.

Scripture quotations marked (NIV) are taken from the Holy Bible, New International Version®, NIV®. Copyright © 1973, 1978, 1984, 2011 by Biblica, Inc.™ Used by permission of Zondervan. All rights reserved worldwide. www.zondervan.com. The "NIV" and "New International Version" are trademarks registered in the United States Patent and Trademark Office by Biblica, Inc.™

Quotations marked (NETS) are taken from *A New English Translation of the Septuagint* ©2000 by the International Organization for Septuagint and Cognate Studies, Inc. Used by permission of Oxford University Press. All rights reserved.

Scripture quotations marked (NASB) are taken from the (NASB®) New American Standard Bible®. Copyright © 1960, 1971, 1977, 1995 by The Lockman Foundation. Used by permission. All rights reserved. lockman.org.

All quotations of the text of the Hebrew Scriptures are from *BHS*[5]. All quotations of the Greek text of the New Testament are from NA[27].

Foreword

THE MORE I READ the New Testament, the more I am persuaded that the Jewish Scriptures used within it are integral to its messages, woven deeply into its fabric and not just accessorizing it. This is why I am pleased and honored to introduce Lyn Nixon's work in this timely and thoughtful book.

I have had the pleasure of knowing Lyn for over twenty years. We met when she was a student at Bethel Seminary where I teach. Lyn was one of those students that you know from early on are going to do exceptional work, and she has.

She was in one of the first cohorts for our Greek program taught in hybrid format, and she excelled at the Greek language even while most of her learning happened remotely. Since our online Greek program from its inception has used student coaches, and since Lyn had great pastoral impulses as well good Greek facility, she served as a Greek coach after graduation. Lyn then moved into teaching Greek and other courses at Bethel Seminary. She did all this while earning her PhD through London School of Theology. More recently, she developed our fully online Greek program, and students have loved her approach and the support she provides throughout their learning.

Picking up and reading *Evoking Story for Transformation* is to dive into the deep waters of intertextuality, hermeneutical theory, and literary analysis, with a learned guide to illuminate the path all along the way. Applying a wide-angle lens to her project, Lyn offers a carefully developed theoretical offering and then shows what difference it makes for interpretive practice. Her insights draw from literary theory, and specifically speech-act theory, to show how a communicative model helps us to understand better the use of the Old Testament in the New. Lyn offers an expansive view of meaning, without losing either side of the balance between authors and readers in contextual relationship.

Analysis of intertextuality—how the New Testament authors use the Jewish Scriptures or Old Testament—is a thriving subdiscipline of New Testament studies. Consider the seminal work of Richard Hays (*Echoes of Scripture in the Letters of Paul*, 1989, and *Echoes of Scripture in the Gospels*, 2016);[1] the continuing T. & T. Clark series begun by Steve Moyise and Maarten Menken (e. g., *The Psalms in the New Testament*, 2004, *Isaiah in the New Testament*, 2005; *Exodus in the New Testament*, 2023 [ed. Seth Ehorn]);[2] and helpful methodological insights from an array of scholars, gathered together by Steve Moyise, B. J. Oropeza, and Max Lee (*Exploring Intertextuality*, 2016; *Practicing Intertextuality*, 2021).[3] Many more scholars and volumes could be added to the list.

Lyn's work in the present book contributes to this conversation. She continues an ongoing interest in storied ways of conceiving how New Testament authors use Old Testament texts, a trend in recent intertextual work begun already with Hays.[4] Lyn follows the promising path that even non-narrative texts are immersed in stories and that the traditions that follow OT texts through time are also storied expressions. New Testament writers use, adapt, and subvert known stories to impact the worldview (the stories) of their audiences.

Lyn offers something new to conversations on intertextuality. Little work has been done using speech-act theory as a foundation for understanding the communicative facets of a biblical author's use of a precursor text. Lyn fills this gap by introducing readers to the important contributions of speech-act theory and brings together Old and New Testament authors in dialogical fashion. A New Testament author who cites an Old Testament text can read it with or without recourse to its context and original purposes. Lyn argues that, in many cases, New Testament authors do follow the original context and purposes of Old Testament texts. Yet she helpfully acknowledges that this attentiveness to the original setting does not necessitate static usage. Instead, using speech-act categories, she suggests that a New Testament writer can retain the Old Testament locution but modify

---

1. R. B. Hays, *Echoes of Scripture in the Letters of Paul*; and R. B. Hays, *Echoes of Scripture in the Gospels*.

2. I have had the privilege of contributing to two of these volumes: see J. K. Brown, "Genesis in Matthew's Gospel"; and J. K. Brown, "Exodus in Matthew's Gospel."

3. Oropeza and Moyise, eds., *Exploring Intertextuality*; Lee and Oropeza, eds., *Practicing Intertextuality*.

4. See also my essay—J. K. Brown, "Metalepsis."

its illocutionary force to fit the new context. In other words, what the Old Testament language *accomplishes* can be shifted to fit the new context.

For example, while in Ps 110:1a, the psalmist envisions Yahweh *commanding* a human actor (David?) to sit at Yahweh's right hand, in New Testament uses of this psalm the command or directive (its original illocution) becomes an assertion (assertive) of what God has already accomplished on Jesus's behalf (e. g., Acts 2:34–36). The original command moves to an affirmation of what has happened in the Messiah.

Lyn also highlights that the end game for biblical authors—in both Old and New Testaments—is transformation. She draws on the speech-act category of perlocutionary effects to highlight that when viewed holistically, the meaning of a text includes *intention for transformation*.[5] She then applies this to the ways New Testament authors use Old Testament citations, not only to affirm existing understandings or provide new ones for their audiences, but also to encourage transformative ways of engaging faith and living it out.

Evoking Story for Transformation offers a wonderful balance between theory and practice. Whether we recognize it or not, each of us brings some interpretive theory to the question of how New Testament authors draw on the Old Testament. This book will help its readers gain greater clarity on their own theoretical assumptions and potentially refine them in the process. But Lyn doesn't leave her readers with only theoretical possibilities and potentials. Lyn's analysis of Ps 110:1 and its use across the New Testament is a stimulating application of her theoretical proposal. In this analysis and in her study of Ps 115:1 LXX in 2 Cor 4:13, she offers fresh insights for curious readers of the New Testament who want to learn more about how its authors interpret the Jewish Scriptures.

JEANNINE K. BROWN
Bethel Seminary, Saint Paul, MN
March 10, 2025

---

5. See my similar affirmation for "perlocutionary intention" in J. K. Brown, *Scripture as Communication*, 2nd ed., 101–5.

Preface

THE IMPETUS FOR THIS study[1] was the strong sense that God was calling me to join in the task of opening the Scriptures to others (Luke 24:32) along with the firm conviction that what we call the "Old" Testament and what we call the "New" Testament are actually parts of one Story of God. So it seemed important to me to explore the claim that the NT authors quoted the OT "out of context" or without regard to the original OT meaning.

It soon became apparent that in order to study this issue in depth, it would be necessary to explore and clarify a number of key concepts, including what quotations do, how authors and readers[2] interact generally, and what is meant by "context," "tradition," "theology," "meaning," and "transformation."

Exploring these concepts led me to create an "action model" of meaning based in Speech Act Theory, and relying, in particular, on the speech-act element of perlocution. A perlocutionary act is an act of a speaker/author that correlates to an intended perlocutionary effect, that is, an intended response of belief and/or action by the hearer/reader. Thus, in my action model, "meaning" includes an intention for transformation, which can be either realignment or subversion/re-creation, and the author and the reader must interact cooperatively in order to successfully communicate that meaning.

Using this model allowed me to determine what was happening at the reader-author "intersection" of specific NT quotations. In the case studies, I first analyzed the quoted OT text in its context to determine what transformation of the implied reader's belief or behavior (the intended

---

1. This book is a slightly revised version of the doctoral dissertation I completed in 2015 at the London School of Theology.

2. Speech Act Theory as it was originally construed concerns speakers and hearers. We demonstrate its applicability to authors and readers in chapter 5.

PREFACE

perlocutionary effect) was intended by the implied OT author.³ And then I analyzed the NT text that quoted that OT text to determine if the intended transformation of the NT audience's belief or behavior indicates that the NT author experienced that intended transformation. In other words, employing the action model to study both the quoted OT text and the quoting NT text allows me to determine whether and, if so, how earlier meaning resonates in the new context.

For my case studies, I chose two examples of NT quotation that scholars have claimed are instances where the NT author quotes the OT in a way that does not correspond to the original meaning of the OT text in its context. These are the quotation of Ps 115:1a LXX in 2 Cor 4:13 and the quotation of Ps 110:1 by various speakers and authors across the NT. In these case studies, I demonstrate that my thesis does hold: in these instances, *NT quotation of the OT promotes transformation on the lifeworld/worldview level by evoking theological tradition.*

Completing this study has allowed me to be a part of "opening the Scriptures to others." I've had the privilege of teaching courses in New Testament, including New Testament Greek, and Hermeneutics at a number of seminaries and graduate schools. I have used the material presented in chapter 7 (the first case study on 2 Cor 4:13) in a variety of courses. The opportunity to offer a course on the New Testament Use of the Old Testament in 2024 enabled me to use some of the theoretical material as well. That helped to convince me that making this study more broadly available might be a way to contribute to the conversation on biblical intertextuality—a conversation that has enriched me both academically and personally.

LYN NIXON
March 2025

---

3. In cases of quotations that include reported speech (in either the quoted or quoting text), this analysis is multi-layered to include the speaker and hearer of the original speech act.

Acknowledgments

"The Lord is my helper" (Heb 13:6 NIV, quoting Ps 118:7). God's whisper that the notion of "opening the Scriptures" to others (Luke 24:32) applied to me started me on this journey. For this and in all things, I give God thanks and praise.

Many, many people have been the eyes and hands and voices of Jesus as I have been engaged with this study. Some of those to whom I owe a debt of gratitude include:

My dissertation supervisor, Thorsten Moritz, whose probing comments and thoughtful reviews often led me to sharpen my thinking and to discover valuable synergies between concepts and theories from various fields of study.

My fellow-travelers in the dissertation process, especially Holly Beers and Justin Winzenburg, who read drafts, made comments, and were persistent in encouraging me to publish this work.

My examiners, Max Turner and Steve Moyise, my professors at Bethel Seminary, the faculty of the London School of Theology, and many others in the academic community, who read and commented on parts or all of the study, allowed me to read and quote from their unpublished works, wrote recommendations, conducted interviews and examinations, and generally provided support and encouragement. A special thanks to Jeannine Brown for writing the Foreword to this volume.

The editors and staff at Wipf & Stock, who offered me the opportunity to publish this study and have patiently and promptly answered my many questions.

You all have been a part of making this possible, and I thank you!

List of Abbreviations

A	an action
AB	Anchor Bible
BCOTWP	Baker Commentary on the Old Testament Wisdom and Psalms
BDAG	Walter Bauer, Frederick W. Danker, W. F. Arndt, and F. W. Gingrich. *Greek-English Lexicon of the New Testament and Other Early Christian Literature.* 3rd ed. Chicago: University of Chicago Press, 2000
BDB	Francis Brown, S. R. Driver, and Charles A. Briggs. *Hebrew and English Lexicon of the Old Testament.* Oxford: Clarendon, 1907
BETL	Bibliotheca Ephemeridum Theologicarum Lovaniensium
BHS[5]	*Biblia Hebraica Stuttgartensia.* 5th ed.
Bib	*Biblica*
BibInt	*Biblical Interpretation*
BibInt	Biblical Interpretation Series
BSac	*Bibliotheca Sacra*
BSL	Biblical Studies Library
CBQ	*Catholic Biblical Quarterly*
CRINT	Compendia Rerum Iudicarum ad Novum Testamentum
DJD	Discoveries in the Judaean Desert
DTIB	*Dictionary for Theological Interpretation of the Bible.* Edited by Kevin J. Vanhoozer. Grand Rapids: Baker Academic, 2005

LIST OF ABBREVIATIONS

ECL	Early Christianity and Its Literature
FIOTL	Formation and Interpretation of Old Testament Literature
GNTE	Guides to New Testament Exegesis
H	the hearer
ISBL	Indiana Studies in Biblical Literature
ISPR	Indiana Series in the Philosophy of Religion
JAAR	*Journal of the American Academy of Religion*
JBL	*Journal of Biblical Literature*
JETS	*Journal of the Evangelical Theological Society*
JPrag	*Journal of Pragmatics*
JSNT	*Journal for the Study of the New Testament*
JSNTSup	Journal for the Study of the New Testament Supplement Series
JSOTSup	Journal for the Study of the Old Testament Supplement Series
LXX	For the Psalms: Alfred Rahlfs, ed., *Psalmi cum Odis*, 3rd ed., Septuaginta: Vetus Testamentum Graecum 10. Göttingen: Vandenhoeck and Ruprecht, 1979
	For all other Old Testament books: Alfred Rahlfs and Robert Hanhart, eds. *Septuaginta*, rev. ed. Stuttgart: Deutsche Bibelgesellschaft, 2006. Also referred to as the Rahlfs-Hanhart LXX
LLL	Longman Linguistics Library
LNTS	Library of New Testament Studies
ModTh	*Modern Theology*
MT	Masoretic Text (of the Hebrew Bible)
NA[27]	*Novum Testamentum Graece*. Nestle-Aland, 27th rev. ed.
NAC	New American Commentary
NETS	*A New English Translation of the Septuagint*. Edited by Albert Pietersma and Benjamin G. Wright. New York: Oxford University Press, 2000
NICNT	New International Commentary on the New Testament

NIGTC	New International Greek Testament Commentary
NLH	*New Literary History: A Journal of Theory and Interpretation*
NovT	*Novum Testamentum*
NovTSup	Supplements to Novum Testamentum
NT	New Testament
NTS	*New Testament Studies*
NTSI	New Testament and the Scriptures of Israel
OT	Old Testament/Hebrew Bible
P	a proposition (is true)
PiL	*Papers in Linguistics*
PT	*Poetics Today*
QJS	*Quarterly Journal of Speech*
RB	*Revue biblique*
S	the speaker
SBLDS	Society of Biblical Literature Dissertation Series
SBLMS	Society of Biblical Literature Monograph Series
SBLSymS	Society of Biblical Literature Symposium Series
SJT	*Scottish Journal of Theology*
SNTSMS	Society for New Testament Studies Monograph Series
SP	Sacra Pagina
SSEJC	Studies in Scripture in Early Judaism and Christianity
TDNT	*Theological Dictionary of the New Testament.* 10 vols. Edited by Gerhard Kittel and Gerhard Friedrich. Translated by Geoffrey W. Bromiley. Grand Rapids: Eerdmans, 1964–76
TNTC	Tyndale New Testament Commentaries
VE	*Verbum et Ecclesia*
VTSup	Supplements to Vetus Testamentum
WBC	Word Biblical Commentary
WUNT	Wissenschaftliche Untersuchungen zum Neuen Testament

1

Introduction

THAT THE JEWISH SCRIPTURES (OT[1]) and the New Testament (NT) are related is evidenced by the frequency with which references, and in particular quotations, from the former are found in the latter. The nature of this relationship has been much discussed. Richard Hays groups the questions that have been asked about the use of the OT into five categories, among which are: which books and passages are quoted by NT authors and what form of the text was used, how NT exegesis relates to that of rabbinic Judaism (midrash or pesher) or to early Christian exegetical traditions, and whether the NT authors "use the Old Testament with exegetical-theological integrity, or . . . rifle it for prooftexts and twist its meaning."[2] Although Hays suggested over twenty years ago that these questions, at least with regard to Paul, "have been either answered in full or played out to a dead end,"[3] the issue of whether the NT authors quote the OT with "exegetical-theological integrity" does still continue to be the subject of fruitful debate, re-fueled in part by Hays's own literary intertextual approach.

In this regard, interesting questions concerning quotation include: the function of a particular quotation; whether the main function of quotation

---

1. Our use of this term is not intended to imply anything about the canonical status of the Jewish/Hebrew Scriptures at the time of the NT writings.

2. See R. B. Hays, *Echoes of Scripture*, 9–10; quote is from p. 9. He explores Paul's work, but his conclusions are valid for all NT authors. From a somewhat different perspective, Bock identifies four different approaches taken by evangelical scholars to the use of the OT in the NT (Bock, "Evangelicals and the Use of the Old Testament," 207–17).

3. R. B. Hays, *Echoes of Scripture*, 9.

is to offer proof via an appeal to authority; and what role is played by the context, co-text, and original meaning of a source (quoted) text in a receptor (quoting) text. In some cases, discussions of these questions are based on the premise or come to the conclusion that the quoting author uses the quoted material without regard for its original meaning.[4]

Given that a quoting author is first a reader of a text, an issue which underlies these questions is whether the author, reader, or text is the locus of "meaning." Some discussions assume adversarial or "power" relationships between the quoted author/text, the quoting author/text, and the audience of the quoting author/text.[5]

Our presupposition instead is that communication, including quotation, tends to be cooperative or dialogical.[6] Therefore, we find it profitable to consider quotation from a fresh perspective. Our thesis is that, in many cases, *NT quotation of the OT promotes transformation on the lifeworld/ worldview level by evoking theological tradition.*

In each of the next four chapters, we develop various aspects of this hypothesis and, in the process, create a new methodology to explore quotation. In chapter 2, we explore intertextuality, and more specifically explicit quotation, from a functional perspective, i.e., what does quotation do? After analyzing pertinent linguistic and literary theories of quotation, we conclude that quotation does not serve primarily as a proof via an appeal to authority or to establish the primacy of the quoter in a power relationship. Rather, a key function of quotation is to evoke Story[7] and, specifically, theological tradition. Our discussion of quotation thus raises the issues of theological tradition, the relationship between the old and new contexts of the quotation, and the interaction between author and reader.

At the beginning of chapter 3, we take up the latter topic, using the construct of the implied author and reader to frame the communicative efforts of the empirical author and reader.[8] This construct makes it possible to determine authorial intention, as revealed by the implied author, without

---

4. The original impetus for this study was Hooker's comment concerning the use of the OT by NT authors: "Often one is left exclaiming: whatever the passage from the Old Testament originally meant, it certainly was not this!" (Hooker, "Beyond the Things that are Written," 295).

5. We explore some of these in chapter 2.

6. For this, we rely on Gadamer, Stuhlmacher, R. B. Hays, N. T. Wright, Snodgrass, Thiselton, and others.

7. We capitalize "Story" to indicate it is not limited to narrative genre.

8. Key resources here are Booth, Chatman, Walhout, Lanser, and Wolterstorff.

requiring retrieval of the motivation of the empirical author. Identifying the implied reader makes it possible to determine intended reader response. Thus, determining what would be fully successful communication is independent of knowing how any empirical reader actually responds.

We then lay the groundwork for our development of the concept of Story by examining "context," first outlining the various types of context (socio-historical and literary context plus linguistic conventions) and then presenting "mutual context" as the subset of context shared by author and reader. Quotation activates (and perhaps first creates) mutual context. Because of the foundational nature of Hays's work, we conclude chapter 3 by interacting with the arguments he makes concerning intertextuality and context in *Echoes of Scripture in the Letters of Paul*.

We develop the concept of theological tradition in chapter 4. After first defining "tradition," we critique works by four ground-breaking scholars who, building to some extent on Hays's work, have explored how a specific NT author makes use of OT tradition.[9] After exploring narrative genre (i.e., "story"), we demonstrate that non-narrative material such as the OT Psalms has the capacity to make a substantial contribution to the tradition mediated by texts. To recognize the contribution of non-narrative material, we call this textual tradition "Story" rather than "story."

A key next step is to develop the relationship of Story to lifeworld/worldview and theology. A lifeworld is the world in which a communicative community shares mutual context, including worldview. "Worldview" encompasses four interrelated elements: Story, symbols, praxis, and the basic questions and answers of human existence.[10] The basic questions and answers deal with the existence and nature of a divine being and the relationship of that deity to humanity; taken together the basic questions and answers comprise "theology." Theology not only asks questions about God and humanity's relationship to God, it answers them with Story. Since, by our definition, those who share a lifeworld share a worldview (and vice versa), lifeworld is created, sustained, and modified by Story and the corresponding theology.

With most of the "pieces" of our model in place, we conclude chapter 4 by integrating those already developed. In the case of NT quotation of the OT, the mutual context activated by the quotation of an element of Story presents theology. Therefore, in our model, quotation stands at the

---

9. These scholars are Keesmaat, R. E. Watts, Pao, and J. R. Wagner.
10. See N. T. Wright, *New Testament and People of God*, 38.

lifeworld intersection of Story and theology. The evoking of an element of Story via quotation has the potential to transform (realign or subvert/re-create) Story, lifeworld/worldview, and the corresponding theology.

To determine *what* transformation is intended and *how* transformation is accomplished, in chapter 5 we create an "action model" of the communication of meaning based on pragmatics, specifically Speech Act Theory.[11] In our action model, we include both the illocutionary and the perlocutionary acts of the implied author as well as those perlocutionary effects (responses) of the implied reader associated with the illocution. In broad categories, these associated perlocutionary responses are either of belief or action. Transformation occurs when communicative interaction is fully successful on both the illocutionary and perlocutionary levels.[12]

By taking the innovative step of including perlocution in the communication of meaning, we are able to creatively distinguish three roles for an empirical reader: (i) the locutionary[13] role of "Independent," (ii) the illocutionary role of "Analyst," and (iii) the perlocutionary role of "Envisager."[14] In brief, an Independent reader creates new meaning using the words or phrases of the locution without regard for the original illocutionary and perlocutionary acts. An Analyst is a cooperative reader who achieves the illocutionary response of understanding (which is the sole illocutionary effect) but is either unwilling or unable to respond with an associated perlocutionary effect. An Envisager not only understands the illocutionary act of the implied author but also responds with an associated perlocutionary effect.[15] It is the Envisaging reader who steps fully into the role of the implied reader.

---

11. Our model has its roots in Vanhoozer's "action model of meaning" (see Vanhoozer, *Is There a Meaning?*, 369–78).

12. Many pragmaticists call perlocution "interaction" rather than "communication." For this reason, we use "communicative interaction" to indicate that illocution and perlocution both play a role.

13. We use the term "locution" to refer to Searle's predicating and referring acts, taken together, rather than to Austin's locutionary act.

14. Since the construct of implied author/reader does not apply to a speech situation, in the case of NT speakers (e.g., Jesus or Peter), we name "Envisaging" those hearers who respond as an implied reader would to the illocutionary and perlocutionary acts of the speaker.

15. The distinction between "Analyst" and "Envisager" is not the same as Steiner's distinction between "critic" and "reader." For Steiner, "criticism labors to transcend relation," and a "critic" is "a 'counterstater' and rival to the work" (Steiner, "'Critic'/'Reader,'" 437). A "reader," on the other hand, "attempts to negate the space between the text and himself. . . . The reader strives for fusion with the text via internalization" (Steiner, 443).

Thus, incorporating the often overlooked and sometimes unhelpfully defined speech-act element of perlocution into our model and hierarchy of reader roles is critical. The intended perlocutionary response of the implied reader, as it corresponds to the perlocutionary intention of the implied author, signals the implied author's transformative intention for Story, theology, and lifeworld/worldview. Therefore, the perlocutionary response of the implied reader sets the standard for the response of the empirical reader. It is by responding at the perlocutionary level (Envisaging) that an empirical reader moves beyond understanding to transformation.[16] In responding with the perlocutionary effect associated with the perlocutionary intention of the implied author, the Envisaging reader "completes the circuit" required for successfully transformative communicative interaction.

Throughout chapter 5, we link our action model to quotation by recognizing that a quoting speaker/author is always first a hearer/reader of the quoted speech or text and/or an intervening interpretive tradition and thus has assumed one of the reader roles vis-à-vis that text and/or interpretive tradition. A NT author may not always read the OT or an intervening interpretation as an Envisager. However, via quotation an implied NT author calls for a response of belief or action intended to transform the current Story and related theological lifeworld/worldview of the NT audience. We not only can assess what transformation is intended but also can evaluate whether a NT author read a passage of the OT as an Envisager by determining whether the theological Story-lines of that passage are evoked via the quotation.

To close chapter 5, we put our action model into our Story/lifeworld framework by defining related groups of speech acts as "speech act complexes." The illocutionary act type of the core speech act of the speech act complex can be considered the illocutionary act type of that speech act complex. Other speech acts in the speech act complex, which may be of different illocutionary act types, play a supporting role. Identifying not only the illocutionary act type of the various speech acts of a speech act complex but also the illocutionary act type of the speech act complex allows us to use Speech Act Theory, originally constructed at the sentence level, at the discourse level of our Story/lifeworld framework.

Our "Analyst" and "Envisager" are different levels of Steiner's "reader."

16   Although illocutionary acts do alter the mutual context of the empirical author and reader, our primary interest is the transformation of belief and/or action that is the *perlocutionary* response associated with the illocution.

The final step in constructing a methodology is its use. Rather than applying our action model to one NT book or the work of one author, we take our examples from a common OT source text, the Psalms. Studying quotations from texts outside the narrative genre allows us to draw stronger conclusions concerning how quotation evokes Story and especially theological tradition to call for reader transformation.

Examples of NT Psalms quotations are used in the first part of this study as illustrations. In the second part, we present two case studies. We introduce these in chapter 6, where we evaluate what role the Psalms generally may have played in the lifeworld and Story of the people of Yahweh and how familiar various groups within the early Church may have been with the Psalms.

In that chapter, we also consolidate our methodological development by summarizing the steps we take in performing our case studies. Our first step is to evaluate the source text of the quotation to determine what the quoted passage, as set within its co-text, contributes to Story, theology, worldview, and lifeworld via the illocution and perlocution of its speech acts as they are addressed to the implied reader by the implied author. We also consider what can be surmised or is implied concerning the socio-historical context as well as what interpretations of that passage may have been current in the middle of the first century CE. We then determine what it would mean to be an Envisaging reader of the quoted text or an intervening interpretation.

Turning to the NT, we consider the passage containing the Psalm quotation, determining its illocutionary and perlocutionary intentions and the associated perlocutionary response of belief or action which would be made by the implied reader and therefore, by definition, the Envisaging empirical reader. We then consider what elements of the theological OT Story-line are evoked by the quotation. Putting this together, we determine (i) what role the quotation plays in the intended transformation of the existing Story, theology, and lifeworld/worldview of the empirical NT audience and (ii) whether the NT author read the OT text (or interpretation) as an Envisager.

Our first case study (chapter 7) is the quotation of Ps 115:1a LXX in 2 Cor 4:13. Recent criticism argues that the sense in which Paul uses this verse "is so far removed from the original context as to raise questions about Paul's reliability as an interpreter."[17] In other words, using our terminology,

---

17. Stanley, *Arguing with Scripture*, 100. In chapter 7, we explore other scholarship which makes similar claims.

the argument is that Paul does not read the quoted passage as an Envisager. Other scholars believe Paul reads the psalm messianically.[18] In our first case study, we use our methodology to investigate the validity of these various claims. We determine that the called-for transformation is consistent with Paul reading Ps 115:1a LXX as an Envisager.

The second case study is the quotation of Ps 110:1 in the Synoptic Gospels, Acts, 1 Corinthians, and Hebrews. Choosing this OT passage allows us to examine the role of a single non-narrative quotation across the transformational efforts of various NT speakers/authors and audiences[19] and to refute the claim that "most application" of Ps 110 to Jesus "in the NT requires it to be understood in a way that would not correspond to its meaning in any OT context."[20]

Some caveats are necessary. First, any model offers only

> partial access to the truth, the truth as viewed within a particular framework and for particular purposes; and it provides orientation for a particular interpretative practice.... No model should claim to offer a comprehensive description of reality, and each may retain its heuristic usefulness even where anomalies and complexities are detected of which it has taken no account.[21]

Other methodologies offer insight into various aspects of quotation; we do not attempt either to synthesize or to replace all other theories or models.

Second, although our model sheds helpful light on NT quotation, we do not claim either that the evoking of tradition is a relevant framework for all quotation or that all NT authors in every case read the passages they quote as Envisagers. Each quotation must be evaluated on its own merits.

However, by including perlocution and especially perlocutionary effect, incorporating the construct of the implied author/reader, and considering Envisaging readers as distinct from Analysts, our model holds the author, reader, and text in creative tension, transcending the false dichotomy between meaning as authorial intention versus reader response and linking quotation as the evoking of Story (textual tradition) to lifeworld/worldview transformation. This offers a new and valuable perspective on quotation and provides the opportunity to gain new insight into the purposes of NT authors and readers in communicative interaction.

---

18. We present some of this scholarship in chapter 7.
19. In some cases, a multi-layered analysis is required.
20. Goldingay, *Psalms 90–150*, 292.
21. Watson, *Text and Truth*, 8.

PART I

Developing a Methodology

2

Quotation

QUOTATION AND INTERTEXTUALITY

The term "intertextualité" was coined by Julia Kristeva, whose concern was "with establishing the manner in which a text is constructed out of already existent discourse. Authors do not create their texts from their own original minds, but rather compile them from pre-existent texts."[1] For Kristeva and some who have followed her, including Roland Barthes, "text" includes all of what might be described as "culture," covering such topics as architecture, art, and "the dominant relations of production and the sociopolitical context."[2] As Barthes describes it, text is "a tissue of quotations drawn from the innumerable centres of culture."[3]

Although we primarily use "text" in its more common linguistic sense,[4] we agree that "the writer is a reader of texts (in the broadest sense) before s/he is a creator of texts, and therefore the work of art is inevitably

---

1. G. Allen, *Intertextuality*, 35. For a discussion of Kristeva and her predecessor, Mikhail Bakhtin, see Pfister, "Konzepte der Intertextualität," 1–11.

2. Still and Worton, "Introduction," 1. As C. B. Hays notes, "when Kristeva speaks of a text, she is not referring merely to literary texts but to historical and social contexts" (C. B. Hays "Echoes of the Ancient Near East," 42).

3. Barthes, *Image, Music, Text*, 146. "For Barthes as for Derrida, 'nothing exists outside the text'" where "text" is "the intertextual" (G. Allen, *Intertextuality*, 74).

4. Generally, by "text," we mean any speech or writing. By "intertext," we refer to any use (quotation, allusion, or echo) of an earlier text.

shot through with references, quotations and influences of every kind."[5] Not only is a writer first a reader of texts, theories of intertextuality highlight the reader in other ways. Gerard Luttikhuisen helpfully notes that "intertextuality plays a significant role not only in the production of texts but also in their reception. In fact, the information of the text cannot be comprehended unless we relate it to what we remember from texts heard or read before. In other words, meaning is assigned to the text in the light of what we know from other texts."[6] More broadly, according to Steve Moyise, "Texts do not present themselves to readers as transparent packages of meaning; readers have to do something in order to interpret them. Intertextuality suggests that what they do is relate them to other intertexts, which might be actual texts or, more generally, events, cultural phenomena, or personal experiences and commitments."[7] In the case of the NT, one of these "texts" is the events of the life, death, resurrection, and exaltation of Jesus Christ.

The reader's experience can have an impact on two other fronts. First, "the reader's experience of some practice or theory unknown to the author may lead to a fresh interpretation."[8] Such "practice or theory" includes instances of intervening interpretation of a text.[9] In the examples we consider of Psalms quotations in the NT, at a minimum, the original text has been interpreted by the Septuagint. In some instances, there also are Jewish interpretations in the Qumran documents and other pre-Christian sources. In addition, not only do NT authors filter their presentation of OT texts through their understanding of the Christ event, in some cases, there may be intervening NT interpretation of an OT text by other NT speakers or authors.

The second possibility is that the reader may not know every text the author knows. To avoid having to determine whether a NT hearer/reader

---

5. Still and Worton, "Introduction," 1. For Pfister also, "der Autor immer zugleich auch Leser ist" (Pfister, "Konzepte der Intertextualität," 21).

6. Luttikhuisen, "Intertextual References," 117. "What is produced at the moment of reading is due to the cross-fertilisation of the packaged textual material (say, a book) by all the texts which the reader brings to it" (Still and Worton, "Introduction," 1–2).

7. Moyise, "Latency and Respect for Context," 134.

8. Still and Worton, "Introduction," 2.

9. As Fishbane points out, "it makes all the difference—all and not some—whether a specific *traditum* has been reused or annotated; or whether, on the contrary, it either contains independent reflexes of common idioms or comments which are original to the particular composition or teaching" (Fishbane, *Biblical Interpretation*, 13).

would recognize the quoted material, we take most of our examples, including the case studies, from marked quotations, that is, "those introduced by an explicit quotation formula, such as 'as it is written.'"[10] With explicit quotation, it is certain both that the quoting author was a reader of the quoted text and/or an interpretation thereof and that the author intends the reader to understand that these words come from a source text.[11]

Intertextuality is not an interpretive method. Rather, it is "a theory (or group of theories) concerning the production of meaning."[12] Some link it irrevocably to poststructuralism,[13] although we do not adopt that perspective here since "an intertextuality that locates meaning in an infinite matrix of possible influences is unable to say anything specific about a text."[14] Rather, we find "intertextuality" helpful because it highlights "the importance of considering the relation between the new context and the old in interpreting allusion and citation."[15] Additionally, we value its focus on the role of the reader. In terms of the five types of intertextuality identified by Moyise, we are interested in the reader-oriented types, i.e., the narrative-frame, dialogical, and "postmodern,"[16] although our goal is to hold them in creative tension rather than considering them as discrete entities.

---

10. Stanley, *Arguing with Scripture*, 47. This is the first of Stanley's categories of quotation. His second is "those accompanied by a clear interpretive gloss (e.g., 1 Cor 15:27)" (Stanley, 47). This category includes 1 Cor 15:25, which we analyze in chapter 8.

11. See Moyise, "Intertextuality and the Study of the Old Testament," 19. As B. L. Tanner notes, "Quotation is an author-generated intertextuality, placed purposefully for a specific effect or effects" (B. L. Tanner, *Book of Psalms*, 6).

12. Moyise, "Intertextuality and Historical Approaches," 447.

13. For example, Hatina criticizes R. B. Hays's use of the word "intertextuality" since it "is certainly not accompanied by a commitment to the poststructuralist framework" (Hatina, "Intertextuality and Historical Criticism," 36).

14. Moyise, "Intertextuality and Historical Approaches," 457.

15. Paul, "Use of the Old Testament," 259. Brawley points out that "by the criteria of intertextuality, . . . the question is no longer how faithful the repetition is to the original. Rather, a reference to an old text locates the modern interpreter in a tensive ambience of echoes between the two texts, and the question is how the two texts reverberate with each other" (Brawley, *Text to Text*, 8).

16. See Moyise, "Intertextuality and Biblical Studies," especially 421, 424, 425–26. In a later work, Moyise identifies three approaches to Paul's quotations: intertextual, narrative, and rhetorical (Moyise, *Paul and Scripture*, 111–25). Herein, we do not explore interpretive techniques like midrash, which belong to Moyise's "exegetical" type. Nor do we deal with "intertextual echo," although we believe that with modification our methodology could be used to study unmarked references such as allusion and echo. However, it would complicate our analysis to establish a process to identify such intertexts.

We have several times referred to "meaning" and its production. Before turning to quotation *per se*, we want to give a brief introduction to the methodology we will develop to determine how "meaning" is produced.

THE PRODUCTION OF MEANING

The arguments of poststructuralists such as Kristeva and Barthes are in part a response to the structuralist insistence that stable meaning can be created and discovered.[17] Thus, in any discussion of intertextuality, context, and the author/reader relationship, "meaning" is a key term, which calls for careful definition. We base our definition of "meaning" on Kevin Vanhoozer's action model, in which meaning is "a three-dimensional communicative action, with form and matter (propositional content), energy and trajectory (illocutionary force), and teleology or final purpose (perlocutionary effect)."[18] These dimensions are elements of a single speech act.

Of these elements, the last two are the most critical in our model. An illocutionary act can be classified as one of five different types (Assertive, Directive, Expressive, Commissive, and Declaration), depending on the illocutionary force with which the content is presented. The sole intended illocutionary effect (response of the hearer/reader) is understanding. Illocutionary acts necessarily have perlocutionary acts associated with them. A perlocutionary act is an act of a speaker/author that correlates to an intended perlocutionary effect (response) of belief and/or action by the hearer/reader.

Our action model holds the three dimensions of meaning in creative tension and, at the levels of the illocution and the perlocution, gives a cooperative role to both the author and the reader in the interactive communication of meaning. We develop our action model further in chapter 5. In the remainder of this chapter, we consider theories or models of the function or purpose of quotation.

---

17. See G. Allen, *Intertextuality*, 69; and Alkier, "Intertextuality and Semiotics," 4. For Barthes's and Derrida's opposition to "structuralist assertions of textual unity and closure," see Beal, "Ideology and Intertextuality," 27.

Poststructuralism is not a monolithic concept. According to C. B. Hays, "the author and the world of the text's production mattered to Bakhtin, and apparently to Kristeva as well" (C. B. Hays, "Echoes of the Ancient Near East," 29). However, Barthes "is famous for announcing the 'death of the Author'" (G. Allen, *Intertextuality*, 74); for Barthes, "the intertextual process is centered in the *reader*" (B. L. Tanner, *Book of Psalms*, 34; emphasis added).

18. Vanhoozer, *Is There a Meaning?*, 218.

THE FUNCTION OF QUOTATION

The traditional approaches to evaluating OT quotations in the NT can be categorized according to the criteria of (i) quantity, i.e., how often specific OT books and passages are quoted by which NT authors and which introductory formulae are used; (ii) "quality," i.e., fidelity to either the MT, a version of the LXX, or another source text; and (iii) interpretive method.[19] Scholars also evaluate OT quotations on the basis of the strength of the intertextual link (explicit quotation, allusion, or "echo")[20] and, recently, purpose or function.

With regard to the latter—the "why" of quotation, Christopher Stanley has offered an intriguing proposal; he argues that "Paul wrote his letters not to lay out a set of theological beliefs, but to motivate specific first-century Christians to believe and/or act (or stop believing or acting) in particular ways."[21] He follows this with the broader idea that "rhetorical speech is . . . *audience-centered speech*; its purpose is to promote action on the part of the audience, not merely to communicate the ideas of a speaker/author."[22] Similarly, in Chaïm Perelman and Lucie Olbrechts-Tyteca's classic work on rhetoric, they present a general goal of argumentation as "obtaining the adherence of the audience."[23]

Since quotations are part of an author's persuasive effort and thus "are meant to affect an audience,"[24] quotation not only reflects culture (or

---

19. For a helpful categorization of some studies which fall into the last category, see Swartley, *Israel's Scripture Traditions*, 10–21.

20. R. B. Hays distinguishes three types of linguistic intertextuality: "Quotation, allusion, and echo may be seen as points along a spectrum of intertextual reference, moving from the explicit to the subliminal" (R. B. Hays, *Echoes of Scripture*, 23).

21. Stanley, *Arguing with Scripture*, 3. Kennedy is another who believes that "the writers of the books of the New Testament had a message to convey and sought to persuade an audience to believe it or to believe it more profoundly" (Kennedy, *New Testament Interpretation*, 3). However, we base our methodology on pragmatics rather than Kennedy's "discipline of rhetoric."

22. Stanley, *Arguing with Scripture*, 16. Stanley starts with Burke's definition of rhetoric as "the use of words by human agents to form attitudes or induce actions in other human agents" (Burke, *Rhetoric of Motives*, 41, as quoted by Stanley, *Arguing with Scripture*, 12n8).

23. Perelman and Olbrechts-Tyteca, *New Rhetoric*, 163. Motsch and Pasch also point out that "der Erfolg des Sprechers, die Realisierung seines Ziels durch den Hörer, hängt vor allem dann, . . . wie es dem Sprecher gelingt, den Hörer positiv zu motivieren" (Motsch and Pasch "Illokutive Handlungen," 74).

24. Stanley, *Arguing with Scripture*, 3. Stanley notes both that little is said about quotation in rhetorical theories and that Perelman and Olbrechts-Tyteca's index lists only four

"lifeworld"),[25] it changes it. Speech and text have the potential to transform the Story they evoke and the lifeworld they represent and also other Stories and lifeworlds with which they interact. We discuss Story, lifeworld, and worldview in greater detail in chapters 3 and 4.

Unfortunately, Stanley does not take full advantage of this promising start. Instead, he unduly narrows his focus, bypassing all theories of how quotations affect an audience other than appeal to authority.[26] Not only does he overlook other possible functions of quotation, he takes the appeal to authority to an extreme, arguing that the function of almost all quotation is to establish the primacy of the speaker in a power relationship.[27] This is a notion he takes from one of the models of quotation he examines, that of Gillian Lane-Mercier. We address this below when we consider specific theories of quotation.

For now, we note that others also find quotation to be primarily an appeal to authority. For Timothy Berkley, it is "characteristic of Paul's use of quotations" that a quotation "serves the separate rhetorical function of a

---

references (Stanley, 12). Although Perelman and Olbrechts-Tyteca describe the "normal role" of quotation as "backing up a statement with the weight of authority," they add that in other circumstances it can be regarded as "a figure relating to communion" with the audience (Perelman and Olbrechts-Tyteca, *New Rhetoric*, 177). Similarly, per Schneider, "the decisive question for an intertextual reading" is "Why was the citation brought in here, and what effect is thereby made possible?" (Schneider, "How Does God Act?," 40). We argue in chapter 5 that being audience-centered and communicating authorial ideas are not mutually exclusive but are instead two complementary aspects of meaning. Additionally, we distinguish between authorial *intention* (as communicated via an author's speech acts) and authorial *motive*.

25. We briefly discussed "culture" above. A shared lifeworld and its corresponding worldview "reside at a very deep level, underlying the character and culture of an entire people" (Naugle, *Worldview*, 150, regarding worldviews).

26. Even where quotation is "used to illustrate or exemplify a point made by a speaker," Stanley feels "the argument from authority is not far from the surface, since the very act of quotation implies that the source of the quotation is respected by the intended audience" (Stanley, *Arguing with Scripture*, 14).

27. According to Stanley, "even quotations that look like innocent ornamental devices can be heavily 'power-coded' when taken from an authoritative source, since they inevitably add an aura of respectability to the speaker/author's pronouncements" (Stanley, *Arguing with Scripture*, 14). Sanborn believes that for Stanley "when someone quotes another passage, either it means the same identical thing it meant in the quoted text or it means something not envisioned in the original text" and is used for the quoter's own "power purposes" (Sanborn, review of *Arguing with Scripture*, 76). But, as Sanborn points out, this either/or position is invalid (Sanborn, 76).

proof-text offering supporting authority for Paul's conclusion."[28] A. T. Hanson makes a similar argument: "One might well ask: If it is not for proof, why does Paul quote Scripture here?"[29] Jeremy Punt believes Paul "invoked (both directly and indirectly) the Scriptures of Israel as an authoritative source. . . . In polemical contexts, he used Scripture as a final court of appeal, since it was for him sacred—proceeding from God—and thus had ultimate authority."[30] Concerning the Synoptic Gospels, Willard Swartley avers that "to varying degrees the authors/narrators cite specific OT texts to document the authority of the tradition. The tradition lives by the Scripture, and citation therefrom conveys authoritative word in the presentation of the narrative."[31] In her study of Hebrews, Cynthia Westfall argues that "quotations generally supply support material or proofs."[32] From the perspective of ancient rhetoric, Burton Mack takes the position that "the purpose of the citation was to show that other recognized authorities had come to the same conclusion or rendered a similar judgment on the same issue."[33]

However, we concur with Anthony Thiselton that "the Old Testament was not simply invoked as a 'support' or a 'proof' in the context of polemical debate for a message which had been understood independently of it."[34] Thomas Hatina also acknowledges that scriptural quotations have other functions than use as "proof-texts or analogies."[35] We combine these ideas with Stanley's thought that quotation can help persuade an audience to believe and/or act (or stop believing or acting) in particular ways[36] in constructing our methodology.

28. Berkley, *From a Broken Covenant*, 139.
29. Hanson, *Studies in Paul's Technique*, 157; see also 147.
30. Punt, "Paul and Postcolonial Hermeneutics," 269.
31. Swartley, *Israel's Scripture Traditions*, 291.
32. Westfall, *Discourse Analysis*, 92.
33. Mack, *Rhetoric and the New Testament*, 46. Amador finds most citations and nontechnical proofs to be "newly invented proofs, often either created or uniquely interpreted to supply authority and legitimation for the new social formations and experimentations taking place" (Amador, *Academic Constraints in Rhetorical Criticism*, 146).
34. Thiselton, *New Horizons in Hermeneutics*, 150; italics omitted. With regard to 1 Corinthians, Heil also argues that "Paul's use of scripture . . . does not merely inform his listeners but performs a rhetorical strategy aimed at persuading and transforming them in various ways" (Heil, *Rhetorical Role of Scripture*, 5).
35. Hatina, *In Search of a Context*, 158.
36. See Stanley, *Arguing with Scripture*, 3, and our discussion of the "why" of quotation above (p. 15).

PART I | DEVELOPING A METHODOLOGY

In the remainder of this chapter, we put a theoretical foundation under our understanding of the function of quotation by engaging with a variety of theories of quotation, some from the field of linguistics and others which take a literary approach.[37] Of particular interest are: (i) the functions of quotation presented by these theories and (ii) what these theories consider to be the relationship between the quoted author and audience and the quoting author (once a reader) and audience.

LINGUISTIC THEORIES OF QUOTATION

Much linguistic work concerning quotation has been from a semantic perspective. Semantic theories of quotations focus on three questions: (i) "In a quotation, what does the referring?," (ii) "How do quotations refer?," i.e., to what linguistic category do quotations belong?, and (iii) "What do quotations refer to?"[38]

Our interest is not in these semantic questions but rather in the pragmatics of quotation, that is, what quotations do. One influential pragmatic theory of quotation is the "demonstration" theory of psycholinguists Herbert Clark and Richard Gerrig.[39]

---

37. Although Stanley is to be commended for bringing scholarship from other disciplines to bear upon NT quotation, it is difficult to understand why he considers the four models he reviews to be "the most important" theories put forward in recent years "to explain how quotations 'work' as part of a literary communication" (Stanley, *Arguing with Scripture*, 24). Two of the papers were written in 1974 and 1982. Both linguistic models he considers, the "dramaturgical" theory of linguist/semanticist Anna Wierzbicka (see Wierzbicka, "Semantics of Direct and Indirect Discourse," 267–307) and the demonstration theory of Clark and Gerrig (see Clark and Gerrig, "Quotations as Demonstrations," 764–805), primarily concern conversation, not literary communication. Plus, Wierzbicka's work is now rarely cited. A decade ago, Récanati described both Wierzbicka's and Clark and Gerrig's theories as providing "a general account of quotation as simulation" (Récanati, "Open Quotation," 652), but in a collection of papers on linguistic and philosophical aspects of quotation, Wierzbicka's work is not mentioned (see Brendel et al., *Understanding Quotation*).

38. Cappelen and Lepore, "Quotation," §2.1.

39. Cappelen and Lepore do not include demonstration theories among the "five kinds of theories of quotation that have been central to the discussion of quotation" (Cappelen and Lepore, "Quotation," §3) although they discuss them briefly under the topic of Mixed Quotation, i.e., a combination of direct and indirect quotation (Cappelen and Lepore, §4; see also their "Varieties of Quotation," 429; and "Varieties of Quotation Revisited," 51). Tannen's description of direct vs. indirect quotation is helpful in understanding these terms: "'Direct quotation' is commonly understood to apply when another's utterance is framed as dialogue in the other's voice. . . . 'Indirect quotation' (or

Quotation as Demonstration

For Clark and Gerrig, the author-reader relationship begins with the quoting author as hearer/reader of the quoted text; they consider quotation to be "a demonstration of what a person did in saying something."[40] For them, direct quotation is "non-serious," that is, the speaker takes "responsibility only for presenting the quoted matter. . . . The responsibility for the depicted aspects themselves belongs to the source speaker. So with quotations speakers can partly or wholly detach themselves from what they depict."[41] This is similar to Anna Wierzbicka's notion that a direct quoter is not a "samesayer" with the original speaker, i.e., the quoter does not commit to the same view as the original speaker and make the same assertion(s).[42]

Even if one agrees that direct quotation is non-serious, that does not mean that the source text is privileged over the receptor text. Nor is Stanley correct that Clark and Gerrig's theory leads to the insight that "quotations lead the audience into a mediated encounter with the original text where a second, more powerful voice speaks on behalf of the quoting author" and that, therefore, with biblical quotations, the audience is brought "into the presence of God, who is shown standing firmly on the side of the speaker."[43] Clark and Gerrig claim neither that the original speaker is a "more powerful voice" nor that in quotation the original speaker "speaks on behalf

---

'indirect discourse' or 'speech') is commonly understood to apply when another's speech is paraphrased in the current speaker's voice" (Tannen, *Talking Voices*, 102).

40. Clark and Gerrig, "Quotations as Demonstrations," 769. They use "demonstrate" in "its everyday sense of 'illustrate by exemplification'" rather than in its "technical linguistic sense of 'point to' or 'indicate'" (Clark and Gerrig, 764, 764n2).

41. Clark and Gerrig, "Quotations as Demonstrations," 792, where they add that this is different from indirect quotation or "description," since "when speakers describe, they take responsibility for their wording."

42. See Wierzbicka, "Semantics of Direct and Indirect Discourse," 286–87. We are not convinced that direct quoters are never samesayers or that direct quotations are always non-serious. For example, linguists Johnson and Lepore argue convincingly that "direct quotations are neither demonstrations nor selective depictions nor non-serious actions" (Johnson and Lepore, "Misrepresenting Misrepresentation," 247).

43. Stanley, *Arguing with Scripture*, 32. Nor do we agree with Stanley that Wierzbicka's theory suggests "an author who quotes from Scripture temporarily lays aside his or her own speech and allows the biblical text to speak directly to the audience. In this way the members of the audience are enabled (in theory) to hear for themselves what the quoting author heard in an earlier encounter with the biblical text" (Stanley, 26). "Allowing the biblical text to speak directly to the audience" and "enabling the audience to hear what the quoting author heard" are not necessarily identical.

of the quoting author."[44] The latter claim leaves no room for irony, other forms of parody, or subversion. It cannot accommodate quotations such as the devil's quotation of Ps 91:11–12 during the temptation of Jesus (Matt 4:6, Luke 4:10–11). Following Stanley here would cause one to argue that this quotation shows God to be speaking on behalf of the devil![45] Instead, Clark and Gerrig's model requires the quoting author to provide sufficient context to enable his or her audience to "hear" the original text. In Matt 4:6, the devil's use of the psalmist's words does not consider the relevant co-text of the source text, i.e., Ps 91:9–10. Using terminology we expand upon in chapter 5, the devil is both reading the source text as an "Independent" and has produced a "defective" speech act.

A useful feature of Clark and Gerrig's theory for our purposes is that it implies the relevance of context by stressing the presence of the shared background required for "solidarity" in interpretation.[46] In chapter 3, we present the existence of mutual context as critical to our model. Direct quotation activates (perhaps first creating) mutual context so that hearers/readers understand a speaker's/author's communicative intent, whether or not agreement/adherence ensues.[47]

---

44. Stanley's claim is incompatible with direct quotation as non-serious action and with a second idea he attempts to derive from Clark and Gerrig: that quotations can "insulate" a speaker "from negative reactions to certain parts of the message" (Stanley, *Arguing with Scripture*, 32). Clark and Gerrig's examples of dissociation of responsibility are not relevant to NT quotation (see, e.g., Clark and Gerrig, "Quotations as Demonstrations," 792–93). Nor do they imply a quoting author can self-insulate from all quotation decisions. Certainly a quoting author is not insulated from a quotation decision that is recognized as misleading.

45. Since this quotation is a direct object clause appearing after a verb of perception, modern translators take ὅτι here to introduce direct discourse. See Wallace, *Greek Grammar*, 454–58. But this is not an instance in which the quoter demonstrates what the original speaker did in saying something. The devil is not demonstrating what the psalmist was doing with his speech but rather is using the psalmist's words manipulatively to tempt Jesus into disobedience.

46. "When speakers demonstrate only a snippet of an event, they tacitly assume that their addressees share the right background to interpret it the same way they do" (Clark and Gerrig, "Quotations as Demonstrations," 793). We rely on H. H. Clark's well-known work on common ground in chapter 3.

47. The word "activate" comes from Brown and Yule, *Discourse Analysis*, 75. Stanley restricts solidarity to situations where both parties are familiar with the original text (see, e.g., Stanley, *Arguing with Scripture*, 31–32); we argue that quotation can be used to create mutual context even when the hearer/reader is not familiar with the source text.

Clark and Gerrig also make a link to Speech Act Theory. However, they omit perlocution in their list of "the selective aspects of the referents that demonstration can depict," which limits the value of their model for us.[48]

François Récanati, who bases his arguments on Herbert Clark's work,[49] points demonstration theories in a new direction with his observation that for open quotation "the demonstration may serve a number of purposes, which can only be determined on a pragmatic basis."[50] Rather than delve into the technical distinctions between open, closed, and mixed quotation, we look further into linguistic theories of quotation by exploring the work of linguist Deborah Tannen, whose research interests include discourse studies, pragmatics, and sociolinguistics.

Involvement and Joint Production

An important element of Tannen's work is "involvement," which occurs in our model as both illocutionary and perlocutionary effect. A key involvement strategy is repetition, defined as "ways that meaning is created by the recurrence and recontextualization of words and phrases in discourse."[51] Involvement develops as repetition, which encompasses quotation, "bonds participants to the discourse and to each other, linking individual speakers in a conversation and in relationships."[52] Ultimately, quotation is "a supremely social act: by appropriating each other's utterances, speakers are bound together in a community of words."[53] We develop the concepts of "a community of words" and of interactional relationships in chapters 4 and 5, respectively.

Although Tannen argues that "even seemingly direct quotation is really 'constructed dialogue,' that is, primarily the creation of the speaker rather than the party quoted,"[54] in all situations, the meaning of the utterance

48. Clark and Gerrig believe "most quotations depict illocutionary acts, including the propositions expressed, and treat the other acts as supportive or incidental" (Clark and Gerrig, "Quotations as Demonstrations," 779; see also 775).

49. This includes both Clark and Gerrig, "Quotations as Demonstrations," and H. H. Clark, *Using Language*.

50. Récanati, "Open Quotation," 665.

51. Tannen, *Talking Voices*, 9. She equates repetition with intertextuality: "Meaning in language results from a complex of relationships linking items within a discourse and linking current to prior instances of language" (Tannen, 9).

52. Tannen, *Talking Voices*, 61.

53. Tannen, *Talking Voices*, 132.

54. Tannen, *Talking Voices*, 103. She adds, "The words have ceased to be those of the

still "resonates with association with its reported context, in keeping with Bakhtin's sense of polyphony."[55] Further, since "the only way we can make sense of the world is to see the connections between things, and between present things and things we have experienced before or hear about,"[56] for Tannen, there is a relationship—albeit perhaps not an equal partnership—between the reporting speech and its context and the reported speech and its context.

Her thoughts concerning the partnership between the speaker and listener set the stage for our discussion of the roles of the author and reader in the coming chapters:

> Listening . . . is an active not a passive enterprise, requiring interpretation comparable to that required in speaking, and speaking entails simultaneously projecting the act of listening: In Bakhtin's sense, all language use is dialogic.
> The theoretical perspective I have in mind is referred to by some as the notion that conversation is "a joint production."[57]

In summary, Tannen's theory introduces us to the concepts of involvement, communicative interaction, the relationship of reported to reporting context, and the role of both speaker/author and hearer/reader in "joint production." We address these in coming chapters. Our next step, however, is to explore further the relationship between reported and reporting speech by evaluating the work of three noted literary theorists who take a literary approach to quotation.

LITERARY THEORIES OF QUOTATION

Strategies of "Humanist Imitation"

For Thomas Greene, a work's intertextuality is "the structural presence within it of elements from earlier works. Since a literary text that draws nothing from its predecessors is inconceivable, intertextuality is a universal

---

speaker to whom they are attributed, having been appropriated by the speaker who is repeating them" (Tannen, 105). This is similar to Sternberg's theory (see below), although Tannen does not reference his work.

55. Tannen, *Talking Voices*, 105.
56. Tannen, "What's in a Frame?," 14–15. In chapter 4, we apply this to evoking tradition.
57. Tannen, *Talking Voices*, 27. This also pertains to written communication; all understanding requires "active interpretation, not passive reception" (Tannen, 103).

literary constant."⁵⁸ Using Renaissance poems as examples, he outlines four strategies of "humanist imitation":

1. The *reproductive* or *sacramental* "celebrates an enshrined primary text by rehearsing it liturgically";
2. The *eclectic* or *exploitative* "treats all traditions as stockpiles to be drawn upon ostensibly at random" so that in it "allusions, echoes, phrases, and images from a large number of authors jostle each other indifferently";
3. In the *heuristic*, having advertised "their derivation from the subtexts they carry with them," the imitations "proceed to distance themselves from the subtexts and force us to recognize the poetic distance traversed";
4. The *dialectical* leaves "room for a two-way current of mutual criticism between authors and between eras."⁵⁹

Hays introduces Greene's typology in the final chapter of his seminal work *Echoes of Scripture in the Letters of Paul*, arguing that Greene's "categories can be applied analogically to any text that performs intertextual reflection."⁶⁰ Other than Galatians, which Hays names heuristic, and a few scattered spots of eclectic reading strategy, Hays finds Paul's intertextuality to be primarily of Greene's "dialectical" type.⁶¹ This dovetails with our interest in the dialogical nature of quotation.⁶²

The other literary theories we explore focus on the locus of power in the relationship between the quoted and quoting authors.

---

58. Greene, *Light in Troy*, 16.
59. Greene, *Light in Troy*, 38, 39, 40, and 45, respectively.
60. R. B. Hays, *Echoes of Scripture*, 174.
61. R. B. Hays, *Echoes of Scripture*, 174–78. Hays abandons his view of the eclectic category as "allusions to various texts and traditions" (R. B. Hays, 173) when he calls 1 Cor 9:8–10 and Rom 10:18 eclectic because "there is no indication that Paul has wrestled seriously with the [single] texts from which the citations are drawn" (R. B. Hays, 175).
62. As Moyise points out, various scholars describe "the interaction between the connotations" a quotation "(may) bring with it and its role or function in the new work" as "dialogical, dialectical, or intertextual" (Moyise, "Quotations," 28, 28n27). For our purposes, it is not necessary to distinguish between the first two terms although "intertextual" is a broader category.

Power in Quotation

At the heart of Meir Sternberg's theory of quotation is that "whatever the surface similarity, the recontextualized inset structurally diverges from the original; whatever the formal autonomy conferred by directness, the inset is communicatively subordinated to the [new] frame" and "the perspectives of the global speaker and his audience are super-imposed on those of the original participants."[63] He adds that "this effectually plays into the hands of quoters interested in drastic and yet unobtrusive manipulation: ironists, parodists, polemicists, not to mention subtle liars."[64] According to Sternberg, "to quote is to mediate, to mediate is to frame, and to frame is to interfere and exploit."[65]

Stanley concludes from Sternberg's argument both that "it is the context of quotation, not the original context, from which the audience obtains the necessary clues for interpreting the work" and that the meaning an author "expects his audience to get from the quoted material . . . may or may not correspond to its 'original meaning.'"[66] We discuss context in the following chapter but point out here that although the co-text is generally important to determining the "meaning" of a text, it does not follow that the original "meaning" of a quotation plays no role in understanding the receptor text.[67]

Sternberg, Tannen, and Stefan Morawski (see below) are all sources for Lane-Mercier's "power" theory.[68] Based on Tannen, Lane-Mercier ar-

---

63. Sternberg, "Proteus in Quotation-Land," 131. For Sternberg, all quotation involves "manifold shifts, if not reversals, of the original meaning and significance. . . . However accurate the wording of the quotation and however pure the quoter's motives, tearing a piece of discourse from its original habitat and reconstructing it within a new network of relations cannot but interfere with its effect" (Sternberg, 108).

64. Sternberg, "Proteus in Quotation-Land," 130, where he calls "verbatim citation . . . a shrewd rhetorical weapon."

65. Sternberg, "Proteus in Quotation-Land," 145.

66. Stanley, *Arguing with Scripture*, 29, 29n32.

67. In a later work, Sternberg hints at the value of the socio-historical context of the quoted text: "The remembrance of the past devolves on the present and determines the future" (Sternberg, *Poetics of Biblical Narrative*, 31).

68. Stanley calls Lane-Mercier's model "the parodic approach" because she argues that "if . . . one accepts the existence of a parodic space within which quotation as play is permitted to flourish, . . . it follows that quotation as play becomes the prototype of reported speech" (Lane-Mercier, "Quotation," 203). Her other category is proof: "The act of quoting from a text considered to be authoritative . . . is . . . equated with the performing of an act of authority or, at the very least, with a display of erudition that only the learned few possess" (Lane-Mercier, 201).

gues that reported speech is "linked to a specifically pragmatic dimension centered upon the production of participatory perlocutionary effects" in the quoter's audience.[69] However, Lane-Mercier admits she goes "beyond Tannen's conclusions, in order to stress the fact that . . . the recontextualization automatically performed by the quoter is accompanied by the implicit subordination of the cited utterance."[70] For her, all quotation "represents an unavowed attempt to exert control over the other. . . . In sum, reported speech relies on a strategy centered on the metaphorical death of the quotee, whose utterance, apparently intact, has nonetheless been decontextualized, severed from its 'origin', and subsumed by the utterance of the quoter."[71] Quotation is thus "a discursive strategy designed to manipulate the listener and, as such, to program the listener's response."[72] Like Sternberg, for Lane-Mercier, the *quoter* has and uses the power in quotation.

A focus on power relationships, and especially the manipulation of both the source text and the audience by the quoter, is a theme of Stanley's work.[73] Stanley argues that "Paul assumed a stance of social and ideological dominance/power over his intended audience, a dominance for which he claimed divine support"[74] and that, "like other Jews," he "believed that a

69. Lane-Mercier, "Quotation," 204. "Quotation is to be construed as an integral component of the discourse of the quoter, designed above all to encourage listener participation" (Lane-Mercier, 204).

70. Lane-Mercier, "Quotation," 205. For Tannen, "seemingly direct quotation is . . . primarily the creation of the speaker rather than the party quoted" (Tannen, *Talking Voices*, 103); Lane-Mercier replaces "primarily" with "automatically" (Lane-Mercier, "Quotation," 204). Although Lane-Mercier notes that "whether the locus of 'power' be conventionally situated in the quotee or in the quoter, the presence of the other can never be entirely erradicated [sic]" (Lane-Mercier, 211), she acknowledges neither any authority of the quotee nor any stability of meaning.

71. Lane-Mercier, "Quotation,"206. Hatina presents Barthes's view of intertextuality as similar: "The entire agenda of displacing traditional structures, even if they are merely viewed as relative instead of contradictory, can be reduced to a struggle for power and authority" (Hatina, *In Search of a Context*, 31).

72. Lane-Mercier, "Quotation," 207; see also 205.

73. "At the heart of the quotation process is a covert attempt by the quoting author to assert power over both the source text and the audience" (Stanley, *Arguing with Scripture*, 34). For Mack, "early Christian rhetoric is packed with stock proofs, strategies, and references to the traditional final topics. The trick was to manipulate these in support of their own propositions. . . . Thus the challenge for early Christians was to (mis)use conventional modes of conviction in the attempt to articulate a new and distinctive ethos" (Mack, *Rhetoric and the New Testament*, 38).

74. Stanley, *Arguing with Scripture*, 171. He sees it as "perhaps no accident that all of Paul's explicit quotations appear in letters to churches in which power relationships

quotation from the holy text should close off all debate on a subject."[75] For him, Lane-Mercier's insistence that quotations are inevitably manipulative "can help us look beyond the apparent innocence of Paul's appeals to Scripture in order to ask questions about his underlying motives."[76]

Others make similar arguments. Punt finds "the Scriptures functioned as the authorizing agent for Paul's own efforts to retain his authority and power within the Corinthian church, providing the mainstay for his rhetoric of power."[77] For Graham Shaw, flattery is "the initial stage of manipulation. . . . Thus what looks like a free offer becomes a means of control. Paul dazzles his readers by the splendour of their status, and thus reconciles them to submitting to the authority of the man who has conferred it upon them."[78] Concerning the New Testament more broadly, J. David Amador, who equates persuasion to a "power engagement," goes so far as to aver that "there is an element of violence in 'persuasion' as an activity of imposing one's own 'point of view' upon another."[79]

Many scholars do not find these arguments compelling. Brian Abasciano uses Stanley's own words to make the strong counter-argument that if Paul "were to misuse Scripture, 'a reader familiar with the original text would invariably have raised questions about the validity of Paul's interpretation. Questions of this sort would have impeded rather than advanced

---

were being contested" (Stanley, 36; see also 88, 92, 122, 178, 182). For Sanborn, Stanley's research is guided by modern rhetorical theory which posits "speakers are engaged in power relationships" rather than attempting "to discover truth and persuade others of it" (Sanborn, review of *Arguing with Scripture*, 76).

75. Stanley, *Arguing with Scripture*, 173; see also 13, 59. For further discussion of quotation as "closing a debate," see p. 87 below, especially n129.

76. Stanley, *Arguing with Scripture*, 36–37. At several points, Stanley moderates Lane-Mercier's position. For example, he notes that "not all quotations are meant to be taken seriously" (Stanley, 36). But he gives no clue as to how to determine which quotations are in which category.

77. Punt, "Paul and Postcolonial Hermeneutics," 286.

78. Shaw, *Cost of Authority*, 31. This assumes Paul's description of his readers' status is a fiction Paul himself has created which does not correspond to reality.

79. Amador, *Academic Constraints in Rhetorical Criticism*, 51, 58. Shaw also believes "the oppressive use of authority derives from the determination to perpetuate a position of power which is threatened by an instability it cannot ultimately evade. . . . Self-perpetuating authority can defend itself from dissolution only by oppression, and the New Testament contains many examples of that ruthless self-defence at work" (Shaw, *Cost of Authority*, 17). We disagree with an understanding of "'persuasion' in terms of sanctioned acts of power/violence" (Amador, *Academic Constraints in Rhetorical Criticism*, 299). Nor do we agree that "power is at play in every . . . attempt at persuasion" (Amador, 86).

Paul's rhetorical purposes."[80] In this regard, Stanley's view of Paul's audiences as irrevocably characterized by their individual initial level of familiarity with Scripture without consideration of their communal interaction is short-sighted. As J. Ross Wagner highlights, "Stanley himself curiously gives pride of place to the least competent hearers imaginable."[81] Not only does Stanley's theory of audience competence presume individual rather than group reading, it is founded on a modern suspicion of expertise. Instead, in Paul's socio-cultural context, the less informed audience would have expected the "informed" audience to have mediated Paul's "meaning" to them. Abasciano says it well:

> It is highly unlikely that Paul would aim his biblical quotations mainly at the scripturally ignorant, intentionally playing fast and loose with Scripture, when the very people who would control the reading and interpretation of Paul's letter would have been those who by Stanley's own admission could have assessed Paul's interpretation and impeded his rhetorical purposes. It is far more likely that Paul would have taken special account of the scripturally learned in his audiences and attempt to craft his biblical argumentation so as to be convincing to those who were familiar with the original contexts of his quotations.[82]

Additionally, "power" arguments overlook the fact that "participants' agreement may be held to play a role with respect to what is to count as being (objectively) the case when matters of right, entitlement, obligation, authority etc. are at issue. . . . Authority does not exist apart from its recognition by relevant social participants."[83] The OT would only be an "authority" for the former pagans among Paul's audience to the extent they accepted it as such.

---

80. Abasciano, "Diamonds in the Rough," 172; quote is from Stanley, "'Pearls before Swine,'" 140.

81. J. R. Wagner, *Heralds of the Good News*, 34n121. We present a different categorization of readers in chapter 5.

82. Abasciano, "Diamonds in the Rough," 172.

83. Sbisà, "Speech Acts in Context," 430. Castelli correctly notes that "all actors in a power relationship possess a critical access to agency. The ascendant figure in a power relationship does not act on the passive, subordinate figure. Although power relationships are asymmetrical, they do not render the subordinate actor without the possibility for action" (Castelli, *Imitating Paul*, 44).

Furthermore, "power is not coterminous with violence."[84] Elizabeth Castelli points out that Paul

> does not possess any special physical means to coerce people to relate to him in a certain way; and he has no state apparatus (police or military) to ensure compliance. Nor obviously would I argue that he actively coerces people against their conscious wills to place themselves in a subordinate relationship to him. Rather he is attempting to persuade them by two simultaneous means—rhetoric and personal authority.[85]

Finally, there are strong ethical counter-arguments; a variety of scholars have pointed out that an oppressive "rhetoric of power" is inconsistent with the relationally transformative message of Scripture. At least in the NT, it does not seem to be the case that "power is at play in every ... attempt at persuasion."[86] For Rikk Watts, the major flaw

> in Stanley's rhetorical model is ... his implicit subordination of Paul's Christ-centered and cruciform ethic to the need to impose his authority. Nothing, it seems to me, could be further from the truth. Rhetoric is the art of persuasion, and the language of "belief" is its focus. It is in being persuaded (cf. Acts 17:4; 18:13; 26:28; Gal 1:10; 2 Cor 5:11) that one is saved.[87]

Watts adds that "to seek to use Scripture as a covert means of establishing his personal authority seems ... totally out of character for one [Paul] who counted all such privilege as dung that he might gain Christ."[88]

More generally, for Clarence Walhout, "the ethical foundation of human action" lies in "the mutually dependent relationships of the self and the other."[89] Kathy Ehrensperger relates this to the role of Scripture:

> To live in the realm of this God means to be in a relationship for which the renunciation of power in the sense of domination is constitutive. ... The character of the relationship and of the dimension of authority and power within it are inseparably intertwined. ... Thus, although the Scriptures are credited with many

---

84. Castelli, *Imitating Paul*, 44.
85. Castelli, *Imitating Paul*, 123.
86. Amador, *Academic Constraints in Rhetorical Criticism*, 86.
87. R. E. Watts, "In Need of a Second Touch?"
88. R. E. Watts, "In Need of a Second Touch?"
89. Walhout, "Narrative Hermeneutics," 123. For him, all actions, presumably including speech and text acts, have ethical implications (see Walhout, 119–20).

divergent roles in the Second Temple period, to attribute to them some force of coercion or dominating power seems unwarranted and inappropriate.[90]

In the NT, "power" is not "dominating power" but "transformative power."[91] Trust is a necessary component of such power: "For transformative power to be power at all, to have an effect on the 'weaker' agent at all, trust is constitutive of its very existence. Trust must be seen as absolutely essential to the establishment and continuation of a truly empowering relation."[92] Along with this comes "respect for the otherness of the other," which "offers a close parallel to *love (agapē)* in the New Testament."[93] This is the "power" generally wielded by Jesus and the NT authors.[94]

Thus, we reject the idea that either the quoted or quoting context or the author or the reader "controls" the other. Instead, we adopt a hermeneutics of cooperation. This means that even in situations where power—or the lack of it—may have a role, we deny that quoting is necessarily exploitative

---

90 Ehrensperger, "Paul and the Authority of Scripture," 311–12. She notes that in the wake of "Max Weber's writings about power, theories of power in the social sciences focused significantly on power as power-over someone—and more specifically on power as domination. . . . Domination, then, is perceived as the ability of an agent to limit the options and choices of others. The means to achieve such domination is through the exercise of force, coercion, or by securing the compliance of the subordinates" (Ehrensperger, *Paul and the Dynamics of Power*, 20).

91. According to Ehrensperger, "the aim of transformative power is to render itself obsolete by means of empowering the subordinate" (Ehrensperger, *Paul and the Dynamics of Power*, 27).

92. Ehrensperger, *Paul and the Dynamics of Power,* 29. "In order for the exercise of power to be empowering, the use of coercion, force, or violence must be ruled out" (Ehrensperger, "Paul and the Authority of Scripture," 299).

93. Thiselton, "Communicative Interaction," 221.

94. R. E. Watts points out that "Paul's discourse is not about domination precisely because his vision of transformation is predicated on exactly the opposite, namely trust. And that trust is in a God whose exercise of power is the very antithesis of domination. To suggest that Paul resorts to the very thing his whole life, often at great personal cost, repudiates, is . . . out of step with Paul" (R. E. Watts, "In Need of a Second Touch?"). Similarly, Strom argues Paul did not focus on personal power/status but rather "led his communities into a new process of framing their identities and purposes. It was a profoundly relational strategy, crafted in the moment to demonstrate what it meant to choose the well-being of others in imitation of the dying and rising of Christ" (Strom, *Reframing Paul*, 194). Along these lines, Thiselton believes "Paul sees his apostleship not as an instrument of power but as a call to become a transparent agency through whom the crucified and raised Christ becomes portrayed through lifestyle, thought, and utterance" (Thiselton, *First Epistle to the Corinthians*, 45).

or that Jesus or the NT authors use quotations in deceitful manipulation. Further, we hold that applying the concept of quotation as a "power play" to any NT author is unhelpful if it leads us to question—or even to attempt to ascertain—an author's motives.[95]

In summary, although Stanley has opened a door to new approaches to the study of quotation, by taking Paul's primary purpose in quoting as the consolidation and manipulation of a power position via an appeal to authority, he leaves what is beyond that door unexplored. Stanley "ignores the various rhetorical ways in which an appeal to authority can be construed, much less the other (sometimes more likely) rhetorical moves in which Paul engages (e.g. narrative posturing or world-projecting)."[96] To explore other moves which can be made via quotation, such as "world-projecting," we turn to the work of philosopher Stefan Morawski.[97]

The Maintenance of Cultural Continuity

Kristeva's work on intertextuality was "set against the prevailing standard of literary theory," which "stressed the autonomy of a text and . . . valued the originality of an author's work as the mark of success. Evidence of influence, then, was seen as a negative factor in literary evaluation."[98] Similar stress on author creativity is a focus of Morawski's work on quotation; he is dismissive of quotation in comparison with the creativity of "art." He believes "philosophy, scholarship and all traditional institutions and their

---

95. We discuss the difference between authorial intention and authorial motivation in chapter 5.

96. Lincicum, review of *Arguing with Scripture*, 430.

97. In a footnote in his final chapter, Stanley mentions Morawski's "frequently cited article" and lists Morawski's four common reasons for quotation (Stanley, *Arguing with Scripture*, 173n4). But since Stanley gives no further details and offers no discussion, it is hard to understand on what basis he concludes that "obviously, this list is too broad and generic to be of much use when applied to the letters of Paul" (Stanley, 173n4).

98. B. L. Tanner, *Book of Psalms*, 6. We find "influence" in its agent-related sense, that is, "whereby people act in a causal manner on other people" (Hatina, "Intertextuality and Historical Criticism," 38), to be helpful as we consider both the function of quotation and the communication of meaning. For discussion of the relationship of influence and intertextuality, see Hatina, "Intertextuality and Historical Criticism," and the essays by Clayton and Rothstein, Clayton, Rajan, and Friedman in Clayton and Rothstein, eds., *Influence and Intertextuality in Literary History*.

attendant ideologies submit to its [quotation's] incursions," while art "resists its pressure" so that the artist "proffers his OWN vision."[99]

Morawski defines textual quotation as "the literal reproduction of a verbal text . . . wherein what is reproduced forms an integral part of some work and can easily be detached from the new whole in which it is incorporated."[100] Although his typology of four functions of quotation bears some similarity to Greene's, his approach is colored by his view of quotation, and his typology lacks a function comparable to Greene's dialectical category.[101] Therefore, we do not use Morawski's typology.

However, his broader view of quotation as evoking tradition is valuable. For Morawski, quotation is "a component element of the stock of culture, anchoring the present to time past."[102] Tradition can be "continued" via quotation, but it also can be "breached."[103] This option is particularly

---

99. Morawski, "Basic Functions of Quotation," 704. For him, quotation is a choice between "innovation and the duplication of canonized exemplars," and the appeal to authority is "a device for ducking independent thought" (Morawski, 691, 692). Although he would include OT quotation as an appeal to authority, we reject the notion that Jesus and the NT authors are "ducking independent thought" and do not characterize their use of quotation as evidence of "intellectual torpor and emotional-ritual assiduity" (Morawski, 692–93).

100. Morawski, "Basic Functions of Quotation," 691, where he adds that quotation is "not so much separate, as separable."

101. Like Greene's sacramental function, with Morawski's *appeal to authority*, the quoter does not produce a personal opinion. Morawski's *erudite* function, in which quotations "serve as evidence" (Morawski, "Basic Functions of Quotation," 694) as the quoter endorses or rebuts the quoted author's views (Morawksi, 695), approximates Greene's heuristic function. Similar to Greene's eclectic function, Morawski's *ornament* function "is an intellectual conceit which sometimes makes no pretence even of accuracy. . . . The quote may be taken out of context or be marginal to the author's views" (Morawski, 695). However, Morawski's *stimulative-amplificatory* function, in which the quoter is an "investigator" for whom quotations "act either as a kind of 'surgical appliance' doing duty for a part of his own argument, or as a springboard for speculations in the same vein, or finally as a reinforcement of the terms in which he poses his problem or the answer which he advances" (Morawski, 694), does not correspond to Greene's dialectical type. Both Morawski's ornament and stimulative-amplificatory functions resemble quotation as described by Sternberg, Lane-Mercier and, to a lesser extent, Tannen and Stanley, in their emphasis on the priority of the quoter. Although Stanley's concept of an appeal to authority is not the same as Morawski's, Stanley agrees with Morawski that there is no need for substantiation with an appeal to authority. For Stanley, the appeal to authority is the substantiation.

102. Morawski, "Basic Functions of Quotation," 704.

103. With quotation considered diachronically, "there takes place a winnowing of the past," and, at the extreme, "a quotation dredged up from the past or extracted from

relevant for NT quotation in cases where an intervening interpretation of the OT may be in view. In general, Morawski argues that

> the situations which prompt literal reference to an original . . . can be summed up simply as MAINTENANCE OF CULTURAL CONTINUITY. It is after all striking how strictly connected quotation is with a sense of traditions. . . . Over and above this, the quotation is a sign of an increasingly alert discernment of questions and answers recurring in human history.[104]

In chapter 4, we look at this from a different perspective, giving the name "theology" to certain of the "questions and answers recurring in human history" and considering quotation to play a role in posing and answering those questions.

In biblical studies, the concept of quotation functioning as a link to tradition was described over fifty years ago by J. A. E. van Dodewaard and C. H. Dodd. We conclude our discussion of quotation by evaluating their contributions and that of Lars Hartman.

Quotation as a Link to Tradition

Van Dodewaard lists three motives for quotation. The first is an appeal to a recognized authority; the second is using someone else's engaging way of making a point. Thirdly, "il est loisible de citer un seul mot ou une seule phrase, non seulement à cause de la signification restreinte de cette phrase ou de cet mot, mais pour évoquer du même coup tout le contexte, toute l'histoire, l'événement même, durant lequel ce mot a été prononcé."[105] Taking the Gospel of Matthew as his example, van Dodewaard considers the third motive particularly applicable to both the words of Matthew and those of Jesus which Matthew reports.

Both van Dodewaard's argument that "tout le contexte, toute l'histoire, l'événement même" is evoked with quotation and C. H. Dodd's similar contention that with regard to certain "fundamental passages," one of which is

---

contemporary records embalming the past can be simply an indictment of the author cited" (Morawski, "Basic Functions of Quotation," 692).

104. Morawski, "Basic Functions of Quotation," 691. For him, this is a spurning of art and innovation.

105. Van Dodewaard, "La force évocatrice," 484. For him, "les moindres allusions elles-mêmes avaient le pouvoir d'évoquer tout un monde à la pensée des auditeurs et des lecteurs" (van Dodewaard, 485-86).

Ps 110, "the *total context* ... is in view, and is the basis of the argument"[106] are stronger claims than we make here. Although we agree that quotation evokes tradition/Story, we do not assert that the entire context of the source text is necessarily in view.[107] We prefer Hartman's less rigorous suggestion that in those situations where "the *tradition*, common to author and reader" permitted an "evocative" function, "the context of a passage quoted or alluded to was somehow evoked in the process of communication."[108] To determine what of the original context is in view, each quotation must be evaluated individually.

Furthermore, like Hartman, we do not limit the evoking of context to Dodd's "fundamental passages." As Morawski argues, "the quotation is never dragged in ... from passages which are of little significance."[109] Prominence is created even with unique quotations, such as Ps 115:1 LXX in 2 Cor 4:13; all quotations can be expected to be significant for understanding a discourse.[110]

Hartman also makes the point that "we ought not to forget how far the OT quoted was an interpreted OT."[111] Every OT source text was read and interpreted by many readers in the centuries since it was originally spoken and subsequently written, and an interpretation may be what is evoked by a NT speaker/author. Although Hartman believes that "in spite of Qumran, Rabbinic traditions, Philo etc., ... we do not know enough to be able to tell with certainty whether or not a quotation has a special nuance of meaning because

---

106. Van Dodewaard, "La force évocatrice," 84; Dodd, *According to the Scriptures*, 126, where he also argues that segments from these passages were quoted "rather as pointers to the whole context than as constituting testimonies in and for themselves."

107. In some cases, the immediate literary context ("co-text") is indispensable to determining the meaning of a text. We discuss co-text and other types of context in chapter 3.

108. Hartman, "Scriptural Exegesis," 151–52. As Plett puts it, "Der Zitat-Kontext bildet dabei das backgrounding, das Zitat selbst das foregrounding" (Plett, "Sprachliche Konstituenten," 86). We name "foregrounding" the "activation of mutual context" and consider it in chapter 3.

109. Morawski, "Basic Functions of Quotation," 695.

110. As Ciampa notes, "Authors have ways of indicating which intertextual relationships are of particular significance for understanding their discourses. This may well be one of the key roles of citation and allusion in a discourse" (Ciampa, "Scriptural Language and Ideas," 41n3).

111. Hartman, "Scriptural Exegesis," 135; cf. Still and Worton, "Introduction," 1. Even the act of recording a speech involves a measure of interpretation.

of an interpretative tradition behind it,"[112] we can at a minimum debate the likelihood of several alternatives. This is important in our case studies.

In this regard, as we pointed out in our evaluation of Morawski's theory, a NT speaker/author does not always evoke tradition to agree with or revitalize it; quotation may evoke tradition to signal a break with it (subversion).[113] We discuss various types of transformation in chapter 4. In any event, we expect the interpretation of the OT by a NT author to reflect the intervening Christ event.

CONCLUSION

Our exploration of intertextuality and quotation in this chapter has established that instead of a power-motivated appeal to authority, biblical quotation can be viewed as evoking tradition in order to create or activate the mutual context of the author and reader, thereby encouraging readers "to believe and/or act (or stop believing or acting) in particular ways."[114] Therefore, important to our methodology are: a dialogical author/reader relationship, the importance of context (and especially co-text), an understanding of textual tradition, and the ability of quotation to support reader transformation. In chapter 3, we explore both the author/reader relationship and the topic of (mutual) context.

---

112. Hartman, "Scriptural Exegesis," 135.

113. Hays and Green also suggest that "engagement with the OT might be parodic, repeating an old pattern or echoing ancient metaphors to signal difference at the very heart of similarity" (Hays and Green, "Use of the Old Testament," 129). This would include the literary technique of irony, which may be behind the decision of both Matthew and Luke to include the devil's quotation of Ps 91:11–12 in their accounts of the temptation. See p. 20 above.

114. Stanley, *Arguing with Scripture*, 3.

3

Context and the Author/Reader Relationship

WE HAVE DETERMINED THAT quotation can evoke tradition, including literary tradition, which we call Story.[1] In turn, tradition/Story is part of the mutual context of the author and reader.[2] Therefore, evoking elements of Story via quotation activates[3] (and perhaps first creates) aspects of mutual context. We continue our discussion of the function of quotation with a more detailed look at mutual context and its activation, beginning by clarifying what we mean by "author" and "reader."

EMPIRICAL AND IMPLIED AUTHOR AND READER[4]

According to Seymour Chatman, the author and reader each entail "three different personages. On the sending end are the empirical author, the

---

1. We capitalize "Story" to indicate we do not limit literary tradition to narrative genre. We define Story further in chapter 4. Note that although our concern is primarily with the textual tradition transmitted by Scripture, we also recognize oral literature as tradition.

2. Although for convenience we refer to the "author" and "reader," our discussion of context applies equally to a speaker and hearer. A major difference is that since a reader's response is not as immediate, mutual context generally changes more slowly with written text.

3. Heimerdinger gives a metaphorical explanation: "An entity is activated to the extent that it is 'lit up' in the consciousness of the hearer" (Heimerdinger, *Topic, Focus and Foreground*, 129).

4. Scholars use "real," "actual," or "historical" as well as "empirical," and "ideal" or "model" as well as "implied." For our purpose, these terms are interchangeable.

implied author, and the narrator (if any); on the receiving end are the empirical audience (listener, reader, viewer), the implied audience, and the narratee" (if any).[5] Chatman, who credits Wayne Booth with the concepts "implied author" and "implied reader," presents this diagram:[6]

Narrative Text

Real ⇢	Implied → (Narrator) → (Narratee) → Implied	⇢ Real
Author	Author	Reader	Reader

The diagram demonstrates that "only the implied author and implied reader are immanent to a narrative, the narrator and narratee are optional (parentheses). The real author and real reader are outside the narrative transaction as such, though, of course, indispensable to it in an ultimate practical sense."[7] The communication of the empirical author and reader takes place "only through their implied counterparts."[8]

Although Chatman, Booth, and others who use this model are primarily concerned with narrative criticism, the construct also has validity in non-narrative genres, including the biblical epistles and the Psalms, both of which are of concern to this study.[9] We describe and evaluate the implied author/reader construct below and follow this with a discussion of the narrator and narratee or "listener."

The Implied Author and Reader

Booth defines the "implied author" as the "second self" the empirical author creates in the literary work.[10] It is the implied author "who has chosen, consciously or unconsciously (so any given reader will infer), every detail, every quality, that is found in the work or implied by its silences."[11] Further-

---

5. Chatman, *Story and Discourse*, 28. See also Lanser, *Narrative Act*, 117–18.
6. Chatman, *Story and Discourse*, 151.
7. Chatman, *Story and Discourse*, 151.
8. Chatman, *Story and Discourse*, 31.
9. See the discussion of Story as more than narrative genre in the following chapter.
10. Booth, *Rhetoric of Fiction*, 429; see also 137–38, 151.
11. Booth, *Rhetoric of Fiction*, 429; see also Chatman, *Story and Discourse*, 148.

more, the implied author "is someone with whose beliefs on all subjects I must largely agree if I am to enjoy his work."[12]

The implied author is constructed by the empirical author and "reconstructed by the reader from the narrative."[13] This reconstruction may be assisted by certain literary strategies, including "the reliability or unreliability of the narrator; pacing . . . ; the knowledge/ignorance contour . . . ; focus . . . ; evaluation . . . ; the use of symbols and of allusions to things and events which occur outside the projected world; and the expression of beliefs concerning the actual world."[14] The implied author also can be revealed through "conventional or formulaic phrasing, genealogical catalogs, and the use of hyperbole and careful documentation" as well as through "less obvious structural patterns involving beginnings and endings, uses of metaphor, symbol, and allusion, sequences of events, and chronological ordering."[15]

The empirical author constructs not only the implied author but also the implied reader—"the audience presupposed by the narrative itself."[16] The implied reader is the one "actual readers must encounter as they encounter the text. The discourse is thus addressed to a readership which it creates itself. . . . The historical reader must, in a sense, read 'through' this textual construct."[17] The identity of the implied reader thus is inferred primarily from the reconstruction of the implied author.

The implied reader can "elucidate" facts suggested by the text and "discern the presence and force of irony, the meaning of metaphors, the suggestions borne by emphasis, the presence of ambiguity (*double entendre*)."[18] The implied reader "'falls for' the implied author's traps; he is surprised by unexpected reversals in the discourse, led astray and brought back onto the right path by the implied author."[19] Furthermore, the implied reader "can

---

12. Booth, *Rhetoric of Fiction*, 137, referring to the novel.

13. Chatman, *Story and Discourse*, 148. After selecting the audience, "the rhetor 'must' then construct her/his argumentative appeals with this audience in mind. In order for argumentation to take place at all, much less be effective, s/he 'must' adapt him/herself to the audience whom s/he has selected. In other words, *the rhetor becomes a construction of the audience*" (Amador, *Academic Constraints in Rhetorical Criticism*, 68).

14. Walhout, "Texts and Actions," 64, with reference to Wolterstorff, *Art in Action*, 139–42.

15. Walhout, "Texts and Actions," 73.

16. Chatman, *Story and Discourse*, 150; cf. Booth, *Rhetoric of Fiction*, 138.

17. Lanser, *Narrative Act*, 116.

18. Wolterstorff, *Works and Worlds of Art*, 116.

19. Tovey, *Narrative Art and Act*, 25–26.

be found as much in the text's silences as in its overt appeals."[20] Where the text is silent about a fact, we infer "that members of the 'authorial audience' already know it," and "what the author feels no need to mention, of the values the story depends on, tells us who he thinks we are before we start to read."[21]

As an example of the use of the implied author/reader construct, we consider the interpretation of Ps 51. Although Ps 51 is introduced as a psalm "of David" and the superscription gives details relating to David's life, David does not need to be considered to be the empirical author of the psalm in order to understand it. Rather, we can learn a great deal about the implied author from an analysis of the text. First, there is no protestation of innocence. The psalmist has sinned and admits his guilt (vv. 2–4), which leads to the penitence so movingly expressed in the psalm. Second, the psalmist understands Yahweh judges sin. In v. 4c–d, the passage quoted in Rom 3:4, the psalmist acknowledges both that Yahweh is justified when Yahweh "speaks" and that Yahweh's judgments are just. The psalmist's fervent plea for Yahweh to forgive his sins implies that the psalmist believes Yahweh has the ability to forgive sin and may do so even where disobedience has been great.

The psalmist presents several reasons designed to motivate Yahweh to perform the desired action of forgiveness.[22] One is Yahweh's own character, in particular, Yahweh's covenant loving-kindness [חסד] and the greatness of Yahweh's compassion [רחם] (v. 1). The implicit argument is that Yahweh's essential being includes forgiveness. In addition, the psalmist offers praise, sacrifice, and correct teaching so that other sinners may also return to Yahweh (vv. 13, 14c, 15b, and 19). This is not a claim to Yahweh's forgiveness but rather a commitment to being in future right relationship with Yahweh. From this characterization of the implied author, we conclude that in this instance the implied reader understands Yahweh's character as well as what

---

20. Booth, *Rhetoric of Fiction*, 423. Turner notes that "if speakers and writers leave much unexpressed, that . . . means that the speaker/writer assumes his addressees share with him a presupposition pool" (Turner, "Historical Criticism and Theological Hermeneutics," 49). Turner's "presupposition pool" is part of our "mutual context" (see n64 below).

21. Booth, *Rhetoric of Fiction*, 423. What is known of the socio-historical context can be important. An unmentioned event may not yet have occurred either in history or from the temporal perspective of the implied author.

22. *Contra* Tate, who argues Ps 51 contains "no motivational appeal to God for action" (Tate, *Psalms 51–100*, 8).

behavior both pleases Yahweh and evidences being in right relationship with Yahweh.

The Narrator and the Listeners

All Scriptural texts not only have an implied author, they contain some narratorial presence. One generally important consideration is the reliability of the narrator. A reliable narrator "speaks for or acts in accordance with the norms of the work (which is to say, the implied author's norms)."[23] Where the narrator is reliable, which we hold to be the case in our case study examples, understanding the narrator is a way to discover the views of the implied author.

The correspondence between the narrator and the listeners[24] is less straightforward than the relationship between the implied author and implied reader. One category of listener is "participants," which includes both direct addressees and side participants (those taking part but currently not directly addressed).[25] The other category of listener is non-participants or "overhearers," that is, those "who have no rights or responsibilities" in the conversation.[26] Overhearers are either "*bystanders* . . . who are openly present but not part of the conversation" or "*eavesdroppers* . . . who listen in without the speaker's awareness."[27]

The existence of listeners of various types is a "device by which the implied author informs the real reader how to perform as implied reader."[28] Therefore, in identifying the implied reader it may be helpful to analyze what types of listeners are present at the episode and discourse levels, although the implied reader may or may not be identified with the direct

---

23. Booth, *Rhetoric of Fiction*, 158–59. Determining that a narrator is reliable does not imply the narrative is non-fiction. In any case, our interest is not in the historical veracity of Scripture but rather in the transformation the various NT speakers/authors attempt to accomplish in their audiences.

24. We use Booth's term here since it is broader than "narratee" (see Booth, *Rhetoric of Fiction*, 423).

25. This terminology comes from H. H. Clark, *Using Language*, 14. For him, the speaker is also a participant.

26. H. H. Clark, *Using Language*, 14.

27. H. H. Clark, *Using Language*, 14.

28. Chatman, *Story and Discourse*, 150. Although he refers to narratees, this applies to all listeners.

addressee or with any of the other listeners.²⁹ We keep this in mind as we consider the identity of the implied reader both in those Psalms passages where the direct addressee is Yahweh and in those NT passages where a speaker directly addresses one audience while the implied NT author addresses a different group. Further, although Paul's arguments are ostensibly directed to his formerly pagan converts, we must take into account the possibility that they also may be indirectly aimed at groups of overhearers, that is, at his opponents and/or Jewish Christians.³⁰

To look ahead several chapters, it is the implied author to whom we refer in discussing the illocutionary and perlocutionary intentions of the speech acts of Scripture. Since the implied author is presented to us via the text, it is not necessary to retrieve the empirical author's personal history or motives to understand the "authorial" speech-act intentions.³¹ The more complete the presentation of the implied author and of the Story and the "lifeworld"³² inhabited by the implied author, the less necessary extra-textual historical reconstruction of the empirical author becomes.

Additionally, we define the terms in our action model relating to the "reader"—particularly perlocutionary effects or responses—in terms of the implied reader and an empirical reader's relationship to the implied reader. As is true for the implied author, identifying the implied reader does not require discovering either the historical identity or the "mind" of any empirical audience.³³ But identifying the implied author and implied reader

---

29. As Reed notes, "Just as the spokesperson may not be the source of a message, the recipient may not be the *target* of address" (Reed, "Modern Linguistics and the New Testament," 236).

30. J. R. Wagner suggests these two groups are the targets of some of Paul's writing (J. R. Wagner, *Heralds of the Good News*, 35–36). Another possibility could be overhearers representing the Roman Empire.

31. "Positing an implied author inhibits the overhasty assumption that the reader has direct access through the fictional text to the real author's intentions and ideology. It does not deny the existence of important connections between the text's and the real author's views" (Chatman, *Coming to Terms*, 76). However, such connections do not include authorial motivation, which often cannot (and need not) be determined even if the empirical author's identity is known. We discuss this further in chapter 5.

32. In a "lifeworld," a "communicative community" shares mutual context. We discuss this further in chapter 4.

33. The empirical reader "is immeasurably complex and largely unknown" (Booth, *Rhetoric of Fiction*, 428). The implied author/reader construct obviates Hatina's concern: "If the recovery of the author's intention is difficult, if not impossible to ascertain, as modern literary criticism points out, then how much more difficult is the recovery of what is in the mind of the audience?" (Hatina, *In Search of a Context*, 339).

within their literary context often does require at least certain minimal assumptions about the context. We turn to this topic next.

CONTEXT

Stanley believes that "Paul often quotes from Scripture in a way that bears little evident relation to the apparent sense of the original passage" and that "we should be careful about assuming that Paul was aware of the 'original context' of every passage that he cites in his letters."[34] Further, he argues against the modern scholarly assumptions that Paul "expected his audiences to refer back to the original context of his quotations" and that his audiences would have been capable of doing so.[35]

This raises the question of defining context. According to communication theorist Em Griffin, "context" is not simply "just a sentence, or even the situation in which the word is spoken. Context is the whole field of experience connected with an event."[36] It includes "the various factors one has to take into consideration together with the text in order to understand the author's intention. Any number of circumstances or contexts might be relevant to this task: historical, linguistic, literary, canonical, sociological, and so forth."[37]

From this, it is clear that context is a "prodigiously elastic term."[38] We need to be precise about how we use "context" since we want to link it to quotation and, ultimately, meaning. Thus, we employ three categories: socio-historical context, literary context ("co-text"), and linguistic conventions.

Socio-Historical Context

The original socio-historical context encompasses more than the situation that brings the speaker/author and first audience together. For example, Francis Watson speaks sweepingly of the "institutional continuum

---

34. Stanley, *Arguing with Scripture*, 53, 54.
35. Stanley, *Arguing with Scripture*, 54–55.
36. Griffin, *First Look at Communication Theory*, 58.
37. Vanhoozer, *Is There a Meaning?*, 250. The actual context of the empirical author may be different from the implied context of the implied author and implied reader. By "context," we refer to the latter.
38. J. B. Green, "Context," 130.

(educational, ecclesial, or whatever) which functions as the comprehensive context within which author, text, and readers are comprised."[39] Similarly, for linguist Richard Ohmann, the use of language is embedded in the broad spectrum of historical relationships so that "to participate in discourse is to set in motion one's whole awareness of institutions, social ties, obligations, responsibilities, manners, rituals, ceremonies."[40]

Locating a text within its socio-historical context can add clarity and richness to an analysis. Ben Meyer notes that "by moving from the description of the common sense of a past age to an explanatory grasp precisely pinpointing that age's insights and oversights, values and biases, the interpreter would no longer find himself surprised by his own findings; for he would have entered, more consciously and securely than he might have thought possible, into the writer's world of meaning."[41] We attempt to read both our example quotations and the Psalms from which they were taken "against the horizons of their own, particular sociohistorical environment," and we use the socio-historical clues available to us.[42] At a minimum, events or traditions described by or alluded to in the text are relevant elements of the socio-historical context.

However, even when "a reconstruction of the stream of life, life-world, or extra-linguistic context which surrounds a text is indispensable to understanding its meaning,"[43] it is not sufficient for such an understanding.[44] And, in general, full socio-historical re-construction is neither necessary nor possible.[45] As the historical and cultural distance widens between the

---

39. Watson, *Text and Truth*, 100, adding that "this institutional continuum is characterized by the phenomenon of 'tradition': author and intended readers are conscious of participating in a tradition which mediates the historical and/or geographical distance that separates them and brings them into a certain proximity to one another." We discuss tradition in the following chapter.

40. Ohmann, "Speech, Literature," 50–51; quote is from p. 51.

41. Meyer, *Critical Realism*, 168; see also his chapter 10.

42. J. B. Green, "Context," 131. Historical and literary approaches "are by no means mutually exclusive; indeed, the most illuminating exegesis employs them together in a complementary fashion" (Hays and Green, "Use of the Old Testament," 130). We do not want to neglect any tool which enriches an analysis.

43. Thiselton, *New Horizons in Hermeneutics*, 560; italics omitted. This is true especially for linguistic conventions (see below).

44. Skinner makes this argument and also presents the potential value of knowing the social context (Skinner, "Meaning and Understanding," 39–49).

45. Concerning the necessity of full socio-historical reconstruction, we agree with Thiselton that "it would be a mistake to conclude that no understanding is possible

production/original reading and subsequent readings of the text, later readers may find it difficult to retrieve the original socio-historical context. Thus, the socio-historical context of many texts, including the Psalms, can be established only quite broadly.[46] A socio-historical gap can even exist between the producer of a text and his or her original audience. Such would be the case for Paul and any of his audience who came to Christianity from paganism. In that situation, quotation may have been employed as a way to bridge the gap.[47] We discuss this below with regard to mutual context.

In general, we are less concerned with the particular historical events that led to the composition of a psalm than we are with the Story which formed and grounded the lives of the author and the original audience and is expressed through the construct of the implied author and reader. Where possible, however, we identify elements of the socio-historical context made available or assumed by the implied author in order to support our reconstruction of the implied author and reader and to determine how the text contributed to the development of Story.

Our second category of "context" is the literary setting or "co-text."[48]

Literary Context (Co-Text)

Paul Ricoeur argues cogently that "a text is more than a linear succession of sentences. It is a cumulative, holistic process."[49] Peter Cotterell and Max Turner define the literary context as "the contribution of all the other parts

---

without historical reconstruction" (Thiselton, *New Horizons in Hermeneutics*, 266). Indeed, in some cases retrieving the original socio-historical context may be unhelpful. According to Moloney, "difficulties are created by the speculative reconstruction of *the world behind the text* (sometimes called a 'diachronic' analysis of the text). Recent scholarship focuses upon *the world in the text* (sometimes called a 'synchronic' analysis of the text) and how it addresses *the world in front of the text*" (Moloney, *Gospel of Mark*, 9).

46. Many Psalms do not identify the historical situation which prompted them. Even with biblical narrative, often "both the actual author and the original situation of communication must be very tentatively reconstructed historically" (White, "Introduction," 11). Thus, *contra* Stroup, it is not always true that "Christian faith and Scripture refer to historical events" (Stroup, *Promise of Narrative Theology*, 144).

47. This is less likely to have been the intended function of allusion or echo since in those situations the presence of material from a previous source is not highlighted.

48. Brown and Yule, *Discourse Analysis*, 46, attribute this term to M. A. K. Halliday (see Halliday, *Language as Social Semiotic*, 133).

49. Ricoeur, "Model of the Text," 212.

of the text to that part under immediate consideration."⁵⁰ The co-text can include a variety of adjacent textual segments (words, phrases, clauses, sentences, paragraphs, pericopes, discourses, books, etc.) and their related intertexts.

Co-text is often critical to determining meaning. As Hans-Georg Gadamer reminds us, the process of "construal" of a sentence is "governed by an expectation of meaning that follows from the context of what has gone before."⁵¹ In situations where the sentence or utterance is "multivocal," it is the co-text that tells the audience which of various possible speech acts the speaker/author intends.⁵²

Unlike socio-historical context, which may be difficult to retrieve, generally some co-text is available to us. But to understand the text and its co-text requires some knowledge of the *linguistic conventions* which governed the creation of the implied reader by the implied author. As an element of culture, linguistic convention bridges socio-historical context and co-text and, therefore, warrants our attention.⁵³

Linguistic Conventions

Roger Fowler defines a convention as "something shared by people" and reminds us that "language is social and conventional both in its origin and in the rules which govern the practices of speaking and writing."⁵⁴ Teun van Dijk also points out that "language systems are CONVENTIONAL systems. Not only do they regulate interaction, but their categories and rules have developed under the influence of the structure of interaction in society."⁵⁵

---

50. Cotterell and Turner, *Linguistics and Biblical Interpretation*, 72. In our model, this includes both a speech act set within a speech act complex as well as the relationship of a speech act complex to the broader discourse (see chapter 5).

51. Gadamer, *Truth and Method*, 291.

52. See Alston, *Illocutionary Acts and Sentence Meaning*, 248. Longacre reminds us of "the natural function of context in resolving most ambiguities" (Longacre, *Grammar of Discourse*, 1).

53. Socio-historical context plus linguistic convention forms Thiselton's "background" (see Thiselton, *New Horizons in Hermeneutics*, 46), a term he takes from Searle, who defines it as "the biological and cultural resources" necessary for the *speaker* to form an intention (Searle, *Intentionality*, 143). Since we are not interested in biological capacity and we wish to include the reader/hearer, we prefer the term "mutual context."

54. Fowler, *Linguistic Criticism*, 40.

55. Van Dijk, *Text and Context*, 167.

Linguistic conventions are necessarily relatively stable; "we can only communicate with one another if we assume that the meanings of signs do not vary substantially from person to person and from day to day."[56] An author "can write meaningfully only within the possibilities provided by the systems of conventions which define the culture."[57]

Literary conventions play a role in the creation of an implied author and reader. Calling literature "highly conventional," Susan Lanser argues convincingly that "the rules and expectations governing the production and reception of a work of art are as much a part of textual structure as the words on the page."[58] This is true for all texts, including biblical texts, even in situations where the flouting of conventions is a rhetorical device.

Literary conventions are also key to a reader's identification of the implied author and reader. Empirical readers "bring not just their 'personal' attitudes and experiences to the work of art, but also sets of linguistic and historical conventions which govern the production of meaning in the text."[59] In his study of biblical narrative, Robert Alter concludes that "a COHERENT READING of any art work . . . requires some detailed awareness of the grid of conventions upon which, and against which, the individual work operates."[60] We use the term "communicative competence" to describe the situation where the author and the reader are mutually aware of and able to use the linguistic conventions that pertain to their communicative situation.[61]

In addition to quotation, a linguistic convention with which we are concerned is figurative language, i.e., those expressions which "associate a

---

56. Fowler, *Linguistic Criticism*, 41.

57. Fowler, *Linguistics and the Novel*, 125. "Even the most revolutionary thinker must speak—and think—in the language of his day" (W. S. Campbell, "Contribution of Traditions," 236).

58. Lanser, *Narrative Act*, 46.

59. Lanser, *Narrative Act*, 54.

60. Alter, *Art of Biblical Narrative*, 47. For a linguist's perspective, see G. Yule, *Pragmatics*, 47. According to Alter, "one of the chief difficulties we encounter as modern readers in perceiving the artistry of biblical narrative is precisely that we have lost most of the keys to the conventions out of which it was shaped" (Alter, *Art of Biblical Narrative*, 47). Thiselton also is correct that we can never become the original audience or recover "the life-world or creative vision that gave rise to the text" (Thiselton, "Communicative Interaction," 201). Although these factors make it more difficult for today's empirical reader to "find" the implied reader, that level of readership remains the standard for fully successful interactive communication. We discuss this further in chapter 5.

61. See Fowler, *Linguistic Criticism*, 248.

concept with a pictorial or analogous representation of its meaning in order to add richness to the statement."[62] Our interest in figurative language is primarily in metaphor, which we discuss in greater detail in the examples where it is found.

MUTUAL CONTEXT AND COOPERATIVE COMMUNICATION

"Mutual context" is the shared and evolving accumulation of these three types of context.[63] It includes "an encyclopedic understanding of the shared social world (including its linguistic and rhetorical conventions) as well as the specific 'context' of the communication," which, in turn, includes both "information constituted from the situative context . . . as well as the new information from the completed part of the discourse itself."[64] Some mutual

---

62. Osborne, *Hermeneutical Spiral*, 122.

63. Lonergan links the process of history to context: "As the process advances, the context within which events are to be understood keeps enlarging. As the context enlarges, perspectives shift" (Lonergan, *Method in Theology*, 192). Gadamer puts it this way: "Horizons change for a person who is moving. Thus the horizon of the past, out of which all human life lives and which exists in the form of tradition, is always in motion" (Gadamer, *Truth and Method*, 303). We prefer "mutual context" to "horizon." Although for Gadamer, "the horizon is the range of vision that includes *everything* that can be seen from a particular vantage point" (Gadamer, 301; emphasis added), in English, the horizon is the junction of the earth and sky, that is, the *farthest* we can see. As Funk describes it, "A horizon represents the limits of a system of meaning, of a world" (Funk, *Poetics of Biblical Narrative*, 291).

64. This is Cotterell and Turner's description of the "Presupposition Pool" (Cotterell and Turner, *Linguistics and Biblical Interpretation*, 49; see also 90). We also incorporate into "mutual context" Turner's thought that when "pragmatics speaks of 'presupposition pools,' it is not driving us back to the hidden psychology of the author or reader, but to things that are known by speaker and hearer, writer and reader, because they are conventional to the society of dialogue partners, or because they are situational elements shared by them. The content of 'presupposition pools' is thus a matter of what is in the public context of a speaker's utterance, and so may be taken to count as part of the utterance meaning" (Turner, "Historical Criticism and Theological Hermeneutics," 50).

The similar concept of "common ground" is attributed to Stalnaker: "Presuppositions are what is taken by the speaker to be the COMMON GROUND of the participants in the conversation, what is treated as their COMMON KNOWLEDGE or MUTUAL KNOWLEDGE" (Stalnaker, "Assertion," 321). Mutual/common knowledge is a very strong requirement; thus, many pragmaticists adopt less stringent criteria. Bach and Harnish use "Mutual Contextual Beliefs" because beliefs "need not be true in order to figure in the speaker's intention and the hearer's inference" (Bach and Harnish, *Linguistic Communication*, 5). Sperber and Wilson also "see the mutual-knowledge hypothesis as untenable"

context is critical to communication: "No text of any kind would be comprehensible without considerable shared context and background."[65] Although the individual contexts of the empirical author/speaker and reader/hearer are different and in different situations overlap to different degrees,[66] in every situation sufficient mutual context must be available or created to permit communication.

This requires a cooperative effort from both an empirical author and reader.[67] An empirical author must understand the intended empirical audience in order to appropriately construct the implied author and implied reader, who, by definition, share mutual context. An empirical author must make "special efforts to insure that the transmission adequately incorporate (sic) his intended meaning and that it meet (sic) in advance the foreseeable receivers' foreseeable problems in construing it."[68] More generally, the empirical author "must take account of which interpretations we are likely to put on his words; he must, in that way and for that reason, take expected

(Sperber and Wilson, *Relevance*, 21) and refer instead to "mutual manifestness" (Sperber and Wilson, 41). Instead of these technical terms, we use "mutual context" to refer to information, events, experiences, etc. available to both the speaker/author and audience.

65. Tannen, *Talking Voices*, 37. "We assume the common knowledge of the respectively indicated world between us and our conversation partner, and we must do that in order to be able [*sic*] say more than one sentence per day" (Alkier, "New Testament Studies," 232). See Brown and Yule for a description of the assumptions made by an author and reader in successful communication (Brown and Yule, *Discourse Analysis*, 206–7).

66. See, e.g., van Dijk, *Text and Context*, 210. We prefer "overlap" to Gadamer's term "fusion" even though Vanhoozer finds evidence that Gadamer "would resist equating a 'fusion' of horizons with an 'assimilation' of horizons" (Vanhoozer, "Discourse on Matter," 34n83).

67. Social psychologist Wendelin Reich believes that for pragmatics, e.g., Speech Act Theory, "the structure of communicative exchanges, and that of individual communicative acts, might reflect their evolutionary-functional roots in social cooperation" (Reich, "Cooperative Nature of Communicative Acts," 1350). Booth correctly points out that "at every point the author depends on inferences about what his reader will likely assume or know—about both his factual knowledge and his experience of literature. And the reader depends on inferences about what the author could assume" (Booth, *Rhetoric of Irony*, 99–100).

68. Meyer, *Critical Realism,* 19. "Nothing the writer does can be finally understood in isolation from his effort to make it all accessible to someone else—his peers, himself as imagined reader, his audience" (Booth, *Rhetoric of Fiction*, 397). "Der Erfolg des Sprechers davon abhängt, ob auch der Hörer die illokutive Absicht des Sprechers versteht und ob er in der Lage ist, die gewünschte Reaktion zu vollziehen" (Motsch and Pasch, "Illokutive Handlungen," 73).

audience reaction into account."[69] "Taking expected audience reaction into account" is a function of understanding the context within which the empirical audience operates—social, cultural, linguistic, literary, etc. To be successful in communication, the empirical author must create an implied reader the empirical audience is capable of becoming. Regarding the biblical authors/speakers, Thiselton notes that "both Jesus and Paul, as well as the author of Luke-Acts, allow their material, vocabulary, and mode of communication to take account of the nature of the audience whom they are addressing."[70]

The reader also assumes responsibilities.[71] "The intrinsically appropriate stance of the interpreter is not doubt nor scepticism nor suspicion, but goodwill, empathy, the readiness to find truth, common understanding, agreement"; the reader must approach the text with "an antecedent stance of openness, receptiveness, empathy vis-à-vis his [the author's] word."[72] Taking such a stance has been variously called a hermeneutics of "consent," "trust," "love" or "hearing"[73]; we call it a hermeneutics of cooperation.[74] In the vocabulary of this study, it is important for empirical readers to be

---

69. Wolterstorff, *Divine Discourse*, 199. "Speakers organize what they want to say in accordance with who they're talking to, where, when, and under what circumstances" (Yule, *Pragmatics*, 3). Motsch and Pasch also speak of "die Fähigkeit des Hörers, das fundamentale Ziel . . . zu realisieren" (Motsch and Pasch, "Illokutive Handlungen," 75). See also Perelman and Olbrechts-Tyteca, *New Rhetoric*, 19–20.

70. Thiselton, *New Horizons in Hermeneutics*, 273.

71. The role of a reader of a text is different from that of a hearer of speech. With speech, "the initiative lies entirely with the speaker, and the hearer may receive his or her communication involuntarily or even unwillingly. Where *A* writes to *B* about *x*, however, the initiative is more evenly distributed between author and reader. One chooses to read or not to read; one does not read involuntarily or against one's will" (Watson, *Text and Truth*, 100).

72. Meyer, *Critical Realism*, 22. "An openness to be willing to listen, to see the other person's point of view, and to be changed, characterizes any hermeneutically sensitive reading of texts" (Thiselton, *New Horizons in Hermeneutics*, 33).

73. See, respectively, Stuhlmacher, *Historical Criticism and Theological Interpretation*, 83–91; R. B. Hays, "Salvation by Trust?," 218–223; N. T. Wright, *New Testament and People of God*, 32–64; and Snodgrass, "Reading to Hear," 9–32.

74. Reich refers to studies in biology, evolutionary psychology, and anthropology which show that "humans are an extraordinarily cooperative species" and "how deeply cooperation with conspecifics is built into human nature" (Reich, "Cooperative Nature of Communicative Acts," 1349). Iser notes that every reader strives "even if unconsciously, to fit everything together in a consistent pattern" (Iser, *Implied Reader*, 283).

willing to think within the framework of the implied author's lifeworld[75]—to be addressed by the implied author and to attempt to respond as the implied reader would.[76]

Although cooperative empirical readers must be prepared for the text to tell them something,[77] "cooperation" is not a giving up of self or identity. Cooperative empirical readers do not transpose themselves "into the author's mind"; rather, they try to transpose themselves "into the perspective within which he [the empirical author] has formed his views,"[78] i.e., the perspective of the implied author. Nor does "cooperation" mean an empirical reader unquestioningly comes to live in the lifeworld presented by the text and adopts its worldview.[79] Cooperation is not an abdication of critical thinking. The empirical reader may be either unwilling or unable to be an implied reader at the perlocutionary level.[80] Using Stanley's argument as his example, Watts relates cooperative yet critical reading to quotation:

---

75. See Thiselton, *New Horizons in Hermeneutics*, 562, although his reference is to the empirical author's lifeworld. From a reader's perspective, "if we fail to transpose ourselves into the historical horizon from which the traditional text speaks, we will misunderstand the significance of what it has to say to us" (Gadamer, *Truth and Method*, 302). We discuss lifeworld and worldview in the following chapter.

76. See Chatman, *Story and Discourse*, 150. This requirement applies to all readers. Thus, "for today's readers this construct, the implied reader, works as a system of guidelines for their reading process" (van Iersel, "Sun, Moon, and Stars," 86). Although he believes that "the image of the original audience is likewise no more than a construct of today's analyst" (van Iersel, 86), this is not the case. Rather, the implied reader is a construct of the implied author as mediated by the text. If today's readers read cooperatively, they discover the implied reader rather than the image or mind of the original audience.

77. This comes from Gadamer, who adds that "we cannot stick blindly to our own fore-meaning about the thing if we want to understand the meaning of another. Of course this does not mean that when we listen to someone or read a book we must forget all our fore-meanings concerning the content and all our own ideas. All that is asked is that we remain open to the meaning of the other person or text" (Gadamer, *Truth and Method*, 271). Snodgrass makes the important point that "humility is part of a hermeneutics of hearing; it seeks to know rather than professes to know" (Snodgrass, "Reading to Hear," 28).

78. Gadamer, *Truth and Method*, 292.

79. "When someone thinks historically, he comes to understand the meaning of what has been handed down without necessarily agreeing with it or seeing himself in it" (Gadamer, *Truth and Method*, 302).

80. Even if the empirical reader refuses "his projected role at some ultimate level, . . . such refusal does not contradict the imaginative or 'as if' acceptance of implied readership necessary to the elementary comprehension of the narrative" (Chatman, *Story and Discourse*, 150).

PART I | DEVELOPING A METHODOLOGY

> It is hard to imagine those who were skeptical of Paul's argument being as easily persuaded as Stanley suggests. Already undaunted by his personal authority—this being precisely why according to Stanley Paul must resort to Scripture—how likely are they simply to take his word without checking to see if said citation does indeed support the view they are resisting?[81]

Communicative cooperation does not require that mutual context be either complete or completely activated. Only certain elements of mutual context are relevant in any given communicative situation. A reader pays attention to those elements which are highlighted in some way, such as by being explicitly quoted. By evoking one or several elements of Story via quotation, an author can create or activate mutual context.

THE ACTIVATION OF MUTUAL CONTEXT BY QUOTATION

There are two situational possibilities for the relationship of quotation to mutual context. For those empirical authors and audiences for whom the quoted matter is part of their individual contexts, an explicit quotation activates the relevant contextual elements.[82] In situations where the quoted material is not known by the audience, an explicit quotation adds that material to mutual context and simultaneously activates it. In either case, by evoking Story and thereby activating elements of mutual context, explicit quotation creates a dialogue with the original text, drawing attention to its themes, or story-lines.[83] This is true even in the common situation where the quotation is not the peak of the discourse but is rather a step in the progress towards a climax or peak.[84]

Our final question regarding context is the extent to which mutual context is activated by quotation. In saying that explicit quotation generally

---

81. R. E. Watts, "In Need of a Second Touch?"

82. "Speakers do, of course, remind each other of knowledge which they share, in order to make that knowledge part of the activated context of discourse" (Brown and Yule, *Discourse Analysis*, 65).

83. While not specifically mentioning quotation, Fowler argues that any "attention-catching" device potentially signals thematization (Fowler, *Linguistic Criticism*, 83).

84. Longacre finds a peak even in "hortatory" discourse, such as NT epistles, where "the struggle is to convince the hearers of the soundness of the advice and to launch them on the course of conduct advocated or to discourage them from a course of conduct which is being proscribed" (Longacre, *Grammar of Discourse*, 84).

activates the thematic tradition of the mutual context, we reject the notion that quotation is "atomistic," i.e., that there is "no regard for the original context."[85] However, this does not mean that the original historical situation that called forth the source text is necessarily in view.[86] If, for example, one takes Ps 51 to have been prompted by David's remorse over his sin with Bathsheba, as the superscription indicates, we would not consider Paul's use of Ps 51:4 in Rom 3:4 to be "atomistic" just because Paul is not concerned with the David-Bathsheba incident. Nor do we consider a quotation to be taken "out of context" simply because the NT author applies it to a new referent, such as something said or written about the Jews in the OT and now applied to the Church or about Yahweh and now applied to Jesus.[87]

Nor is the purpose of explicit quotation always to call into the reader's mind every detail of the literary context of the source text, especially if one considers the co-text to be the entire OT or even an entire psalm.[88]

---

85. See Hatina, *In Search of a Context*, 158. "Atomistic" quotation is evidence of "Independent" reading (see chapter 5) and is quotation as a form of play (see chapter 2).

86. Moyise correctly points out that "allusions and quotations are always out of context *to some degree* because they have been loosed from their original linguistic and historical moorings," i.e., their socio-historical and linguistic contexts (Moyise, "Use of Analogy," 33–34).

87. Although Moyise considers the opposite of "fixed meaning" to be the application of words concerning one person to a different person (see, e.g., Moyise, *Jesus and Scripture*, 119; and "Does the NT Quote the OT Out Of Context?," 138, 141), our action model does not tie meaning to a single referent. This is *contra*, for example, Mead, who argues that Jesus "thoroughly disregards" the historical OT situation with his allusion to Ps 62:12 in Matt 16:27, where "instead of God, the *Son of man* . . . will requite each man his activities" (Mead, "Dissenting Opinion about Respect for Context," 281). But even if ἀποδώσει in Matt 16:27 is taken to refer to the Son of Man rather than to τοῦ πατρὸς αὐτοῦ (the immediately preceding singular noun), this may be an attempt by Matthew or Jesus to identify Jesus with the "Lord" of Ps 62:12 and thereby implicitly claim divinity for Jesus.

88. *Contra* Shires, who claims "every quotation or allusion may presuppose both its immediate context and its relation to the entire Hebrew tradition" (Shires, *Finding the Old Testament*, 32–33). Even if the latter statement could be demonstrated generally, in individual cases the relationship to at least some elements of the tradition would be so faint as to be, for all practical purposes, undetectable. Nor do we agree that with quotation the entire co-text "is in view, and is the basis of the argument" (Dodd, *According to the Scriptures*, 126, with regard to certain "fundamental passages," one of which is Ps 110). Referring to Dodd and others, Doble claims that "what in the text of the New Testament appear to be citations or allusions, are, in fact, markers, or signals, or headlines which call into play a larger, *whole* [literary] context" (Doble, "Something Greater than Solomon," 190–91; emphasis added). A similar overly broad claim is made by Pfister, who argues that "mit dem pointiert ausgewählten Detail wird der Gesamtkontext abgerufen, dem es entstammt, mit dem knappen Zitat wird der ganze Prätext in die neue Sinnkonstitution

Although we hold that for all explicit quotation "*some* connotations or associations will carry over from previous contexts" since "if this were not the case, then the concept of quotation would be 'sense-less,'"[89] how much of context is in view differs in various situations. In some cases, following Herbert Clark's notion that "contributors project the most economical evidence they think they need for current purposes," a brief reference, particularly to an opening, peak or topic verse, may point to the broader source text.[90] Brevity may also foster involvement.[91] But whether an OT passage is a shorthand which evokes the literary or socio-historical context more broadly must be considered on a case-by-case basis. We do not assume maximal context (i.e., that a quotation references all of the work quoted, the entire OT, or even a specific tradition, such as the Exodus or an intervening interpretation of it) unless there are clear indications from the verse which contains the quotation or its co-text that more of the literary or socio-historical context is in view.[92]

Furthermore, although in general, we agree with Hatina's caution that "the literary context in which the quotation is embedded must be the final arbiter"[93] and with George Savran's similar thought that the significance both of alterations to quoted material and of verbatim repetition "can be

einbezogen" (Pfister, "Konzepte der Intertextualität," 29).

89. Moyise, *Evoking Scripture*, 20. As Plett notes, "Wo keine einzige Gemeinsamkeit existiert, läßt sich keine Beziehung herstellen" (Plett, "Sprachliche Konstituenten," 93). However, "Hatina has demonstrated that we should not move from this commonsense observation to much larger claims that a quotation necessarily evokes all of its surrounding context" (Moyise, *Evoking Scripture*, 20).

90. H. H. Clark, *Using Language*, 250. Since the cost of communication includes processing time, "participants try to minimize total joint processing time. Other things being equal, the briefer the evidence, the better" (H. H. Clark, 250).

91. According to Tannen, "the necessity of filling in unstated information has long been regarded as a crucial part of literary discourse. . . . This makes discourse effective because the more work readers or hearers do to supply meaning, the deeper their understanding and the greater their sense of involvement with both text and author" (Tannen, *Talking Voices*, 37). See also Iser concerning the "gaps" in texts which allow the reader to "experience the text as a reality" (Iser, *Implied Reader*, 40).

92. Hatina, *In Search of a Context*, 161. Moyise uses "maximalist" and "minimalist" (and "moderate") to refer to various views concerning the accuracy with which the Gospel authors recorded Jesus's use of Scripture (see Moyise, *Jesus and Scripture*, 7–10).

93. Hatina, *In Search of a Context*, 161. Although "both contexts are important," he believes one should begin with the receptor text in order to avoid "a forced transference of meaning" (Hatina, 2, 160). We instead begin with the source text so that we are not influenced in our reading of that text by the receptor text.

assessed only in light of the context in which the quotation is placed,"[94] we hold to the notion of quotation as "dialogical."[95] By this we mean that there is a complex and dynamic relationship between the quoted text and the quoting text, such that "the context and connotations of the original are not entirely left behind, but are brought to bear (*positively or negatively*) in the reading of the citation or allusion."[96] Therefore, in our case studies, we examine sufficient co-text to permit an understanding of the function of the quoted passage in the source and receptor texts and to determine what that passage contributes to Story in each case.

One example of a dialogical approach to intertextuality is that of Hays, who finds that Paul works "to bring Scripture and gospel into a mutually interpretive relation."[97] Because Hays links intertextuality and context to tradition/Story and theology as well as to the creation of meaning, we lead into chapter 4 by evaluating his seminal work, *Echoes of Scripture in the Letters of Paul*.[98]

---

94. Savran, *Telling and Retelling*, 36. Moyise points out that although allusions and quotations "often evoke something of the old context, their meaning is now largely determined by the role and function they have in their new context" (Moyise, "Use of Analogy," 34).

95. Perrin also uses this term and suggests the fruitfulness of considering the NT authors as "addressees" of the OT authors. See Perrin, "Dialogic Conceptions of Language," especially pp. 216–24.

96. Paul, "Use of the Old Testament," 258; emphasis added. For Savran, "although the quoted words take on meaning ascribed to them by their new context, they still retain some autonomy as identifiable prior direct speech, which carries within it some of the sense of its original context" (Savran, *Telling and Retelling*, 110–11). Moyise avers "it is probably best to seek the 'meaning' or 'significance' of a quotation in the interaction between the connotations it (may) bring with it and its role or function in the new work" (Moyise, "Quotations," 28). As Plett points out, "Indem der rezipient im Leseakt den abwesenden Prätext-Kontext des Zitats mitvergegenwärtigt, schafft er zusätzliche Konnotationen des ihm vorliegenden Textes" (Plett, "Sprachliche Konstituenten," 82). Here we disagree with Evans, who believes "the NT writers were rarely concerned with the question of what . . . the text originally meant" (Evans, "Function of the Old Testament," 193). In general, we reject those "postmodern understandings of intertextuality, which . . . contend that later references to earlier texts interact in such a way that new meanings are produced that are completely unlinked and dislodged from the originally intended meaning of the earlier text" (Beale, *New Testament Biblical Theology*, 3). Such readings are "Independent" (see chapter 5). Instead, we follow R. E. Watts in assuming the NT authors are "not unaware of the original contexts and contemporary understandings of Israel's scriptures and that these often provide hermeneutical clues as to the significance of the surrounding New Testament material" (R. E. Watts, "Psalms in Mark's Gospel," 25).

97. R. B. Hays, *Echoes of Scripture*, 176.

98. Others of R. B. Hays's works, including his 1983 dissertation, also have informed

PART I | DEVELOPING A METHODOLOGY

ECHOES OF SCRIPTURE IN THE LETTERS OF PAUL BY RICHARD B. HAYS

Hays approaches "the task of interpretation . . . by reading the letters as literary texts shaped by complex intertextual relations with Scripture."[99] Rather than "seeing quotations and allusions as subsidiary to Paul's main arguments, Hays sees letters like Romans, Galatians, and Corinthians as an ongoing conversation with Scripture,"[100] a conversation set against the backdrop of the changes in the socio-historical context brought about by the life, death, and resurrection of Jesus Christ.[101]

Taking an inductive literary-intertextual approach, Hays considers the "rhetorical and semantic effects" of "poetic allusions."[102] Reminiscent of Lane-Mercier's description of quotation as "play,"[103] Hays claims an interest in quotation as "an act of figuration, establishing a metaphorical resonance between drama and life."[104]

---

this study.

99. R. B. Hays, *Echoes of Scripture*, xi. Israel's Scripture is the "single great textual precursor" which created the symbolic field within which "Paul repeatedly situates his discourse" (R. B. Hays, 15).

100. Moyise, *Evoking Scripture*, 1.

101. The impact of the Christ-event demonstrates why texts "always demand and generate new interpretation" (R. B. Hays, *Echoes of Scripture*, 4).

102. R. B. Hays, *Echoes of Scripture*, 19. Moyise notes that "what is different in Hays's analysis is that he does not present this as yet another proof text for Paul's gospel; rather he turns to literature and poetry to describe the subtle effects of such echoes" (Moyise, *Paul and Scripture*, 112). Some criticize Hays for paying too little attention to the historical-critical method. According to Hübner, "Seine bewußt angesprochene Abwertung der Methode gegenüber der—in der Tat unverzichtbaren!—Sensibilität bringt ihn z. T. um die Früchte seines eigenen so verheißungsvollen neuen Ansatzes" (Hübner, "Intertextualität," 895). On the one hand, this criticism seems to demand too much from Hays's methodology. On the other, it is not entirely accurate. Although Hays admits history is not his main interest, he acknowledges that "attention to intertextuality . . . compels respect for diachronic concerns," and he correctly claims his "treatment of Paul . . . is not ahistorical" (R. B. Hays, *Echoes of Scripture*, xii).

103. See chapter 2.

104. R. B. Hays, *Echoes of Scripture*, 33. Using J. Hollander's *The Figure of Echo: A Mode of Allusion in Milton and After* as a model for reading Paul's intertextual allusions leads Hays to argue that "Paul's citations of Scripture often function not as proofs but as tropes; they generate new meanings by linking the earlier text (Scripture) to the later (Paul's discourse) in such a way as to produce unexpected correspondences, correspondences that suggest more than they assert" (R. B. Hays *Echoes of Scripture*, 24). He finds it "unimaginative" that commentators "ascribe to Paul's intertextual tropes a literal

However, Hays also holds to "a single key hermeneutical axiom: that there is an authentic analogy—though not a simple identity—between what the text meant and what it means."[105] He believes Paul uses "the rhetorical figure of *metalepsis*, a device that requires the reader to interpret a citation or allusion by recalling aspects of the original context that are not explicitly quoted."[106] This happens at different levels.

The first level is the obvious connection between a quotation and its OT co-text. For example, with regard to Paul's use of Ps 51 in Rom 3, Hays believes "no reader familiar with the psalter could possibly fail to hear the resonance of the psalm's unquoted verses with the themes of Romans 3. Rather than spelling out all the connections, Paul opts for metaphorical understatement, allowing this well-known psalm's echoes to sound subliminally beneath the overt argument."[107] Similarly, regarding Rom 15:7–13, which contains quotations from various OT texts, including Pss 18:49 and 117:1, Hays argues that "even here . . . where the significance of the [OT] passages for Paul's case is evident, we will miss important intertextual echoes if we ignore the loci from which the quotations originate."[108]

---

assertive weight that they cannot and should not bear" (R. B. Hays, 175).

105. R. B. Hays, *Echoes of Scripture*, 27.

106. R. B. Hays, "*Echoes of Scripture*: Abstract," 43.

107. R. B. Hays, *Echoes of Scripture*, 49. He elaborates: "The point made explicitly by Paul's citation of Ps. 51:4 is that Scripture proclaims the justice of God's judgment. The point made implicitly is that Psalm 51 . . . models the appropriate human posture before this righteous God: not challenging his just sentence of condemnation but repenting and acknowledging desperate need" (R. B. Hays, 50). Whether or not Hays sees these connections as intentional is unclear. On the one hand, he presents Paul as making deliberate choices; on the other, he finds "little evidence in Romans to suggest these structural parallels are deliberately crafted by Paul" (R. B. Hays, 49). Also confusing is his reference to Paul's use of Ps 51:4 in Rom 3 as adducing "a prooftext" (R. B. Hays, 48). Later, he calls prooftexting a "pejorative label" and describes it as the appropriation of OT language "with minimal attention to the integrity of the semiotic universe of the precursor" (R. B. Hays, 175). Since these comments contradict his thoughts about the connection between this quotation and its OT co-text, it seems he uses "prooftext" somewhat injudiciously with regard to Rom 3.

108. R. B. Hays, *Echoes of Scripture*, 71. See also Hays's thoughts regarding Paul's echo of Ps 97:2 LXX in Rom 1:16–17 (R. B. Hays, 36). He makes a stronger argument concerning the allusion to Ps 143 in Rom 3:20, which he says anticipates "the next turn in the argument," and thus bridges "paragraphs that are often read in disjunction from one another" (R. B. Hays, 52). This allusion is key to Hays's view of Rom 3:21 as "the climax of a continuous discussion that goes back at least to the beginning of the chapter, or indeed all the way back to Rom. 1:16–17" (R. B. Hays, 52).

PART I | DEVELOPING A METHODOLOGY

Craig Evans raises the question of whether Hays sufficiently considers to what extent Paul interacts with Jewish interpretive tradition. For Evans, "it would be more accurate to speak of the echoes of *interpreted* Scripture in the letters of Paul."[109] Paul and other NT authors did not approach the Scriptures of Israel *tabula rasa*; they may have been interacting with interpretations of an OT text. We consider this sometimes overlooked issue in our case studies.

Hays's second level of connection between a quotation and its OT co-text are situations where the pertinence of the Scripture Paul adduces

> is not immediately evident. In some cases the logic of the quotation depends on a preexisting conceptual/theological structure, presupposed by Paul and his intended readers but not explained in the text. The convention of reading the lament psalms as prophetic anticipations of the Messiah's suffering provides a good illustration of this phenomenon (e.g., Rom. 15:3, quoting Ps. 68:10 LXX).[110]

The weakest level of connection includes instances in which "dissonances between the sacred texts and Paul's rendering of them" create an "undeniable gap between the 'original sense' of the Old Testament texts and Paul's interpretation, even in cases where the citations are in verbatim agreement with the LXX."[111] For example, in two instances, including the citation of Ps 19:4 in Rom 10:18, Hays finds "no indication that Paul has wrestled seriously with the texts from which the citations are drawn. He has simply appropriated their language to lend rhetorical force to his own discourse, with minimal attention to the integrity of the semiotic universe of the precursor."[112]

---

109. Evans, "Listening for Echoes," 50; emphasis added. However, Beker's criticism of Hays for not providing "a more detailed critique of the shortcomings of the pesher and midrashic methods" (Beker, "Echoes and Intertextuality," 65) is invalid. Hays argues correctly that "Paul's own hermeneutical practices are sufficiently different from theirs [the pesherists and midrashists] to demand independent investigation" (R. B. Hays, "On the Rebound," 87).

110. R. B. Hays, *Echoes of Scripture*, 87.

111. R. B. Hays, *Echoes of Scripture*, 6. He calls some of Paul's wording changes deliberate "manipulations" which "should not be explained away by appealing to some hypothetical textual tradition not otherwise attested or by saying that Paul was just quoting from memory" (R. B. Hays, 147). Rather, Paul works to achieve a desired reading by "tinkering with the text" (R. B. Hays, 67; see also 80–81, 112–13, 147, 153, 160).

112. R. B. Hays, *Echoes of Scripture*, 175. We evaluate J. R. Wagner's arguments concerning this quotation in chapter 4.

This example points to a tension in Hays's understanding of Paul's interpretive method. On one hand, Hays concludes that Paul "seems to have leaped—in moments of metaphorical insight—to intuitive apprehensions of the meanings of texts without the aid or encumbrance of systematic reflection about his own hermeneutics."[113] Only slightly more tamely, he also contends Paul believed the proper reading of Israel's sacred texts was Paul's own reappropriation of them and that Paul's interpretive practice presupposes "the legitimacy of innovative readings that disclose truth previously latent in Scripture."[114] Furthermore, Hays argues that "Paul's readings of Scripture are not constrained by a historical scrupulousness about the original meaning of the text," and he is adamant that "for Paul, original intention is not a primary hermeneutical concern."[115] Such remarks lead to James Scott's charge that Hays presents Paul as "basically an idiosyncratic reader of the Old Testament with some Christian presuppositions and a few hermeneutical constraints."[116]

On the other hand, Hays acknowledges that if Paul's readings of Scripture were predominantly of the "eclectic" type represented by the citation of Ps 19:4 in Rom 10:18, "his discourse would lose much of its gravity."[117] Rather, Hays believes Paul's intertextuality is primarily of Greene's "dialectical" type: "Paul's great struggle is not a struggle to assert his own authority over Scripture; it is, rather, a dialectical struggle to maintain the integrity of his proclamation in relation to Scripture and the integrity of Scripture in relation to that proclamation, to justify his startling claims about what the God of Israel had elected to do in Jesus Christ."[118] Hays adds that while Paul was "undergoing a profound disjuncture with his own religious tradition," he "insistently sought to show that his proclamation of the gospel was

---

113. R. B. Hays, *Echoes of Scripture*, 161.

114. R. B. Hays, *Echoes of Scripture*, 2, 4.

115. R. B. Hays, *Echoes of Scripture*, 156. In addition to "intuitive" and "innovative," other terms Hays applies in *Echoes of Scripture* to Paul's treatment of the OT include: "revisionary" (R. B. Hays, 67, 81, 120), "casual audacity" (R. B. Hays, 68), "adducing prooftexts" (R. B. Hays, 68, 82, 87) "subversive" (R. B. Hays, 79, 111), "outrageous" (R. B. Hays, 82, 157), "fanciful" (R. B. Hays, 97, 140), "whimsical" (R. B. Hays, 165), "novel" (R. B. Hays, 155), and "daring" (R. B. Hays, 129). Not all of these seem complimentary. In many of them, quotation is presented as "play."

116. J. M. Scott, "'For as Many as are of Works of the Law,'" 191n18.

117. R. B. Hays, *Echoes of Scripture*, 174–78; quote is from p. 175. For Hays's apparent modification of Greene's "eclectic" category, see chapter 2 n61.

118. R. B. Hays, *Echoes of Scripture*, 158–59.

PART I | DEVELOPING A METHODOLOGY

grounded in the witness of Israel's sacred texts" and that "fundamental to Paul's whole theological project is the claim that his gospel represents the authentic fulfillment of God's revelation to Israel."[119] This dialectical perspective is the direction we take here.

A final point which deserves comment is the issue of "meaning." Hays gives five possibilities for the "intertextual fusion that generates new meaning": (i) Paul's mind, (ii) the letter's original readers, (iii) the text, (iv) any personal act of reading, and (v) a community of interpretation.[120] Although Hays claims the "working method" of his book is an attempt to hold all five options "together in creative tension,"[121] in his concluding chapter he privileges reading communities as the locus of meaning since "texts have meaning only as they are read and used by communities of readers."[122] However, the original author and readers and the text do play a strong supporting role: "Claims about intertextual meaning effects are strongest where it can credibly be demonstrated that they occur within the literary structure of the text and that they can plausibly be ascribed to the intention

---

119. R. B. Hays, *Echoes of Scripture*, 2, 60. We agree with this conclusion despite the fact that in response to W. S. Green's criticism (W. S. Green, "Doing the Text's Work," 63), Hays agrees his work "might occasionally overstate the case for continuity" (R. B. Hays, "On the Rebound," 93). Moyise summarizes Hays's understanding of Paul's theme as "God's purpose to raise up a worldwide community of people who confess his sovereignty and manifest his justice," and he argues that this theme makes continuity between Paul's thought and the OT "more easily discernible" (Moyise, *Old Testament in the New*, 135).

120. R. B. Hays, *Echoes of Scripture*, 26. The last of these includes all communities of readers/interpreters subsequent to the original readers. Thus, the tradition evoked by quotation may involve the interpretation of a great many subsequent reading communities. We discuss this in chapter 4 and the case studies.

121. R. B. Hays, *Echoes of Scripture*, 27. This leads D. B. Martin to ask "how Hays intends to enjoy such diverse bedfellows as E. D. Hirsch, Jr. (authorial intention), T. S. Eliot (the text itself), and Stanley Fish (community of interpretation and reader-response) all at the same time" (D. B. Martin, review of *Echoes of Scripture in the Letters of Paul*, 291). Martin concludes that "Hays's rhetoric . . . is New Critical" (D. B. Martin, 292). We do not agree with Martin's assessment.

122. R. B. Hays, *Echoes of Scripture*, 189. This constraint apparently does not apply to Paul, whose readings are "abidingly valid figurations" (R. B. Hays, 187), despite being revisionary, subversive, outrageous, etc. (See n115 above). Hays also argues that "recognizing the metaphorical character of the intertextual relation will prevent *us* from literalizing or absolutizing *Paul's* reading," and he adds that "Paul's own example would lead us to expect that the community, under the guidance of the Spirit, will remain open to fresh readings of the same text, through which God will continue to speak" (R. B. Hays, 186–87; emphasis added). Although there is much to admire about Hays's work, this conclusion is difficult.

of the author and the competence of the original readers."[123] Thus, Hays can claim, "I fail to fall in line with the currently fashionable skepticism about the stability of meaning in texts."[124]

Inspired by a desire to maintain Hays's "creative tension" and by his thought that "Scripture really does retain its own voice and power to challenge and shape Paul's unfolding discourse,"[125] in chapter 5 we develop a theory of interactive communication based in linguistic pragmatics, in which "meaning" is co-created by the author and reader through the construct of the implied author and reader as mediated by the text. We also create a typology of readers in connection with this model of meaning.

With regard to Paul's allusion to Ps 143:2 in Rom 3:20, Hays contends that "the psalm is not adduced as a proof for Paul's assertion, but his assertion echoes the psalm, activating Israel's canonical memory."[126] This thought bridges our move to chapter 4, in which we explore how an author uses quotation to evoke elements of textual tradition or "Story," thus activating its "Story-lines" or theological themes.

---

123. R. B. Hays, *Echoes of Scripture,* 28. The hermeneutical conventions of Hays's interpretive community include the conviction that "a proposed interpretation must be justified with reference to evidence provided both by the text's rhetorical structure and by what can be known through critical investigation about the author and original readers" (R. B. Hays, *Echoes of Scripture,* 28).

124. R. B. Hays, "On the Rebound," 81.

125. R. B. Hays, "On the Rebound," 83.

126. R. B. Hays, *Echoes of Scripture,* 51. By "story" Hays means the Christ-story, which he considers the narrative substructure underlying Paul's writings. We find an "older" level of substructure—as did Jesus and the NT authors—in the ongoing Story of God's people as developed in the OT and interpretations thereof.

4

Tradition, Story, Lifeworld, and Theology

TRADITION AND STORY

TRADITION IS "ANYTHING IN the heritage from the past that is delivered down to the present and can contribute to the makeup of the new ethos."[1] It "provides for cultural continuity and cohesion by *preserving* the authoritative memories of the past,"[2] and it "delivers the framework—intellectual, historical, religious, hermeneutical—needed for a new event or word to be meaningful."[3] In the NT, it is the Jesus event which tradition—both the OT and intervening interpretation[4]—makes meaningful.[5] At the same time, the Jesus event reshapes tradition as it moves into the future.[6]

---

1. Knight, "Introduction," 2.
2. Fishbane, "Torah and Tradition," 286.
3. Knight, "Revelation through Tradition," 165.
4. This concept—although not all of the terminology—comes from Barr, *Concept of Biblical Theology*, 280. We construe "intervening interpretation" quite loosely and investigate apocryphal, Qumranian, and other intertestamental Jewish textual traditions in our case studies.
5. "Jesus' story is told within the structure and language of Israel's faith story. Israel's story shapes Jesus' story, as presented in the Synoptics. Indeed, the OT is a precondition for the Synoptics' story of Jesus" (Swartley, *Israel's Scripture Traditions*, 282).
6. See chapter 3 and the case studies.

In chapter 3, we argued that by evoking textual tradition or "Story," quotation activates mutual context. In this chapter, we explore how evoking Story and activating mutual context transforms lifeworld/worldview, theology (the basic questions and answers), and, ultimately, Story itself. These relationships are not linear but rather simultaneously multi-dimensional and interwoven. Lifeworld, Story, theology, and worldview are both the basis for and the outcome of human action.

We begin by examining the ground-breaking work of four scholars who take a possible function of intertextuality to be the activation of textual tradition.[7] Our goal is to evaluate how their thoughts on quotation, intertextuality, context, and tradition might inform our developing methodology.

FOUR WORKS ON "TRADITION"

Paul's Use of the Exodus Tradition

Like Hays, Sylvia Keesmaat takes intertextuality as her methodological basis. As she observes, "There has been a welcome shift in the discussion in such a way that Israel's scriptures are understood less as an 'authority' to which the New Testament writers were appealing and more as a major component of the symbolic world within which they were thinking."[8] This aligns with our thoughts about quotation evoking tradition rather than serving a power relationship via an appeal to authority. We also agree that intertextuality can produce tension in tradition since intertextuality "both 'disrupts' and 'regenerates' a given textual tradition" and is therefore "one means by which a tradition is transformed and revivified for a new context and situation."[9] Her categories of tension resolution are "(1) alienation, or

---

7. The works by Keesmaat, R. E. Watts, and Pao are foundational to a study of the NT use of OT tradition. We add J. R. Wagner to demonstrate that "tradition" is not limited to the Exodus/New Exodus. Although N. T. Wright's worldview theory also is important to our model, we reserve it for our discussion of "Story" and of the connection between worldview, story/Story, and theology later in this chapter.

8. Keesmaat, *Paul and His Story*, 31–32.

9. Keesmaat, *Paul and His Story*, 51. Paul "was struggling with the question of what it meant to serve God in Jesus Christ and was doing so in fundamental continuity with the traditions and scriptures of his people, Israel. However, the invasive action of God in Jesus Christ introduced a new element into the story, an unexpected twist in the plot, which meant that Paul's dialogue with Scripture involved a transformation and reappropriation of the tradition for the new communities which had come into being in Jesus Christ. . . . The tradition has been transformed in such a way that it is revivified"

an abandonment of the tradition; (2) reversion, or fidelity to the tradition unchanged; and (3) transformation of the tradition."[10] We create a different typology of transformation below.

Keesmaat defines tradition as "those events, stories, rituals and symbols that shape the collective identity of a community, that are passed down in a community from generation to generation and that are rooted in the foundational past of that community."[11] Although we concur that "the power of a story to create a world and shape reality for people is clear,"[12] her notion of the "foundational" past is overly narrow. For her, "the exodus tradition came to express all that was contained in Israelite historical understanding; it was *the* tradition, *the* story which embodied the past, present and future of the Israelites."[13] Although Jonathan Whitlock's criticism that "at its weakest" Keesmaat's study "becomes a prisoner of its own conceit, relating images and language back to the exodus which are better explained otherwise and thus obscuring rather than elucidating Paul's meaning"[14] is overly harsh, it is true that she does not generally consider the possibility "that Paul could in many cases be referring to prophetic writings without consciously intending to invoke the exodus story."[15] Although Keesmaat

---

(Keesmaat, 233).

10. Keesmaat, *Paul and His Story*, 20; see also 33.

11. Keesmaat, *Paul and His Story*, 17.

12. Keesmaat, *Paul and His Story*, 326. I. W. Scott places Keesmaat's work among the recent "full-blooded treatments of Paul's thought using narrative as a central structural feature" (I. W. Scott, *Implicit Epistemology in the Letters of Paul*, 96n3).

13. Keesmaat, *Paul and His Story*, 36. Harrelson makes a similar argument (see Harrelson, "Life, Faith, and the Emergence of Tradition," 20).

14. Whitlock, review of *Paul and His Story*, para. 9. He believes only two of the images in Rom 8:14–17 "which Keesmaat traces back to the exodus tradition . . . are plausibly taken from there directly. For the others the connection is a stretch." Moyise finds Keesmaat's argument concerning Rom 8:18–39 more compelling, since the themes she finds in this passage, namely "adoption, being led by the Spirit, crying out to God as father, suffering, inheritance and glory . . . are all themes associated with the exodus story. She freely admits that Israel's story has ended in 'an unexpected way' and so one cannot simply stress continuity between new and old in an uncritical way. But it is the story that governs the shape of Paul's use of the Old Testament" (Moyise, "Use of Analogy," 40). However, the story Keesmaat refers to in her concluding chapter is "the basic story of the righteous God who called Abraham, promised him many descendants and the inheritance of the whole world, revealed God's nature in the exodus and God's faithfulness throughout Israel's history and in the new exodus in Christ" (Keesmaat, *Paul and His Story*, 237). This Story is broader than the Exodus.

15. Whitlock, review of *Paul and His Story*, para. 4.

broadens her concept of the tradition in her conclusion,[16] her use of the Exodus as *the* structural feature behind Paul's letters is too restrictive.

An example is Paul's quotation of Ps 44:22[17] in Rom 8:36. This is the only explicit quotation in Rom 8:18–39, a passage to which Keesmaat devotes an entire chapter. She links the Exodus to Rom 8 on the basis of the echo she finds there of a "central lament" from Jer 11:18—12:6 along with the thought she takes from Walter Brueggemann that all "subsequent laments in Israel rely upon and appeal to the paradigmatic beginnings of Exodus 2."[18] The "paradigmatic" lament is Exodus 2:23b–25, in which the Israelites "groan" under their slavery, raise a cry for help to Yahweh, who then hears, remembers the covenant, and responds. But not only is this at most a proto-lament in form,[19] to claim on this basis that all biblical laments refer to the Exodus is unjustified. Although Keesmaat's thoughts about tradition and the response to tradition are helpful, we do not follow her in connecting all OT quotation to the Exodus.

Furthermore, Keesmaat not only argues that all Paul's quotations refer to the Exodus, she posits a co-textually maximalist view of those references. For her, Paul "is evoking a whole intertextual matrix, a larger narrative world made up of the whole exodus story, from bondage and suffering in Egypt, to the wanderings and rebellion in the wilderness, to the inheritance of the promised land."[20] Although we agree that quotation can and often does point to a broader context, we find Keesmaat's understanding of not only quotations but even allusions and echoes as evoking "the whole world" of the text to be too sweeping.[21] Rather, we believe that what and how much of Story is evoked by quotation must be evaluated on a case-by-case basis.[22]

16. See n14 above.

17. In *Paul and His Story*, Keesmaat mistakenly identifies this quotation as Ps 44:2, not 44:22 (Keesmaat, *Paul and His Story*, 130, 266). She discusses Ps 44:22 quite briefly and gives no explanation as to why Paul does not quote Jer 11:19a if it is Jeremiah's lament Paul has in mind.

18. Keesmaat, *Paul and His Story*, 129, quoting W. Brueggemann, *Israel's Praise*, 141.

19. According to Westermann, as a Lament of the People, Ps 44 contains five elements: address, lament, confession of trust or assurance of being heard, petition, and vow of praise (Westermann, *Praise and Lament*, 52). Only the lament and petition elements are found in Exod 2.

20. Keesmaat, *Paul and His Story*, 218.

21. "Texts exist in certain contexts, therefore, in alluding to or echoing a specific text the whole world of that text is evoked" (Keesmaat, *Paul and His Story*, 51).

22. Here we agree with Paul that "only study of the texts in question can show the way in which the contexts interrelate" (Paul, "Use of the Old Testament," 259).

PART I | DEVELOPING A METHODOLOGY

Mark's Use of the Isaianic New Exodus

In his ground-breaking work *Isaiah's New Exodus in Mark*, Rikk Watts focuses on Mark's use of the Exodus theme as transformed by Isaiah's prophetic vision into the promise of the Isaianic New Exodus. As we also argue, he finds some OT texts are appealed to "because they invoke, within an ideologically schematised memory of Israel's history, some aspect of Yahweh and Israel's historical relationship to which that text bears witness."[23]

Watts's methodology is based on "the relationship between a community's founding moment and ideology's role in maintaining social cohesion."[24] For Watts, ideology is not content, i.e., "what the group understands about the world"; rather, it is the "lens through which the world is understood."[25] Of particular interest is his proposal that ideology creates a community's unique identity and "provides the interpretive framework through which a given community both understands and shapes its internal relations, its history and its environment; that is, ideology provides a total world view."[26] This is similar to our concept of worldview. However, unlike N. T. Wright, Watts does not link worldview/ideology with theology. Since this link is critical to our model, we rely more heavily on Wright's work.

Watts's belief that all other concerns, motifs, and OT themes in Mark are "presented within the larger literary and theological theme" of the Isaianic New Exodus[27] causes him to stretch the Isaianic New Exodus to cover quite a bit of territory. For him, the Isaianic New Exodus reflects the schema of the first Exodus, e.g., "deliverance, journey, and arrival in Jerusalem" as

---

23. R. E. Watts, *Isaiah's New Exodus*, 50. In at least one instance (the quotation of Isa 29), Hatina argues Watts mistakenly considers that the quotation "acquires its meaning from the Isaian literary context . . . and not Mark" (Hatina, *In Search of a Context*, 252). This criticism seems unfounded although admittedly Watts's interest is not in exploring the dialogical nature of the two texts/contexts. See chapter 3 for a discussion of Hatina's insistence that the receptor text is the final arbiter of meaning.

24. R. E. Watts, *Isaiah's New Exodus*, 28.

25. R. E. Watts, *Isaiah's New Exodus*, 40. Watts does not consider "ideology" to be a pejorative term. This differs from most understandings of that term as represented by Plett's consideration of an "ideological" quotation as one where the "claim to authority is not questioned at all" (Plett, "Intertextualities," 13).

26. R. E. Watts, *Isaiah's New Exodus*, 377; see also 36. For Watts, "the convictions and energies of the founding moment become the 'overall' interpretive schema for the group not only for internal interaction but also for its understanding of history, and indeed the whole world" (R. E. Watts, 39).

27. R. E. Watts, *Isaiah's New Exodus*, 4.

"delineated further with their attendant motifs of, for example, Yahweh as warrior and shepherd," Yahweh as king and servant, the return of Yahweh's actual presence, and the Messiah.[28]

Watts may extend the theme of the Isaianic New Exodus beyond its natural boundaries in his treatment of Jesus's use of Ps 118:22-23 in the Parable of the Wicked Tenants (Mark 12:10-11).[29] According to Watts, Ps 118:22-23 "functions as the 'capstone' to the story"; he concludes that "we may have here intimations that the Markan Jesus sees himself as the one who fulfils the NE [New Exodus] hope of Isaiah 2:2 and 56:7 (cf. 11:16)."[30]

28. R. E. Watts, *Isaiah's New Exodus*, 43; see also 80, 90, 119-20, 347. Although "Israel's view of her history ... seems ... to be structured around several major events or periods: Creation, Patriarchs, Exodus-Conquest, Monarchy, Exile, Return, with the culmination to be found in some sort of expectation of a greater restoration," Watts argues these events "tend to be described in ways which bring out their continuity with the concerns, themes, and trajectories of the founding moment," that is, the Exodus (R. E. Watts, 41). His primary interest, however, is in Isaiah's interpretation of that founding moment. Further, despite claiming that he does not propose "that every appeal to the OT necessarily functions in this way" (R. E. Watts, 51), he does not mention any Markan OT reference that functions in any other way. Even Watts's suggestions for future research concern whether other OT motifs have "consilience" with the theme of the Isaianic New Exodus (R. E. Watts, 388).

29. Another example is Mark 14:62. Since this verse is climactic in the narrative (see chapter 8), it is interesting that Watts finds only "possible" allusions to Isa 50 and 53 in the co-text (Mark 14:58, 60, and 61) (R. E. Watts, *Isaiah's New Exodus*, 364).

30. R. E. Watts, *Isaiah's New Exodus*, 344-45, 346. Space precludes us from investigating Watts's claims that (i) Ps 118 focuses particularly "on the Temple as the goal of the eschatological new exodus," and (ii) "Mark's unselfconscious messianic application within a new exodus framework, suggests that Psalm 118 was already understood along these lines" (R. E. Watts, "Psalms in Mark's Gospel," 30-31; see also 35). With regard to the latter, see Witherington, who argues that "there was early Jewish messianic interpretation of Ps. 118:25-26 referring it to the final Davidide and the redemption wrought by him" (Witherington, *Gospel of Mark*, 310). Marcus adds that older scholars (for example, Strack and Billerbeck, and Jeremias) "assert that a messianic understanding of Ps 118:26 was already present in the Judaism of Jesus' time. This is possible, since the NT passages that use Ps 118:26 ... assume rather than argue for a messianic interpretation, and other NT and early Christian passages (Mark 12:10; Acts 4:11; 1 Pet 2:7; *Barn*. 6:4; *Acts of Peter* 24) reveal a tendency to read Psalm 118 Christologically" (Marcus, *Mark 8-16*, 774-75). However, Marcus concludes that "the Jewish texts cited by Jeremias et al. (*b. Pesaḥ.* 118a; *Pes. Rab.* 31:6; *Midrash Psalms*; etc.) are later than the NT period and prove only that the Hallel psalms were read *eschatologically*, not *messianically*" (Marcus, 775). For Witherington, too, it is "not at all clear that we are to think the crowds understood that all this symbolized that Jesus was the Messiah; not least because Jesus is not conforming to the expectations of the warrior messianic figure of *Pss. Sol.* 17-18 and other early Jewish texts (*b. Sanh.* 98a)" (Witherington, *Gospel of Mark*, 310, referring to Mark 11:9). On the other hand, in an earlier work Marcus suggests that behind Mark's citation of Ps 118 in

PART I | DEVELOPING A METHODOLOGY

But if the Psalm quotation is the "capstone" of the parable, then Watts's claim for a theme of the *Isaianic* New Exodus seems overstated.[31] Although there are links to Isa 5 in the parable,[32] the focus in Mark 12 on Ps 118:22–23 implies a more basic Exodus/New Exodus theme.[33]

Like Keesmaat, Watts takes a maximalist view of context, arguing that

---

Mark 12:10–11 may be "Jewish exegetical traditions interpreting the psalm as a prophecy of eschatological victory. As in 1:2–3 and 1:11, the passage would here be making use of the Old Testament picture of God coming in triumphant holy war to save his people" (Marcus, *Way of the Lord*, 115).

31. It would be more logical to argue Mark meant to invoke the theme of the Isaianic New Exodus if he had quoted Isa 28 and not Ps 118. In Isa 28:16 LXX, the stone (λίθος/ ἀκρογωνιαῖος) is laid for a foundation (θεμέλιον) stone. But in Mark 12:10, which corresponds exactly to Ps 118:22 LXX, the "λίθον has become the κεφαλὴν γωνίας, 'head of the corner,' which probably refers to either a capstone that completes an arch or a capital that sits atop a column or pinnacle of the building. It is not a foundation stone" (Evans, *Mark 8:27—16:20*, 238).

32. See Moyise, *Jesus and Scripture*, 22–23.

33. In several commentaries on Mark which use Watts's book as a resource, this passage is not discussed with reference to the Exodus/Isaianic New Exodus. See Donahue and Harrington, *Gospel of Mark*; Stein, *Mark*; and Marcus, *Mark 8–16*. Moloney notes only that Watts provides "a strong evaluation of the impact of the Isaianic background on 11:27—12:12" (Moloney, *Gospel of Mark*, 232n86). Others who find that Ps 118 points to the Exodus do not mention the Isaianic New Exodus. Hatina, for example, notes that "several studies have convincingly documented that Mark was indebted to the story of the first exodus" (Hatina, *In Search of a Context*, 160, with reference especially to Swartley, *Israel's Scripture Traditions*). L. C. Allen believes Ps 118 was incorporated into the Hallel "due to its many echoes of Exod 15" (L. C. Allen, *Psalms 101–150*, 165; see also McCann, *Theological Introduction to the Book of Psalms*, 166–67). Fuhrmann believes that "by citing Exod 15:2, David recalls the communal story of God's deliverance and salvation over Egypt at the Reed Sea and connects his personal story with the foundation story of Israel's deliverance" (Fuhrmann, "Use of Psalm 118:22–23," 75; see also 69, 81n52).

It would have strengthened Watts's argument if he had considered Isaiah more broadly. Fuhrmann points out that not only is Ps 118:14 an "exact quote of MT Exod 15:2," Isa 12:2 also quotes Exod 15:2 (Fuhrmann, "Use of Psalm 118:22–23," 75). Constant believes that the presence "du nom divin יָהּ" in both Isa 12:2 and Exod 15:2, "jointe à la répétition d'Exod 15:2 en Ésa 12:2, atteste une influence probable du cantique d'Exode 15 sur ce psaume de louange concluant la promesse du retour de l'exil et des temps messianiques" (Constant, "Le Psaume 118," 130; see also 65).

However, although the Isaianic New Exodus may be "not as basic for Mark as Watts makes it out to be" (D. H. Johnson, review of *Isaiah's New Exodus in Mark*, 108; cf. Ahearne-Kroll, *Psalms of Lament*, 170n7), it is important in Mark (see, e.g., Evans, "Beginning of the Good News," 86). For Hatina, the incorporation of both exodus narratives is "part of Mark's larger sphere of influence" (Hatina, *In Search of a Context*, 159). Strauss concludes that Watts's work has alerted scholars "to the possible influence of the Isaianic new exodus in the Gospels" (Strauss, *Davidic Messiah in Luke-Acts*, 304n2).

the true significance of a brief and even fragmentary citation may go far beyond what might otherwise appear to be the case. Although to the untutored the citation might seem of little importance, the fact remains that to trained hearers it has considerable allusive power and thereby serves to invoke a comprehensive hermeneutical framework.[34]

For him, citations "provide a shorthand method of referring to whole fields of meaning which themselves are located within the on-going schema of Israel's 'story.'"[35]

Here, too, in some cases Watts stretches a little.[36] For example, again with regard to the quotation of Ps 118:22–23 in Mark 12:10b–11, Watts

---

34. R. E. Watts, *Isaiah's New Exodus*, 32. Watts references Jeremias, Cranfield, Marcus, and Dodd for his argument that Mark followed a rabbinic practice and quoted "the first section of a verse while *the latter unstated section is actually in mind*" (R. E. Watts, 135; emphasis added). This goes beyond Watts's earlier claims. Plus, Watts's evidence is not totally convincing. Dodd and Marcus make only the vague point that "the conjuring up of the larger context of a passage through the citation of a specific verse or two . . . corresponds to a method of citation found in rabbinic literature" (Marcus, *Way of the Lord*, 199–200; cf. Dodd, *According to the Scriptures*, 126). Jeremias's claim is also weaker than Watts's: "In the Judaism of this period, when large parts of scripture were known off by heart, it was regularly the custom to quote only the beginning of a passage, even if its continuation were kept in mind" (Jeremias, *New Testament Theology*, 54–55). With regard to Isa 42:1 in Matt 12:18, Jeremias states that "as so often in OT quotations, e.g., in Rabb. Literature, the continuation . . . is implied but not directly cited" (Jeremias, "παῖς θεοῦ," 5:701). Since Jeremias is Cranfield's source, Cranfield's evidence is not independent (see Cranfield, "Study of St Mark," 59). None of these scholars gives a rabbinic example. Nor does the example Jeremias gives in *New Testament Theology* of the quotation of Ps 51:4b in Rom 3:4b support his claim since the source text is not the beginning of a passage or even the beginning of a verse. In sum, this argument is too slender a branch to bear the weight Watts tries to hang on it.

35. R. E. Watts, *Isaiah's New Exodus*, 382. This appears to be his only use of "story" although he may refer to it indirectly in his two references to Dodd's "text plots" (R. E. Watts, 50, 382) and in describing "ideology's account of the founding moment," "ideology's account of subsequent events," and "Israel's retelling of its inaugural event" (R. E. Watts, 40, 42, 43). In general, his concern is icon and symbol (the "media of ideology") along with ritual re-enactment ("symbolic revivification") rather than story (see R. E. Watts, 40–46).

36. As Hatina queries, "Do individual terms like 'gospel' and broad themes like forgiveness and wilderness necessarily point to the literary context from which the quotation is borrowed? If Mark wanted to show a continuity between the exodus of Second Isaiah and Jesus' ministry, why did he not explicitly mention the exodus or deliverance in his prologue? And why would he not quote from either Isa 40:9, 10 or 11 since these texts express the theme of the exodus more than all the others?" (Hatina, *In Search of a Context*, 159–60).

believes that "in the light of the messianic overtones of the immediately following verses (118:25f) as used in 11:9, Mark probably means that these verses here should recall that acclamation and likewise be messianically construed (cf. Acts 4:11; 1 Pet 2:7)."[37] Certainly the fact that Ps 118:25–26 was recently quoted in Mark increases the likelihood that passage may still be in mind as a nearby verse is cited. However, even if one agrees that the use of Ps 118:25–26 in Mark 11:9 has messianic "overtones," does this mean a reference to *other* verses of Ps 118 is also necessarily messianic?[38] We take up a similar question in our case study of the NT quotation of Ps 110:1.

In summary, some of Watts's thoughts about ideology/worldview are helpful. In particular, his notion that quotation highlights elements of the on-going relationship between God and God's people is in line with our argument that a function of quotation is to evoke tradition as it is textually represented by Story and thereby to activate mutual context. However, we are not convinced either that every OT quotation in Mark is a reference to the Isaianic New Exodus or that a quotation generally refers to the "whole context." We hold instead that each quotation is to be evaluated on a case-by-case basis.

The Isaianic New Exodus in Acts

David Pao, who references Watts's work, also argues for understanding "scriptural statements" as pointers "toward a wider story" with which the narrative of Acts interacts.[39] Like Watts, Pao contends that "the scriptural story which provides the hermeneutical framework for Acts is none other than the foundation story of Exodus as developed and transformed through the Isaianic corpus."[40] Pao, however, ventures beyond the Isaianic New Exodus, noting that "in ancient Israelite traditions, . . . the Exodus narrative is not understood as being entirely distinct from the Creation story; and a strict separation between the two should not be made."[41]

---

37. R. E. Watts, *Isaiah's New Exodus*, 346.

38. For example, Elliott believes 1QS 8.5, which draws on the "stone" imagery of Isa 26:1, Isa 28:16, and Ps 118:22, provides "evidence of the use of stone motifs prior to the New Testament that may actually refer to the saved community rather than a messiah" (Elliott, *Survivors of Israel*, 332–33).

39. Pao, *Acts and the Isaianic New Exodus*, 4.

40. Pao, *Acts and the Isaianic New Exodus*, 5.

41. Pao, *Acts and the Isaianic New Exodus*, 57. For Pao, "in the evocation of both the

Although, as Pao correctly notes, some Psalms contain creation language, these are not the Psalms quoted in Acts.[42] Since, by Pao's own count, more explicit OT quotations in Acts come from the Psalms than from any other source,[43] this raises a question as to whether Pao has truly captured the "wider story" with his amalgam of the Exodus narrative as transformed in Isaiah plus the Creation story. Somewhat ironically, Watts is among the questioners: "Since most of his [Pao's] explicit Davidic references invoke the Psalms and as Isa. 55:3 is the only explicit Davidic reference in Isaiah 40–66 one wonders if the link with Isaiah's new exodus is as straightforward as Pao implies."[44]

An example may be helpful. Pao analyzes several passages that present Jesus as "a royal figure in the line of David" and "highlight the Davidic kingdom in the restoration program in Acts."[45] These include the series of quotations in Paul's speech in Acts 13:33–35, which Paul uses to describe the raising of Jesus. The first quotation is of Ps 2:7. The second, from Isa 55:3, concerns God's promises to David. The final quotation, from Ps 15:10 LXX, restates the promise that Yahweh's holy one would not see decay. Pao aptly notes that "the cluster of these three quotations, together with the explicit mention of David in vs 36, point to the significance of the David tradition for understanding the status of the exalted Christ."[46]

But since there is no overt mention in this quotation sequence of the Isaianic New Exodus, the link Pao attempts to create to an Isaianic motif

---

Exodus and Creation traditions, the concern with the creation of a new people of God is highlighted" (Pao, 57; see also 251). See Beale for an argument that the New Exodus theme in the NT "is another metaphor for the new-creational kingdom" (Beale, *New Testament Biblical Theology*, 172). However, exploring the relationship between the New Exodus and the new creation would take us too far afield.

42. The psalms which contain creation language are "Pss 74:12–17; 77:12–20; 89:5–37; and 114" (Pao, *Acts and the Isaianic New Exodus*, 57n67), and Ps 145[146]:6 (Pao, 204n62). The only explicit references to Exodus events in the NT Psalms quotations are Ps 78:24 (John 6:31) and Ps 95:7–11 (Hebrews).

43. Pao lists the twenty OT (LXX) quotations in Acts (Pao, *Acts and the Isaianic New Exodus*, 4n15). Seven Psalms are the source of six quotations, and five quotations come from Isaiah, while seven other OT books each provide one or two quotations.

44. R. E. Watts, review of *Acts and the Isaianic New Exodus*, 260. Similar criticism has been levied against Watts himself, as we discussed above.

45. Pao, *Acts and the Isaianic New Exodus*, 135.

46. Pao, *Acts and the Isaianic New Exodus*, 135. Pao confusingly refers to several Psalms quotations, such as Ps 16:10 in Acts 13:35, as "Isaianic passages" (Pao, 85n86). One such "Isaianic passage" (Acts 2) has no explicit quotation of Isaiah.

of restoration is fragile. Not only is the book of Psalms the only identified source text, the Psalms quotations carry more of the content of Paul's argument. The more general quotation from Isa 55:3d, with its reference to the promises given to David now fulfilled in Jesus, can as logically be considered to support the Psalms quotations as vice versa.[47] And, although this passage is bookended with promises of salvation and forgiveness of sins (Acts 13:26 and Acts 13:39–40), which support a restoration motif, Paul's references are to Abraham (v. 26) and David (vv. 34, 36) rather than to the Exodus or Isaianic New Exodus.[48]

Although, overall, we agree with Watts that in Acts "the connection between Davidic hopes and the specifically Isaianic version of the new exodus remains tenuous,"[49] Pao is correct that "an emphasis on the typological use of Scripture that focuses primarily on individual figures of Israel's past should be balanced by an approach that emphasizes the broader story in which the individuals play a part."[50] This is similar to our argument that quotation evokes textual tradition (Story). Although Pao does look at Story beyond the Isaianic New Exodus, we construe Story even more broadly and determine on a case-by-case basis which Story-lines are evoked by quotation.

An issue we raised previously is that scholars question whether the receptor or source text should be primary in determining the meaning of a quotation. In this regard, Gregory Beale contends Pao wrongly believes "the NT text exercises its power over its OT source text."[51] But this criticism

---

47. Here we disagree with Strauss, who finds the New Exodus restoration is in view in Luke's use of Isa 55:3d LXX in Acts 13:34 (see Strauss, *Davidic Messiah in Luke-Acts*, 297).

48. Admittedly, the Exodus is described several verses earlier (Acts 13:17–20). However, Keener, who believes Isaiah is "more dominant at key points in Acts' structure" than the Davidic story, does not list Acts 13:33–35 as a "programmatic text" in which Isaiah is used (Keener, *Acts*, 1:482). And he feels that Pao "may limit Luke too much to a single 'primary grid'" (Keener, 1:482). For Strauss also, "the eschatological new exodus which is described in Isaiah and the Prophets" is not "*the* controlling theme of Luke's work" (Strauss, *Davidic Messiah in Luke-Acts*, 304).

It may be that there are two interrelated themes rather than a single focus on the Isaianic New Exodus. Mallen believes that "Luke uses Isaiah to clarify the nature of Jesus' mission and message of salvation, and the surprising destiny of Israel and the nations" and "appears to use Psalms to provide focused support for Jesus' suffering and resurrection as the Davidic Messiah and his enthronement as Lord" (Mallen, *Reading and Transformation of Isaiah*, 105; see also 189). See also Moyise, *Later New Testament Writings*, 41.

49. R. E. Watts, review of *Acts and the Isaianic New Exodus*, 260.

50. Pao, *Acts and the Isaianic New Exodus*, 253, 251.

51. Beale, review of *Acts and the Isaianic New Exodus*, 96.

is not justified. Pao refers not to the power of the NT text over the OT text, but rather to the power of the OT text in its NT context to accomplish the goal of the implied author: "In the development of the identity of the early Christian movement, the appropriation of ancient Israel's foundation story provides grounds for a claim by the early Christian community to be the true people of God in the face of other competing voices."[52] Secondly, Pao's thought that "in any use of 'ancient' texts, the embedded meaning of the source text is both affirmed and qualified"[53] presents both contexts as important. Pao sees the scriptural tradition as both valuable to and transformed for the current situation, in which the socio-historical context has been altered, most notably by the advent of Jesus Christ. In this, Pao takes a step towards what we argue is the dialogical nature of the relationship between an OT text and the receptor texts in which it is quoted. Wagner opens this door further.

Paul's Use of the Old Testament in Rom 9–11

Building on Hays's work in intertextuality, Ross Wagner examines Paul's use of Isaiah in Rom 9–11 and 15. However, Wagner does not focus on the Isaianic New Exodus but instead considers the interweaving of Isaianic material with other OT material (notably from Deuteronomy and the Psalms). He emphasizes that "other scriptural voices . . . play a crucial role in shaping the meaning and force of Isaiah's words in Paul's argument."[54]

In general, Wagner finds Paul's citations and allusions to be coherent "with the larger narrative and structural patterns found in their scriptural contexts" and considers that the gospel Paul preaches "stands in deep continuity with the witness of the biblical texts to God's continuing faithfulness to the covenant with Israel."[55] However, he calls some of Paul's readings of Scripture "radical" in comparison to the readings of Paul's Jewish contemporaries.

---

52. Pao, *Acts and the Isaianic New Exodus*, 5.

53. Pao, *Acts and the Isaianic New Exodus*, 251.

54. J. R. Wagner, *Heralds of the Good News*, 352.

55. J. R. Wagner, *Heralds of the Good News*, 11. Wagner cites R. B. Hays, *Echoes of Scripture*, 157–58, to support this argument and refers to Keesmaat and others in the related footnote where he adds that "the view that Paul normally paid no regard to the larger context of his citations continues to live on happily in many quarters" (J. R. Wagner, *Heralds of the Good News*, 11n40). Wagner rightly calls "incredible . . . Stanley's assumption that once Paul expended the labor to find and excerpt a passage, he promptly forgot all about its original setting" (J. R. Wagner, 25).

PART I | DEVELOPING A METHODOLOGY

According to Wagner, some of Paul's "radical re-readings" emerge from one of his "fundamental interpretive strategies": reading the OT "as testimony to the surprising reversal wrought by God's grace, in which those apparently outside the scope of God's mercy are included among the people God has redeemed for himself."[56] We consider "reversal" to be a legitimate form of continuity,[57] and we use this concept, along with Keesmaat's notion of a range of possible responses to tension within tradition, in our discussion of the possible transformative goals/results of recontextualizing a source text.[58]

Wagner's characterization of Paul's readings as "radical," "stunning," "brazen," "scandalous," "tendentious," etc. or even as "misreadings" appears to support Stanley's criticism of Paul's quotation technique. Stanley argues that Paul's "decision to include so many 'brazen misreadings of Scripture' in his letters must be judged a major rhetorical miscalculation" since it means the relation of Paul's quotations "to the source text would have been

---

56. J. R. Wagner, *Heralds of the Good News*, 83. Wagner believes "the 'foreignness' of Paul's interpretations to the original scriptural contexts of the citations is best explained, not by assuming that at the moment of writing he did not recall the wider setting of a verse he had previously copied into his notebook, but by recognizing that Paul's gospel and mission have driven him to a radical rereading of scripture" (J. R. Wagner, 52). Wagner also refers to "the shocking nature" of Paul's interpretation of Hos 2:23 and 1:10 in Rom 9:25–26 and to "strong 'misreadings' of this prophetic oracle" (J. R. Wagner, 82, 83), as well as to Paul's "stunning" and "brazen" "misreading" of Isa 65:1–2 in Rom 10:19–21 (J. R. Wagner, 205, 213). At least twice, Wagner fails to put "misreading" in quotation marks (J. R. Wagner, 205, 211); this omission appears unintentional.

According to Wagner, other "radical re-readings" stem from the fact that "on the face of it, Paul's radical claim that the Law can be divorced from the 'works' it commands brazenly contradicts the scriptures, certainly as they were read by most of his contemporaries" (J. R. Wagner, 159; see also 154). We cannot evaluate the law-works issue here although this could prove an interesting future use of our methodology.

It is not clear against what benchmark Wagner considers Paul to "re-read" (especially as compared to his "reading"). Is it Paul's own first reading, an amalgam of all his readings prior to his conversion, the reading of the original audience, the reading of the reading community to which Paul previously belonged, or the reading of a reading community which has developed differently from the one to which he now belongs? Because of this, we avoid the idea of "re-reading" and instead develop a hierarchy of reader roles within the framework of Speech Act Theory (see chapter 5).

57. Per Chazon, continuity can be "of identity or . . . of dissonance"; in either case, it "engages the biblical context and imports it into the new composition" (Chazon, "Use of the Bible," 96).

58. By "recontextualization," we mean using spoken or written words in a new literary context.

difficult, if not impossible, for a knowledgeable reader to figure out."[59] One of Stanley's examples is the quotations in Rom 10:18–21, among which is Ps 18:5 LXX.[60] Here, Stanley believes Wagner "has to strain . . . to maintain his position that Paul took seriously the context of his quotations."[61]

Wagner concedes that

> at first glance, it would appear that Paul has merely torn this sentence [Ps 18:5] from its context . . . and forced it to say something quite different than it does in its original setting. Paul's interpretation would probably have struck a person who was familiar with the psalm as extremely tendentious, since it is obvious that the "voice" and "words" spoken of by the psalmist belong not to Christian missionaries, but to the "heavens."[62]

But Wagner argues that, to the contrary, "Psalm 18, with its cosmic celebration of God as creator, . . . quite appropriately answers the question [in Rom 10:18] drawn from Isaiah 40:28" and that the "citation of Psalm 18:5 implies, not just that messengers of the gospel have gone out all over the world, but more specifically that Israel, knowing the truth about God as creator and entrusted with the inestimable gift of God's νόμος, should have been particularly receptive to the good news of God's salvation for Jew and Gentile alike through Christ."[63]

In general, Wagner does not believe Paul ignores the co-text of the OT passages he quotes.[64] Rather, he finds that the OT "texts exercise a pervasive influence on Paul's conception of the gospel. Particularly where Paul employs the device of intertextual echo, scripture maintains its own voice

---

59. Stanley, *Arguing with Scripture*, 56n46, adding that this poses "serious problems for Wagner's presumption (*Heralds,* 36–37) that Paul expected the literate members of his congregation to retrace, approve, and explain the intricacies of his biblical argumentation to the majority who had little or no formal education and little free time to devote to the task."

60. The other Psalm quotation among Stanley's "notable examples" is Ps 115:1 LXX in 2 Cor 4:13, which we take up as our first case study.

61. Stanley, review of *Heralds of the Good News,* 779; cf. R. B. Hays, *Arguing with Scripture*, 3, 53n39, 56n46, 160–69. As we noted in chapter 3, Hays finds Paul's reading in this instance to be of the eclectic type (R. B. Hays, *Echoes of Scripture,* 175).

62. J. R. Wagner, *Heralds of the Good News,* 185.

63. J. R. Wagner, *Heralds of the Good News,* 185, 186.

64. In the subtitle of his book, J. R. Wagner claims Paul and Isaiah are "in concert" in Romans. This "implies harmony rather than discord" (Moyise, "Quotations," 25).

PART I | DEVELOPING A METHODOLOGY

over against Paul's, continually forcing the apostle to articulate his gospel in terms that are faithful to the scriptural story of God's election of Israel."[65]

This leads Florian Wilk to a different criticism of Wagner's work. Wilk calls "exceedingly questionable" Wagner's approach of beginning "with the analysis of the Old Testament passages" and specifying "the place and function of the statement quoted by Paul in its original context in order to understand the character of the Pauline interpretation of that statement on this basis."[66] He also feels Wagner's maximalist view of the relevant co-text gives undue attention to the OT context.[67] For his part, Wilk considers context quite narrowly, arguing it is only "possible and sensible to reconstruct his [Paul's] understanding of this context in strict orientation toward the elements that coincide with his text."[68]

We concur that "how Paul implemented the reading and interpretation of a section" of the OT "and whether this happened in the same way every time are questions that cannot be answered *a priori*."[69] We do not want to pre-select a mold and attempt to fit Paul or any NT author into it; we continue to hold that the extent to which the OT co-text is relevant must be determined for each NT quotation. However, Wilk's claim that because Wagner begins his analysis with the source text he must therefore derive the meaning of the receptor text from the meaning of the source text is unjustified. Nor do we believe that a redefinition of the referent in reversal necessarily means that the original context is being ignored or bypassed.[70]

Although Wagner's focus is on Paul as author, he does consider Paul's audience. Wagner identifies the "ideal reader" of Romans and considers

---

65. J. R. Wagner, *Heralds of the Good News*, 10, with reference to Hays's work.

66. Wilk, "Paul as User, Interpreter, and Reader," 87, 88.

67. In this, J. R. Wagner follows Hays. As an example, see Wagner's suggestion that in Rom 9–11, Paul "brings to fulfillment the essential story, not only of Deuteronomy 32, but of Israel's scriptures in their entirety" (J. R. Wagner, *Heralds of the Good News*, 201). Wilk has also criticized Wagner on the grounds that "zudem wird die (sinnvolle) Absicht, im Sinne von Hays' 'intertextual echoes' die Resonanzen der jesajanischen Kontexte im Römerbrief aufzuspüren, nur selten ausgeführt" (Wilk, review of *Heralds of the Good News*, 50).

68. Wilk, "Paul as User, Interpreter, and Reader," 88.

69. Wilk, "Paul as User, Interpreter, and Reader," 87.

70. In his review, Wilk does not take account of the possibility of reversal: "Demgemäß ist das Unternehmen, Stellung und Funktion eines Jesajawortes in seinem Kontext zu bestimmen, um diese dazu mit seiner Verwendung bei Paulus zu vergleichen, wenig sinnvoll—und das Verfahren, auf dieser Basis seine Deutung durch Paulus zu klären, verfehlt" (Wilk, review of *Heralds of the Good News*, 51).

which groups among the original audience might have filled the roles of direct addressees and overhearers.[71] In a footnote, he acknowledges that "readers and reading communities contribute an essential element to the interpretive process," and, as we noted in chapter 2, he advocates for a "'hermeneutic of love,' in which we approach the task of interpretation much as we would a conversation with someone we respect and admire."[72] This aligns with our approach; we put the final pieces of the author/reader partnership into our model in chapter 5.

In general, Wagner's thought that Paul finds a larger cultural "story' of God's relationship with Israel" in Isaiah, Deuteronomy, the Psalms, and elsewhere in Scripture points to our understanding of the "Story" of Israel as not one particular narrative but as a richly interwoven tradition, mediated through the OT texts.[73] The quotation of OT texts by NT speakers/authors reflects the relationship perceived between the OT Story of Yahweh's people and subsequent events, especially the Jesus-event. This leads us to further discussion of Story, the role of the Psalms and other non-narrative texts therein, how Story relates to theology, and how Story is transformed.

STORY AND LIFEWORLD/WORLDVIEW

We begin our exploration of literary tradition (Story) with a look at "story," that is, narrative.[74] Hays contends that we "reflect the character of the *kerygma* more faithfully by treating its elements not as atomized facts but as moments in a story."[75] He suggests the way to a narrative approach to

71. See J. R. Wagner, *Heralds of the Good News*, 35–37.

72. J. R. Wagner, *Heralds of the Good News*, 13n51.

73. J. R. Wagner, *Heralds of the Good News*, 31. As we have said, we do not take any one narrative, such as the Exodus, to be the sole substructure for the non-narrative OT material. Nor do we follow Dodd in considering only a few "fundamental" OT passages to be "the substructure of all Christian theology" (Dodd, *According to the Scriptures*, 127). Rather, we agree with Litwak: "This study does not require that every intertextual echo maps to a specific theme" (Litwak, *Echoes of Scripture*, ix).

74. This terminology does not imply anything about the historicity of Scripture: "Story/story" and "fiction" are not equivalent. As R. B. Hays correctly points out, "We should not be misled into supposing that the description of Paul's gospel as 'story' necessarily implies that it is 'only' the product of human ingenuity" (R. B. Hays, *Faith of Jesus Christ*, 21).

75. R. B. Hays, *Faith of Jesus Christ*, 64. Although he is correct that "'story' . . . does not necessarily refer to an actual narrated text; it can refer to the ordered series of events which forms the basis for various possible narrations" (R. B. Hays, 18), this distinction

Paul is via those who believe "*all* ordered worlds are shaped by narrative. This view is stated in its baldest and most radical form by Stephen Crites, who claims that 'the formal quality of experience through time is inherently narrative.'"[76]

Other scholars have noted the role of narrative in creating and sustaining personal and social identity. For example, David Horrell believes stories both "construct a sense of human identity and shape human interaction."[77] Joel Green argues that "narrative is central to identity formation; who we are as human beings is narratively and relationally shaped and embodied."[78] Of particular interest are Crites's sacred stories, those "fundamental narrative forms" through which "men's sense of self and world is created."[79]

---

is not significant for us.

76. R. B. Hays, *Faith of Jesus Christ*, 20, quoting Crites, "Narrative Quality of Experience," 291. N. T. Wright makes a similar claim for the value of story in epistemology: "Stories . . . provide a vital framework for experiencing the world," and thus "the stories which characterize the worldview itself are . . . located, on the map of human knowing, at a more fundamental level than explicitly formulated beliefs, including theological beliefs" (N. T. Wright, *New Testament and People of God*, 38). Wright bases his epistemological model on critical realism, which is "a way of describing the process of 'knowing' that acknowledges the *reality of the thing known, as something other than the knower* (hence 'realism'), while also fully acknowledging that the only access we have to this reality lies along the spiraling path of *appropriate dialogue or conversation between the knower and the thing known* (hence 'critical')" (N. T. Wright, 35). Although we use insights from Wright's model (below), our concern is not epistemology but communicative interaction. Therefore, we do not explore critical realism in detail.

77. Horrell, "Significance of 'Paul's Story,'" 170. Tannen concurs: "Storytelling . . . is a means by which humans organize and understand the world, and feel connected to each other" (Tannen, *Talking Voices*, 105).

78. J. B. Green, "Practicing the Gospel," 393–94.

79. Crites, "Narrative Quality of Experience," 295. Some scholars reject this because of their narrow construal of narrative. For example, in response to Hays's *Echoes of Scripture*, Hübner comments negatively that "Paulus erzählt im Röm ja keine 'story about δικαιοσύνη θεοῦ', er bietet vielmehr einen theologischen Diskurs" (Hübner, "Intertextualität," 892). More basically, Beaumont rejects the idea that "human experience itself is already narrative in its form," which he considers to be the basic argument of Crites, Hauerwas and Burrell, and MacIntyre (Beaumont, "Modality of Narrative," 133). (For Hauerwas and Burrell, see "From System to Story." For MacIntyre, see "Virtues"). For the most part, Beaumont agrees with Ricoeur's more modest claim that "since human experience (including experience of the divine) is temporal, narrative is the most suitable form of discourse to express its temporality" (Beaumont, "Modality of Narrative," 133).

However to say we "live in" Story is not to say that all texts are narrative or that the only textual tradition which undergirds lifeworld is the narrative genre. As we discuss below, our interest in textual tradition is in what we name "Story," in which biblical narratives and non-narrative textual elements all have a place.

Such stories project symbolic worlds, which "are not like monuments that men behold, but like dwelling-places. People *live in them*."[80] To borrow (and slightly modify) a phrase from Brian Wicker, all humanity lives in a "Story-shaped world."[81]

This understanding of story leads us to the concept of *lifeworld*, "the world of our *common experience.*"[82] According to Jürgen Habermas, "the world gains objectivity only through *counting* as one and the same world *for* a community of speaking and acting subjects. . . . Through this *communicative practice* they assure themselves at the same time of their common life-relations, of an intersubjectively shared *lifeworld.*"[83] Because of its communicative focus, lifeworld is a construct which fits our methodology particularly well. In terms of our earlier discussion, the lifeworld is the world in which a "community of words" or "communicative community" shares mutual context.

How a community that shares a lifeworld perceives the world "out there" and determines how to relate to that world is its "worldview."[84] David Naugle links worldview back to lifeworld with this pragmatic test: "Does the worldview work? Is it livable? . . . Can it be applied helpfully to the most important areas of human life and experience?"[85]

---

80. Crites, "Narrative Quality of Experience," 295; emphasis added.

81. This phrase comes from the title of Wicker's *The Story-Shaped World*.

82. Schutz and Luckmann, *Structures of the Life-World*, 1:68.

83. Habermas, *Reason*, 12–13. See also Habermas, *Lifeworld and System*, 113–52. We do not agree that "the different aspects of communicative action (understanding, coordination, sociation)" are "rooted in the structural components of speech acts (propositional, illocutionary, expressive)" (Habermas, *Lifeworld and System*, xxv). In particular, the third component of a speech act is not "expressive" but perlocution—a dimension critical to the model we finalize in chapter 5. We also prefer communicative "interaction" to communicative "action."

84. According to N. T. Wright, worldviews "form the grid through which humans, both individually and in social groupings, perceive all of reality" (N. T. Wright, *New Testament and People of God*, 32). For philosopher James Olthuis, "A worldview (or vision of life) is a framework or set of fundamental beliefs through which we view the world and our calling and future in it. . . . It is the integrative and interpretative framework by which order and disorder are judged; it is the standard by which reality is managed and pursued; it is the set of hinges on which all our everyday thinking and doing turns" (Olthuis, "On Worldviews," 155). "Since a worldview gives the terms of reference by which the world and our place in it can be structured and illumined, a worldview binds its adherents together into community. Allegiance to a common vision promotes the integration of individuals into a group" (Olthuis, 156).

85. Naugle, *Worldview*, 327.

PART I | DEVELOPING A METHODOLOGY

Before we consider the relationship of lifeworld to intertextuality, we must first define Story and then articulate its role in lifeworld and worldview.

"STORY"

We define "Story" as the aggregate of those elements of a communicative community's literary tradition that help define its lifeworld and thus its worldview. With this, we broaden "Story" beyond "story" to include non-narrative literary tradition.[86] "Story" encompasses not only narrative genre but also non-narrative speech and text, such as the Psalms and biblical epistles.[87] It also can include intervening interpretations of a text.[88]

Non-narrative material plays a role in Story from two related vantage points. First, there may be a narrative substructure to non-narrative literary tradition.[89] As Crites points out, resonances of the sacred story "sound in poetic productions that seem to defy all traditional forms of storytelling."[90]

---

86. This seems preferable to attempting to fit all NT writing into narrative genre. Adams's claim that Romans is "story" in the sense of narrative is not plausible, and his attempt to identify elements of plot, setting, and characterization therein using a Greimasian scheme is awkward (see Adams, "Paul's Story"). Hays also flirts with this when he attempts to locate narrative *structure* in Galatians 4:3–6, 3:13–14, and 3:21–22 as a means of demonstrating that Paul's theology rests on a narrative *substructure* (cf. R. B. Hays, *Faith of Jesus Christ*, chapters 3–5).

87. "A people's story is not necessarily purely narrative: materials of many kinds may be slotted into a narrative structure, and this is done in the Hebrew Bible. Thus legal materials are inserted and appear, almost entirely, as part of the Moses story. In this case they are incorporated into the narrative. Others are more loosely attached: songs and hymns of the temple and of individuals, mostly collected in the Book of Psalms but some slotted into the narratives as in Samuel, Kings and Chronicles" (Barr, *Concept of Biblical Theology*, 356).

88. Bock believes that "to be complete, intertextuality should continue to glance at the historical interpretive tradition behind an Old Testament text" (Bock, *Proclamation from Prophecy and Pattern*, 273).

89. According to J. B. Green "even those texts that do not exhibit an explicitly narrative mode of discourse—say, the latter prophets or letters—have a storied character about them" (J. B. Green, "Scripture and Theology," 17; cf. Beale, *New Testament Biblical Theology*, 166). To use R. B. Hays's term, "reflective discourse" can be "rooted in and shaped by a story" (or Story) (R. B. Hays, *Faith of Jesus Christ*, 95) without exhibiting narrative characteristics.

90. Crites, "Narrative Quality of Experience," 297. Referring to Ps 42, Watson points out that the common tendency to see poetry "as a communing with self for the sake of self . . . ignores the fact that as communicative action writing is normally directed towards others, with the intention of conveying a communicable, public meaning that

Secondly, Paul Ricoeur identifies a critical role for non-narrative material in developing the lasting significance of stories: "Laws, prophecies, wisdom sayings, and hymns, by contributing to the full *meaningfulness* of biblical narratives, start the transfer from mere storytelling to the grasping of the enduring signification of the stories themselves."[91] By contributing to Story, non-narratives help define lifeworld/worldview.

George Lindbeck connects non-narrative texts to lifeworld: "A habitable text need not have a primarily narrative structure" but must only "in some fashion be construable as a guide to thought and action in the encounter with changing circumstances. It must supply followable directions for coherent patterns of life in new situations."[92] Using our terminology, the implied author of a "habitable"[93] text must create an implied reader whose lifeworld/worldview and related Story serve as a guide for thought and behavior.[94] Such "habitable" texts include the Psalms.

In this regard, Arvid Kapelrud highlights the criticality of the Psalms to tradition/Story: "No investigation of Israelite traditions can be done without a discussion of the material found in the psalms.... A picture of the religion of ancient Israel is not complete, not even correct, if it does not make a comprehensive use of the psalms. There the traditions were welded together in a theological form which was directive in Israelite religion."[95] This leads to our next step: to explore what we mean here by "theology" and how it relates to the biblical Story, lifeworld, and worldview.

---

evokes a definite response. This text is intended for *use*" (Watson, *Text and Truth*, 117).

91. Ricoeur, *Figuring the Sacred*, 246; see also 37. "God is named in diverse ways in narration that recounts the divine acts, prophecy that speaks in the divine name, prescription that designates God as the source of the imperative, wisdom that seeks God as the meaning of meaning, and the hymn that invokes God in the second person" (Ricoeur, 227). Goldingay adds that "nonnarrative books such as the Psalms, the Prophets, and the epistles abound in material that has taken the first step from narrative to discursive statement" (Goldingay, "Biblical Narrative," 134).

92. Lindbeck, "Scripture, Consensus, and Community," 97.

93. Ricoeur also speaks of "inhabiting" and "dwelling in" a text and the world it intends (see Ricoeur, *Figuring the Sacred*, 232–34).

94. The implied author and implied audience, by definition, share a lifeworld and worldview. With regard to the relationship of the implied author to the empirical author, Thiselton reminds us that "what is important is not our knowledge of the name and biography of an author, but that the text which the author produces is understood ... as a wholeness which represents the vision of a human mind and which belongs to some larger context or life-world" (Thiselton, *New Horizons in Hermeneutics*, 261).

95. Kapelrud, "Tradition and Worship," 123.

PART I | DEVELOPING A METHODOLOGY

LIFEWORLD/WORLDVIEW, STORY, AND THEOLOGY

To discuss the relationships among lifeworld/worldview, Story, and theology, we adapt N. T. Wright's model in which worldview consists of four elements: the stories we tell ourselves and one another, basic questions and answers concerning human existence, symbols, and praxis.[96] Although Wright refers to stories as the "irreducible narrative element,"[97] he allows room in worldview for other types of literature and, therefore, for Story. For example, he finds that "short poems and aphorisms are to worldviews what snapshots are to the *story* of a holiday, a childhood, a marriage."[98]

Wright makes explicit the connection between worldview, story (here, Story), and theology, arguing convincingly that "worldviews are . . . profoundly *theological*" since "'worldview' . . . embraces all deep-level human perceptions of reality."[99] In our model, theology stands at the intersection of two worldview elements: Story and the basic questions and their answers. The "basic questions" concern both the existence and attributes of a divine being, in our case Yahweh, and the relationship of Yahweh to the world. More specifically, they cover Yahweh's character and work:

- whether or not Yahweh exists,
- if so, what Yahweh is like,
- how Yahweh relates to the world, and
- what Yahweh is doing or will do about putting the world to rights;

---

96. See N. T. Wright, *New Testament and People of God*, 38. For Wright, stories are the organizing focus and "most characteristic expression of worldview," and "symbol and praxis point beyond themselves to a controlling story or set of controlling stories which invest them with wider significance" (N. T. Wright, 123; see also 45, 125).

97. N. T. Wright, *New Testament and People of God*, 38. For Naugle, "since people are storytelling creatures who define themselves and the cosmos in a narrative fashion, the content of a worldview seems best associated with this most relevant activity" (Naugle, *Worldview*, 291).

98. N. T. Wright, *New Testament and People of God*, 65. He speaks primarily of "stories" or the "category" or "element" of story, by which he refers to narrative genre. Only rarely does he refer to "Story" (see, e.g., N. T. Wright, 6).

99. N. T. Wright, *New Testament and People of God*, 122, 123. Theology "provides an essential ingredient in the stories that encapsulate worldviews; in the answers that are given to the fundamental worldview questions; in the symbolic world which gives the worldview cultural expression; and in the practical agenda to which the worldview gives rise" (N. T. Wright, 130).

and also human existence:

- who are we,
- where are we,
- what is wrong, and
- what is the solution, i.e., how are we to relate to Yahweh and each other?[100]

Not only are these questions about Yahweh and humanity's relationship to Yahweh theological, the answers are elements of Story.[101] The Story of Yahweh's people, which is comprised of answers to the theological questions, gives rise to a certain lifeworld/worldview and determines and sustains appropriate praxis.[102]

---

100. These questions are adapted from N. T. Wright, *New Testament and People of God*, 127, 123.

101. By construing the answers to the basic theological questions as the Story of Israel, we avoid L. T. Johnson's criticism that N. T. Wright's method demands "an artificial unification into a single story that he can term 'the authentic first-century Jewish worldview' (p. 149)" (L. T. Johnson, review of *The New Testament and the People of God*, 537).
Various scholars have attempted to outline the "single story" of Israel. We evaluated several examples earlier in this chapter. Beale also outlines a very general "story" (see Beale, *New Testament Biblical Theology*, 116). For N. T. Wright, the OT story includes: Adam and the fall, Abraham, the descent into Egypt, the exodus rescue/liberation under Moses's leadership, the conquest, the period of the judges, David and the establishment of the monarchy, David's successors and the division of the kingdom, the exile, and the return from exile under Zerubbabel and the high priest Joshua and also under Ezra and Nehemiah (see N. T. Wright, *New Testament and People of God*, 216). Others argue instead for one basic theme. For R. B. Hays, "Scripture is . . . a story about *dikaiosynē theou*, God's righteousness, which is the ground of the narrative unity between law and gospel" (R. B. Hays, *Echoes of Scripture*, 157). Harrelson finds the basic theme of the core tradition to be "Yahweh's Promise on the Way to Consummation" (Harrelson, "Life, Faith, and the Emergence of Tradition," 30), although, oddly, he does "not understand the core tradition to provide anything like a 'center' of the Old Testament, theologically viewed" (Harrelson, 30n17).
Here, we identify Story by its theological Story-lines, and we do not limit it to one foundational narrative or central theme. Instead, all answers to the basic theological questions contribute to Story.

102. Theology is also instrumental in *interpreting* worldview: It "suggests certain ways of telling the story, explores certain ways of answering the questions, offers particular interpretations of the symbols, and suggests and critiques certain forms of praxis" (N. T. Wright, *New Testament and People of God*, 126). With quotation, however, our interest is in theology's role in (trans)forming Story, worldview/lifeworld, and praxis.

By providing answers to the basic questions, the Psalms contribute to theology.[103] Therefore, the mutual context created/activated by the quotation of a psalm has a theological dimension, and the theology mediated via such a quotation is lifeworld/ worldview transformative for the NT audience.[104] Story and theology also are transformed. Before exploring how this happens, we need both to establish the connection between lifeworld, Story, and quotation and to define what we mean by "transformation."

EVOKING STORY BY QUOTATION

Luke Timothy Johnson connects Story and lifeworld to intertextuality: "The world which the text produces is . . . a complex network of literary interconnections" which "create a world of metaphoric structures within which humans can live in a distinctive manner."[105] For NT authors to refer to or quote the OT is

> an indication that they perceive themselves as participating in a discourse that is shaped by a perception of life and the world according to the Scriptures, that is, according to a Jewish social and symbolic universe. At the center is the relationship with the one God who has committed himself in his covenant and promises to his people Israel. To refer to the Scriptures as a way of participating in a relationship is something entirely different from a so-called "use" of Scripture as prooftext or a reference to divine authority on the part of the interpreter. It could better be described as a reference to one's foremost loyalty and an acknowledgement of being a response-able participant in a life and discourse rooted in the guidance of the God of Israel.[106]

---

103. Goldingay calls the Psalms "arguably the densest theology in Scripture" (Goldingay, "Biblical Narrative," 137). According to McCann, the Psalms "instruct the people of God about God, about themselves and the world, and about the life of faith" (McCann, *Theological Introduction to the Book of Psalms*, 20–21). Since the Psalms universalize the emotions attached to situations of praise, thanksgiving, and lament without being limited to specific historical circumstances, they are valuable to all Yahweh's people.

104. Since the psalms "expound a theme through repetition and poetic imagery," they provide "a medium whereby theological notions could be imparted to and remembered by the people" (J. W. Watts, *Psalm and Story*, 28, 81).

105. L. T. Johnson, "Imagining the World Scripture Imagines," 175.

106. Ehrensperger, "Paul and the Authority of Scripture," 310–11. With regard to Hays's work, W. S. Green asks, "Does a literary relationship between two texts necessarily imply a comparable theological one?" (W. S. Green, "Doing the Text's Work," 62). We

TRADITION, STORY, LIFEWORLD, AND THEOLOGY

Quotation plays a key role in sharing Story because worlds can be accessed "through the explicit presence of expressions of previous sentences."[107] OT quotations thus evoke the story/Story the NT speakers and authors are *living* and into which they are now inviting (or reminding) their audiences to live.[108]

TRANSFORMATION

Our understanding of lifeworld and of story/Story is less static than that of Habermas, for whom the lifeworld is "presupposed as unproblematic" and within which "subjects acting communicatively always come to an understanding."[109] Rather, we believe that "no experience is in essence definable as 'unproblematic'" and, further, that all "acts which gear into the everyday life-world change it."[110] However, to look ahead to the next chapter, we consider "full" transformation to involve more than a change in the mutual context of the hearer/reader.[111]

Our interest is in the transformation of lifeworld/worldview, Story, and theology which occurs in response to tension. Tension can stem from a new event, such as the Jesus-event, or another element, such as the interposition of another Story.[112] Quotation is an impetus for transformation since

---

concur with R. B. Hays that "if the literary is not co-essential with the theological, it is at least organically fused.... Intertextual literary linkages both reflect and create theological convictions" (R. B. Hays, "On the Rebound," 83).

107. Van Dijk, *Text and Context*, 229, where he refers to "certain worlds" which can be accessed only in this way.

108. As an example, for Neufeld, the author of 1 John "makes and shapes a world with definite ethical responsibilities, which his readers are invited to enter" (Neufeld, *Reconceiving Texts as Speech Acts*, 4).

109. Habermas, *Reason*, 70.

110. Schutz and Luckmann, *Structures of the Life-World*, 1:265, 1:272.

111. Perelman and Olbrechts-Tyteca are correct that an unfolding argument "changes the situation of the audience, and this no matter what its reception of the arguments.... A speech does not leave the hearer the same as he was at the beginning" (Perelman and Olbrechts-Tyteca, *New Rhetoric*, 491). But this is not the "transformation" we consider.

112. These are interrelated. Story is a means by which one's own or others' views of the world may be reinforced, modified, or challenged (see, e.g., N. T. Wright, *New Testament and People of God*, 39). Wright theorizes, for example, that Paul's "repeated use of the Old Testament is designed to suggest new ways of reading well-known stories, and to suggest that they find a more natural climax in the Jesus-story than elsewhere" (N. T. Wright, 79).

tension is "the inevitable product of engaging more than one context."[113] Thus, whenever Story is evoked and mutual context is created and/or activated, there is the potential for transformation of the empirical audience.

We base our typology of transformation on communication theorist Walter Fisher's categorization of the functions of stories: "(1) to give birth to—to gain acceptance of—ideas/images, *affirmation*; (2) to revitalize or to reinforce ideas/images, *reaffirmation*; (3) to heal or to cleanse ideas/images, *purification*; and (4) to undermine or to discredit ideas/images, *subversion*."[114] These can be consolidated into two basic types of transformation. Fisher's second and third categories, in which a "later experience . . . does not suppress and replace the earlier experience,"[115] can be combined as "realignment."[116] The second type of transformation is subversion, where existing ideas are undermined.[117] But subversion does not leave a vacuum in the socio-cultural fabric. Rather, the subverted ideas are replaced by other ideas. Subversion is irrevocably linked to affirmation or re-creation.[118]

In the same way that reaffirmation and purification are different subtypes of realignment, there are different subtypes of subversion. In addition to "reversal," which we discussed earlier in this chapter, another key type is "inversion," which

> was frequently practiced by Israel's classical prophets. When in Rom. 11.9–10 Paul cites imprecatory Psalms originally directed

---

113. Moyise, *Evoking Scripture*, 32.

114. Fisher, *Human Communication as Narration*, 144. Fisher is credited with introducing narrative theory to the field of communication.

115. Gese, "Tradition and Biblical Theology," 314.

116. Realignment is Fishbane's term (see Fishbane, *Biblical Interpretation*, 409). It is a type of transformation since it generally occurs in response to some "disorder, either disparity between or disharmony within orientations. Some turmoil needs to be calmed, some order restored, some trouble resolved" (Crafton, "Dancing of an Attitude," 436).

117. As Hays and Green point out, it is not necessarily the case that "via the phenomenon of intertextuality a NT writer simply agrees with and builds on an earlier writing" (Hays and Green, "Use of the Old Testament," 129).

118. Although Thiselton believes "many narratives . . . *found and create*, rather than *subvert*, worlds" (Thiselton, *New Horizons in Hermeneutics*, 571), in actuality, all hearers/readers already belong to a lifeworld and have a worldview. As Schutz and Luckmann point out, "the actor is 'always already' within society" (Schutz and Luckmann, *Structures of the Life-World*, 2:66). Thus, subversion and creation are linked, and "explicit intertextuality can carry with it both 'disruptive' and 'reconstructive' features" (Boyarin, "Old Wine in New Bottles," 541).

against Israel's enemies (Pss. 69.22–23 and 35.8) and applies them against Israel herself, he has employed the hermeneutics of prophetic criticism. He has done what Isaiah did centuries earlier when the seventh-century prophet, for example, alluded to David's great victories, implying that God would once again defeat his enemies—only this time Israel was God's enemy (see Isa. 28.21).[119]

Another subtype is parody, i.e., "repeating an old pattern or echoing ancient metaphors to signal difference at the very heart of similarity."[120] Subversion also occurs "when a particular retelling of the community's story . . . challenges or transforms accepted readings in the service of a revisionary vision for the community's life."[121] Such transformation may be highly beneficial. As Ben Meyer notes, the "new ascertainment . . . may . . . be welcomed as a liberation, a life-saver, a pearl of great price."[122]

Wright downplays subversion with his argument that in order to make sense of a story, event or datum that conflicts with one's worldview, one generally invents a new story to explain "how the evidence for the *challenging* story is in fact deceptive."[123] For him, subversion is a slow and stubbornly resisted process. Only eventually do "some worldviews become progressively harder and harder to retain, needing more and more conspiracy theories in order to stay in place, until they (sometimes) collapse under their own weight."[124] We, however, believe Story is evoked not only to support or realign lifeworld and worldview, but also to alter them more substantially—to "mediate, challenge, confront, reshape"[125] them—and that this can happen more immediately.

---

119. Evans, "Listening for Echoes," 51.

120. Hays and Green, "Use of the Old Testament," 129.

121. R. B. Hays, "Liberation of Israel," 102.

122. Meyer, *Reality and Illusion*, 52.

123. N. T. Wright, *New Testament and People of God*, 42; emphasis added. Although Moritz links Wright's "spiralling path of dialogue" to "hypothesis-verification/falsification" (Moritz, "Critical but Real," 179), Wright's model of hypothesis/verification does not include falsification.

124. N. T. Wright, *New Testament and People of God*, 117. Although Wright acknowledges that "stories are . . . peculiarly good at modifying or subverting other stories and their worldviews" (N. T. Wright, 40), his model calls for the subversion of worldview to be a lengthy process which is often successfully deflected.

125. Moritz, "Critical but Real," 186.

Whether realignment or subversion pertains in any particular situation depends in part upon to what extent the speaker/author and audience already share a lifeworld. Watson points out that

> it makes a considerable difference whether this relationship to existing language and knowledge is understood in terms of *repetition and supplementation* on the one hand or *antithesis and eclecticism* on the other. In the first case, an existing knowledge is given retrospective sanction by the gospel, which presents itself as the completion of that which already exists.... In the second case, existing knowledge is declared to consist largely in distortion and falsehood.[126]

Thus, subversion appears to be in view in NT situations where Story is evoked via quotation for an audience whose lifeworld/worldview is dramatically different from the author's. In such cases, "the telling of stories in the Bible has among its chief aims the subversion of the hearers' and readers' worldviews."[127] In other words, the message of the NT may have been equally challenging for Jews who were not yet Christians and for Gentiles; for both groups, transformation would be of the subversion type.

TRANSFORMATION AND POWER

Our argument is that OT quotation evokes theological elements of Story to invite the empirical audience (via the implied author and reader) to live into the lifeworld of the people of God as that lifeworld is redefined by the life, death, and resurrection of Jesus.[128] Although changes in lifeworld are most obvious in the situation of subversion, realignment also has an impact on lifeworld, worldview, and Story.

---

126. Watson, *Text and Truth*, 250–51.

127. Moritz, "Critical but Real," 179. Although N. T. Wright distinguishes "between those who share a worldview (who tell one another stories to confirm and fine-tune the worldview) and between holders of different worldviews (who tell one another stories designed to subvert one another's positions)," he believes a "subversive" story must be "close enough to the story already believed by the hearer for a spark to jump between them" (N. T. Wright, *New Testament and People of God*, 45, 40). But it is hard to imagine how a "spark" could cross the vast gap from polytheism to monotheism. Such subversion is more dramatic than Wright describes.

128. *Contra* to what he sees as Lindars's notion that the earliest OT use by Jesus's followers was apologetic, Juel argues cogently that OT quotation clarifies "the implications of faith in Jesus for one's relationship with Israel's God and with the world" (Juel, *Messianic Exegesis*, 1, with reference to Lindars, *New Testament Apologetic*).

But in neither case is the transformation accomplished via quotation necessarily the result of domination or manipulation. With regard to Paul, Ehrensperger points out that he "did not refer to the Scriptures in order to introduce prooftexts or to issue a final word that cannot be challenged. . . . For Paul, the word of God is alive, not static, and thus a word of God would never close a debate. It would serve rather to empower the debaters and thus to promote a response-able hearing by the community involved."[129] In other words, the interaction between author and reader generally is dialogic; communication is not a one-way street. "The Biblical text . . . seeks to persuade its readers to accept the depicted world as their world."[130] Since evoking Story calls for a transformative response of belief and/or action on the part of the audience, "telling" is not the only dimension of communication; "hearing" and "responding" are also critical.[131]

How the transforming communicative interaction occurs is the final piece of our methodology. We use linguistic pragmatics—and especially the often-neglected speech-act element of perlocution—to develop an "action" model which allows us to evaluate how quotation, by evoking Story and activating mutual context, calls the audience to live into the reconfigured lifeworld of the people of Yahweh.[132]

---

129. Ehrensperger, "Paul and the Authority of Scripture," 319. "Never" may be too strong a word. A potential example of Paul using Scripture to close debate is 1 Cor 11:3–16, which contains an allusion to Gen 2:18–23 (1 Cor 11:8–9) and where Paul closes the argument (1 Cor 11:16) with what may be a presumption of authority. However, Stanley finds that although Paul in 1 Cor 11 "adopts a more challenging tone," it appears to him to be an argument which appeals "to the audience's understanding instead of simply insisting on obedience and threatening those who hold a different view" (Stanley, *Arguing with Scripture*, 84n19). Another possible instance is 1 Cor 3:19–20; Shaw finds that in these verses "internal debate and discrimination are ruled out of order by appeals to Scripture"—in this case Job 5:13 and Ps 94:11 (Shaw, *Cost of Authority*, 67).

130. Patrick and Scult, *Rhetoric and Biblical Interpretation*, 19.

131. As R. B. Hays avers, "In depicting Paul as a thinker who lived in a 'story-shaped world,' I do not intend to relativize the truth-claims of his gospel, which still confront the reader with the demand for decision and commitment" (R. B. Hays, *Faith of Jesus Christ*, 20). The response of the empirical reader may be negative; the lifeworld that is offered "may be inhabited or rejected" (Snodgrass, "Reading to Hear," 21). We address this in chapter 5.

132. This would include former pagans. As J. R. Wagner points out, it is "difficult to believe that these Gentiles who shared a common life with Jewish believers who presumably *were* concerned to understand their confession of Jesus as the Christ in relation to Israel's scriptures and traditions would have been completely unfamiliar with or uninterested in these sacred texts" (J. R. Wagner, *Heralds of the Good News*, 34).

5

Communicative Interaction and Reader Roles

SINCE WE TAKE COMMUNICATION generally to be dialogical, cooperative, and transformative, our definition of communication is interactive: Communication is "an activity in which symbolic content is not merely transmitted from one source to another, but exchanged between human agents, who interact within a shared situational and/or discursive context."[1] However, although this definition tells us *how* communication happens, it does not tell us *why*. Therefore, to complete our definition of communication, we add: "for the purpose of creating meaning."[2]

Linguistic pragmatics[3] underlies the analytical apparatus for our model of how quotation effects transformation since recent work in this field presents meaning in a way that aligns with our definition of communication, i.e., as "jointly construed by the speaker and the hearer."[4] Specifically,

---

1. Price, *Communication Studies*, 5; italics and bold omitted.

2. We take this from Frey et al. who define communication as "the management of messages for the purpose of creating meaning" (Frey et al., *Investigating Communication*, 28; italics omitted).

3. Linguistic pragmatics is "the subfield of linguistics that studies the use of words (and phrases and sentences) in the actual context of discourse" (Akmajian et al., *Linguistics*, 13).

4. Carassa and Colombetti, "Joint Meaning," 1852. "Joint meaning is a joint commitment of two or more subjects, who are then obligated to each other to act coherently; in other words, joint meaning entails directed obligations, rights, and entitlements" (Carassa and Colombetti, 1851). Carassa and Colombetti's work is based on that of H. H. Clark, for whom "communicative acts are inherently joint acts" (H. H. Clark, *Using Language*, 125).

we adapt Vanhoozer's action model of the communication of meaning, which is based on Speech Act Theory,[5] to (i) define "meaning," (ii) outline three possible reader roles in communicative interaction, and (iii) provide a framework for our analyses.

THE COMMUNICATION OF MEANING

There has been much debate over whether "meaning" (i) is to be found in authorial intention, (ii) is encoded in the text, or (iii) is determined by the response of the reader.[6] Vanhoozer's action model holds these three

---

5. "A branch of the theory of communication" (Bierwisch, "Semantic Structure," 3; cf. Tilley, *Evils of Theodicy*, 17), Speech Act Theory is one of two major subcategories of linguistic pragmatics. The other subcategory is "implicature theories" (see Reed, "Modern Linguistics and the New Testament," 238–42), which includes Gricean pragmatics (named for its most famous proponent, H. Paul Grice) and relevance theory (the best-known formulation is that of Sperber and Wilson). Speech Act Theory and implicature theories can be roughly distinguished by which of the participants in the communicative process is emphasized. Speech Act Theory focuses on the speaker's acts, while implicature theories examine how a hearer infers a speaker's intentions. See Dominicy and Franken, "Speech Acts," and G. H. Bird, "Relevance Theory," for comparisons of the two groups of theories. Wilson and Sperber provide a helpful comparison of Gricean pragmatics and relevance theory (see Wilson and Sperber, "Relevance Theory," especially page 607). In contrast to conventional Speech Act Theory, our model includes the reader as an active agent in constructing meaning via perlocutionary effect.

6. Cotterell and Turner identify three aspects of the human communication process: "the (two) participants and the communication" (Cotterell and Turner, *Linguistics and Biblical Interpretation*, 39). Other scholars refer to the author as sender or addresser; the receptor is also called reader, receiver, audience, or addressee. Although these terms are generally interchangeable, we use "author" and "reader" to align with the implied author/reader construct introduced in chapter 3. Note that Cotterell and Turner's "competent" reader is a type of empirical reader and is not the same as the implied reader.

Corresponding to the communication process, Cotterell and Turner distinguish three "aspects" of meaning: author's meaning, receptor's meaning, and textual meaning (Cotterell and Turner, *Linguistics and Biblical Interpretation*, 39). They propose Hirsch as "perhaps the leading proponent of the theory of the determination of author's intention" (Cotterell and Turner, 42; see also Hirsch, *Validity in Interpretation* and "Meaning and Significance Reinterpreted"). Ricoeur and Gadamer are among those who locate "intentionality" in the text. Famously, Ricoeur adduces that "writing renders the text autonomous with respect to the intention of the author. What the text signifies no longer coincides with what the author meant; henceforth, textual meaning and psychological meaning have different destinies" (Ricoeur, "Hermeneutical Function of Distanciation," 139). The text is also seen as autonomous in relation to "the original audience and the discursive situation common to the interlocutors" (Ricoeur, "Response by Paul Ricoeur," 37). Although Ricoeur speaks of the "three aspects of the act of discourse" (i.e., the locutionary, illocutionary, and

PART I | DEVELOPING A METHODOLOGY

loci in creative tension.[7] He defines meaning as "a three-dimensional communicative action, with form and matter (propositional content), energy and trajectory (illocutionary force), and teleology or final purpose (perlocutionary effect)."[8] These action model dimensions are different elements of a single speech act.[9]

---

perlocutionary acts) as "having the same meaning" (Ricoeur, "Hermeneutical Function of Distanciation," 135), in general, "theories of textual autonomy typically subordinate the importance of authorial intention and frequently ignore the significance of authorship altogether" (Walhout, "Texts and Actions," 48). Fish is among the reader-response theorists who believe readers independently create meaning, while Eco and Iser more conservatively believe the text limits which reader responses are valid. We discuss "intentionality" below, and we incorporate some of Eco's thoughts into our model. Although there is much to admire about Cotterell and Turner's model, it compartmentalizes the three aspects of meaning, which then must somehow be reconciled. To avoid this, we use Vanhoozer's action model as a framework for our methodology.

7. See chapter 3 for our discussion of R. B. Hays's efforts along these lines. We find Vanhoozer's model more robust. Other scholars recognize the benefits of an action model. For Walhout, hermeneutics "must not conceive of texts simply as objects which have certain properties but also as instruments which we use to perform various kinds of actions" (Walhout, "Texts and Actions," 44). Thiselton sees an action model as a guard against radical reader-response theory: "The action model allows us to separate out different levels and dimensions of language use without necessarily opening the door to the mistaken view that the 'meaning' of a text is simply what any reader cares to do with it" (Thiselton, "Reader-Response Hermeneutics," 107).

8. Vanhoozer, *Is There a Meaning?*, 218. Our speech-act terminology is somewhat different; we discuss the relationship of "propositional content" and "locution" below. Vanhoozer follows Jakobson's schema which, like other sender/text/receiver models, shows the sending of a message from an addresser to an addressee within a certain context and requiring both a point of connection ("contact") and a common code. (See Jakobson, "Concluding Statement," 353). Such a "message" model is, for some, irrevocably connected to the flawed concept of communication as the coding and decoding of transmissions by the sender and receiver, respectively. Akmajian et al. summarize six critical shortcomings of such a "code/decode" model (Akmajian et al., *Linguistics*, 366–69). However, Jakobson's model is not irrevocably linked to communication as coding and decoding since it "subordinates the code function to the overarching function of communication" (Vanhoozer, *Is There a Meaning?*, 271n103). In Jakobson's model, "code" receives no greater attention than any other element of text and much less than "message," for example. In any event, we do not present communication as uni-directional or based on coding and decoding. Rather, our action model of communicative meaning is *interactional*.

9. For this, see also Moritz, "Scripture and Theological Exegesis," 121. He presents perlocution as "the intended response by the communicative partner" without distinguishing between associated and non-associated perlocution (see below). We disagree with Thiselton, who separates "illocutionary" speech acts from "perlocutionary" speech acts and says the latter "depend for their effectiveness on *sheer causal (psychological or*

Speech Act Theory takes its name from its characteristic idea that speech *does* something—in other words, that *speech* is *action*. Thus, according to Vanhoozer and others, what a text *does* is what it *means*.[10] Moreover, "strictly speaking it is people, not texts, who mean things. Texts mean something only when they are used in some way by someone."[11] We therefore follow Vanhoozer's suggestion: "Let us henceforth think of meaning not as something that words and texts have (*meaning* as noun) but rather as something people do (*meaning* as verb)."[12]

In presenting meaning as a *unity*, our action model holds the three dimensions of meaning in creative tension, doing justice to each dimension "without missing the distinctive ways each contributes to the communication process"[13] or privileging any of the dimensions.[14] Since one of the dimensions is perlocutionary *effect*, the effect produced in or by the *reader/hearer* in response to the perlocutionary act of the author/speaker, our action model, including the implied author/reader construct, explicitly recognizes the contribution of the reader/hearer to the communication of meaning.

The three dimensions of a speech act allow us to identify three possible roles for an empirical reader: (i) Independent, (ii) Analyst, and (iii) Envisager.[15] An Independent generates "meaning" from the locution without

---

rhetorical) persuasive power" (Thiselton, *First Epistle to the Corinthians*, 51).

10. When Iser argues that "what is important to readers, critics, and authors alike, is what literature *does* and not what it *means*" (Iser, *Act of Reading*, 53), he uses a concept of "meaning" that "connotes the idea of a self-contained 'sense' lodged within the sentences of a text" (Walhout, "Texts and Actions," 44). Walhout suggests that instead "the proper question for hermeneutics is 'What actions are being performed by the making and use of this text?'" (Walhout, 44). Alston is another who argues that "an expression's having a certain meaning consists in its being usable to play a certain role (to do certain things) in communication" (Alston, *Illocutionary Acts and Sentence Meaning*, 154; italics and bold omitted).

11. Loughlin, *Telling God's Story*, 132.

12. Vanhoozer, *Is There a Meaning?*, 202.

13. J. K. Brown, *Scripture as Communication*, 1st ed., 27.

14. Here we diverge from Vanhoozer since his model "entails a view of interpretation that gives primacy to the author as communicative agent," (Vanhoozer, *Is There a Meaning?*, 218). Although his formulation of "a theological general hermeneutic that sought to restore certain authorial rights, especially the right to be heard" (Vanhoozer, "Imprisoned or Free?," 59) helpfully counters certain moves of deconstructionism, his claim that "meaning is the result of intentional (illocutionary) action" (Vanhoozer, "From Speech Acts to Scripture Acts," 18) is too narrow.

15. This concept comes from Vanhoozer, *Is There a Meaning?*, 369–78, although we rename the categories and define them in Speech Act Theory terms. The term "Envisager" comes from Callow, *Man and Message*. Although Callow uses the term to describe

regard for the author/speaker's illocutionary act, an Analyst understands the illocutionary act, and an Envisager understands the illocutionary act and also responds with the perlocutionary effect (belief and/or action) associated with the perlocutionary act. Only with perlocution does a reader move beyond understanding to adherence and lifeworld transformation.[16]

To lay the groundwork to elaborate on the three reader roles, we next discuss the action model dimensions of locution (*propositional content*), illocution (*illocutionary force*), and perlocution (*perlocutionary effect*).

SPEECH ACTS

J. L. Austin introduced the concept of speech as action in a 1955 lecture series later published as *How to Do Things with Words*, a title which identifies Speech Act Theory's main thrust—that words *do* things. One of Austin's students, John Searle, revised and expanded Austin's theory. Searle's version is widely regarded today as "Speech Act Theory." However, we adapt Austin's terms *locution, illocution*, and *perlocution* to frame our description of how words do things.[17] With regard to locution, we provide a brief evaluation of Austin's original theory in light of Searle's subsequent work, since this and their taxonomies are arguably the points of greatest divergence between the two. With regard to perlocution, we go beyond Austin, Searle, and pragmatic theories generally and consider that the entirety of perlocution contributes to meaning.

In our model, we use "act" (e.g., "illocutionary act") to describe what is done by the speaker/author and "effect" (e.g., "perlocutionary effect") to describe the audience response. A response may be a linguistic, mental, or physical act. The terms "illocution" and "perlocution" refer to the total

---

authorial knowledge of the empirical audience, her thought that envisaging involves "the potential for matching without inconsistency" (Callow, 66) is also appropriate for the reader.

16. Although we reserve the term "understanding" for the sole intended illocutionary effect, Vanhoozer's use points to our Envisager role: "In a broader sense, . . . understanding discourse goes beyond merely recognizing illocutions and includes right reception and right response" (Vanhoozer, "Imprisoned or Free?," 72). We take the term "adherence" from Perelman and Olbrechts-Tyteca (see, e.g., Perelman and Olbrechts-Tyteca, *New Rhetoric*, 14).

17. See Austin, *How To Do Things with Words*, chapters 8–10; and Vanhoozer, *Is There a Meaning?*, chapter 5.

action, i.e., the act of the speaker/author together with the effect/response of the audience.

Since Speech Act Theory focuses on conversation, before we embark on a discussion of what words do, we must show Speech Act Theory to be a viable approach to text.[18]

Speech Acts and "Text" Acts

Searle considers "writing in a language" to be the performance of an illocutionary act,[19] a claim that does not seem to be challenged as regards "non-literary" (i.e., nonfiction) texts. Speaking, for example, of newspaper stories, Ohmann states that in such a case "the usual rules of illocutionary action all apply."[20] However, since some parts of Scripture, including the Psalms, are "literature,"[21] in order to be able to apply our methodology to such texts, we must refute the contentions of those who deny that "literary language figures among the words that do things."[22]

Mary Louise Pratt provides a decisive argument for the validity of applying speech-act analysis to texts: "Unless we are foolish enough to claim that people organize their oral anecdotes around patterns they learn from reading literature, we are obliged to draw the more obvious conclusion that the formal similarities between natural narrative and literary narrative derive from the fact that at some level of analysis they are utterances

---

18. Since, as originally constructed, Speech Act Theory does not deal with texts, authors, or readers, Gilfillan Upton puts the cart before the horse when she argues that "because Speech Act Theory is a form of communication theory, it considers the process of the transmission of a message between the implied author and the implied audience" (Gilfillan Upton, *Hearing Mark's Endings*, 196). However, after demonstrating the applicability of Speech Act Theory to text, we integrate the implied author/reader construct into our action model.

19. Searle, *Expression and Meaning*, 58.

20. Ohmann, "Speech, Literature," 57.

21. Ohmann defines "literature" as "poems, plays, novels, jokes, fairy tales, fantasies, etc." (Ohmann, "Speech, Literature," 53). For Scripture, this would at least include psalms, hymns, and parables.

22. Petrey places Austin in this category (Petrey, *Speech Acts*, 50). In part, this issue exists because "the primary question posed by the intersection of illocution and literature" is taken to be "how fiction is different from lies" (Petrey, 64–65). But, as Walhout points out, "Fiction is not . . . the same as falsehood" (Walhout, "Narrative Hermeneutics," 102).

of the same type."²³ Furthermore, "all the problems of coherence, chronology, causality, foregrounding, plausibility, selection of detail, tense, point of view, and emotional intensity . . . are problems whose solutions can readily be adapted from spoken to written discourse."²⁴ As a result, "a speech act approach to literature offers the important possibility of integrating literary discourse into the same basic model of language as all our other communicative activities."²⁵

Some scholars do not consider Speech Act Theory to be useful in analyzing texts on the basis that the writing-reading relation is not "dialogue,"²⁶ where "dialogue" is defined as the immediate occurrence of multiple exchanges. However, not only does Thiselton argue that much of Scripture originated as a record of oral discourse,²⁷ we believe that dialogue occurs with a single exchange. Further, both Watson and Vanhoozer recognize writing as a "technology that makes possible the extension of a particular speech act in time and space."²⁸ Thus, time and distance do not obviate the applicability of Speech Act Theory to texts; a speech-act approach can profitably be used to analyze biblical texts.²⁹

23. Pratt, *Towards a Speech Act Theory*, 69.

24. Pratt, *Towards a Speech Act Theory*, 66–67.

25. Pratt, *Towards a Speech Act Theory*, 88.

26. Ricoeur argues that "dialogue is an exchange of questions and answers; there is no exchange of this sort between the writer and the reader. The writer does not respond to the reader" (Ricoeur, "What is a Text?," 146). For Young and Ford, with writing-reading "the text is independent of the author who no longer has control over it. . . . Dialogue is not possible" (Young and Ford, *Meaning and Truth in 2 Corinthians*, 87).

27. Thiselton, *New Horizons in Hermeneutics*, 17. He remains "unconvinced by those who try to restrict speech-act theory to oral discourse" (Thiselton, 2).

28. Watson, *Text and Truth*, 98; cf. Vanhoozer, *Is There a Meaning?*, 214. It is also certainly true that "if oral speech-acts presuppose a state of affairs that is a matter of shared concern, the same is true of their written equivalents" (Watson, *Text and Truth*, 100).

29. "In the last couple of decades Christian scholars have attempted to draw upon speech act theory as either a tool for exegesis or more systemically as a tool to reconceptualise theological hermeneutics" (Barker, "Speech Act Theory," 3). In the latter category, Vanhoozer and Wolterstorff are frequently mentioned. In the former category, Tovey's approach comes closest to our model in the areas of authorial intentionality, the role of the reader, and the use of the implied author/reader construct. However, none of these exegetical studies use Speech Act Theory, particularly perlocution, in the way we do. For example, we disagree with Tovey's claims that illocutionary force "approximates to the perlocutionary effect, except that force is perhaps more within the control of the speaker than the effect" (Tovey, *Narrative Art and Act*, 71) and, with regard to Assertives, that "the illocutionary act is to persuade, the perlocutionary act is to convince and confirm belief" (Tovey, 89).

In order to apply Speech Act Theory to texts, we need to clarify our terminology. Following C. K. Grant, we construe any Speech Act Theory reference to the "speaker" to include "the utterer of any word or sentence, whether written or spoken, or the user of any non-verbal symbol or combination of symbols that could be translated into a word or sentence."[30] In the case studies, the term "speaker" refers to a participant in a verbal exchange whose speech is set out in the text. We use the term "author" with regard to the written text. We recognize that where an author quotes a speaker, each may be performing a distinct speech act.

Similarly, a Speech Act Theory reference to the "hearer" may "refer either to the person to whom a statement is directly addressed, as in a conversation or letter, or to . . . people who understand a statement not directly addressed to them."[31] The latter may be side participants to a conversation, overhearers of a verbal exchange, the original readers of a verbal exchange in a text, or later readers of a text. In the case studies, we use the term "hearer" or "listener" to refer to any participant in a verbal exchange described in the text, while the term "reader" refers to the audience of the text, even though some of the empirical audience may actually have had the text read to them.

"Locutionary" Acts

For Austin, performing "a *locutionary act* . . . is roughly equivalent to uttering a certain sentence with a certain sense and reference, which again is roughly equivalent to 'meaning' in the traditional sense."[32] Searle, however, objects to Austin's locating meaning in the locutionary act.[33] Instead, Searle divides this speech-act segment into the *utterance* act and the *propositional*

---

30. C. K. Grant, "Pragmatic Implication," 304.

31. C. K. Grant, "Pragmatic Implication," 304.

32. Austin, *How To Do Things with Words*, 109. By "the traditional sense," Austin apparently refers to Gottlob Frege's linguistic theory, in which the components of meaning are "sense" and "reference" (see, e.g., Austin, 93, 149). Following Austin, P. N. Campbell situates meaning in the locution and then separates meaning and force: "Meaning is a property of locutions and force a property of illocutions" (P. N. Campbell, "Rhetorical View," 287). We disagree.

33. Cf. Searle, "Austin on Locutionary and Illocutionary Acts," 149. We agree with Searle that "'saying' something, in the full sense of 'say'" (as per Austin, *How To Do Things with Words*, 92) is not found in the locutionary act, and we find valid Searle's objection to Austin's notion of "locutionary meaning."

act.³⁴ However, because Austin's symmetry is so memorable, we term Searle's utterance and propositional acts, taken together, as locutionary acts.³⁵

Regarding the propositional act,³⁶ Searle names its two components "referring" and "predicating." A referring expression is "any expression which serves to identify any thing, process, event, action, or any other kind of 'individual' or 'particular.' . . . Referring expressions point to particular things; they answer the questions 'Who?' 'What?' 'Which?'"³⁷ The predicating component "presents a certain content"³⁸ without implying a particular illocutionary force. Rather, "different illocutionary acts can have a common content,"³⁹ i.e., one propositional act can form the basis of a variety of illocutionary acts, depending on the illocutionary force with which it is presented. Therefore, a propositional act is only a statement, that is, an Assertive illocutionary act, when it is presented with assertive (truth-valued) illocutionary force.⁴⁰

34. Searle, *Speech Acts*, 23–24.

35. Whether a NT speaker/author followed the MT, the LXX, a targum, or an unknown form has occupied generations of diligent scholars. Here we investigate only those locutionary (i.e., text-critical) issues which bear on how a particular quotation communicates meaning.

36. The utterance act includes uttering (or writing) morphemes and sentences.

37. Searle, *Speech Acts*, 26–27. Cotterell and Turner define "the *referent* of a word or expression in an utterance" as "the *thing in the world which is intentionally signified by that word or expression*" where "the *thing* in question may be an object, an event or a process" (Cotterell and Turner, *Linguistics and Biblical Interpretation*, 84).

38. Searle, *Speech Acts*, 123. This term is related to the grammatical predicate. The first dimension of Vanhoozer's action model, "propositional content," appears to equate to Searle's propositional act although Vanhoozer does not mention the referring component.

39. Searle, *Speech Acts*, 123.

40. "A proposition, then, is to be distinguished from an assertion or statement of it. Asserting a proposition means the speaker . . . is committed to its truth. . . . In other words, speakers can do more than one thing with the same propositions; they can assert, question, command or wish. . . . 'The illocutionary force indicator shows how the proposition is to be taken'" (Vanhoozer, *Is There a Meaning?*, 210; quoting Searle, *Speech Acts*, 30). Steinmann is another who points out "the propositional act—expressing a proposition—must not (as it sometimes is) be confused with asserting the proposition, which is an illocutionary act. . . . The illocutionary act . . . is the act of doing something with the proposition expressed. Asserting that this proposition is true is one kind of illocutionary act" (Steinmann, "Perlocutionary Acts," 113).

In a later work, Searle and Vanderveken move away from the proposition as the content of various illocutionary acts and instead confusingly argue that "all propositions are either true or false" (Searle and Vanderveken, *Foundations of Illocutionary Logic*, 32).

Earlier in this chapter, we defined an Independent as a reader who creates meaning from the locution without considering the illocutionary act. Therefore, distinguishing the Independent reader from the Analyst requires a deeper understanding of the illocutionary act.

Illocutionary Acts and Illocutionary Force

Much of the work of Speech Act Theory has focused on the second dimension of our action model of meaning, the illocutionary act, which has been described as "probably the most significant analytical tool offered by speech-act theory."[41] Following Austin, scholars define the illocutionary act as "doing" something via language. For example, Vanhoozer defines the illocutionary act as "what we do in saying something (e.g., greeting, promising, commanding, etc.)"[42]

In contrast to those who consider words, propositions, or locutionary acts to be the locus of meaning, Searle situates meaning in the illocutionary act: "Saying something and meaning it is a matter of intending to perform an illocutionary act."[43] Searle's sometime collaborator Daniel Vanderveken is even more explicit; he takes as his "fundamental hypothesis" that "complete illocutionary acts (and not only propositions or truth conditions) are the primary units of literal meaning in the use and comprehension of natural languages."[44] Using the example of Jesus's teaching, Richard Briggs

---

This conflates the preparatory conditions concerning propositional content with the sincerity condition and leads to problems first in categorizing a speech act and then in determining whether it is defective and/or unsuccessful (see below). See Récanati for a successful counter-argument to Searle and Vanderveken's claim (Récanati, "Content, Mode, and Self-Reference," 49–63).

41. Briggs, "Speech-Act Theory," 763.

42. Vanhoozer, *Is There a Meaning?*, 209.

43. Searle, *Speech Acts*, 46; cf. Searle, "Austin on Locutionary and Illocutionary Acts," 153. Here we disagree with Wolterstorff, who believes that "since the meaning of a sentence is identical with the propositional content of the illocutionary act that the inscription of the sentence was used to perform, we can just as well say that the goal of interpretation is to identify and grasp the propositional content of the illocutionary act. To grasp the one is to grasp the other" (Wolterstorff, "Resuscitating the Author," 41).

44. Vanderveken, *Meaning and Speech Acts*, 11. A. Wagner, who uses Speech Act Theory in his OT analyses, considers more broadly that "die Berücksichtigung der Handlungszusammenhänge von sprachlichen Äußerungen macht klar, daβ Bedeutungsfragen nicht nur auf der Ebene der Semantik oder der Syntax liegen, sondern daβ sie auch abhängen vom 'Gebrauch' einer Äußerung" (A. Wagner, "Der Lobaufruf im israelitischen

illustrates the difference between locution and illocution: "It is the illocutionary act and not just the content of Jesus' teaching which should occupy the interpreter, and which perhaps provides a useful step forward in understanding what Jesus is trying to *do* in any particular case."[45]

The components of the "full blown" illocutionary act are "illocutionary force and propositional content."[46] These two elements work together: "Predication presents a certain content, and the mode in which the content is presented is determined by the illocutionary force of the sentence."[47] Illocutionary force is one of the most important elements in Searle's taxonomic system for illocutionary acts. Since his system is generally considered the "standard,"[48] we outline it below.

Searle's Taxonomy of Illocutionary Acts

Although Searle outlines "twelve significant dimensions of variation" between illocutionary acts,[49] within his taxonomic system the most im-

---

Hymnus," 154). We use the adjective "lexical" to distinguish the sense or meaning of a word or expression from the communicative meaning of a speech act (see Cotterell and Turner, *Linguistics and Biblical Interpretation*, 164-65, 145).

45. Briggs, *Words in Action*, 263. This is not to say that we can ignore the locution. As A. Wagner points out, "Sprechhandlungstheoretische Analysen können aber nicht an die Stelle syntaktischer Forschung treten! Ebensolches gilt für semantische Fragen, für die Lexikographie, auch sie werden nicht durch die sprechakttheoretische Untersuchung überflüssig gemacht, sondern ergänzt" (A. Wagner, "Die Stellung der Sprachakttheorie," 73). Here we explore only those questions of the lexical meaning of words and of syntax/grammar that bear on the communication of meaning.

46. Searle, *Expression and Meaning*, vii. It would probably be more accurate to call the second element the "propositional act." Although Searle believes "not all illocutionary acts have a propositional content" (Searle, *Speech Acts*, 30), if such illocutionary acts exist, they do not interest us.

47. Searle, *Speech Acts*, 123. He holds it is not possible to "*just* refer and predicate without making an assertion or asking a question or performing some other illocutionary act" (Searle, 25).

48. Searle's typology "remains the most influential" (Huang, *Pragmatics*, 106) and is the only taxonomy "tied to a general theory of illocutionary acts" (Bach and Harnish, *Linguistic Communication*, 40). Petrey calls Austin's taxonomy "complex (not to say chaotic)" (Petrey, *Speech Acts*, 59), and except for Commissives, Searle abandons it because it has "no clear or consistent principle or set of principles" (Searle, *Expression and Meaning*, 10; cf. Bach and Harnish, *Linguistic Communication*, 40).

49. Searle's description of the illocutionary act is quite vague (see Harnish, "Speech Acts and Intentionality," 174). We use the insights of other scholars (see below) to support our understanding of illocution.

portant criterion is "illocutionary force," of which "illocutionary point/ purpose" or the "essential condition" or what the utterance "counts as" is the most important element.[50] Other important criteria include the "sincerity condition"[51] and the satisfaction of certain preparatory conditions which the speaker "*implies* in the performance of the act."[52]

Searle identifies five basic categories of speech acts: *Assertives, Directives, Expressives, Commissives* and *Declarations*.[53] Since we use these

---

50. See Searle, *Expression and Meaning*, 2; and Searle, *Speech Acts*, 66–67. For him, illocutionary force determines "what illocutionary act the speaker is performing in the utterance of the sentence" (Searle, *Speech Acts*, 30). Bach and Harnish also equate "force" and "illocutionary act type" (Bach and Harnish, *Linguistic Communication*, 6). Vanhoozer's description of illocutionary force as "the stance adopted by the speaker" toward the propositional content (Vanhoozer, *Is There a Meaning?*, 210) has the advantage of not using the word "illocutionary" but does not adequately explain "stance." Tovey incorrectly considers illocutionary force and illocutionary point as different aspects of a speech act (see, e.g., Tovey, *Narrative Art and Act*, 71).

51. The sincerity condition is "the psychological state expressed in the performance of the illocutionary act" (Searle, *Expression and Meaning*, 5). Tsohatzidis points out that "confusingly, Searle sometimes . . . uses the term 'sincerity condition' to refer both to the possession and to the mere expression of mental states (see, for example, Searle and Vanderveken 1985:22), though it is only the first usage, inaugurated in Searle 1969, that is clearly intelligible: a *sincerity* condition on a speech act is, presumably, a condition whose non-satisfaction would make that act *insincere,* and what makes, for example, an assertion insincere is not that its speaker does not *express* a belief in the truth of its content, but rather that he does not *have* this expressed belief. (Indeed, since, on Searle's later views, assertions are necessarily expressions of belief in their contents, the idea that the mere expression of such a belief would be sufficient to make any assertion *sincere* would have the absurd consequence that it is impossible for any assertion to ever be insincere—a consequence that Searle explicitly rejects)" (Tsohatzidis, "Gap between Speech Acts and Mental States," 232n4). Here we follow early Searle in using the term "sincerity condition" to indicate the possession of a certain psychological state.

52. Searle, *Speech Acts*, 65. Although every illocutionary act has an essential condition and preparatory conditions, some have "no sincerity and no propositional content conditions" (Harnish, "Speech Acts and Intentionality," 174). In addition to the three criteria outlined here, early Searle includes a criterion he calls "direction of fit" between the illocutionary act and the actual state of affairs in the world (see Searle, *Expression and Meaning*, 3–4). Burkhardt is correct that "the 'direction of fit' in reality does not enrich our stock of categories, but is just another way of describing the 'propositional content rule'" (Burkhardt, "Speech Act Theory," 107). Other criteria include the relationship of the illocution to the context, the strength of the illocutionary point, and the role of authority. Many of the criteria distinguish illocutionary acts within the taxonomic categories rather than across categories (see Searle, *Expression and Meaning*, 3, 13). For a helpful discussion of Searle's twelve dimensions, see Connor-Linton, "Sociolinguistic Model," 98–100.

53. In context, each speech act has a single illocutionary purpose/essential condition,

categories to analyze the NT psalm quotations in both their OT and NT settings, we describe them briefly below.

Assertives are characterized by the speaker's commitment to the truth of the stated proposition *p*. "The simplest test of an assertive is this: can you literally characterize it (inter alia) as true or false."[54] The psychological state is Belief (that *p*).[55]

Directives are attempts "by the speaker to get the hearer to do something. . . . The sincerity condition is want (or wish or desire). The propositional content is . . . that the hearer *H* does some future action *A*."[56]

Commissives commit the speaker to some future course of action. "The sincerity condition is Intention," and "the propositional content is always that the speaker *S* does some future action *A*."[57]

Expressives express the "psychological state specified in the sincerity condition about a state of affairs specified in the propositional content," which "ascribes some property (not necessarily an action) to either *S* or *H*."[58] "The truth of the expressed proposition is presupposed."[59] Expressives cover a wide variety of "psychological states," including thanking, congratulating, apologizing, and welcoming.

Declarations are illocutions for which "the successful performance . . . brings about the correspondence between the propositional content and reality," i.e., "the status or condition of the referred to object or objects"[60] is

---

no matter its form (*contra* Poythress, "Canon and Speech Act," 344–46). For example, "Can you pass the salt?" is a request (Directive) even though in form it is an inquiry about physical capabilities. Using what we know of the socio-historical context and the conventions of language (see chapter 3) allows us to determine the illocutionary force of an indirect speech act such as a metaphor.

54. Searle, *Expression and Meaning*, 13. By "it," Searle apparently refers to the propositional act contained in an Assertive since he points out it is not the illocutionary act of stating which is true or false but the "statement-object" or proposition (Searle, "Austin on Locutionary and Illocutionary Acts," 158–59).

55. Searle, *Expression and Meaning*, 12. This corresponds to Austin's constative (see Searle, 12, and also n62 below).

56. Searle, *Expression and Meaning*, 13–14.

57. Searle, *Expression and Meaning*, 14.

58. Searle, *Expression and Meaning*, 15, 16.

59. Searle, *Expression and Meaning*, 15. We find confusing Vanderveken's later notion that since "every successful performance of a speech act is an expression of mental states . . . any type of illocutionary act strongly commits the speaker to an expressive" (Vanderveken, "Universal Grammar and Speech Act Theory," 45).

60. Searle, *Expression and Meaning*, 16–17.

altered. These are "cases where one brings a state of affairs into existence by declaring it to exist, cases where, so to speak, 'saying makes it so.'"[61]

Since the Psalms are prayers, it might seem they would be Expressives. But this is not the case. The majority of the Psalm passages quoted (and the speech act complexes of which they are a part) are either Assertives or Directives. Since Assertives are particularly important in our analysis, we explain below their "tellability."

The Tellability of Assertives

We agree with those, like Searle, who argue that making a statement (an Assertive) is truly a speech act.[62] Assertives are "doing something"—often something significant. According to Pratt, some Assertives "represent states of affairs that are held to be unusual, contrary to expectations, or otherwise problematic."[63] In contrast to "informing" assertions, with such "tellable" Assertives a speaker is "verbally displaying a state of affairs, inviting his addressee(s) to join him in contemplating it, evaluating it, and responding to it. His point is to produce in his hearers not only belief but also an imaginative and affective involvement in the state of affairs he is representing and an evaluative stance toward it."[64] Similar to Tannen's concept of involvement (see chapter 2), the communicative purpose of a tellable assertive is that "the addressee will respond affectively in the intended way, adopt the intended evaluation and interpretation, take pleasure in doing so, and generally find the whole undertaking worth it."[65]

---

61. Searle, *Expression and Meaning*, 16.

62. Although Austin initially found a distinction between *saying* things with words (the "constative") and *doing* things with words (the "performative"), he came to understand that "stating is performing an act" (Austin, *How To Do Things with Words*, 139). Searle agrees: "Making a statement is as much performing an illocutionary act as making a promise, a bet, a warning or what have you" (Searle, *Expression and Meaning*, 17–18).

63. Pratt, *Towards a Speech Act Theory*, 36.

64. Pratt, *Towards a Speech Act Theory*, 136. She finds it "ironic that speech act philosophers and linguists have been so slow to recognize the extent to which assertions and representative discourse in general are used for purposes other than informing, reminding, or displaying knowledge at exams" (Pratt, 149).

65. Pratt, *Towards a Speech Act Theory*, 148. "An assertion that is both true and non-obvious will still be pointless if it has no real or supposed relation to the interests of the hearer" (Pratt, 134).

With regard to Scripture, Briggs correctly points out that Assertives are tellable "in even the most apparently unpromising of biblical texts. In other words: assertion can hardly be 'mere assertion,' unless perhaps we were discussing some idling form of language, utterances 'said for no conceivable reason.'"[66]

Assertives are the only category of illocutionary acts in which the essential condition is a commitment to the truth of the propositional content.[67] However, all speech acts can be both defective and/or unsuccessful.[68]

Non-Defective and Successful Illocutionary Acts

In a defective illocutionary act, a condition "intrinsic to the notion of the action in question," such as the sincerity condition or a preparatory condition, is not satisfied.[69] With explicit quotation, an example of a potentially defective speech act would be the implied NT author misquoting the OT. If the implied NT reader is not to take this as a deliberate alteration,[70] such an illocutionary act would be defective. For example, some scholars argue the quotation of Ps 68:18 in Eph 4:8 is defective.[71]

---

66. Briggs, *Words in Action*, 269.

67. "Assertions . . . differ from (almost) all other types of speech acts in that they prima facie imply an unmistakable validity claim, a claim to truth" (Habermas, *On the Pragmatics of Communication*, 74). In some situations, the illocutionary force of non-Assertives also "depends on contextual realities described by true propositions and understood by believers as part of background knowledge" (D. Clark, "Beyond Inerrancy," 123). However, here we consider only Assertives "true" or "false"; other speech acts are "sincere" or "insincere."

68. *Contra* Leech, who argues that "pragmatics is concerned only with publicly conveyed meaning, and does not take account . . . of miscommunication" (Leech, *Principles of Pragmatics*, 35). Although we cannot concern ourselves with private or secret communications (which by definition are unavailable), we have an interest in defective and unsuccessful speech acts to the extent we suspect their existence.

69. Searle, *Speech Acts*, 54; see also 65. Tovey correctly notes that "the implied author's purpose is to fulfill the appropriateness conditions for his assertions" (Tovey, *Narrative Art and Act*, 263).

70. Examples of deliberate alteration include punning, parody, and irony. This "can point to an intensification, climactic development, acceleration of the actions and attitudes initially represented, or . . . to some unexpected, perhaps unsettling, new revelation of character or plot" (Alter, *Art of Biblical Narrative*, 97–98).

71. Moritz summarizes the variety of explanations that been offered for the reversal of the verb in Eph 4:8 from Ps. 67:19c LXX (ἔλαβες to ἔδωκεν) (Moritz, *Profound Mystery*, 73). One plausible argument is that Eph 4:8 "rejects the MT and LXX rendering 'take' or

A defective illocutionary act is not necessarily unsuccessful.[72] Illocutionary act success is not defined as an absence of defects. The sole condition for illocutionary act success is that a "the hearer understands it in the way that the speaker intended it."[73] Hearer understanding is both necessary and sufficient for illocutionary act success; "the fulfillment of illocutionary intentions consists in hearer understanding."[74]

To clarify the role of illocution in communicating meaning, we must more precisely define illocutionary intention (author) and illocutionary effect (reader).

Illocutionary Intention

For Searle, authorial intention is foundational to the meaning of an illocution: "The speaker intends to produce a certain effect by means of getting the hearer to recognize his intention to produce that effect."[75] This has generated controversy. Some believe Speech Act Theory falls afoul of the intentional fallacy, i.e., considering intention as bound to the author's psychology.[76] However, though later Searle speaks of "fundamental psycho-

---

'receive' in favour of the translation 'give' found in the Targum and Peshitta" (Ellis, *Paul's Use*, 144; cf. Evans, "Praise and Prophecy," 577). That the tradition represented by Targum Psalms is also found in Midr. Pss. 68§11 supports Moritz's own argument that the quotation "relates not directly to Ps 68, but to an early Christian polemic, formulated in response to what was perceived to be a Jewish misuse of Ps 68.18" (Moritz, *Profound Mystery*, 73).

72. The three possibilities are: "A speech act may be unsuccessful, it may be successful but defective, and it may be successful and nondefective" (Searle and Vanderveken, *Foundations of Illocutionary Logic*, 13). Tilley gives an example with regard to Assertives: "While any assertive which asserts what is false is defective, that does not cause its failure. If a challenger can show an assertive to be seriously defective, that may undercut its effectiveness. If an asserter can justify the assertion, that may enhance its effectiveness. However, neither of these rhetorical moves affects the truth of what is asserted" (Tilley, *Evils of Theodicy*, 78).

73. Searle, "Literary Theory," 647; see also Searle, *Speech Acts*, 47; and Lee, "Perlocution and Illocution," 38n2.

74. Bach and Harnish, *Linguistic Communication*, 5. Bakhtin also argues that understanding is a goal of speech/text: "From the very beginning, the speaker expects a response from them [those for whom the utterance is constructed], an active responsive understanding. The entire utterance is constructed, as it were, in anticipation of encountering this response" (Bakhtin, "Problem of Speech Genres," 94). One biblical scholar who has adopted this position is Briggs (see Briggs, *Words in Action*, 66).

75. Searle, *Speech Acts*, 45.

76. See, e.g., Black, "Meaning and Intention," 258. For the intentional fallacy, see

logical notions such as belief, intention, and desire," and he terms these "Intentional,"[77] at no point does Searle enter the murky waters of motive in an attempt to determine *why* a speaker utters a certain speech act. Searle takes the performance of a speech act as evidence for the intention behind it rather than looking behind the speech act to discern the motives of its author.[78] This coheres with Sternberg's understanding of the biblical inter-

---

Wimsatt and Beardsley, "Intentional Fallacy," 4. Although Booth is correct that Wimsatt and Beardsley "rule out only statements made by the author outside the work about his motives or purposes or plans or hopes for value" (Booth, *Rhetoric of Irony*, 126n13), for many, "intention" remains linked to "the psychologizing approaches of F. Schleiermacher and others and the Romanticist ideas of getting into the mind of an author so that the interpreter knows the author's mind better than he himself or she herself did" (Snodgrass, "Reading to Hear," 16). As Patte has noted, "The mention of 'mind,' 'brain,' and 'mental states' makes us cringe" since this appears to equate "intentionality" with "subjectivity" (Patte, "Speech Act Theory," 95).

77. Searle, "Intentionality and Method," 720, where he names these notions the sincerity conditions of statements, promises, and desires, respectively. In this article, Searle often confusingly refers to "intentionality" rather than "Intentionality" even when not discussing Commissives. This becomes more puzzling when one compares early Searle, in which "Intention" is the sincerity condition of a Commissive (see, e.g., Searle, *Expression and Meaning*, 14). Here we agree with Thiselton that "there are ways of expressing intention which identify the directedness of a speech-act without presupposing some pychological [sic] notion of 'inner mental states'" (Thiselton, *New Horizons in Hermeneutics*, 59; cf. Vanhoozer, "Discourse on Matter," 21, who refers to the "psychological sense of the term" as "planned to" and the "technical sense" as "directing their consciousness toward"). Like Briggs, we avoid adopting Searle's "framework of intentionality and mental states," but still find it "possible to utilise the insights of his philosophy of language" (Briggs, *Words in Action*, 55).

78. Unlike Castelli, who equates "author's intent" to "the motive residing in the mind of the writer" and finds intent to be "unattainable because it involves inaccessible aspects of the author's psychology" (Castelli, *Imitating Paul*, 120; cf. Walhout, "Narrative Hermeneutics," 71, 100; and Wolterstorff, "Resuscitating the Author," 37), Skinner correctly avers that "an agent's motives *for* writing (though not his intentions *in* writing) can be said to stand 'outside' his works, and in a contingent relationship to them, in such a way that their recovery does seem to be irrelevant to the determination of the meaning of the works" (Skinner, "Motives, Intentions and the Interpretation of Texts," 402). Similarly, for Ricoeur, "the hermeneutical task is to discern the 'matter' of the text (Gadamer) and not the psychology of the author" (Ricoeur, "Phenomenology and Hermeneutics," 111). Vanhoozer agrees "there is a difference between understanding *why* someone says something (a question for historians and psychologists) and *what* a person said—his or her speech act" (Vanhoozer, "Imprisoned or Free?," 61n26). We concur with this thought: "I am not interested in recreating the inner life of the author or in reconstructing the author's motives but in giving a description, as thick as it is correct, of the author's *Akt des Redens* (speech act, discourse)" (Vanhoozer, "Discourse on Matter," 21).

In a later work, Skinner finds value in investigating motive: "We can . . . seek further

preter's only concern being "'embodied' or 'objectified' intention. . . . 'Intention' no longer figures as a psychological state consciously or unconsciously translated into words. Rather, it is a shorthand for the structure of meaning and effect supported by the conventions that the text appeals to or devises: for the sense that the language makes in terms of the communicative context as a whole."[79]

Nicholas Wolterstorff puts this back into speech-act terminology with the thought that reading a text for "authorial discourse" is not "to enter the dark world of the author's psyche" but rather "to discover what assertings, what promisings, what requestings, what commandings, are rightly to be ascribed to the author on the ground of her having set down the words that she did in the situation in which she set them down."[80]

Any residual concern over "intentionality" is dispelled by the use of the implied author and reader construct since this "is a tool which rescues and places in a proper perspective the concept of an intent behind the production of a literary work."[81] Thus, the illocutionary acts of the implied author—those "assertings," "promisings," "requestings," and "commandings"—reveal to the empirical reader, via the construct of the implied reader, the implied author's intentions.[82]

---

corroboration for such ascriptions of intentionality by enquiring into the motives and beliefs of the agent in question" (Skinner, "Reply to My Critics," 280; see also 266-67). We argue below that the implied author/reader construct makes such inquiry into the motives of an author unnecessary.

79. Sternberg, *Poetics of Biblical Narrative*, 9.

80. Wolterstorff, *Divine Discourse*, 93. Even radical reader-response theorist Stanley Fish recognizes Speech Act Theory does not link authorial intention to motivation: "Intention, in the view of . . . [speech act] theory, is a matter of what one takes responsibility for by performing certain conventional (speech) acts. The question of what is going on inside, the question of the '*inward* performance' is simply bypassed; speech-act theory does not rule on it. This means that intentions are available to anyone who invokes the proper (publicly known and agreed upon) procedures, and it also means that anyone who invokes these procedures (knowing that they will be recognized as such) takes responsibility for having those intentions" (Fish, *Is There a Text?*, 203-4). We discuss linguistic conventions with regard to author intention/audience understanding below.

81. Tovey, *Narrative Art and Act*, 79, adding that thus "it is no longer the case that the 'Intentional fallacy' bulks large in literary criticism." See also Meyer, *Reality and Illusion*, 97-98.

82. This does not speak to the possible communicative inadequacy of an empirical author, i.e., the failure to create the appropriate implied author. However, we assume the empirical author is competent unless evidence is found to the contrary (see BeDuhn, "Historical Assessment of Speech Acts," 93, 95).

Turner relates intention to the NT writings (specifically to Paul):

> When we ask concerning authorial intention, we are not seeking information about Paul's unexpressed psychological motivations (interesting though they may be), which may or may not have been realized. We are inquiring rather about what intentional acts he has indeed performed in and through what he has actually said, understood within the linguistic/cultural world in which he uttered/inscribed the words.[83]

Turner makes it clear that not only are intentional acts performed through speech or text but that the goal of those acts is they be "understood." "Understanding" is the intended illocutionary effect.

The Illocutionary Effect of Understanding

We argued above that the illocutionary effect of understanding is both necessary and sufficient for illocutionary act success. The questions now before us are: What do we mean by "understanding," and what makes understanding possible?

To answer the first question, we look to Bach and Harnish, who "restrict illocutionary intentions to those intentions whose fulfillment consists in nothing more than their recognition."[84] Thus, to "understand" means the empirical reader grasps the purport of the locutionary act and recognizes what type of illocutionary act is being performed.[85] Since the implied

---

83. Turner, "Historical Criticism and Theological Hermeneutics," 47.

84. Bach and Harnish, *Linguistic Communication*, xv. This differs from Austin's three types of illocutionary effects: "securing uptake, taking effect, and inviting a response" (Austin, *How To Do Things with Words*, 118). Only "securing uptake," which equates to Searle's illocutionary effect of understanding, occurs in every instance (Austin, 139). "Taking effect" refers to changes in social reality caused by Declarations (Austin, 117) and is not of concern here. Austin describes "inviting a response" with an example: "Many illocutionary acts invite by convention a response or sequel. Thus an order invites the response of obedience" (Austin, 117). However, considering "inviting a response" to be an illocutionary effect of a Directive blurs the distinction between illocutionary and perlocutionary effects. Although Austin argues "we must distinguish 'I ordered him and he obeyed' from 'I got him to obey'" (Austin, 117), such a distinction is difficult to make or defend—and Austin does not explain how to do it. Indeed, by Austin's definition, a Directive illocutionary act would be illocutionarily unsuccessful if the hearer does not do what is asked. *Contra* Austin, we consider "inviting a response" to be a perlocutionary intention and the response to be a perlocutionary effect (see below).

85. See, e.g., Bach and Harnish, *Linguistic Communication*, 56. We reject Habermas's

reader, by definition, is of the same mind as the implied author, in our action model "understanding" involves the empirical reader discovering the implied author and implied reader and "the world which it [the text] intends to disclose," i.e., the lifeworld.[86] When understanding happens, mutual context is activated and one becomes "immersed in conversation with a tradition and engaged in that form of life which the tradition has assumed."[87]

To determine what makes understanding possible, we begin with Paul Ricoeur's thought that the "intention of being identified, acknowledged, and recognized as such by the other is part of the intention itself."[88] Bach and Harnish's "Communicative Presumption" expands on this idea:

> The communicative presumption is the mutual belief prevailing in a linguistic community to the effect that whenever someone says something to somebody, he intends to be performing some identifiable illocutionary act. . . . People . . . do mutually believe that speakers speak with overt intentions, and this mutual belief figures in ordinary communication situations. People do rely on others to have identifiable intentions in their utterances, and they expect others to rely on them to have such intentions.[89]

Understanding, then, is made possible when the empirical author constructs an implied author whose illocutionary acts the empirical audience

---

definition of understanding [*Verständigung*] in which "reaching understanding is considered to be a process of reaching agreement [*Einigung*] among speaking and acting subjects" (Habermas, *Reason*, 286–87; brackets original). We do not agree that the illocutionary aim is both "that the hearer understand what is said *and undertake the obligations* connected with the acceptance of the offer contained in the speech act" (Habermas, 293–94; emphasis added; cf. n84, where we reject Austin's similar ideas). Reaching agreement and undertaking obligations are perlocutionary effects (see below).

86. Walhout, "Texts and Actions," 47, with reference to Ricoeur. Vanhoozer also points out that "what the reader receives according to Ricoeur is not the author's intention but the 'world of the text'—that is, a proposed way of being-in-the-world" (Vanhoozer, "Reader in New Testament Interpretation," 267). In our terms, this is the lifeworld presented in/by the text.

87. Stroup, *Promise of Narrative Theology*, 208. To the extent understanding is considered an "act," with successful illocution we already have participation in communication, i.e., in joint action (see H. H. Clark, *Using Language*, 219).

88. Ricoeur, *Interpretation Theory*, 18. This is similar to Searle's argument (see, e. g., Searle, *Speech Acts*, 45).

89. Bach and Harnish, *Linguistic Communication*, 12.

PART I | DEVELOPING A METHODOLOGY

can identify.[90] "The utterance must be made with the intention that H can find the inference route, and part of what the hearer takes into account in trying to find the route is that the utterance is made with that intention."[91] But the empirical reader also has a role; s/he must be willing to enter into the reading "contract." A certain cooperation is therefore required.

The cooperative effort which underpins understanding relies in part on linguistic conventions (an element of context).[92] Searle defines the conventions of language as those constitutive rules related to illocutionary force and the essential condition which generally have the form "X counts as Y in context C."[93] The existence of linguistic conventions common to both author and audience is critical to achieving the illocutionary effect of understanding. As Briggs puts it, "If there is any agreement on what illocutionary analysis achieves, it is that it draws together the issues of authorial (or speaker's) intention and the audience's understanding, by examining what conventions exist within the public domain of both the author and the audience."[94]

90. Schutz and Luckmann remind us that "steering one's own behavior toward anticipated interpretation by others is a basic presupposition of communicative action" (Schutz and Luckmann, *Structures of the Life-World*, 2:8).

91. Bach and Harnish, *Linguistic Communication*, 80; cf. Brown and Yule, *Discourse Analysis*, 33. Like authorial intention, reader understanding is "less a mental state than something like an ability, or a competency" (Briggs, *Words in Action*, 54).

92. "Meaning is more than a matter of intention, it is also a matter of convention" (Searle, "What is a Speech Act?," 230).

93. Searle, *Speech Acts*, 35. Searle, who considers language to be "rule-governed intentional behavior" (Searle, 16), defines "constitutive" rules as those rules which "constitute (and also regulate) an activity the existence of which is logically dependent on the rules" (Searle, 34). According to van Dijk, "the rules are CONVENTIONAL in the sense of being shared by most members of a linguistic community: they KNOW these rules implicitly and are able to *use* them" (van Dijk, *Text and Context*, 1).

Our concept of "convention" is weaker than that of Bach and Harnish (see Bach and Harish, *Linguistic Communication*, 108–9; cf. Briggs, *Words in Action*, 64). For us, "rules" can be simply practices, norms or, as Cotterell terms them, "regularities" (Cotterell, "Sociolinguistics and Biblical Interpretation," 75n12; cf. Alston, *Illocutionary Acts and Sentence Meaning*, 264). We follow H. H. Clark in considering convention to be "a regularity . . . in behavior . . . that is common ground in a given community C . . . as a coordination device" (H. H. Clark, *Using Language*, 71).

94. Briggs, "Speech-Act Theory," 764; cf. Tovey, *Narrative Art and Act*, 79. "One of the necessary conditions for understanding in any situation what it is that S in uttering utterance x must be doing to [audience] A must be some understanding of what it is that people in general, when behaving in a conventional manner, are usually doing in that society and in that situation in uttering such utterances" (Skinner, "Conventions

This does not mean all empirical readers will necessarily agree "about the kind of illocutionary act which is being performed in a specific utterance."[95] But using our action model means that disagreements about an illocutionary act are not about different understandings of the author's motivations. Rather, they are founded in different premises about the relevant context or linguistic/literary conventions, and they center on what role a particular illocutionary act plays in creating the implied author and implied reader. Such disagreements are more productive than those which concern the empirical author's unrecoverable "mental acts."

As we have defined reader roles, accomplishing "understanding" means the empirical reader reads as an Analyst. We conclude our discussion of illocutionary acts by distinguishing between the reader roles of Independent and Analyst.

The Reader Roles of Independent and Analyst

Based on our discussions of illocution and illocutionary success, we add to our definition of reader roles that an Independent reader does not evidence having arrived at (or possibly even attempted) the illocutionary effect of understanding.[96] Therefore, vis-à-vis an Independent reader, the illocutionary act is unsuccessful, and illocutionary meaning has not been communicated.[97] To claim a reader-now-author quotes "out of context" is the equivalent in our model of naming the quoting author an Independent

---

and the Understanding of Speech Acts," 133; cf. Skinner, "Motives, Intentions and the Interpretation of Texts," 406). This extends beyond linguistic conventions. As A. Wagner notes, "so ist z. B. die Handlungsstruktur von Äußerungen (also die Frage nach dem Zweck einer Äußerung, ob sie zu etwas auffordern soll, etwas mitteilen will, etwas ausdrücken soll usw.) bestimmt von allen Gesetzen und Gegebenheiten, die das Handeln in einer Gesellschaft insgesamt bestimmen: Kommunkationsgegebenheiten, sprachliche Konventionen, Werte, institutionelle Gegebenheiten, etc." (A. Wagner, "Der Lobaufruf im israelitischen Hymnus," 151).

95. Lanser, *Narrative Act*, 68n9.

96. An Independent reader is very similar to the reader described by radical reader-response theories. According to Fish, "the reader's response is not *to* the meaning: it *is* the meaning" (Fish, *Is There a Text?*, 3). Rorty believes that "a text just has whatever coherence it happened to acquire during the last roll of the hermeneutic wheel" (Rorty, "The Pragmatist's Progress," 97).

97. An Independent reader may achieve understanding but choose to disregard the illocution. The result is the same as for a reader who does not understand.

PART I | DEVELOPING A METHODOLOGY

reader of the source text.[98] The way Stanley describes Paul's use of Ps 115:1 LXX in 2 Cor 4:13 dovetails with calling Paul an Independent reader: "The sense in which he uses the verse is so far removed from the original context as to raise questions about Paul's reliability as an interpreter."[99] We take up this example as a case study.

An Analyst, on the other hand, is a reader who recognizes the illocutionary intentions of the implied author and achieves the intended illocutionary effect of understanding the illocutionary act. When a reader reads as an Analyst, the illocutionary act is successful.

Even if a reader reads as an Analyst (or Envisager), this does not mean that the illocutionary force of the original speech act is retained in a quotation. Most quotations are Assertives, i.e., they report earlier speech acts, which may have been Assertives, Commissives, Directives, etc.[100] Even if the locution is replicated verbatim, the illocutionary act (and therefore the perlocutionary act) in the reporting context may be different. Further, the referent may be redefined by reversal, inversion, or expansion. Thus, a quotation does not necessarily reproduce earlier meaning (as we have defined "meaning"). Instead, our question is whether and, if so, how earlier meaning resonates in the new context.

We believe that in many instances of biblical quotation, the NT author evokes the OT Story, thereby activating mutual context, in support of his invitation to the NT audience to read as Envisagers and experience transformation. To describe the Envisager more precisely we must plunge into perlocution.

---

98. Our characterization of a NT author as a reader of an OT text is based on the NT quotation of that text. Whether any NT authors are fully Independent OT readers is unclear. As Moyise points out concerning the "eclectic" quotation in Matt 2:15, "There is far more involved than Matthew taking a verse out of context with no interest in the original meaning" (Moyise, "Does the NT Quote the OT Out of Context?," 139).

99. Stanley, *Arguing with Scripture*, 100. Stanley does not consider Paul in an interpretive role of either Analyst or Envisager (see below); he believes "Paul often quotes from Scripture in a way that bears little evident relation to the apparent sense of the original passage" (Stanley, 53).

100. See Becker, *Letter Hermeneutics in 2 Corinthians*, 88; and Grey, "Acts of the Spirit," 78.

Perlocutionary Acts and Effects

The final dimension of our action model is *perlocution*, another term coined by Austin. However, he, Searle, and others not only focus their efforts on illocution, they deny perlocution a role in communicating meaning.[101] Other linguists split the speech act into two elements: linguistic, i.e., "communication" (illocution), and potentially non-linguistic, i.e., "interaction" (perlocution).[102] But Frans van Eemeren and Rob Grootendorst are

---

101. Very little was done with perlocution in the early development of Speech Act Theory. In the 36-page bibliography published by Meyers and Hopkins in 1977, fewer than ten entries contain "perlocution" in the title. (See Meyers and Hopkins, "Speech-Act Theory Bibliography"). Although Austin and Searle include perlocution in the total speech act, they argue meaning is communicated via a successful *illocutionary* act. In opposing Grice's inclusion of the perlocutionary act in meaning, early Searle argues that (i) "even where there generally is a correlated perlocutionary effect, I may say something and mean it without in fact intending to produce that effect" (Searle, *Speech Acts*, 46) and (ii) "the characteristic intended effect of meaning is understanding" which "is not a perlocutionary effect" (Searle, 47). Austin's argument that "perlocutionary acts do not have stable meaning" is based on his assumption that "perlocutionary acts are *not* conventional" (Austin, *How To Do Things with Words*, 120; cf. Searle and Vanderveken, *Foundations of Illocutionary Logic*, 12). Similarly, Steinmann argues that "there are no rules that the writer can follow that guarantee performance of the intended perlocutionary act" (Steinmann, "Perlocutionary Acts," 113–14). However, as Rolf notes, "The fact that there is no way that a conventional procedure can guarantee that the intended [perlocutionary] effect will be achieved does not represent any peculiar property of speech acts at all. It is a common characteristic of all actions that there is no such guarantee. The actor, though he (in general) takes for granted that there is no guarantee that the effects he intends will be achieved, does what he wants to do, i.e. *tries* to achieve the effect he intends to be realized" (Rolf, "On the Concept of Action," 164). Alston's approach also considers that "a necessary and sufficient condition of performing an illocutionary act of a certain type is not that one succeed in producing a certain effect in the addressee (actually perform an [sic] perlocutionary act), but only that one *have the intention* to produce that effect (to perform the correlated perlocutionary act)" (Alston, *Illocutionary Acts and Sentence Meaning*, 37). Furthermore, Verschueren finds perlocution to be "relevant on condition that (i) we redefine perlocutionary effects in terms of the speaker's intentions, (ii) we restrict ourselves to those intended effects which are typically associated with the speech act type involved, and (iii) we recognize that the intended typically associated effects are not necessarily achieved" (Verschueren, "Lexical Decomposition," 353). Along these lines, in our inclusion of perlocution in meaning we use a looser concept of convention, allow for perlocutionary intentions, and consider only associated perlocutionary effects.

102. Some linguists refuse to include perlocution in communication because they take communication as only linguistic and perlocutionary effects can be non-verbal (see Gu, "Impasse of Perlocution," 427; and Bach and Harnish, *Linguistic Communication*, 16). According to van Rees, "Illocutionary acts involve the attainment of a *communicative* effect by producing verbal utterances with the intention of getting a listener to

correct that "communication" and "interaction" are both "in principle part of a complete speech act and therefore must be included in an adequate theory of speech acts."[103] Thus, in referring to meaning as created in fully successful *communicative interaction*, we consider meaning to result from illocution and perlocution taken together. For both illocution and perlocution, we include acts and effects, even if the intended perlocutionary effect is non-linguistic.[104] In our action model, "full" meaning is situated in the successful completion of the total speech act.

---

recognize, by recognizing that one has that intention, what particular attitude (belief, want, intention, affect) with respect to a particular state of affairs one is trying to express. Perlocutionary acts involve the attainment of an *interactional* effect by trying to bring about further effects on the cognitive, affective, or conative state of the listener by way of a communicative act" (van Rees, "Adequacy of Speech Act Theory," 40; bold omitted).

Although later Searle defines "speech acts proper" as illocutionary acts (see Searle and Vanderveken, *Foundations of Illocutionary Logic*, 12) and restricts meaning to "speaker meaning," (see Searle, "What is Language," 31), he agrees that "communicating is a matter of producing certain effects on one's hearers" (Searle, *Intentionality*, 165). Then, in order to sustain his argument that only illocution matters in producing meaning, he adds that "one can intend to represent something without caring at all about the effects on one's hearers" (Searle, *Intentionality*, 165). He goes so far as to aver that "one can make a statement . . . without even intending to get them [one's hearers] to understand it at all" (Searle, *Intentionality*, 165), a notion which seems to eliminate speaker intentionality. These are not the normal situations of communication or of intentionality and do not concern us (cf. Tilley, *Evils of Theodicy*, 16). Nor are we interested in the example of sentences uttered in solitude (Alston, *Illocutionary Acts and Sentence Meaning*, 30); utterances not involving a listener are not communication.

Others who equate speech acts only with illocutionary acts include van Dijk (see, e.g., van Dijk, *Text and Context*, 195) and Kurzon, who goes so far as to argue "perlocutionary acts . . . are not part of speech act theory, and as such are not part of pragmatics" (Kurzon, "Speech Act Status of Incitement," 595). Vanhoozer also appears to include only illocution in communication: "The proper function of our communicative faculties, I contend, is to produce true interpretation—understanding" (Vanhoozer, *Is There a Meaning?*, 205). However, he opens the door to perlocution as "strategic action" a few pages later when he states that "speakers and authors . . . are both perlocutionary and illocutionary agents. Interpreting texts is thus a matter of understanding purposive action—communicative and strategic. When I speak of communicative action in relation to texts, therefore, I am referring to the full-fledged, four-dimensional reality described by speech act theory and not only to the illocutionary dimension" (Vanhoozer, 224–25). This last sentence corresponds to our use of perlocution.

103. Van Eemeren and Grootendorst, *Speech Acts*, 25; see also 23.

104. Generally, even those who include perlocution in communicative meaning do not include the reader. Instead, they use one of two approaches: (i) the communication of meaning involves only the perlocutionary acts/intentions of the author/speaker, or (ii) perlocutionary effects are attributed to the efforts of the speaker/author who, in essence, causes them. We discuss and reject causality below. An example of the former approach

This accords with recent thinking about pragmatics. According to social psychologist Wendelin Reich, "the problematic status of perlocutionary acts in SAT [Speech Act Theory] can only be rectified if we give up the assumption that speech acts are produced by speakers alone, together with the related assumption that meanings (illocutionary level) rather than effects (perlocutionary level) are all that matters."[105] Our action model thus goes beyond traditional pragmatic theories—both Speech Act Theory and implicature theories—in which communicating meaning is a function only of authorial intention and reader recognition (understanding). Because perlocution is a critical element of our action model and because it has often been ignored or excluded, we look more closely at perlocutionary acts and effects —beginning with their relationship to illocution.

Like illocutionary acts, perlocutionary acts are acts of the speaker/author. Max Black defines a perlocutionary act as "something we may do by producing an illocutionary act (e.g., persuading, getting somebody to do something, checking somebody, annoying him, etc.)"[106] We go further than Black in arguing that a perlocutionary act *necessarily* occurs in connection

---

is Grice. He defines nonnatural ("NN") meaning on the basis of intentional *perlocutionary* acts: "'A [a speaker] meant$_{NN}$ something by x' is (roughly) equivalent to 'A intended the utterance of x to produce some effect in an audience by means of the recognition of this intention'" (Grice, *Studies in the Way of Words*, 220). See also Verschueren, "Lexical Decomposition," 347; and Connor-Linton, "Sociolinguistic Model," 96.

Within biblical scholarship, Watson expresses a Gricean view of meaning: "The *literal sense* of the biblical texts comprises (*i*) verbal meaning, (*ii*) illocutionary and perlocutionary force, and (*iii*) the relation to the centre. As communicative actions, the texts seek to convey a meaning in order to evoke a particular response" (Watson, *Text and Truth*, 123). Although he adds that "the true end of communicative action . . . is responsive action" (Watson, 116), for him the audience's role is passive: "Readers can only *receive* meaning, they cannot *create* it" (Watson, 104). Other biblical scholars/theologians who recognize perlocutionary intentionality include Meyer, *Critical Realism*, 22; Gilfillan Upton, *Hearing Mark's Endings*, 93; and Tovey, *Narrative Art and Act*, 264.

105. Reich, "Cooperative Nature of Communicative Acts," 1352. Tilley puts it more strongly: "A theory of speech acts cannot . . . equate the meaning of the act performed to the illocutionary intent of the agent. That would be as flawed as a general theory of human acts which neglected the essential links between act and results or which equated the act performed to the bare intention of the agent. . . . Hence, part of the meaning of communicative speech acts is their perlocutionary results" (Tilley, *Evils of Theodicy*, 23).

106. Black, "Austin on Performatives," 224; cf. Searle, *Speech Acts*, 25. *Contra* C. Tanner, "Climbing the Lampstand-Witness-Trees," 88; and Vorster, "Toward an Interactional Model," 111–12, we reject an understanding of illocution as the intended effect on the audience and perlocution as the actual effect. Similarly, we find misleading Tovey's assignment of illocutionary intent to the implied author and perlocutionary effect to the story (see Tovey, *Narrative Art and Act*, 263).

with an illocutionary act, that is, all illocutionary acts have intentional perlocutionary acts associated with them.[107]

Although the full range of perlocutionary effects includes all reader responses except the illocutionary effect of understanding,[108] in this study, our concern is associated perlocutionary effects, i.e., those the implied author intends for the implied reader which are directly and conventionally correlated with understanding the illocutionary act and recognizing its related perlocutionary act.[109] We do not consider other perlocutionary acts and effects, i.e., either unintentional perlocutionary effects or "effects or consequences of speech acts that are *not* brought about on the basis of *understanding of an illocutionary act.*"[110] This means we reject Habermas's

---

107. *Contra* Botha's concept of the perlocutionary act as "sometimes ... performed" (Botha, *Jesus and the Samaritan Woman*, 48; cf. Vorster, "Toward an Interactional Model," 111). Rather, as van Eemeren and Grootendorst point out, "Language users performing speech acts do not, in principle, do so with the sole intention of making the persons to whom they address themselves understand what speech act they are performing: rather, by means of those speech acts they hope to elicit from their listeners a particular response (verbal or otherwise)" (van Eemeren and Grootendorst, *Speech Acts*, 23). Similarly, "when the listener perceives and understands the meaning (the language meaning) of speech, he simultaneously takes an active, responsive attitude toward it. He either agrees or disagrees with it (completely or partially), augments it, applies it, prepares for its execution, and so on.... Thus, all real and integral understanding is actively responsive, and constitutes nothing other than the initial preparatory stage of a response (in whatever form it may be actualized)" (Bakhtin, "Problem of Speech Genres," 68–69).

108. See S. Davis, "Perlocutions," 54.

109. *Contra* Irsigler, who considers that "perlokutive Effekte oder Zwecke, das, was der Sprecher tatsächlich beim Hörer/Adressaten bewirken will, sind bzw. ist nicht konstitutiv mit bestimmten Illokutionen verbunden" (Irsigler, "Psalm-Rede," 69). Rather, we follow Cohen in considering "standard" perlocution to be directly "associated" with the illocution (Cohen, "Illocutions and Perlocutions," 494–99; cf. van Eemeren and Grootendorst, "Study of Argumentation," 155). In this, "perlokutive Akte [i.e. perlokutionäre Effekte ...] schließen sich irgendwie konventionell an den illokutiven Akt an" (Luge, "Perlokutionäre Effekte/Perlocutionary Effects," 75, quoting Völzing, "Gebrauchstexte, Linguistik und perlokutive Akte," 103, with the material in brackets added by Luge).

Cohen identifies two other types of perlocution: unintentional perlocution and indirect perlocution. In the latter, the perlocution stems from the locution (Cohen, "Illocutions and Perlocutions," 495–97). Indirect perlocution fits Tovey's view of "perlocutionary acts (perlocutions)" as "the intended effects that locutions are conventionally expected to have or to achieve" (Tovey, *Narrative Art and Act*, 71; cf. Lee, "Perlocution and Illocution," 37; and Luge, "Perlokutionäre Effekte/Perlocutionary Effects," 74, 83). Our concept of perlocution is narrower than that of Botha, who includes some non-associated perlocution (see Botha, *Jesus and the Samaritan Woman*, 99, 104).

110. Van Eemeren and Grootendorst, *Speech Acts*, 27. See also Vanhoozer, *First Theology*, 185. We do not find helpful either Burkhardt's redefining perlocution as the

model, since in it only non-associated perlocutionary effects are the goal of perlocutionary intention, and associated perlocutionary effects are included in illocution.[111]

The three-way correlation between each illocutionary act type and the associated perlocutionary act and perlocutionary effect is as follows:

Assertive: that H believe that P.

Directive: that H (intend to) do A.

Commissive: that H believe S intends to fulfill his obligation to do A.

Expressive: either (i) H believe S has the appropriate feeling or (ii) H respond with the appropriate feeling.[112]

"intra-illocutionary effect" or the "illocutionary point" (Burkhardt, "Speech Act Theory," 98n117, 98n119) or the notion that illocution is "a special type of perlocution" (Lee, "Perlocution and Illocution," 38n2).

111. For Habermas, perlocutionary acts are not speech acts but instead "constitute a subclass of teleological actions which must be carried out *by means of* speech acts, under the condition that the actor does not declare or admit to his aims as such" (Habermas, *Reason*, 292; emphasis added; see also 293–94, and Habermas, *On the Pragmatics of Communication*, 126). Habermas considers perlocution to be *strategic* action, i.e., concealed action which involves exerting influence and manipulation while *communicative* action is "linguistically mediated interactions in which all participants pursue . . . *only* illocutionary aims" (Habermas, *Reason*, 295).

In his later work, Habermas modifies this slightly, distinguishing three classes of perlocutionary effects (Habermas, *On the Pragmatics of Communication*, 320). The first resembles associated perlocution, the second are unintentional perlocutionary effects, and the third are strategic actions, which "come about only if they are not declared or if they are brought about by deceptive speech acts that merely pretend to be valid" (Habermas, 202). However, Habermas emphasizes "that *the distinction between communicative and strategic action* is not influenced by this revision" (Habermas, 203). Moreover, for him, "the agreement reached with the hearer, that is, the hearer's acceptance of the speech-act offer" is "achieved solely through the performance of the illocutionary act" (Habermas, 202). Thus, "the illocutionary meaning of an utterance is not that the hearer should take note of S's belief (or intention) but rather that she should come to hold the *same* view as S (or that she should take seriously S's announcement)" (Habermas, 320). For us, this is perlocution, not illocution.

112. Adapted from Bach and Harnish, *Linguistic Communication*, 81. With texts these correlations apply to the implied reader. Although Rolf uses Searle's title of "extra-linguistic purposes" (see Searle, *Intentionality*, 178) instead of "perlocution," his similar correlation includes Declarations. We agree with him that "the so-called extra-linguistic purposes . . . have to be considered at all costs, if one wants to describe adequately what makes a speech act an action" (Rolf, "On the Concept of Action," 163).

PART I | DEVELOPING A METHODOLOGY

This correlation between illocutionary acts, perlocutionary acts, and associated perlocutionary effects[113] is key to our action model of meaning since it shows the intended perlocutionary effect of every speech act to be transformation of beliefs or behavior.

As with illocutionary intention,

> discernment of what perlocutionary acts a speaker is attempting to commit requires neither direct nor inferential access to the speaker's cognitive or affective states. This is because it may be inferred pragmatically that the speaker attempts the same perlocutions with the speech act that any rational speaker would be attempting with such an act in identical circumstances.[114]

Therefore, perlocutionary intentions are expressed through the correlated illocutionary intentions of the implied author and reveal the associated perlocutionary effects (responses) of the implied reader.[115]

Because perlocution occurs in correlation with illocution, different types of illocutionary acts have different intended perlocutionary effects. With an Assertive, for example, the intended illocutionary effect is that the hearer/reader understand the illocutionary act, that is, understand that the illocutionary act is an Assertive and also what content is presented and with what degree of force. The intended perlocutionary effect is that hearers/readers adhere to the truth of the Assertive and transform their lifeworld/worldview accordingly.[116]

---

113. *Contra* S. Davis, who gives promising and thanking as examples of illocutionary acts without perlocutionary purposes (S. Davis, "Perlocutions," 47), all illocutionary acts have associated perlocution. As Alston puts it, "For every illocutionary act type there is some type of belief or action such that the intention to elicit a belief or action of that type in [addressee] A normally accompanies illocutionary acts of that type" (Alston, *Illocutionary Acts and Sentence Meaning*, 44).

114. Gaines, "Doing By Saying," 214n25. We do not mean to imply by this that the making of a perlocutionary act depends on its success. Rolf names "absurde" those views in which "den Vollzug perlokutionärer Akte in irgendeiner Form abhängig machen vom faktischen Eintreten beabsichtigter Wirkungen auf seiten des Adressaten einer solchen Handlung" (Rolf, "Perlokutionäre Akte und perlokutionäre Effekte," 264). He adds that "der Erfolg, das Erreichen des Ziels einer Handlung für deren Vollzug keine Bedingung darstellen kann" (Rolf, 267).

115. This is what we take "understanding" a perlocutionary act to mean.

116. The mutual context of the speaker and hearer is altered at the illocutionary level (see chapter 4, n111) as a result both of the presentation of an illocutionary act with its preparatory and sincerity conditions and of hearer/reader understanding (see Thiselton, *New Horizons in Hermeneutics*, 565; Gadamer, *Truth and Method*, 570; Lee, "Perlocution and Illocution," 38n2; Wunderlich, "Methodological Remarks on Speech

In this regard, Directives are unique. They are the only illocutionary acts "definable in terms of the intended perlocutionary effect"; in other words, the intended perlocutionary effect of a Directive is a key element of the essential condition of a Directive illocutionary act.[117] Additionally, unlike other speech acts where the intended perlocution relates to transformation of the hearer's knowledge base or belief system, the intended perlocutionary effect of a Directive is transformation of the hearer/reader's actions. For this reason, Directives can be particularly important.

Some illocutionary acts are indirect, i.e., their function is not evidenced by their grammar. Such illocutionary acts still have a single illocutionary force and perlocution. For example, "Blessed is he whose transgressions are forgiven, whose sins are covered" (Ps 32:1 NIV, quoted in Rom 4:7–8) is, on its surface, an Assertive. But taken within its OT co-text, and especially considering Ps 32:5–6, it is a warning (or, minimally, a suggestion) and thus is a Directive.[118] The intended perlocutionary effect is not audience adherence to the truth of the statement. Rather, as a Directive, the intended perlocutionary effect is the action of confession and seeking forgiveness; this is what the implied reader does upon both understanding and adhering to the warning.

Successful Perlocution and the Interactive Communication of Meaning

A speech act is fully successful only when it is perlocutionarily successful. We define a successful perlocutionary act as one where the empirical reader/hearer responds with the intended perlocutionary response (belief or action) called for from the implied reader.[119] This we term "adherence."

Act Theory," 292; Ward, *Word and Supplement*, 99; and Sbisà, "Speech Acts in Context," 433). As Alston notes, "Just by virtue of being an act it [an illocutionary act] will have consequences" (Alston, *Illocutionary Acts and Sentence Meaning*, 32). But this is not the transformation which occurs with full perlocutionary act success.

117. Searle, *Speech Acts*, 71. This refutes his contention that perlocution never plays a role in meaning.

118. See Bach and Harnish, *Linguistic Communication*, 49, for a discussion of the "Advisories" subtype of Directive.

119. We follow Rolf in speaking "vom Erfolge einer Handlung" as "wenn die intendierte und die faktisch erzielte Wirkung zusammenfallen" (Rolf, "Perlokutionäre Akte und perlokutionäre Effekte," 265), with the caveat that regarding perlocution we refer only to associated perlocution. Rolf adds that "wenn meine Worte jedoch nicht gehört und nicht verstanden wurden, dann läβt sich dennoch nicht sagen, ich hätte nicht gehandelt . . . ; feststellen läβt sich lediglich, daβ ich mit meiner Handlung den mit ihr verfolgten Zweck nicht erreicht habe und insofern nicht erfolgreich war" (Rolf, 266).

Because perlocutionary acts are both intentional and direct, illocutionary success is *necessary* for perlocutionary success. This means that for empirical readers to make the intended perlocutionary response, they must first respond with the illocutionary effect of understanding.[120] However, illocutionary success is not *sufficient* for perlocutionary success.[121] As Gadamer points out using the example of a Directive, "The intended recipient of the order . . . is well able to distinguish between understanding and obeying an order. It is possible for him not to obey even when—indeed, precisely when—he has understood it."[122]

Perlocutionary intentionality does not imply causality. Perlocution "is a joint endeavour between S and H. It involves S's performance of speech acts and H's performance of response-acts."[123] Perlocutionary effects are

---

120. See S. Davis, "Perlocutions," 44. Although a reader/hearer who does not understand the illocution could make the appropriate perlocutionary response by chance, "accidental" perlocution does not concern us. Nor are we interested in the possible success of a non-associated perlocutionary act.

121. See van Eemeren and Grootendorst, *Speech Acts*, 25. As Bach points out, "We need to distinguish the success of a speech act as an illocutionary and as a perlocutionary act" (Bach, "Pragmatics," 469).

122. Gadamer, *Truth and Method*, 330; cf. Houston, "What Did the Prophets Think They Were Doing?," 177). This is a difficulty with Habermas's model, in which successful *illocution* includes adherence (see n111).

123. Gu, "Impasse of Perlocution," 422, arguing against Austin's claim that since "mental events . . . are not acts," a hearer "has no claim of agency concerning the effects produced in him." Like Gu, Rolf argues that "kann generell festgestellt werden, daß— in analytischer Perspektive gesehen—eine Handlung und der mit ihr verfolgte Zweck beziehungsweise die mit ihr intendierte Wirkung eines ist, die erzielte Wirkung jedoch ein anderes" (Rolf, "Perlokutionäre Akte und perlokutionäre Effekte," 265). Marcu calls "attaching little or no importance to the role of the hearer in the perlocutionary act" a fallacy (Marcu, "Perlocutions," 1726; italics omitted).

"actively produced by H, who has the claim to the agency of the effects."[124] The success of a perlocution depends on hearer cooperation.[125]

In our model, neither authorial intention (even including perlocutionary intention) nor reader response is the sole determinant of communicative meaning. Although we agree the author "created and patterned the set of relations being analyzed, had a purpose in doing so, and still has a relation to the text him or herself that is important for interpretation,"[126] communication is not a one-way transmittal from author to reader. Nor does the hearer/reader create meaning unilaterally; we disagree with the radical reader-response positions of theorists such as Stanley Fish and Richard Rorty[127] as well as with the notion that "the autonomy of the text . . . hands writing over to the sole interpretation of the reader."[128] Rather, the empirical reader plays

---

124. Gu, "Impasse of Perlocution," 422; cf. Luge, "Perlokutionäre Effekte/Perlocutionary Effects," 76. Similarly, Cohen and Perrault argue that "while a speaker often has performed illocutionary acts with the goal of achieving certain perlocutionary effects, the actual securing of those effects is beyond his control. Thus, it is entirely possible for a speaker to make an assertion, and for the audience to recognize the force of the utterance as an assertion and yet not be convinced" (Cohen and Perrault, "Elements of a Plan-Based Theory," 187). P. N. Campbell asserts that "each party to a language or communicative act possesses language and, therefore, is not simply manipulated by others, but participates in the acts of persuading, ordering, etc." (P. N. Campbell, "Rhetorical View," 296). This is in contrast to the passive role allotted to the reader by Bach and Harnish: "If the hearer forms a corresponding attitude that the speaker intended him to form, the *speaker* has achieved a perlocutionary effect in addition to illocutionary uptake" (Bach and Harnish, *Linguistic Communication*, 39, emphasis added; cf. Austin, *How To Do Things with Words*, 121).

125. See Kurzon, "Speech Act Status of Incitement," 571, 574–575.

126. Snodgrass, "Reading to Hear," 19.

127. See n96 above. For a summary of various reader-response arguments, including Barthes's *lisible* and *scriptible* texts and deconstructionism, see Sherwood, *The Prostitute and the Prophet*, especially chapters 1–3. Witherington points out that even ardent reader-response theorists "like S. Fish, have been willing to object that they have been misquoted or misunderstood at times and that we must think in terms of interpretive communities which guide our reading. But no complaints about being *misunderstood* can be allowed to stand unless one has intended some specific meaning in the first place which was misheard or misinterpreted. And why should we need interpretive communities if the meaning simply happens between the reader and the text?" (Witherington, *Gospel of Mark*, 57).

128. Ricoeur, "Metaphor," 174. (See n6 above). Our difficulty is with the word "sole" since, in general, Ricoeur neither unleashes the reader nor ignores the author. For example, he finds that "to interpret is to explicate the type of being-in-the-world unfolded in front of the text" (Ricoeur, "Hermeneutical Function of Distanciation," 141), and he warns against forgetting "that a text remains a discourse told by somebody, said by

a role in the interactive communication of meaning first by understanding the identity of the implied reader created by the implied author and presented in the text and then, in situations of fully successful communicative interaction, by *envisaging* himself or herself as that reader.

In this, there are similarities between our model and the thoughts of conservative reader-response theorist Umberto Eco. As we do, Eco uses the construct of the implied reader.[129] Similarly, he sees pragmatics as concerned

> not only with the phenomenon of interpretation (of signs, sentences, or texts) or of indexical expressions, but also with the "essential dependence of communication in natural languages on speaker and hearer, on *linguistic context and extralinguistic context [cotext]* ..., on the availability of background knowledge, on readiness to obtain this background knowledge and on the good will of the participants in the [a] communication act."[130]

Eco does not privilege the reader to the extent of considering every reading to be valid,[131] and in his focus on the interaction of the text and the reader, he equates the intentions of the text with those of the implied author.[132] His concept of pragmatics accords with our ideas about mutual context and author/reader cooperation.

Our action model, in which meaning is a three-dimensional communicative interaction mediated through text via the construction of the implied author and the implied reader, does not present the communication

---

someone to someone else about something" (Ricoeur, *Interpretation Theory*, 18). For the empirical reader, "it is not a question of imposing upon the text our finite capacity of understanding, but of exposing ourselves to the text and receiving from it an enlarged self" (Ricoeur, "Hermeneutical Function of Distanciation," 143). Walhout suggests the way "to defend textual autonomy" is "to ignore authorial intention and posit the presence of an 'implied author'" (Walhout, "Texts and Actions," 48). But we argue instead that it is via the implied author that we discover the intentions of the empirical author.

129. Eco calls this the "Model Reader." See, e.g., Eco, *Role of the Reader*, 7–10.

130. Eco, *Limits of Interpretation*, 213, quoting Bar-Hillel, "Communication and Argumentation," 270–271. The words in brackets are original to Bar-Hillel's essay.

131. According to Eco, there are "bad" readings; any interpretation is to be checked against "the text as a coherent whole" (Eco, *Limits of Interpretation*, 60, 149).

132. See, e.g., Eco, "Between Author and Text," 69; and Eco, *Limits of Interpretation*, 59. Although Eco says that "in this dialectics between the intention of the reader and the intention of the text, the intention of the empirical author has been totally disregarded" (Eco, "Between Author and Text," 65), this reference to "intention" appears to be to authorial "motive," which we agree is not necessary to recover.

of meaning as the sole purview of *either* the author *or* the reader but of *both/and*. Our action model recognizes both the author and the reader as active agents in the co-creation of meaning.[133] And it does not consider just the dimension of illocution; we see meaning as fully communicated only when the speech act in its totality, including perlocution, is successful. Since successful perlocution occurs only when the empirical reader responds with the perlocutionary response (effect) intended for the implied reader by the implied author, speech acts which are only understood (the illocutionary response) are not fully successful communicative interactions. This understanding of the role of the author and reader in both illocution and perlocution is the foundation of the reader role of Envisager.

The Reader as Envisager

The implied reader is an Envisager since, by definition, the implied reader responds with the illocutionary effect of understanding and also with the perlocutionary effect corresponding to the perlocutionary intention of the implied author.[134] Therefore, for Envisaging to be accomplished empirically, there must be full communicative interaction, i.e., the speech act must be both illocutionarily and perlocutionarily successful. An Envisaging empirical reader not only understands the force of the illocutionary act but also responds with the intended perlocutionary effect.[135] Only Envisaging readers undertake the necessary transformation of beliefs/thoughts or action to "live into" or "inhabit" the lifeworld and Story presented by the implied author.[136] What transformation is required of the Envisager can be

---

133. Our model of communication "treats speakers and addressees as partners" (H. H. Clark, *Using Language*, 132).

134. When empirical readers envisage themselves as the implied or "ideal" reader, they "experience the intended perlocutionary effect" (Steinmann, "Speech-Act Theory and Writing," 310). Although the construct of implied author/reader does not apply to conversation, we call hearers "envisaging" if they respond appropriately to a NT speaker's illocutionary and perlocutionary acts.

135. An Envisaging empirical reader does not have to form an intention to be an Envisager. It is the result that determines what role an empirical reader adopts.

136. L. T. Johnson avers that "if Scripture is ever again to be a living source for theology, those who practice theology must become less preoccupied with the world that produced Scripture and learn again how to live in the world Scripture produces" (L. T. Johnson, "Imagining the World Scripture Imagines," 165). More specifically, Möller concludes with regard to Ps 101 that "in singing or praying this psalm, we, its modern readers, are ourselves making a pledge; we are committing ourselves to the behaviour the ancient

examined on a theoretical basis, without knowing the actual response of any empirical reader or whether any particular speech act has been fully successful.[137]

Empirical readers may have difficulty undertaking the called-for transformation. Not only is "the perlocutionary function . . . the least communicable,"[138] i.e., a speech act has the greatest chance to be unsuccessful in the dimension of perlocution, reading cooperatively "does not foreclose critique."[139] Hays relates this to the faithful reading of Scripture: "Is all questioning to be excluded, all critical reading banished? By no means. Asking necessary and difficult questions is not to be equated with *apistia*."[140] In some cases, even if understanding is accomplished, the empirical reader may choose not to make the intended perlocutionary response. Even a cooperative reader may conclude that the role of Envisager must be rejected, i.e., that the world being offered is not one that can be "inhabited" with integrity or coherence.[141] In such a case, the potential Envisager remains at the level of Analyst, someone who understands the intention of the implied

---

psalmist thought appropriate for a king" (Möller "Reading, Singing and Praying the Law," 135–36). With regard to Directives, Gadamer notes that if the contemporary reader "really wants to understand the order," i.e., if the order is to be perlocutionarily successful for that reader, that reader must "perform the same act as that performed by the intended recipient of the order" (Gadamer, *Truth and Method*, 330). One of our goals in interpretation is to discern what it might mean for the modern reader to "perform the same act."

137. *Contra* Vorster, who argues that "perlocutionary acts are relevant for New Testament studies only in an intratextual conversational situation where the effect of an illocutionary act is given" (Vorster, "Toward an Interactional Model," 112). Polk treats "meaning" differently than we do when he adds actual reader response. For him, a text's "ultimate meaning . . . is only completed in the reader's living. How s/he responds to the summons and pursues the intended transformation become part of the work's scope. In fact, that response becomes one criterion for evaluating what the text is and does, what it ultimately means" (Polk, *Prophetic Persona*, 174).

138. Ricoeur, *Interpretation Theory*, 18.

139. Meyer, *Critical Realism*, 22; cf. Vanhoozer, *Is There a Meaning?*, 227.

140. R. B. Hays, "Salvation by Trust?," 221.

141. Tovey points out that "readers are at liberty to accept or reject at all levels" (Tovey, *Narrative Art and Act*, 97). For Vanhoozer, "readers must not only respond but respond *responsibly*. . . . It may be that, once having grasped the text's intended sense, the reader will recoil in disgust" (Vanhoozer, "Reader in New Testament Interpretation," 273). These references are to the empirical reader since the implied reader always makes the response intended by the implied author. The more divergent the goals and interests of the empirical author and reader, the more difficult it may be for an empirical reader to be envisaging (see Pratt, "Ideology and Speech-Act Theory," 68–69).

author but does not respond with the intended perlocutionary effect and the requisite lifeworld transformation.

We tie Envisaging to quotation with Stanley's thought that "Paul wrote his letters not to lay out a set of theological beliefs, but to motivate specific first-century Christians to believe and/or act (or stop believing or acting) in particular ways."[142] As Derek Tovey asks, "Is it the case that the primary intention of the Fourth Gospel is to display a state of affairs with no intention that this should have an impact on the reader which is world-changing, or action-inducing?"[143] He answers his own question: "The purpose of his [the implied author's] narrative is so to affect their worldview that they orient their lives in accordance with what follows from accepting his assertions."[144] Lifeworld/worldview and theology are transformed when reading is Envisaging.

As the final step in creating our methodology, we put our action model on the same linguistic level as our theological framework and the implied author/reader construct. In other words, we consider "how speech act functions are realized in larger text units"[145] since those are the building blocks of Story.

SPEECH ACT COMPLEXES

In the 1960s there was a move from the word to the sentence as the unit of communication. This is reflected in Searle's belief that "the characteristic grammatical form of the illocutionary act is the complete sentence. . . . Sentences, not words, are used to say things."[146] Linguistics has gone

---

142. Stanley, *Arguing with Scripture*, 3. This thought inspired some of our discussion of quotation in chapter 2.

143. Tovey, *Narrative Art and Act*, 196.

144. Tovey, *Narrative Art and Act*, 89. "The narrative is a theological display which, in setting forth the state of affairs it represents, seeks an affective response. This response is not to be at the level of aesthetic enjoyment but of belief and self-involvement in the 'world' which is represented in the story" (Tovey, 265).

145. Hatch, *Discourse and Language Education*, 152.

146. Searle, *Speech Acts*, 25. "The history of linguistics shows that for semantics *the word* was first regarded as the practical unit of communication" (Louw, "Discourse Analysis," 102). Prior to Searle, "Frege pointed out . . . sentences and not words are the primary units of meaning of a language" (Vanderveken, *Meaning and Speech Acts*, 7; see also n32 above). Austin also argued that "it appears correct to say that what 'has meaning' in the primary sense is the sentence" (Austin, *Philosophical Papers,* 56).

further and now operates "from the assumption that communication occurs in discourses, not in isolated or random sentences."[147] Although some scholars name the paragraph "the developmental unit of discourse,"[148] because "paragraph" is a grammatical term, we instead consider the "speech act complex" to be that portion of a text which has homogeneity and cohesiveness.[149]

The speech acts in a speech act complex are not generally equally weighted. Speech acts "do not merely follow each other at the same level: ... some acts may have secondary rank with respect to others."[150] Our name for "the main act intended in a sequence of speech acts, such that the other speech acts are components or auxiliary/preparatory for that act" is the *core speech act*.[151] The illocutionary act type of the core speech act determines the illocutionary function of the speech act complex.[152] Tellability also can

---

147. Porter, "Greek Grammar and Syntax," 99. G. H. Guthrie refers to discourse analysts David Allen and Talmy Givón in pointing out that "*the primary locus of discourse meaning resides above the sentence level*" (G. H. Guthrie, "Discourse Analysis," 256). Similarly, Walhout asserts that we "have to go beyond the sentence in order to determine the illocutionary force of its utterance" (Walhout, "Narrative Hermeneutics," 67).

148. Longacre, *Grammar of Discourse*, 288. See also Osborne, for whom the paragraph is "the key to the thought development of biblical books" (Osborne, *Hermeneutical Spiral*, 41).

149. We adapt "speech act complex" from van Eemeren and Grootendorst's discussion of illocutionary act complexes (see, e.g., van Eemeren and Grootendorst, *Speech Acts*, 34). The notion that "homogeneity and cohesiveness" define its boundaries comes from Louw ("Discourse Analysis," 103). In a later work, van Eemeren and Grootendorst tie these "'higher' textual levels" to Speech Act Theory (see, e.g., van Eemeren and Grootendorst, "Study of Argumentation," 154).

A speech act complex is generally a smaller unit than van Dijk's macro or global speech act (see, e.g., van Dijk, *Text and Context*, 238), which is similar to Brown and Yule's "speech event," i.e., "an activity in which participants interact via language in some conventional way to arrive at some outcome" (Brown and Yule, *Discourse Analysis*, 57; see also 47, 135, and Hatch, *Discourse and Language Education*, 136). Conventionally patterned interactions such as Brigg's examples of confessing faith, forgiving sin, and teaching (see Briggs, *Words in Action*, chapters 6–8) are beyond the scope of this study. Not only are they not related to quotation, they would require an expansion of our action model.

150. Van Dijk, *Text and Context*, 216. As Chatman describes it, the various "text-types routinely operate *at each other's service*" (Chatman, *Coming to Terms*, 10).

151. Van Dijk, *Text and Context*, 226. The core speech act equates to the topic sentence of a paragraph. However, "topic" has the sense only of content, i.e., "what a discourse or part of it 'is about'" (van Dijk, 6) whereas the core speech act includes not only propositional content but also illocution and perlocution.

152. Often, a "sequence of (various) speech acts *as a whole* has the function of a command, advice, etc." (van Dijk, *Text and Context*, 233; cf. Brown and Yule, *Discourse*

be extended into speech act complexes since it "can be meaningfully applied to utterances of more than a single sentence, utterances whose individual sentences probably represent a wide variety of speech act types."[153]

Whether there is a natural hierarchy of speech acts in a speech act complex is debated.[154] But Kathleen Callow and John Callow find that

> cohesive prominence occurs when two units are joined in a coherence relation: unless this is a purely additive relationship, it is normal for one member of the pairing to carry more impact, more cognitive weight, than the other. Thus *result* is more naturally prominent than *reason*, *response* than *stimulus*, and so on.... The naturally prominent elements constitute the structural core of the unit, to which the less prominent units relate.[155]

From a speech-act perspective, Alessandro Ferrera argues that "the hierarchic status of a speech act in a sequence corresponds to the hierarchic status of the extra-illocutionary [i.e., perlocutionary] goal that it is meant

---

Analysis, 233). Pratt convincingly argues that there is "a level of analysis at which utterances with a single point or purpose must be treated as single speech acts, or 'discourse acts,' or 'texts,' if we wish" (Pratt, *Towards a Speech Act Theory*, 141). See also Irsigler, who argues with regard to Psalm 13 that "von der Feststellung 6d her, d.h. von der Ebene des erreichten Wirkungszwecks her, erscheint die ganze Psalmrede nachträglich als ein einziger komplexer perlokutiver Akt" (Irsigler, "Psalm-Rede," 87) and Tovey, who speaks of "the perlocutionary effect intended by the narrative [of John's Gospel] taken as a whole" (Tovey, *Narrative Art and Act*, 92).

153. Pratt, *Towards a Speech Act Theory*, 141. In some cases, it is helpful to further identify the illocutionary force of the speech acts and/or the speech act complex according to the subtypes proposed by Bach and Harnish.

154. In response to the questions "Was aber, wenn in einem Text aufgrund seiner Komplexität verschiedene Illokutionen vorkommen... ? Welche Illokution ist dann die dominante?," A. Wagner suggests several possibilities: "Die einen beschreiten den Weg, einen Text mit einer Äußerung gleichzusetzen und nach der dominanten zugrundeliegenden Illokution zu fragen.... Ein zweiter Weg, sich der Sprechaktseite eines Textes zu nähern, is es, auf die Kombination und Abfolge von Illokutionen einzelner Äußerungen/Sätze in Texten zu achten.... Ein weiterer Weg besteht darin, die sprechakttheoretische Dimension eines Texts nicht aus der Addition seiner Einzelteile, sondern aus der (in sich heterogenen) Gesamtheit des Textes zu gewinnen" (A. Wagner, "Die Stellung der Sprachakttheorie," 80–81). We prefer those options which recognize that individual speech acts retain their illocutionary force.

155. Callow and Callow, "Text as Purposive Communication," 11. Motsch and Pasch believe "offenbar ist jeweils eine der beiden illokutiven Handlungen dominierend, d.h., sie gibt an, was der Sprecher mit der Textäußerung erreichen will" (Motsch and Pasch, "Illokutive Handlungen," 72). Further, "ergibt sich die Möglichkeit von Hierarchien illokutiver Handlungen" (Motsch and Pasch, 73). This seems intuitively likely.

to achieve."[156] This means Directives are likely to have some sort of "purposive prominence." Therefore, in our analysis, we generally consider how other speech acts support any Directives in either the speech act complex or the related speech event.

Thiselton notes that "a speech-act, or series of speech-acts, may be able simultaneously to project narrative-worlds and assert states of affairs and transform the perceptions of readers."[157] This we believe is the goal of an envisaging OT reader who is now a NT author and who quotes an OT passage. An Envisaging NT speaker/author moves beyond understanding the message of the text to live into the world presented by the implied OT author. By subsequently quoting that passage, the envisaging NT speaker/author evokes an OT Story-line or an intervening interpretation of it in order to invite the NT audience to hear/read the recontextualized Story as Envisagers and then to live into that lifeworld and adopt the theological worldview of its Story.[158] Because an Envisaging empirical reader responds with the intended perlocutionary effect of belief and/or action, that reader moves towards adopting the Story and worldview presented in the text and inhabiting its lifeworld.

In our two case studies, we use our methodology to explore how a particular quotation is intended to transform the Story, theology, and lifeworld/worldview of the Envisaging empirical NT audience. In the next chapter, we introduce the case studies by outlining the steps of our analysis and laying some groundwork concerning the Psalms generally.

---

156. Ferrera, "Pragmatics," 144. Along these lines, Searle and Vanderveken argue that "expressives are the weakest" type of speech act (Searle and Vanderveken, *Foundations of Illocutionary Logic*, 178).

157. Thiselton, "Reader-Response Hermeneutics," 100–101; cf. Thiselton, *First Epistle to the Corinthians*, 41; and Thiselton, *New Horizons in Hermeneutics*, 154, 558–620.

158. Although the NT writings were no doubt crafted with certain audience characteristics in mind, we do not limit "empirical" to "original." "Empirical" refers to all flesh-and-blood readers or potential readers. "Audience" includes not only hearers and readers of the written text, but also hearers of speeches and conversations the text records.

PART II

Case Studies

6

Introduction to the Case Studies

OUR FINAL STEP IS to demonstrate the applicability of our methodology. In addition to the examples we have already presented from the NT Psalms quotations to illustrate various aspects of our methodology, as case studies we use our full methodology to examine two Psalms passages quoted in the NT. The first is Ps 115:1 LXX as quoted by Paul in 2 Cor 4:13. The second is Ps 110:1 [109:1 LXX] as quoted by Jesus in the Synoptic Gospels, by Peter in Acts 2:34–35, by Paul in 1 Cor 15:25, and by the author of Hebrews in Heb 1:13.

THE ORGANIZATION OF THE CASE STUDIES

In each case study, we first determine the contribution of the source (OT) speech acts within their speech act complex to Story and thus to lifeworld/ worldview and theology. In keeping with our pragmatic focus, we use Ernst Wendland's five major Psalm functions: "petition, thanksgiving, praise, instruction, and profession of trust" and his five minor functions: "repentance, remembrance, retribution, royalty, and liturgy"[1] to estab-

---

1. Wendland, *Analyzing the Psalms*, 33. We prefer Wendland's schema to Gunkel's more complicated typology (see Gunkel, *Introduction to Psalms*, 1998). We also find that typologies which contain three or fewer categories are not sufficiently detailed for the analysis of speech act complexes. Examples include: Westermann, *Praise and Lament*; Weiser, *Psalms*; W. Brueggemann, *Message of the Psalms*; and Wendland's earlier work, "Continuity and Discontinuity in Hebrew Poetic Design."

lish the boundaries of the speech act complex which contains the quoted passage.

We next ascertain what role is played by each speech act. This involves applying our action model. We first discuss any critical issues of locution, and then we determine the illocutionary and perlocutionary intentions and desired perlocutionary response, using the construct of the implied author/reader and remembering the implied reader is not necessarily the direct addressee.[2] As part of this analysis, we consider relevant elements, if any, of the socio-cultural context along with literary conventions and the immediate and broader co-text.[3] We also evaluate what is known of any subsequent interpretations of the passage which may have been available in the NT period.

Determining illocutionary and perlocutionary intention and desired perlocutionary response allows us to identify what it would mean for an empirical hearer/reader to respond as an Envisager, i.e., a hearer/reader who understands the illocutionary acts and also responds with the perlocutionary effects associated with the perlocutionary acts of the speech act complex. This allows us to evaluate the theological import of the speech act complex, i.e., what answers to the basic theological questions are implied, as well as how the speech act complex contributes to the Story of God's people and ultimately to lifeworld and worldview.

Turning to the NT quotation, we follow the same process to determine the illocutionary and perlocutionary intentions and desired perlocutionary response of the speech act complex which contains the quotation. We then consider what elements of the theological OT Story-line are evoked by the quotation and what perlocutionary responses of belief and/or action would be made by the implied reader and, by definition, the Envisaging empirical reader. From this, we can ascertain both whether the NT author reads the OT as an Envisager and what transformation of lifeworld/worldview and corresponding Story is in view for those in the NT audience who read as Envisagers.

Whenever a text contains a report of direct speech, there are two levels of discourse. These are not entirely separable since what we know of the original dialogue is mediated and framed by the implied author of the reporting text. Nevertheless, we must attend to both levels. This is the

---

2. In Psalms passages where God is the original direct addressee, the implied reader is most likely a side participant or an overhearer.

3. In each case study, we discuss which elements of co-text are relevant.

situation in our second case study where the source text (Ps 110:1) contains a quotation. Additionally, both in what has become known as the *Davidssohnfrage* in the Synoptic Gospels and in Acts 2, the NT author (Matthew, Mark, or Luke) reports direct speech of either Jesus or Peter, and that direct speech includes a quotation of Ps 110:1.

To introduce the case studies, we consider the role the Psalms may have played in the lifeworld and Story of Yahweh's[4] people, both ethnic Jews and God-fearers.

THE PSALMS WITHIN THE JEWISH LIFEWORLD

In their original setting the Psalms are primarily non-narrative and non-historical.[5] In general, they do not recount events that occurred in the history of Yahweh's relationship with Israel. Their connection to the Story of Israel is not via its stories. However, the Story of Yahweh and Yahweh's people not only underpins the Psalms, the Psalms contribute to that Story in a significant way by providing answers to the basic theological questions.

On the one hand, the Psalms answer the basic theological questions about the deity: "whether there is a god, what relation this god has to the world in which we live, and what if anything this god is doing, or will do, about putting it to rights."[6] The Psalms define and describe what can be expected of Yahweh, presenting Yahweh as a god of righteousness and justice as well as the covenant people's source of help and comfort in times of trouble, whether that trouble comes from external sources or results from the psalmist's or the people's own behavior.

On the other hand, the Psalms also provide answers to the basic theological questions of human existence: "who are we, where are we, what is

---

4. Although some Psalms use "Elohim" (אלהים) to refer to the Israelite deity, the case study Psalms use "Yahweh" (יהוה). Where clarity is needed, we use "Yahweh."

5. There are a few exceptions. Of the eighteen historical psalms identified by Wendland or Anderson, six are explicitly quoted in the NT. (See Wendland, *Analyzing the Psalms*, 48; and Anderson, "Psalms," 59). In three instances, Pss 78:24b, 89:20, and 95:7–11, the quoted passage references an historical event. However, these quotations do not figure in our study.

6. N. T. Wright, *New Testament and People of God*, 127. As McCann notes, "The Psalms are not just human words *to* God. They are also words *about* God. They teach us about God; they reveal who God is" (McCann, *Theological Introduction to the Book of Psalms*, 16).

wrong, and what is the solution?"[7] Often, the answers to these questions given in the Psalms involve worship (i.e., praxis). As Watson describes it, "In the context of the covenant, it is the Book of Psalms that best represents the full range of human worship of God."[8] Every human emotion is included: "From anger to adulation, the various psalms cover the gamut of human emotion and response to God's presence in the world, or lack thereof."[9] More than simply describing how a person or group has interacted with Yahweh in a specific situation, the Psalms call for an integrated life in relationship with Yahweh.

William Brown argues that the Psalms are "the theological center of the Old Testament. . . . On David's many-stringed lyre, as it were, there can be heard almost every theological chord that resounds throughout the Hebrew Scriptures, from covenant and history to creation and wisdom."[10] Although some scholars have attempted to identify one major theological theme of the Psalter,[11] it is more helpful first to determine how the speech act complexes with which we are concerned contribute to Story and then to determine whether and, if so, how the NT quotation re-presents those elements of Story.

To demonstrate that the Psalms inhabited the lifeworld/worldview intersection of Story, theology, and praxis for the people of Yahweh at the end of the Second Temple period, we need to briefly assess the role the Psalms played.

---

7. N. T. Wright, *New Testament and People of God*, 123.

8. Watson, *Text and Truth*, 240.

9. W. P. Brown, *Seeing the Psalms*, 2.

10. W. P. Brown, *Seeing the Psalms*, 1. According to Terrien, the themes of the Psalter "are articulated together according to an unspoken architecture of theocentricity" (Terrien, *Psalms*, 44).

11. Some central themes scholars argue for the Psalms include: the cult of the Covenant, the presence of Yahweh, and Yahweh as king. The first of these is Weiser's thesis and also encompasses Mowinckel's cult functional approach (see Mowinckel, *Psalms in Israel's Worship*). The second is the foundation of Terrien's argument (see, e.g., Terrien, *Psalms*, 57). For the central theme of Yahweh as king, see H. H. Guthrie, *Israel's Sacred Songs*, 23; Mays, "Centre of the Psalms," 232; Howard, "Psalms and Current Study," 27; and McCann, *Theological Introduction to the Book of Psalms*, 163.

However, we do not presuppose any single theme for the Psalms or Psalms quotations. Nor do we accept Waltke's notion that "the specific predictions of some psalms that find their fulfillment in Jesus Christ combined with the use of the Psalter in the New Testament suggest that the entire Psalter pertains to Jesus Christ and his church" (Waltke, "Christ in the Psalms," 41). Instead, we evaluate each quotation on its own merits.

INTRODUCTION TO THE CASE STUDIES

THE PSALMS IN THE PRAXIS OF THE FIRST-CENTURY PEOPLE OF YAHWEH

Worship and prayer were a vital part of first-century praxis in Jerusalem. There were daily sacrifices in the Temple, with special requirements for the Sabbath; other festivals were celebrated monthly or annually.[12] The postexilic books of Chronicles and Nehemiah tell us that "in the period of the Second Temple, during the rule of the Persians, Greeks, and Romans, the singing of psalms and sacred music had a privileged place among all the liturgical celebrations, sacrifices, fasts, vigils, pilgrimages, etc., in Jerusalem."[13] Since a goal of the Chronicler was to encourage true worship of Yahweh, the importance placed on singing Psalms and other hymns highlights proper worship praxis in the Second Temple period.[14] Additionally, there are numerous allusions to the Psalms and psalmic language in the postexilic OT prophets, most notably in the later chapters of Isaiah and in Haggai, Zechariah, and Malachi.[15]

The Psalms appear to have been used not only in the Temple in Jerusalem but also in domestic devotional practices. Domestically, J. A. Smith believes the Psalms were sung during the Second Temple period in the Passover ritual, at weddings and funerals, and, based on 4 Macc 18:15, as part of a father's religious instruction of his children. He concludes that "psalm singing may therefore be considered to have been a normal concomitant of the religious life of the family in the home."[16] Another indication that the Psalter was "the meditation book of pious groups and of private individuals" comes from the use of a portion of Ps 136 in 1 Maccabees.[17]

---

12. For a discussion of the worship use of the psalms, see McKinnon, "On the Question of Psalmody," 163.

13. Tournay, *Seeing and Hearing God*, 27. Tournay also refers to the book of Ezra (probably Ezra 3:11). Second Maccabees 2:13 attributes to Nehemiah the collection of "the books about the kings and prophets, and the writings of David, and letters of kings about votive offerings."

14. See Terrien, *Psalms*, 60n200.

15. See Gillingham, "From Liturgy to Prophecy," 474–76.

16. Smith, "Ancient Synagogue," 10. In 4 Macc 18:15, a pious father is remembered as singing or chanting (ἐμελῴδει) words of David, the "hymn-writer" (ὑμνογράφος), from Ps 34:19 LXX.

17. Maher, "Psalms in Jewish Worship," 34.

As regards synagogue use, Samuel Terrien claims "the book of Chronicles reflects an epoch when the Psalms were intoned not only in the temple ceremonies but also among the synagogues of the Diaspora."[18] Lawrence Schiffman concurs that "throughout the Second Temple period, increasing emphasis was placed on the requirement of daily prayer for all Jews. For many Jews it was the emerging synagogue that served as the locus of their prayers."[19] More cautiously, Lee Levine suggests first century synagogue worship was "limited to Sabbaths and holidays. Pre-70 sources speak almost exclusively about the Sabbath and in several instances, both in Berenice, to New Moon and Sukkot gatherings. Other holiday gatherings—although unattested—can reasonably be assumed."[20]

Another question is the content of synagogue worship. Given the early-attested name "proseuche" ("place of prayer"), it seems safe to conclude that synagogue worship at least "consisted of prayers and Scripture reading."[21] Further, it is likely—although not certain—that by the late

---

18. Terrien, *Psalms*, 20. According to Levine, "the earliest 'hard' evidence we have for the existence of a synagogue appears in a number of inscriptions from Ptolemaic Egypt which mention a *proseuche*, commencing with the third century BCE. To date, about twelve such inscriptions and papyri have been discovered from the Hellenistic period" (Levine, *Ancient Synagogue*, 19). Flesher agrees the synagogue "arose in a region without access to the Temple cult (i.e., in Egypt) and in a sense comprised a substitute for it. It served as a gathering place for all Israelites—priests and commoners—where they took part in worship" (Flesher, "Palestinian Synagogues," 28).

We do not rely on rabbinic evidence concerning the pre-70 synagogue, following Binder, who concludes that "what probably constitutes the earliest and most reliable stratum of evidence from the rabbinic writings yields us no useful information about pre-70 synagogues" (Binder, *Into the Temple Courts*, 12).

19. Schiffman, "Foreword," xxviii. See also Maher, who believes the practice of regular daily worship grew out of sending *ma 'amadot* to serve in the Temple in Jerusalem "during a particular week. On the days when the *ma 'amad* was in Jerusalem the people who remained at home refrained from work, came together to worship, and recited the same biblical passages from Genesis (cf. *t. Ta 'anit* 4[3], 3)" (Maher, "Psalms in Jewish Worship," 13). Levine finds "the division into *ma 'amadot* was already known to the author of I Chronicles (24:1-18) in the fourth or third century BCE." (Levine, *Ancient Synagogue*, 36n64; *contra* Grabbe, who, without considering 1 Chronicles, believes "passages which speak of the *ma 'āmādôt* do not occur in the pre-70 stratum of tradition" [Grabbe, "Synagogues in Pre-70 Palestine," 22n20]). Levine takes a middle perspective, i.e., that "presumably, the Torah was read twice a year in the towns and villages whose local priestly courses were officiating in the Jerusalem Temple" (Levine, *Ancient Synagogue*, 141).

20. Levine, *Ancient Synagogue*, 134.

21. Flesher, "Palestinian Synagogues," 28. According to Levine, in the Diaspora "proseuche" was a more common term to describe the institution than "synagogue,"

Second Temple period, those prayers included psalms. Certainly, the evidence is overwhelming that the canonical psalms were important to the inhabitants of Qumran. "Among the almost nine hundred scrolls that were discovered in the Judean desert, no book is represented by more manuscripts than the book of Psalms."[22] That "the Psalms scrolls represent nearly 20% of biblical manuscripts found" indicates "the important place of the Psalms in the life of the community that copied and preserved them."[23] Additionally, 11QPs^a

> informs us that David "wrote 3,600 psalms (*thlym*); and songs (*shir*) to sing before the altar over the whole-burnt *tamid* offering every day, for all the days of the year, 364; and for the *qorban* of the Sabbaths, 52 songs; and for the *qorban* of the New Moons and for all the Solemn Assemblies and for the Day of Atonement, 30 songs." . . . This text takes it for granted that psalms and songs formed part of the worship on weekdays, Sabbaths and feastdays.[24]

Other evidence of psalm usage (although not necessarily the canonical psalms) in connection with first-century worship is found in the NT.[25]

---

which may "indicate a desire by Diaspora synagogues to highlight a religious dimension" (Levine, *Ancient Synagogue*, 127).

22. Flint, "Psalms and Psalters," 233. Of the 150 canonical psalms, "126 are at least partially preserved in the forty Psalms scrolls or other relevant manuscripts such as the pesharim. All the remaining twenty-four psalms were most likely included, but are now lost because of the damaged state of most of the scrolls. . . . The reason for this discrepancy is because the beginnings of scrolls are usually on the outside and are thus far more prone to deterioration" (Flint, 234).

23. Swanson, "Qumran and the Psalms," 248-49. In addition to the manuscripts that contain only Psalms, "there are seven other texts that include significant citations of the psalms" (Swanson, 248), including "three pesharim, 4QFlorilegium, 4QTanhumim, 4QCatena A, and 11QMelchizedek" (Swanson, 260). The biblical psalms were not the only prayers at Qumran; "the remains of over two hundred non-biblical prayers, psalms, and hymns . . . have been recovered from among the Qumran manuscripts" (Levine, *Ancient Synagogue*, 60).

24. Maher, "Psalms in Jewish Worship," 19, quoting J. A. Sanders, *Psalms Scroll of Qumrân Cave 11*, 92; words in parentheses added by Maher. We concur with Maher that the arguments for a triennial cycle for the Sabbath reading of the psalms in the pre-70 synagogue are not convincing (Maher, "Psalms in Jewish Worship," 32; cf. McKinnon, "On the Question of Psalmody," 188-90; and Grabbe, "Synagogues in Pre-70 Palestine," 24). Although synagogue worship "probably included reading of the Scriptures and the recitation of the Daily Psalm" (Maher, "Psalms in Jewish Worship," 13), daily use of the psalms in the synagogue is not established by documentary evidence until the eighth-century tractate *Soferim* (see Maher, 27).

25. Although Stanley argues that due to their great expense, "it seems highly unlikely

PART II | CASE STUDIES

In the context of the gathering of the church, Paul refers in 1 Cor 14:15 (twice) to "singing psalms" (ψάλλω) and in 14:26 to a "psalm" (ψαλμός). Eph 5:19 speaks of singing "psalms and hymns and spiritual songs among yourselves."[26] Other NT references to speaking or singing psalms include Rom 15:9, Col 3:16, and Jas 5:13.[27]

From what is known of Second Temple practices, along with those of local households and probably at least the Diaspora synagogues, plus the evidence from Qumran and the NT, it appears the canonical Psalms were well-known to first century Yahweh-worshippers. N. T. Wright concludes that the Psalms were an important part of the worship and prayer life of even the "average" Jew, who "would grow up knowing the basic prayers, and a good many psalms."[28] The Psalms would have been known not only by the NT authors (especially Paul and Matthew, whose Jewish roots are unquestioned) but also by all observant Jews, including those in the Diaspora, and by God-fearers among the Gentiles.

---

that anyone (including Paul and the members of his churches) would have had access to a full complement of 'Septuagint' scrolls in the middle of the first century CE" (Stanley, "Pearls before Swine," 127), Abasciano's counter-arguments are more convincing (see especially Abasciano, "Diamonds in the Rough," 156–61).

26. According to E. P. Sanders, since Paul's "view of group worship was almost certainly influenced by the synagogue services that he had attended, we may add singing to prayers and the reading and exposition of scripture as possible synagogal activities" (E. P. Sanders, *Judaism*, 202).

27. Although not a reference to the Psalms, Jesus speaks of those who "stand and pray [ἑστῶτες προσεύχεσθαι] in the synagogues [συναγωγαῖς]" (Matt 6:5). Furthermore, the NT evidence is clear that "by the first century CE at the very latest, readings from the Torah were accompanied by readings from the Prophets" in the synagogue context (Levine, *Ancient Synagogue*, 142, referring to Luke 4:16–21 and Acts 13:14–15).

28. N. T. Wright, *New Testament and People of God*, 233.

We reserve our discussion of how familiar a first-century audience of Jews, God-fearers, and/or former pagans might have been with a specific Psalm for our case study examples.[29] In both examples, it is likely that Diaspora God-fearers and even Jews were more familiar with the Septuagint translation (LXX) than with the Hebrew text.[30] We begin with Ps 115:1 LXX [116:10 MT] as quoted by Paul in 2 Cor 4:13.

---

29. Most evidence for the use of specific Psalms comes from what is known of the cultic practices of the Temple. Despite the fact that Terrien and others refer to the Psalter as "the hymn book of the second temple" and even of the synagogue, (see Terrien, *Psalms*, 60), there is direct evidence for use of only a few individual Psalms.

30. According to Jobes and Silva, "since the New Testament authors were writing in Greek, they would naturally quote, allude to, and otherwise use the Greek version of the Hebrew Bible" (Jobes and Silva, *Invitation to the Septuagint*, 23). Ahearne-Kroll makes the excellent point that an ancient native reader of Greek would have analyzed the Greek text of the OT in its own right rather than reading it through the lens of its MT counterpart (Ahearne-Kroll, *Psalms of Lament*, 84).

Jobes and Silva argue that "the current consensus among Septuagint scholars, with few exceptions, is that only one 'original' Greek translation was made of each book prior to the Christian era, and that whatever differences are found between surviving texts of the same book reflect a revision of the Greek" (Jobes and Silva, *Invitation to the Septuagint*, 45–46). For the Psalms, Eaton believes the LXX translation was "completed by about 200 BCE" (Eaton, *Psalms*, 43). At the other end of the spectrum, Hay believes "scholars increasingly emphasize the fact that there was no single unified Greek translation of the Jewish scriptures in the pre-Christian era" (Hay, *Glory at the Right Hand*, 21n9). In either case, today we have multiple texts. In referring to "LXX," "the Greek text" or, for the Hebrew, "MT," we do not intend to imply there is only one such document.

7

Ps 115:1a LXX as Quoted in 2 Cor 4:13[1]

IN THIS CHAPTER, WE use our action model to study Paul's use of Ps 115:1a LXX in 2 Cor 4:13. Although this is a "small" quotation—the only NT quotation from Ps 115 LXX[2]—it has been the subject of quite varied discussion. On the one hand, some scholars charge that, using our terminology, Paul reads as an Independent but presents his reading as Envisaging. According to C. K. Barrett, "Paul pays no heed to the context, but picks out the two significant words."[3] From another perspective, Jan Lambrecht posits that "since in the psalm the 'speaking out' addresses God it is rather unlikely that Paul, who changes that speaking into preaching to people, intends

---

1. Since 2 Corinthians is an undisputed Pauline letter, we refer to its author as "Paul." Whether it was originally one or several letters does not affect our argument since scholars generally agree 1:1—7:4 was a single letter. For the argument that the letter was a unity from its inception, see Hughes, *Paul's Second Epistle to the Corinthians*, xxx; Barnett, *Second Epistle to the Corinthians*, 16–26, 40; Witherington, *Conflict and Community*, 333; and Harris, *Second Epistle to the Corinthians*, xiii. Those who agree with Hay that 2 Corinthians is "a combination of Pauline letter fragments" (Hay, "Shaping of Theology," 139) include Barrett, *Commentary on the Second Epistle to the Corinthians*, 9; Furnish, *II Corinthians*, 35; and Murphy-O'Connor, *Theology of the Second Letter to the Corinthians*, 66. Watson's argument that 2 Cor 1–9 was written after 2 Cor 10–13 (Watson, *Paul and the Hermeneutics of Faith*, 150–51) might affect the mutual context of what are now the earlier chapters, but we are not able to explore that here.

2. Some scholars find an allusion to Ps 115:2 LXX in Rom 3:4a. (See, e.g., Hanson, *Studies in Paul's Technique*, 17; and R. B. Hays, *Echoes of Scripture*, 204n33). There also may be an echo of Ps 116:3 MT in Acts 2:24.

3. Barrett, *Commentary on the Second Epistle to the Corinthians*, 143. R. P. Martin also argues Paul "fastens on the two verbs, 'believe,' 'speak,' in order to justify his apostolic ministry as proclamation" (R. P. Martin, *2 Corinthians*, 83).

to refer to the broader context of that psalm (situation of need)."[4] Stanley incorporates elements of both arguments into his forceful criticism of Paul's handling of this quotation: "The sense in which he uses the verse is so far removed from the original context as to raise questions about Paul's reliability as an interpreter.... In a context in which Paul's motives were already under a cloud, this kind of observation would have given ammunition to those who argued that Paul could not be trusted."[5]

At the other end of the spectrum, Hays, Thomas Stegman, Kenneth Schenck, and Douglas Campbell all have taken hold of A. T. Hanson's notion that in 2 Cor 4:13, Paul reads Ps 115:1 LXX messianically.[6] The first to do so was Hays, who calls this "christological ventriloquism."[7] For him, the passage "is greatly clarified if we see in it another instance of Christ as the praying voice in the psalm quotation."[8]

In addressing these varied Pauline readings, our first step is to determine what it would mean to read Ps 115:1a LXX or an interpretation thereof as an Envisager. Following this, we identify what audience transformation Paul encourages by evoking this OT Story-line and assess whether Paul reads this OT text as an Envisager.

---

4. Lambrecht, *Second Corinthians*, 74.

5. Stanley, *Arguing with Scripture*, 100–101; see also 100n7, 100n8. He finds this to be an instance in which Paul "quotes verses in such a way that their relation to the source text would have been difficult, if not impossible, for a knowledgeable reader to figure out" (Stanley, 56n46). In a later work, Stanley repeats much of his argument verbatim but softens this criticism: "An audience that was familiar with the psalm might well have been disturbed by the discrepancy between the original sense of the words that Paul cites and the way in which he uses them in his argument. This in turn could have led them to question whether they could trust Paul's skills as an interpreter" (Stanley, "Paul's 'Use' of Scripture," 148).

6. We discuss Hays's, Stegman's, Schenk's, and D. A. Campbell's arguments below. It should be noted that Hanson's discussion of this quotation is inconsistent. On the one hand, he argues the psalm predicts the Messiah's death and resurrection, that Ps 115:2 LXX is uttered by the pre-existent Messiah, and that 2 Cor 4:13–15 is "midrash" on Ps 116:8–19 MT; on the other, he claims that "we need not imagine that in such passages Paul is intentionally commenting on Scripture, or even that he expects his readers to recognize his scriptural allusions" (Hanson, *Studies in Paul's Technique*, 167). However these comments are to be taken, we agree with Furnish that "it is certainly too much to describe vv. 13–15 as a 'midrash' on Ps 116:8–19 [MT]" (Furnish, *II Corinthians*, 285).

7. R. B. Hays, "Christ Prays the Psalms," 104n14.

8. R. B. Hays, "Christ Prays the Psalms," 108.

PART II | CASE STUDIES

PS 115 LXX [116:10-19 MT]

Although "in the standard 'LXX' text, the verse that Paul quotes is the first verse in a new psalm (Ps 115:1) rather than the midpoint as in the Hebrew (Ps 116:10),"[9] both Pss 116 MT and 115 LXX are Psalms of Individual Thanksgiving.[10] They contain: (i) praise of Yahweh for Yahweh's glorious attributes or acts of deliverance, (ii) a description of the distress experienced by Yahweh's people and how they called upon Yahweh, (iii) a profession of trust in Yahweh or a testimony that Yahweh has responded, and (iv) an expression of thanksgiving and/or a promise to praise Yahweh.[11]

In their OT setting, the speech acts later quoted describe the psalmist's distress and also tell us about the lifeworld/worldview of the psalmist—most notably, that the psalmist professes faith in Yahweh.[12] The speech act complex includes an acknowledgement of the help Yahweh has provided and is followed by a vow to give praise and offer thanks.

---

9. Stanley, *Arguing with Scripture*, 100. The various versions of the LXX give "united testimony" as to the division of Ps 116 MT into two parts (Stanley, *Paul and the Language of Scripture*, 216). Ps 116:14 MT is omitted in the LXX, but that is not an issue here. Interestingly, in fragment 2 of 4Q96=4QPs°, "the alignment of text on lines 4-5 shows that a long interval followed Ps 116:9, indicating that vv 10 onwards most likely constitute a new Psalm" (Skehan et al., "Psalms," 139; see also 140). Thus, the LXX may preserve an older tradition than does the MT.

10. According to Bullock, Ps 116 MT is one of only three psalms categorized as a psalm of individual thanksgiving by Gunkel, Mowinckel, Westermann, and Kraus (Bullock, *Encountering the Book of Psalms*, 154).

11. See Wendland, *Analyzing the Psalms*, 38-40, 58, 60.

12. We discuss lifeworld/worldview and Story in greater detail below.

PS 115:1A LXX AS QUOTED IN 2 COR 4:13

The Locution

Although there are some locutionary issues surrounding the relationship of the MT and LXX texts,[13] since Paul quotes the LXX,[14] we use that text to evaluate the illocution and perlocution of the source text. There are five

---

13. According to Skehan et al., "Psalms," 140, only a few letters of Ps 116:10 MT were found at Qumran (4Q96=4QPs° contains the first two letters and perhaps the last of the first word "I believe" as well as the first letter of the third word "I spoke"). Therefore, the LXX may translate a non-MT Hebrew text. If the LXX does translate the MT, two translation decisions in Ps 115:1 LXX often result in different English renderings of the MT and LXX. This has led to comments such as: "The meaning of the Hebrew is problematic . . . but it is certainly not given correctly in the LXX" (Furnish, *II Corinthians*, 258; cf. Hooker, "Interchange and Suffering," 78n11). Because this can lead to the charge that Paul chose the LXX in order to manipulate his audience, we briefly examine these possible translation decisions.

The first is the translation of כי, the conjunction connecting vv. 10a and 10b MT. Of the three common English lexical meanings for כי (BDB, s.v. "כִּי"), "when" (including with concessive force, "even when") is the most common English translation of this verse. However, the LXX Psalter renders כי here—and only in this verse, according to L. C. Allen, *Psalms 101–150*, 152—with the Greek διό, an "inferential conjunction" with a lexical meaning of "therefore" or "for this reason" (BDAG, s.v. "διό"). NETS gives "and so" for διό in Ps 115:1 LXX, which also is inferential.

Often this is seen as a discrepancy between the MT and LXX. But, according to Waltke and O'Connor, "a result clause can be introduced by כִּי" (Waltke and O'Connor, *Introduction to Biblical Hebrew Syntax*, 639). This correlates with an option BDB gives for כי as "that": "expressing consecution." "With the result that" gives a coherent rendering of Ps 116:10 MT and approaches the lexical meaning of "therefore" or "so" (i.e., διό). Kraus believes that "כי is correctly rendered with διό in Gk" (Kraus, *Psalms 60–150*, 387). Several English translations do give an inferential meaning for כי here. NKJV renders כי as "therefore" as did the 1984 NIV; NLT and NCV give "so."

The second decision is the addition in Ps 115:1 LXX of the conjunction δέ prior to ἐταπεινώθην. This does not correspond to a word in the MT and may have been added for clarity. It makes it impossible to read the third clause of the LXX verse as the content of the "speaking," which generally is the translation decision of English versions. (NETS is an exception). We discuss this further below.

14. As a self-identified "Hebrew of Hebrews; in regard to the law, a Pharisee" (Phil 3:5 NIV), a pupil of the Pharisee Gamaliel (Acts 22:3–4), a member of the Sanhedrin, and a teacher of the law (Acts 5:34), Paul would have known the Hebrew. Presumably he quotes the LXX because his Greek-speaking audience knew that translation. For this, see Binder, who finds that one of the few differences "in the reading practices of the diaspora synagogues . . . was the use of the Septuagint for the sacred scriptures" (Binder, *Into the Temple Courts*, 402, with reference to Tov, "Septuagint," 161–87. See especially Tov, 163, 168).

speech acts in this speech act complex, vv. 1a, 1b, 1c, 2, and 3.[15] The LXX and NETS of this speech act complex are presented in Appendix §1.

The Illocution

The first four speech acts are Assertives.[16] As δέ in v. 1c makes plain, they describe a series of events: believing (v. 1a), then speaking (v. 1b), followed by affliction (v. 1c), and, finally, complaint—presumably about those causing the affliction (v. 2). The final speech act is a Commissive, set against the background of an unstated but assumed event, i.e., that Yahweh has delivered the psalmist (v. 7).

Verse 1a signals that this speech act complex serves as a Profession of Trust. The content of the psalmist's "belief" (ἐπίστευσα, v. 1a) is debated. Pierre Auffret construes v. 1c as describing "I" ("qui étais trop humilié") and considers that v. 2 presents the content of the psalmist's belief, i.e., "le caractère trompeur de l'homme."[17] But the presence of δέ in v. 1c causes his argument to fail for the LXX. John Eaton considers the psalmist "believed that I should perish"[18] based on the Hebrew verb having "not the usual sense 'speak', but (as in the Arabic counterpart) 'be carried away, pass away, die.'"[19] This also seems unlikely.

Others consider the psalmist's "belief" to be trust that Yahweh would rescue[20] or had rescued him.[21] However, for the psalmist to be "speaking" of

---

15. All references to psalm verses in this chapter are to Ps 115 LXX unless otherwise noted.

16. Since these Assertives recount an event, they are Retrodictives (see Bach and Harnish, *Linguistic Communication*, 44).

17. Auffret, "'Je marcherai à la face de Yahvé,'" 390.

18. Eaton, *Psalms*, 399, where he adds that those around the psalmist are "earthly helpers" who "fail."

19. Eaton, *Psalms*, 400.

20. See, e.g., L. C. Allen, *Psalms 101–150*, 155–56. Goldingay considers that the psalmist's trust in Yahweh comes because "there was nowhere else to turn" (Goldingay, *Psalms 90–150*, 343). For Stegman, the "story" of Pss 114–115 LXX suggests "two things: first, the psalmist *trusted* in God to rescue him; and second, he *has been faithful* to God" (Stegman, "Ἐπίστευσα, διὸ ἐλάλησα," 732). Although the latter seems possible (see n24 below), the former is less likely, and the combination of the two is overly complicated.

21. Barnett's position is that the psalmist "believed" God had delivered him from death, and therefore he "spoke" of it (Barnett, *Second Epistle to the Corinthians*, 241). According to Clifford, "people entrusted themselves to a particular deity on the basis of the deity's ability to save them," and in Ps 116 MT "Yahweh, the Savior of Israel, has proved

his deliverance is inconsistent with the LXX text. The presence of δέ in v. 1c means both the psalmist's troubles and Yahweh's saving action result from (or at least follow) his speaking, which in turn is preceded by his belief/trust.[22]

Since a Profession of Trust can concern *who God is*,[23] it is more likely that Yahweh or Yahweh's character is the object of the psalmist's belief. For the implication of v. 1 to be "I believed/put my faith [in Yahweh], therefore I spoke" is more probable than "I believed [that Yahweh would rescue/had rescued me], therefore I spoke."[24]

The result of the psalmist's faith was speaking (ἐλάλησα, v. 1b). Since the implied content of what was "spoken" relates to the "belief" of v. 1a, presumably the psalmist spoke of his faith or of Yahweh, the object of his faith. There is no basis in the LXX text for considering that the "speaking" was directed towards Yahweh since the result of speaking was the psalmist's affliction.[25] Thus, Stanley's notion that the psalmist was "'humbled' *by God*" is not a valid understanding of the Greek text.[26] The almost certain implica-

---

to be a saving God" (Clifford, *Psalms 73–150*, 198).

22. We are given no information in Ps 115 LXX as to what has prompted the psalmist's belief in Yahweh. According to Goldingay, psalms are not tied to a socio-historical context but rather are designed to be used "as the vehicles for praise and prayer throughout the story of God's people" (Goldingay, *Psalms 1–41*, 25). Similarly, J. A. Grant believes "the ahistoricity of the psalms" means "they are designed to be appropriated in the way that is most relevant to the community of believers in their setting" (J. A. Grant, "Interpreting the Psalms," 112). It is common in Psalms of Thanksgiving for the psalmist's purpose to be not "to relate what happened to him, but to testify what God has done for him" (Westermann, *Praise and Lament*, 109). Ps 116 MT is "more indefinite than usual" and "was deliberately framed indefinitely to cover more than one occasion for thanksgiving" (L. C. Allen, *Psalms 101–150*, 153).

23. See Wendland, *Analyzing the Psalms*, 33, 45, for a brief description of a Profession of Trust.

24. N. T. Wright finds that the "point" of Ps 116:10 MT is "a statement of 'faith,'" and he considers that the best translation of that verse in 2 Cor 4:13 may be "*I kept faith*, and so I spoke" (N. T. Wright, "Faith, Virtue, Justification," 485). However, Wright does not consider the LXX text, and his suggestion seems to require that Pss 114 and 115 LXX be read together. But other than an implication that the psalmist's faith has already weathered some trials, this alternative is not too different from what we propose here unless "keeping" faith is equated with obeying rules.

25. There is no reason to consider the "speaking" (v. 1b) to have the same audience as the "saying" (v. 2). Not only is this a chain of events in the Greek text, the Greek verbs are different.

26. Stanley, *Arguing with Scripture*, 100; emphasis added. Although he is correct that v. 1c is a "statement of what transpired after the 'speaking' ('and I was greatly humbled')," it does not follow that God humbled the psalmist (Stanley, 100n5). As Abasciano puts it,

tion of v. 3 is that Yahweh is the psalmist's rescuer and not the source of his difficulty.[27]

As to the tellability of these Assertives, the first Assertive is foundational to the discourse. Absent the faith/belief of the psalmist there would be nothing to relate; this Assertive motivates the subsequent sequence of events. As the opening phrase and the foundational thought of the psalm, the faith/belief of the psalmist is both structurally and naturally prominent. Because the second Assertive (v. 1b) gives the result of the psalmist's belief, it also has natural prominence. Thus, the first two Assertives are both tellable. Whether or not the psalmist's speaking was considered normal, it may have been unusual for the psalmist to have been brought low or afflicted (ἐταπεινώθην σφόδρα, v. 1c) by those who heard him. Even if this negative result was not unexpected, it certainly was unwelcome. This explains the tellability of the third Assertive (v. 1c).

The final Assertive, v. 2, describes the consequences of the situation in v. 1c. Here it is clear the psalmist's alarm (τῇ ἐκστάσει μου) is caused by humans since the psalmist voices the complaint that πᾶς ἄνθρωπος ψεύστης. If the psalmist's alarm stems from his being brought low (v. 1c), the persons about whom he complains are most likely the perpetrators of his affliction.[28] The complaint is part of the "description of distress" common to a Thanksgiving psalm. Yahweh must be its audience, since v. 3 is logically understood against the background of Yahweh's rescue (made explicit in v. 7).

Although the interrogative form is somewhat unusual, v. 3 is a Commissive.[29] Yahweh's salvific action has produced a thankful spirit in the

---

"The psalmist's words are not a complaint for which God humbled him as Stanley claims. Quite to the contrary, they are an expression of faith in God despite suffering and opposition contained in a psalm of thanksgiving which does indeed breathe a spirit of praise and joy.... The fact that the psalmist grounds (διό) his speech on faith ensures that he is not suffering God's judgment for what he says.... This interpretation is confirmed by the fact that the psalm goes on to thank and praise the Lord for deliverance, presumably from the affliction of his lying enemies and in response to his faith-filled prayer making known his wretched state" (Abasciano, "Diamonds in the Rough," 174). Stanley's later attempt (see Stanley, "Paul's 'Use' of Scripture," 147) to rebut Abasciano's argument is unconvincing.

27. Auffret agrees that "Yahvé a sorti son fidèle" (Auffret, "'Je marcherai à la face de Yahvé,'" 390).

28. Since the psalmist complains that lies are being told about him, his affliction may have included the humiliation of slander. It is also likely he experienced physical suffering since he speaks of death in v. 6. This combination dovetails with Booij's evaluation of "the experience denoted by '*nh*" as "often, perhaps always, the suffering from hard, oppressive, threatening or humiliating treatment" (Booij, "Psalm 116,10–11," 390).

29. This is a non-rhetorical question. Whether this Commissive is a Promise or an

psalmist, and the psalmist is pondering how to best express his thanksgiving. Verse 3 thus both includes "a *testimony* that God has indeed helped and delivered"[30] and looks forward to the following speech act complex, which has the function of a vow to give praise.[31]

This understanding of the function of the speech acts of this speech act complex helps identify the implied author and audience. As to the implied author, faith in Yahweh led to or even impelled speech (v. 1a–b). The implied author was not angry with Yahweh for not having prevented the serious negative consequences which resulted from this speaking. Nor did he lose faith in Yahweh's providence. Rather than retaliating against his persecutors, he complained to Yahweh about those who were spreading malicious lies about him (v. 2), and, ultimately, his hopes of rescue were realized. In response, the implied author expresses an attitude of thanksgiving (v. 3) rather than entitlement. The implied author calls on Yahweh's name (v. 4) and gives or promises Yahweh thanks, praise, sacrifice, and, ultimately, eternal devotion (vv. 7–10).

We infer the identity of the implied audience from both the construction of the implied author and other elements of the text and co-text. For the majority of the Psalm, including this speech act complex, the psalmist directly addresses a human audience. As the implied audience, these direct addressees understand what the psalmist has done and that these actions are appropriate for followers of Yahweh.

The knowledge assumed in the co-text adds information about the implied audience. They understand what "a cup of salvation" (v. 4) and "a sacrifice of praise" (v. 8) are. They know the importance of fulfilling one's vows (v. 9), who the Lord's people are (v. 9), and where "the courts of the house of the Lord" are located (v. 10). In the closing verses of the Psalm, "before all his people" and "the courts of the Lord" are equated to "*your* midst, O Ierousalem" [NETS; emphasis added]. Taken together, the implied audience is seen to be a group of faithful Yahweh-followers united in fellowship with the implied author.[32]

Offer is not critical, although we favor the latter (see Bach and Harnish, *Linguistic Communication*, 50–51).

30. Wendland, *Analyzing the Psalms*, 39.

31. Prinsloo makes a semantic argument that Ps 116:12 MT [115:3 LXX] should be taken as part of the next speech act complex, the vow of praise (Prinsloo, "Psalm 116," 80). Although Ps 115:3 LXX is a bridge to the vow of praise, we include it in the first speech act complex since it includes the testimony of God's response to the distress.

32. The implied audience does not necessarily (and in some cases cannot) possess

By definition, the implied audience responds with the desired illocutionary effect of understanding. For empirical hearers/readers to read at the Analyst level, they must understand the implied author's illocutionary act in the way the implied audience would. So to read this speech act complex as an Analyst, an empirical reader would understand that Yahweh's followers are those who believe in and trust Yahweh and are willing to speak of their faith even if the consequences are unpleasant. The Analyst also understands that the faithful believe Yahweh will rescue them from their distress and that the appropriate response in those circumstances is to thank and praise Yahweh.[33]

To determine the Envisaging reading, we evaluate the perlocution of this speech act complex.

The Perlocution

The Envisaging reader enacts an appropriate perlocutionary response. The associated perlocution of an Assertive is "that H believe that P" and that of a Commissive is "that H believe S intends to fulfil his obligation to do A."[34]

As regards the Assertives in this speech act complex, "believing that P" is more than the Envisaging reader agreeing that the psalmist's account of the situation is factual. For the Assertives in Ps 115:1–3 LXX, successful perlocution requires the reader to live into a lifeworld in which: (i) faith leads to or motivates speaking of one's faith, (ii) one acknowledges that Yahweh's lordship and preservation does not mean protection from affliction, including affliction resulting from the proclamation of faith, and (iii) one knows that Yahweh ultimately rescues and preserves Yahweh's people.

For the Commissive, an Envisager recognizes the psalmist is obligated to "return" (ἀνταποδώσω, v. 3a) something to Yahweh since Yahweh has "returned" (ἀνταπέδωκεν, v. 3b)[35] something to him or her, and such a

---

the exact characteristics of the original empirical audience, who were Jews in the Temple grounds in Jerusalem.

33. If we define prayer as speech addressed to God, this speech act complex is not a prayer, *per se*. "In Ps 116 ... God is as much the one spoken about as the one spoken to. What this tells us is that thanksgiving and praise are features of Christian worship that are to be heard by God but especially by others" (Miller, *The Way of the Lord*, 212).

34. Bach and Harnish, *Linguistic Communication*, 81.

35. The use of ἀνταπέδωκεν in v. 3b raises the question of how rescue by Yahweh is a "return." (This is not a translation issue since the Hebrew root גמל can have the sense of "recompense" [BDB, s.v., "גָּמַל"; cf. Ps 18:21 MT]). The answer is found in the mutuality

reader lives into the lifeworld where this is true. Potentially relevant here is Αλληλουια ("Praise Yahweh") at the beginning of the Psalm.[36] If this is a genuine request (Directive), its desired perlocutionary response would be that listeners join in worship of Yahweh. This gives a communal aspect to the requirement to give praise and thanksgiving to Yahweh for both the deliverance of the psalmist and the relationship Yahweh has initiated and maintains with Yahweh's people.[37] In the following speech act complex, the psalmist determines that to "take a cup of salvation and call on the name of the Lord," to "sacrifice to you a sacrifice of praise," and to "pay . . . vows to the Lord before all his people" satisfies the obligation of the Commissive. Thus, the recital of the psalm may not only describe the vow but may also fulfill it.[38]

To identify the intended transformation, we recall our description of the implied audience as faithful Yahweh-followers. The Psalm appears to be a realignment of that audience's understanding of Yahweh and the relationship they are to have with Yahweh, either by reaffirming beliefs under attack from some source or restoring a belief system which has deteriorated. This may also be subversion if the audience did not previously realize the causal connection between belief and speech or if they expected Yahweh to *prevent* any difficulties resulting from faith-driven speaking. The transformation of the Envisager's belief system—and the actions that flow from that transformation—are linked to Story, lifeworld, and theology.

THE CONTRIBUTION OF PS 115:1-3 LXX TO STORY, LIFEWORLD, AND THEOLOGY

Psalm 115:1–3 LXX speaks to the basic theological question of how Yahweh's people are to relate to their god. The speech acts later quoted contribute to

---

of the psalmist's relationship with Yahweh; for both parties to have privileges and responsibilities helps make sense of the otherwise puzzling v. 6.

36. This transliterates the Hebrew imperative הַלְלוּ־יָהּ.

37. The ending of Ps 116 MT "s'impose d'en rendre grâces dans ce peuple qui est celui de l'Alliance, et d'en appeler en conséquence au Nom de Yahvé non plus seulement dans le cadre d'une détresse individuelle, mais dans ce contexte où le peuple élu peut exprimer cette Alliance dont il est l'un des partenaires" (Auffret, "'Je marcherai à la face de Yahvé,'" 394).

38. *Contra* Dahood's understanding that the "whole trend" of the psalm is that "the Psalmist, placed in extreme danger and abandoned by men, did not despair, but relying on the divine promises, he pleaded for help from God and was saved" (Dahood, "Two Pauline Quotations," 23), the psalm's movement is toward the response of thanksgiving and praise.

PART II | CASE STUDIES

Story the information that the psalmist's speaking to others of Yahweh or of faith in Yahweh was a natural result of belief and that Yahweh does not prevent trouble from occurring in the life of the faithful even under these circumstances. Further, even in a situation of distress, the believer is not to take matters into his or her own hands but to turn to Yahweh for help. Yahweh hears and responds to the complaints of the faithful and is the ultimate source of protection and rescue. The appropriate response to Yahweh's saving acts is an attitude of thanksgiving and the offering of praise.

Understanding the contribution of this speech act complex to Story leads to quite profound conclusions about the relationship Yahweh's people are to have with Yahweh and with others. Both the lifeworld and worldview of the Envisager incorporate these Story-lines—an Envisager agrees that the psalmist has behaved appropriately and lives his or her own relationship with Yahweh and in the world according to these precepts.

INTERVENING INTERPRETATION

Psalm 115 LXX has no obvious link to the narrative of Scripture. It is not a historical psalm; it makes no reference to any specific incident and has no superscription. Most do not consider it a royal psalm.[39] However, Ps 116 MT [114–115 LXX] is part of the Egyptian Hallel, which was sung in the Temple and probably elsewhere during Passover and perhaps also for other cultic occasions.[40] Because Passover was "associated with Israel's national liberation from bondage in Egypt," the Hallel psalms may have been "linked with the hope of a future eschatological liberation and the coming of a new king."[41] But there is no explicit evidence for this with regard to Ps 115 LXX.

---

39. According to Day, some add Ps 116 MT "to Gunkel's irreducible minimum" of royal psalms (Day, *Psalms*, 88).

40. During the first century, the Hallel was sung in the Temple while the Passover lambs were sacrificed (see Maher, "Psalms in Jewish Worship," 14; E. P. Sanders, *Judaism*, 135; and Smith, "Ancient Synagogue," 9). Per McKinnon, it "was sung in the Temple on about eighteen days of the year: the eve of Passover, possibly the first day of Weeks, the eight days of Tabernacles and probably the eight days of Hanukkah" (McKinnon, "On the Question of Psalmody," 164).

41. R. B. Hays, "Liberation of Israel," 109; cf. Swanson, "Qumran and the Psalms," 242. Although J. R. Wagner finds that for Jeremias, the entire Hallel "was understood as having eschatological and messianic connotations by the time of Jesus," Wagner himself argues convincingly that "the rabbinic evidence traditionally used to support this contention is problematic" since "the earliest authorities cited for eschatological interpretations of the *Hallel*" range between late second century CE and fourth century CE (J. R.

We next evaluate the speech act complex which includes Paul's quotation of Ps 115:1a LXX.

THE QUOTATION OF PS 115:1A LXX IN 2 COR 4:13

Stanley directs some of his harshest criticism of Paul at this verbatim quotation from Ps 115 LXX: "To an informed audience, the discrepancy of the original sense of the words and the way Paul used them in his argument would have been jarring."[42] Further, "the freedom with which he manipulates the biblical text to support his positions might have induced a person with a deeper knowledge of Scripture (the 'informed audience') to challenge or reject some of the arguments in which his quotations were embedded. . . . Fortunately for Paul, it appears that few people in his churches fit this description."[43] Barrett and Lambrecht also argue that with this quotation Paul is, in our terminology, acting as an Independent reader rather than an Envisager. In contrast, some scholars believe Paul read this psalm messianically, i.e., that Paul took the words of the psalm as the words of Jesus. Thus, this quotation makes a good case study of our methodology.

To begin to evaluate these arguments, we assess the degree of familiarity the original empirical audience might have had with Ps 115 LXX.

Would the Corinthian Church Have Known Ps 115 LXX?

Some members of the Corinthian church were no doubt very familiar with the Jewish Scriptures. A devout, well-educated, and prominent Jew like Crispus, the former synagogue leader (Acts 18:8, 1 Cor 1:14), would have worshiped in the Jerusalem Temple—perhaps regularly. Since it is likely that the Egyptian Hallel (Pss 113–118 MT [111–117 LXX]) was used in Temple worship at the time 2 Corinthians was written,[44] Crispus most

---

Wagner, "Psalm 118 in Luke-Acts," 158).

While Moses is referred to several times in 2 Cor 3 and the letter as a whole contains a Story-line of rescue/redemption from suffering, a link to the Exodus in 2 Cor 4:12 is very faint. In any case, unlike the psalmist, Moses's suffering did not result from his speaking; rather, the initial suffering of the Israelites was the *cause* of Moses's speaking, and their later suffering followed their disobedience.

42. Stanley, *Arguing with Scripture*, 100.
43. Stanley, *Arguing with Scripture*, 178.
44. According to R. P. Martin, "2 Corinthians (at least chaps. 1–9), [was] written in the autumn of A. D. 55 or, less likely, 56, and the last four chapters a short while later" (R.

PART II | CASE STUDIES

likely knew those Psalms.[45] Other Diaspora Jews and even God-fearers, like Titius Justus (Acts 18:7)[46] and Stephanas (1 Cor 16:15), probably knew the Hallel since some scholars believe it was recited in the Diaspora synagogues on a variety of festival days and during the Seder.[47] Thus, Paul could have expected those in the Corinthian church with synagogue ties to have known Ps 115 LXX. Further, because the first-century churches read and studied Scripture corporately (see, e.g., 1 Cor 14:26, Eph 5:19, Col 3:15), those in the Corinthian church without a synagogue background would have learned from those who did.[48] Rather than trying to bypass those who had prior knowledge of the Jewish Scriptures, Paul encourages the Corinthians to submit to Stephanas's leadership (1 Cor 16:16). Given the importance of the Hallel in Jewish worship and the way first-century churches read Scripture, if there is any OT Scripture with which Paul could have expected his entire Corinthian audience to have been familiar, it would have been a passage from a Hallel psalm like Ps 115:1 LXX.

Knowledge of Ps 115 LXX appears to be an element of the mutual context of Paul and his empirical audience; this helps us identify the implied author and implied audience. We begin our analysis of the illocution of the speech act complex containing the quotation by taking a closer look at what else we learn about the implied author and audience from this letter—especially the segments prior to and within this speech act complex[49]—as well as

---

P. Martin, *2 Corinthians*, xxxv).

45. See n40 above.

46. If Titius Justus is the person later referred to as "Gaius" (Rom 16:23, 1 Cor 1:14), as some argue (see, e.g., Barnett, *Second Epistle to the Corinthians*, 5), he remained an important part of the Corinthian church.

47. See chapter 6 concerning the use of the Psalms in intertestamental and first-century domestic devotional practices and possibly in at least the Diaspora synagogues. For some thoughts about the domestic singing of the Hallel during the Passover/Seder meal, see Smith, "Ancient Synagogue," 9–10; and Maher, "Psalms in Jewish Worship," 14, 26. As to synagogal use, Rabinowitz, who believes the Psalms were used very little in the synagogue as late as the Talmudic period (c. 70–500 CE), does find evidence for the recitation of the Hallel "on 18 days of the year in Palestine, and on 21 days in the Diaspora, viz., the first day(s) of Passover, Pentecost, every day of Tabernacles and Hanukkah" (Rabinowitz, "Psalms in Jewish Liturgy," 110; cf. Maher, "Psalms in Jewish Worship," 25–26).

48. See Abasciano, "Diamonds in the Rough," 156–69. Of the NT references to speaking/singing psalms listed in chapter 6, half have a corporate dimension.

49. On a first reading, the empirical audience would only have learned about the implied author and implied reader from what had been already presented in the letter. However, we assume multiple readings, and so we reference the remainder of the letter in some cases.

from a previous letter, 1 Corinthians, the contents of which would have been part of the mutual context of Paul and the original recipients of this letter.

The Implied Author and Audience

From 1 Corinthians, we learn the implied author of the Corinthian correspondence was called to be "an apostle of Christ Jesus by the will of God" (1 Cor 1:1).[50] However, he is "the least of the apostles, unfit to be called an apostle," because he "persecuted the church of God" (1 Cor 15:9). But by God's grace, his life has been redirected (1 Cor 15:10), and now his calling is to preach the gospel (1 Cor 2:45, 15:11), a task set him by God and Jesus Christ (1 Cor 1:17, 3:5). This call is not based on his superior speaking abilities; he is not an eloquent or confident speaker (1 Cor 2:5). Rather, he speaks "in words not taught by human wisdom but taught by the Spirit" (1 Cor 2:12–13; see also 1 Cor 1:17, 25–30; 2:1; 3:18–21, etc.).

In the present letter, the implied author is presented as a follower of Jesus, who is called "Christ" (or "Messiah") (2 Cor 1:1, 2, 3, 5), "Lord" (2 Cor 1:2, 3), and "Son of God" (2 Cor 1:19). Jesus is the climactic fulfillment of the promises of the faithful God (2 Cor 1:18–20). Among Paul's "working assumptions" are that "he everywhere presupposes that God exists and acts (or has acted) in a decisive and reconciling way in Jesus, especially through his death (2 Cor 5:14–15, 18, 21)" and resurrection.[51]

The hardships Paul experienced in his ministry were so severe that "we felt that we had received the sentence of death" (2 Cor 1:9). In those situations, his reliance on God for strength and consolation and his trust in God for deliverance were justified (2 Cor 1:3–5, 8–10). He remains confident that God "will continue to rescue us" (2 Cor 1:10; see also 2:14, 5:5–8).

Paul's planned visit to Corinth (1 Cor 16:7) was painful (2 Cor 2:1). A subsequent visit (2 Cor 1:15–16) has not materialized (2 Cor 1:23). This "broken promise" plus the painful visit and a painful letter (2 Cor 2:4), along with divisions within the Corinthian church (1 Cor 1:10–11, 3:3, 11:18) and church discipline problems, have strained Paul's relationship with the Corinthian believers and caused him emotional pain and anguish (2 Cor 2:4).[52] Paul's detractors accuse him of vacillating when he fails to

---

50. This is repeated verbatim in the opening verse of 2 Corinthians.

51. Hay, "Shaping of Theology," 140. For others of Paul's "working assumptions," see Hay, 140–41.

52. The relationships among the Corinthians also are strained (see 1 Cor 1:10–11,

make another visit (2 Cor 1:15–18, 23) and also of being self-aggrandizing (2 Cor 1:24, 3:1) and inappropriate in his handling of God's message (2 Cor 2:17).[53] In particular, since the Corinthian value system "perceived suffering and weakness as signs of failure,"[54] Paul's suffering, affliction, and near-death experience (2 Cor 1:4–9, 4:7–11; see also 1 Cor 4:9–17) have raised questions about his ministry and his status as an apostle.[55]

In addressing these pressing questions,[56] Paul's implied audience is not his opponents but rather the Christians in Corinth and Achaia (2 Cor 1:1) who are tempted to fall away from the message Paul has brought them, believing instead those who are "peddlers [καπηλεύοντες] of God's word" (2 Cor 2:17). Despite the fact that, in general, the Corinthian Christians are neither well-educated nor of high social status (1 Cor 1:26),[57] they have become arrogant, thinking they know more than they do (1 Cor 4:18–19, 14:36), placing themselves above others (1 Cor 11:20–22, 14:26), excusing sinful behavior (1 Cor 5:1–2), and even flirting with (or more!) the worship of other gods (1 Cor 10:14). Surrounded by inhabitants of a lifeworld that is "external, if not hostile, to the story,"[58] the former pagans seem to have not

---

2 Cor 2:7–8).

53. The identity of Paul's "enemies" is debated. Furnish summarizes the three major viewpoints (Furnish, *II Corinthians*, 48–54) and concludes Paul's opponents "were of Jewish background" and probably "Christian missionaries" (Furnish, 53). Similar conclusions are reached by Harris, *Second Epistle to the Corinthians*, 71. However, Georgi's argument that "the adversaries in 1 Cor. were Gnostics, and those of 2 Cor. were shaped by Hellenistic-Jewish Apologetics" (Georgi, *Opponents of Paul*, 317) outruns the available evidence, as does Murphy-O'Connor's position that the opponents are "Corinthianized" Judaizers (see Murphy-O'Connor, *Theology of the Second Letter to the Corinthians*, 12–15). In any event, our concern is the charges against which Paul defends himself and the reasons that he does so rather than the identity or belief system of his opponents.

54. Ehrensperger, "Paul and the Authority of Scripture," 316.

55. "Paul's sufferings reveal him to be anything but 'glorious'; therefore, his theology of 'fulfillment' must be questioned. Paul is the living denial of what he preaches" (Barnett, *Second Epistle to the Corinthians*, 37; cf. Hay, "Shaping of Theology," 146; and Furnish, *II Corinthians*, 277).

56. Paul's defense of his apostleship "deals with two issues: the relationship between suffering and ministry, and the prospect of death" (Murphy-O'Connor, *Theology of the Second Letter to the Corinthians*, 44; cf. Furnish, *II Corinthians*, 277). According to Ehrensperger, Paul tries to demonstrate that the negative experiences he has had "are inherent to life in Christ under the contextual circumstances of life under Roman rule" (Ehrensperger, "Paul and the Authority of Scripture," 316).

57. Murphy-O'Connor, *Theology of the Second Letter to the Corinthians*, 8, highlights the class distinctions found in 1 Cor 1:26–28.

58. Hartt, "Theological Investments in Story," 291.

broken completely with their past. Although Paul assumes "the Corinthian church is functioning and has a general sense of Christian purpose,"[59] the Corinthians are progressing quite slowly in faith (1 Cor 3:1–2).

The implied audience remembers Paul's behavior when he was with them as well as his previous preaching, both in person and through written or oral messages sent via ministry colleagues. They know that Paul has been given authority or power (ἐξουσία) by Jesus and in the gospel.[60] That this is not dominating power but rather the power to transform can be seen in his reliance on persuasion (πείθομεν, 2 Cor 5:11) rather than on force or coercion.[61] Paul uses his power to build up (οἰκοδομή, 2 Cor 10:8) the Corinthians rather than to tear them down (καθαίρεσις, 2 Cor 13:10) or for personal financial gain (2 Cor 11:7–9; cf. 1 Cor 9:18).[62] At its core, the relationship of the implied audience to Paul is based on mutual faith in God and in Jesus (2 Cor 1:24). Paul refers to God as *our* father (2 Cor 1:2) and the father of *our* Lord Jesus Christ (2 Cor 1:3). The Corinthians understand they participate in Paul's experience (2 Cor 1:7) to their benefit (2 Cor 1:4–6, 2:10, 4:12; cf. 1 Cor 4:10). Paul is a sacrifice for them, "the aroma of Christ to God" (2 Cor 2:15).[63]

On a literary level, the implied audience is able to "recognize all or many of his [Paul's] references to . . . [the Jewish] scriptures (and perhaps to special exegetical traditions)."[64] Although David Hay believes Paul

59. Hay, "Shaping of Theology," 140.

60. The Corinthians recognize this since they have written to Paul for guidance (1 Cor 7:1).

61. "Paul is urging, cajoling, remonstrating, using every kind of rhetorical device, to get this community both to see things his way and to conform their behavior accordingly, that is, in keeping with the gospel" (Fee, "Toward a Theology of 1 Corinthians," 38). Paul may not have the power to excommunicate/restore since in 1 Cor 5:2 he calls on the Corinthians to remove an errant member and in 2 Cor 2:6–8 he urges them to restore a member. If Paul does have authority to compel these actions, it may be that he instead "wants them to respond voluntarily to his discourse" (Witherington, *Conflict and Community*, 358).

62. Amador finds that "Paul is genuinely interested in building up the community, both through outreach and through practices that take into account the need to address those who are spiritually weak. . . . It is nowhere apparent that his appeals to community benefit and his use of the spiritually weak to curb the authority of the strong in the community are appeals for his sake or for the sake of his followers. They instead appear to be genuine concern for those in the community who are at the time of the writing the most (spiritually and/or socially) disadvantaged (8.10–13; 10.24–29; 11.22)" (Amador, *Academic Constraints in Rhetorical Criticism*, 232).

63. See H. H. D. Williams, "Psalms in 1 and 2 Corinthians," 173.

64. Hay, "Shaping of Theology," 140. Those among the empirical audience who did not

"assumes without argument that the Jewish scriptures have continuing authority for Christians,"[65] our position is instead that Paul assumes the OT Story frames the lifeworld and worldview of the Christians in Corinth, throughout Achaia (2 Cor 1:1b), and everywhere (1 Cor 1:2). The broad Story underlying the letter is the Story of Yahweh and the relationship of a Yahweh-follower to Yahweh, as the character both of Yahweh and of this relationship have been further revealed through the life, death, and resurrection of Jesus Christ.[66]

Our next step is to evaluate which theological Story-lines are particularly relevant in the first speech event of this letter, 2 Cor 1:8—7:16.[67]

The Theological Story-Lines of 2 Cor 1:8—7:16

In our model, a text's theological Story-lines are revealed by determining which basic questions about Yahweh and humanity's relationship to Yahweh the text answers.[68] In the first speech event of 2 Corinthians, the relevant theological questions include: who Yahweh is, how Yahweh relates to the world, and how Yahweh's people are to relate to Yahweh. Several interrelated theological Story-lines emerge from exploring these questions.

First, the side-by-side presentation of Jesus Christ and God in 2 Cor 5:20 demonstrates that "who Yahweh is" and "how Yahweh relates to the world" are now answerable only through the lens of Jesus Messiah, the "likeness of God" (2 Cor 4:4; see also 4:6). Jesus is foundational to the speech or "preaching" of the implied author and his colleagues (2 Cor 1:19; 2:12, 17).[69] Paul proclaims "Jesus Christ as Lord" (2 Cor 4:5; see also 1:3)[70] and calls himself and his colleagues "ambassadors for Christ" (2 Cor 5:20a).

---

have this familiarity would have learned from those who did (see the discussion on p. 152).

65. Hay, "Shaping of Theology," 140.

66. As R. B. Hays notes, "The history of God's dealings with Israel is always read by Paul retrospectively through the lens of God's act of reconciling the world to himself through the death of Jesus Christ" (R. B. Hays, "On the Rebound," 78).

67. Kruse comes close to our linguistic/pragmatic division, calling 1:12—7:16 "The Body of the Response" (Kruse, *Second Epistle of Paul to the Corinthians*, 54).

68. See chapter 4.

69. Mack notes that "whereas Paul had to argue for his authority as an apostle, he never argued for the authority of the kerygma" (Mack, *Rhetoric and the New Testament*, 98).

70. The implied topic of Paul's preaching is described as: "'the word of God' (2:17; 4:2), 'the gospel' (4:4), 'Jesus Christ as Lord' (4:5)" (Barnett, *Second Epistle to the Corinthians*, 241).

The "ambassadors" speak not only *about* Jesus Christ but also *in* him; Jesus is both the content and the ground of their message, which is given by God in God's power (see, e.g., 2 Cor 2:17; 3:46; 4:1, 7; 12:19).[71]

Paul's ministry is to proclaim that message (see, e.g., 2 Cor 2:17, 4:2, 5:20). He has "laid a foundation as an expert builder" (2 Cor 3:10), and Christians are to hold fast to the good news he proclaimed to them (2 Cor 15:1-11) and the teaching he passed on to them (2 Cor 11:2).[72] Ultimately, Paul is confident that God will rescue (2 Cor 1:10; see also 2:14, 5:5-8), that God's promises, of which the gift of the Spirit is a "first installment" (2 Cor 1:20-22), will be fulfilled, and that God has granted a new covenant, through which the Spirit brings life (2 Cor 3:6). Since "it is by God's mercy that we are engaged in this ministry," God can be expected to provide what is necessary for its success; therefore, Paul and his colleagues "do not lose heart" (2 Cor 4:1). This phrase is repeated in 2 Cor 4:16, thus book-ending this sub-section of the letter with Paul's continued ministry resolve.

At this writing, Paul is weak and suffering (2 Cor 4:8-10). But his apparent "lack of glory" is not, as the Corinthians assume, evidence of a defective ministry. Rather, Paul's suffering demonstrates his solidarity with the Savior and therefore, the rightness of his message (2 Cor 13:3-4).[73] Paul's weakness reveals divine power (2 Cor 1:9, 3:5, 4:7, 12:8). In the co-text immediately preceding the quotation, Paul highlights the benefits to

---

71. From the outset of the letter, it is Messiah Jesus who is both the content of Paul's speaking (1:19, 2:12, 4:5) and the one who makes it possible (2:17). He is the one for whom Paul and his colleagues suffer (1:5, 4:10-11), through whom they are consoled (1:5) and have confidence (3:4), and in whom both they and the Corinthians stand firm (1:21). The emphasis on Jesus Christ continues past 4:13. It is "the judgment seat of Christ" before which believers all must appear (5:10), the "love of Christ" that "urges us on" (5:14), "for him" that believers live (5:15), "in Christ" that "there is a new creation" (5:17), and through Christ that believers are reconciled to God (5:18-19).

72. Paul received some of his teaching from Jesus (1 Cor 11:23), but he does not indicate the source of all his teaching (see, e.g., 1 Cor 15:3-11). For his teaching topics, see 1 Cor 5:1, 6:19-20, 7:19, 10:7-8.

73. Paul interprets "these mortal adversities . . . as an integral and appropriate part of true apostleship (4:7-15)" (Furnish, *II Corinthians*, 277). Further, his "endurance in the sufferings of ministry" marks him "as a genuine servant of Christ, whose own sufferings are now reproduced in the ministry of the one who represents him" (Barnett, *Second Epistle to the Corinthians*, 212; cf. Furnish, *II Corinthians*, 285-286). However, it goes too far to say that "there is a divine purpose for apostolic suffering, namely, that Paul might testify to God's deliverance (1:11; 4:12-15)" (Barnett, *Second Epistle to the Corinthians*, 236) or that "these adversities are for the ultimate purpose of the overflowing of 'thanksgiving to the glory of God'" (Kraftchick, "Death in Us," 171).

the Corinthians of the affliction and peril he and his colleagues have experienced (2 Cor 4:12).[74]

For Paul, the messenger matters only as a vehicle for the message. His "defence . . . of the integrity of his personal character and apostleship" was "dictated not by self-interest but by the necessity for protecting the church God had founded through him from forces and doctrines which were essentially inimical to the gospel committed to Paul and to the spiritual welfare of those whose lives, through response to that gospel, had been transformed and set free."[75] The goal of Paul's ministry is "that those to whom he came might have the 'life' that Christ's death made possible for them to have."[76] Paul defends himself and his ministry not to preserve his own reputation (1 Cor 4:3) but rather to remove any barriers that might keep the Corinthians from trusting his message and, through it, his Lord.[77]

Using these identifications of the implied author and audience and of some major theological Story-lines of this letter section, we turn to a more detailed analysis of the quotation and its speech act complex. Our goal is first to determine what transformation of the lifeworld/worldview, theology, and Story of the audience is intended by Paul's quotation of Ps 115:1 LXX, i.e., what it would mean for Paul's readers to be Envisagers. From this, we can assess whether Paul himself reads the OT text as an Envisager.

---

74. Paul suffers on behalf of the Corinthians so they, like him, might experience the "life, or deliverance, of Jesus" (Barnett, *Second Epistle to the Corinthians*, 227). In 5:21, Paul reminds them that "God made him who had no sin to be sin for *us*, so that in him *we* might become the righteousness of God" (NIV; emphasis added).

75. Hughes, *Paul's Second Epistle to the Corinthians*, xvi–xvii. Similarly, Witherington argues that "to call Paul's apostleship into question would be for the Corinthians to call their own Christian existence into question" and that this is what calls for Paul's response in 2 Corinthians rather than Paul's concern for his own reputation or status (Witherington, *Conflict and Community*, 207). Barrett's thought that "nothing appears more powerfully in 2 Corinthians than the strength of Paul's vocation" (Barrett, *Commentary on the Second Epistle to the Corinthians*, 32) misses the mark slightly. Nothing appears more powerfully in the letter than the importance of Paul's *message*. His ministry serves the message he is called to proclaim.

76. Barnett, *Second Epistle to the Corinthians*, 238.

77. As Hay notes, "a decision against Paul implies a rejection of the Jesus and the God whose ambassador Paul is" (Hay, "Shaping of Theology," 141; see also 135. Also see Barnett, *Second Epistle to the Corinthians*, 301, 311). Witherington adds that "to be alienated from the agent was to be alienated from the one who sent him" (Witherington, *Conflict and Community*, 328; see also 396–97).

The Illocution of the Quotation and its Speech Act Complex[78]

Second Corinthians 4:13 is part of a speech act complex which includes v. 14[79] and is composed of four Assertive illocutionary acts: (i) the quotation and its introduction (v. 13a), (ii) καὶ ἡμεῖς πιστεύομεν (v. 13b), (iii) διὸ καὶ λαλοῦμεν (v. 13c), and (iv) the reason statement (v. 14).[80] The speech acts of this passage in both NA²⁷ and the NSRV are presented in Appendix §2 in parallel columns.

What is the tellability of these Assertives?[81] The first Assertive includes the quotation from Ps 115:1a LXX. Since ἐπίστευσα, διὸ ἐλάλησα is a marked quotation and also the first explicit OT quotation in the letter,[82] it has rhetorical prominence. Paul uses the quotation to equate the "spirit of faith"[83] he and his ministry colleagues possess to that of the psalmist, who also experienced suffering and came close to death.[84] This is either a new way for Paul to describe faith or a reaffirmation of previous teaching.

---

78. Stanley puts this in his "U+" category as a quotation in "full agreement with the standard printed edition of the author's normal *Vorlage*, with no significant variations in either text" (Stanley, *Paul and the Language of Scripture*, 58; see also 216; cf. Furnish, *II Corinthians*, 258). We find no locutionary issues in 2 Cor 4:13.

79. *Contra* Barnett, who believes the "the unity of vv. 13–15 is indicated by the conjunctions" (Barnett, *Second Epistle to the Corinthians*, 239), we agree with Lambrecht that "a division of 4:7–15 into three (unequal) parts appears to be justified: vv. 7–12, 13–14, and 15" (Lambrecht, *Second Corinthians*, 76). However, as the immediately following co-text, we consider v. 15 in our analysis.

80. Verse 14 could be considered two speech acts. But it simplifies the analysis to consider it as one, and nothing is lost by doing so.

81. Identifying the subcategory of these Assertives is not critical.

82. See Furnish, *II Corinthians*, 258.

83. Stegman asks: "Does πνεῦμα refer to a human quality or to the Spirit of God?" (Stegman, "Ἐπίστευσα, διὸ ἐλάλησα," 732). Furnish convincingly argues that these are intertwined: "Paul means to identify the *Spirit of faith* he has experienced with *the same one* known to the psalmist from whom he proceeds to quote. . . . It is preferable . . . to read this as a reference to the (Holy) Spirit, in and with which faith comes, as in 1 Cor 12:9; Rom 8:14–16; Gal 3:2, 5, 14; 5:5; cf. 1 Cor 2:4–5; 1 Thess 1:5–7" (Furnish, *II Corinthians*, 258; see also 286). We do note that nowhere else in the NT is the Holy Spirit referred to as the "spirit of faith." There are three later uses of "spirit" in the letter (2 Cor 7:1, 13; 11:4) which do not refer to the Holy Spirit.

84. Although Moyise is correct that "it is unlikely that they [the original recipients] would know the Hebrew text," (Moyise, *Paul and Scripture*, 107), it seems quite likely that some (many?) of them would have understood Ps 115 LXX against the backdrop of the psalmist's suffering since that suffering is the subject of v. 1c and his rescue is alluded to in vv. 3 and 7. While Paul does not explicitly quote Ps 115:1c LXX, it is clear

From the next two Assertives we learn that because Paul and his colleagues have the same spirit of faith as the psalmist, they are impelled to speak as the psalmist did.[85] The tellability of these Assertives lies in the way they present Paul and his colleagues as successors to the psalmist in belief and subsequent speech.[86]

Although Ralph Martin feels that "the centerpiece is the assertion, πιστεύομεν, 'we believe' (v 13),"[87] it seems more plausible that the following speech act, "and so we speak" is the core.[88] Not only does this have natural prominence as an implication, result, or consequence, it aligns with how the letter has developed thus far. *All* of Paul's experiences—not only the ministry success evidenced in the faith of the Corinthian believers (2 Cor 3:2–3) but also the persecution Paul has endured (2 Cor 1:3–9; 4:8–12, 16–17) and the pain and grief he and the Corinthians have suffered due to difficulties in their relationship (2 Cor 2:1–4)—stem from Paul's speaking the truth of the gospel, i.e., that Jesus Christ is Lord (2 Cor 4:2–5).

---

throughout the letter that he has been "brought very low"; he uses ταπεινός in 7:6, 10:1, and 12:21. As Murphy-O'Connor points out, the "majority of commentators have seen that *to auto pneuma tês pisteôs* means that Paul identifies with the faith of the psalmist. This necessarily implies that he perceived the similarity of their situations because he was still thinking of his sufferings" (Murphy-O'Connor, "Faith and Resurrection," 547; cf. Furnish, *II Corinthians*, 285).

85. Unlike Young and Ford, *Meaning and Truth in 2 Corinthians*, 64, we do not assume Paul considers David to be the psalmist. In Rom 4:6 and 11:9, Paul attributes to David two sayings from psalms with Davidic superscriptions. But Paul makes no such attribution here in quoting from a psalm with no superscription.

86. According to Dahood, "of the various interpretations of the Pauline intention in quoting these words from the Psalter (Ps 116,10), that which places a relationship of cause and effect between faith and preaching seems best to fit the context" (Dahood, "Two Pauline Quotations," 23; see also Kruse, *Second Epistle of Paul to the Corinthians*, 108; and Thrall, *Introduction and Commentary on II Corinthians I–VII*, 338). Even Barrett, who argues that Paul uses this quotation out of context, recognizes that "Paul thinks of faith that leads to speech" (Barrett, *Commentary on the Second Epistle to the Corinthians*, 142). This is not, however, as Clifford takes it, a situation of "faith authorizing one to instruct others" (Clifford, *Psalms 73–150*, 200). Nor, *contra* Murphy-O'Connor, is it significant that Paul uses λαλέω in 4:13 rather than κηρύσσω as in 4:5. (He believes Paul uses λαλέω not to refer to his preaching but to what he has just said in 4:7–12; see Murphy-O'Connor "Faith and Resurrection," 547). Not only does Paul use λαλέω regarding his ministry in 1 Cor 2:6–7, 13, and 2 Cor 2:17, 12:19, since Paul is emphasizing the similarities between himself and the psalmist, it is important that he use the same verb as Ps 115:1 LXX.

87. R. P. Martin, *2 Corinthians*, 89.

88. See Furnish, *II Corinthians*, 286.

The final Assertive, v. 14, stands in a causal relationship to the core speech act. This Assertive is tellable in part because in it, "Paul identifies the object of faith and thus the ultimate source of apostolic boldness as the God *who raised [the Lord] Jesus* and *will raise us also with Jesus.*"[89] Paul and his colleagues see their righteous suffering in the same light as the psalmist considered his righteous suffering—a negative consequence of faith-fueled speech from which the speaker is ultimately redeemed by Yahweh.[90] Although Paul has already lauded Yahweh for his earthly deliverance (2 Cor 1:10), in 2 Cor 4:14 he adds a broader, eternal perspective. He returns to this in 2 Cor 4:17 where he compares "this slight momentary affliction" to "an eternal weight of glory beyond all measure." That Paul and his colleagues will be raised with Jesus is a link to both the immediately preceding and succeeding co-text of this speech act complex, especially 2 Cor 4:8–11 and 4:16b–5:5, as well as to earlier passages, such as 2 Cor 1:8–10 and 2:16. Yahweh's rescue or deliverance, of which the resurrection of believers is the ultimate, final, and eternal example, is the reason for Paul's hope (2 Cor 4:1, 16).[91]

---

89. Furnish, *II Corinthians*, 286. Jesus's resurrection was a core element of Paul's preaching (cf. 1 Cor 15:4), and, according to Shaw, "the resurrection and vindication of Jesus is the pledge of Paul's vindication and the Corinthians' also, so that the origin of his authority is also the source of their hope. . . . We see here the way in which a quite tangential text was used by the early church to indicate that Jesus' resurrection was indeed 'according to the Scriptures'" (Shaw, *Cost of Authority*, 104–5). We concur with his argument without agreeing that this quotation is "tangential."

90. Furnish highlights that "courage to speak out despite adversity" is the point both in the psalm and "in 2 Cor 4:13, which . . . does not sit loosely in its context but helps to support the statements about apostolic boldness Paul has already made (3:12; 4:1) and will make again (4:16; 5:6, 8)" (Furnish, *II Corinthians*, 285). As Kleinknecht puts it, "In ihm [Ps 115] sieht er denselben Geist des Glaubens wirksam, so daß er ein Entsprechungsverhältnis zwischen seiner Heilserwartung und der Rettung des leidenden Gerechten sowie zwischen seinem und dessen λαλεῖν postuliert" (Kleinknecht, *Der leidende Gerechtfertigte*, 261).

91. As Young and Ford correctly note, "Paul's confidence explicitly depends upon the resurrection, as he has already indicated in 1.9, and will again in 13.4" (Young and Ford, *Meaning and Truth in 2 Corinthians*, 64). However, this does not mean "the basis and motive for Paul's 'speaking' are eschatological, specifically in reference to judgment" (Barnett, *Second Epistle to the Corinthians*, 243). Paul wants the Corinthians to live a life of grace and thanksgiving *now*. But, in turn, that does not imply "the 'resurrection' of Paul in v. 14b takes place within the framework of terrestrial existence" or that Paul depicts "his arrival at Corinth as a 'resurrection'" (Murphy-O'Connor, "Faith and Resurrection," 546, 549). Rather, Paul believes both that God has rescued (ἐρρύσατο) Paul and his colleagues from death and will continue to deliver (ῥύσεται) them (1:10) *and* that God raises (ἐγείροντι) the dead (1:9) and in the future will raise (ἐγερεῖ) believers (4:14; see also 4:17—5:1). Also see Hay, "Shaping of Theology," 140.

PART II | CASE STUDIES

The links in 2 Cor 4 to Ps 115 LXX extend beyond this speech act complex.[92] The clearest and most relevant example is the immediately following co-text, v. 15. There, Paul presents the overarching purpose of his ministry as the increase of thanksgiving to the glory of God.[93] This ties back to 2 Cor 1:11, where many are to give thanks because God has rescued and will continue to rescue Paul, and also to 2 Cor 2:14, where thanks are due to God who causes ultimate triumph for those who know God. Thanksgiving is also the central focus of Ps 115 LXX. Of the psalm's ten verses, six concern giving thanks and praise, honoring vows, etc. Because Ps 115 LXX "is a hymn of thanksgiving for deliverance from death," it fits Paul's situation particularly well.[94] Like the psalmist, Paul has been rescued by Yahweh and recognizes that thanks and praise are due to the God who sustains.

In summary, this speech act complex, situated immediately after Paul's expanded description of affliction in 2 Cor 4:8–12 and just prior to his call to increase thanksgiving to Yahweh, ties together believing, speaking, suffering, and confident hope of rescue, including future resurrection, the "eternal" rescue. These interrelated Story-lines are also those of the original psalm and especially the speech act complex which contains the quoted passage.[95] With the quotation, Paul connects himself and his col-

92. Kleinknecht finds it "sehr wahrscheinlich, daβ Paulus mit dem Zitat des zunächst recht unmotiviert erscheinenden Psalmwortes mehr zitiert als nur jene drei Wörter" (Kleinknecht, *Der leidende Gerechtfertigte*, 261).

93. Verse 15 also picks up the Story-line of 2 Cor 1:6 and 4:12 regarding the benefit to the Corinthians of Paul's suffering (see Barrett, *Commentary on the Second Epistle to the Corinthians*, 143–44). "Everything," including Paul's ministry of speaking/preaching the Gospel and the suffering that ensues, occurs so the Corinthians may have the life faith brings, both in the present and eternally (see also v. 17). Lambrecht ably ties this together: "With v. 15 Paul both summarizes and motivates the main ideas of the first two parts. Suffering and preaching occur for the sake of the Corinthians. Then, . . . the last purpose clause points out the ultimate aim of all apostolic activity, namely the glory of God. People are to be persuaded to be thankful. God's free gift of the ministry should lead to giving thanks to God" (Lambrecht, *Second Corinthians*, 77).

Verse 15 also connects the discussion of glory in 2 Cor 3:7—4:6 to 4:16–18. Although God's glory is not mentioned in Ps 115 LXX, it is present in other Hallel psalms, including Ps 111:9 LXX, which Paul quotes in 2 Cor 9:9. These and other allusions Young and Ford find to the Hallel psalms lead to their conclusion that "Paul almost seems to follow themes in progression from a group of Psalms of which the core might well be particularly familiar and significant to him" (Young and Ford, *Meaning and Truth in 2 Corinthians*, 68). We cannot explore this here.

94. Hughes, *Paul's Second Epistle to the Corinthians*, 146, referring to Ps 116 MT.

95. Hooker incorrectly believes Paul "is using the quotation atomistically" arguing that the sufferings of the psalmist are described in Ps 116:1–9 MT while Paul instead

leagues to the Story of the psalmist, who was compelled to speak because of his belief, subsequently experienced serious negative consequences, and was ultimately rescued by Yahweh. Yahweh's response led the psalmist to further proclamation of his faith in and loyalty to Yahweh and to make and fulfill vows to praise Yahweh. Like the psalmist, Paul and his colleagues continue in both faith and the ministry to which Yahweh has called them, despite the ensuing afflictions. They are confident that Yahweh will rescue them and will, ultimately, bring the faithful into Yahweh's very presence. Using our terminology, our conclusion is that via this quotation Paul successfully evokes a key element of the Story of Yahweh's people.

Contra Stanley, the quotation does not play "a fairly minor position in a lengthy chain of arguments that Paul brings forward to defend his ministry."[96] At the other end of the spectrum, it also "does not serve as a proof imbued with claims to divine authority" or "serve the purpose of closing the debate, of being the final word that would allow no further discussion."[97] The quotation is not designed either to dominate or to manipulate.[98] Rather,

---

uses Ps 115 LXX, which is "a psalm of deliverance" (Hooker, "Interchange and Suffering," 78n11). Furnish points to a number of scholars who believe Paul has the broader Psalm in mind and notes just one, Barrett, who disagrees (see Furnish, *II Corinthians*, 285). On the one hand, we do not find it necessary to consider the broader psalm since Ps 115 LXX does refer to the psalmist's suffering (vv. 1c, 2, 6, 7c). On the other, we do not find sustainable Young and Ford's "almost claim" that Ps 115 LXX "is the text of Paul's second letter to the Corinthians" (Young and Ford, *Meaning and Truth in 2 Corinthians*, 66), which is based on this quotation and such links as ἐκστάσει/ἐξέστημεν (Ps 115:2 LXX/2 Cor 5:13), σωτηρίου/σωτηρίας (Ps 115:4 LXX/2 Cor 1:6, 6:2), and the inexact parallel δοῦλος/διάκονοι (Ps 115:7 LXX/2 Cor 6:4) (Young and Ford, 65).

96. Stanley, "Paul's 'Use' of Scripture," 146; see also Stanley, *Arguing with Scripture*, 99. He refers to 2 Cor 4:13–14 as an "obscure" quotation/reference (Stanley, *Arguing with Scripture*, 98; cf. Stanley, "Paul's 'Use' of Scripture," 146). R. B. Hays also calls it an "obscure Pauline passage" (R. B. Hays, "Christ Prays the Psalms,"108).

97. Ehrensperger, "Paul and the Authority of Scripture," 316, 318. *Contra* Hooker, it is not "an ordinary proof-text" (Hooker, "Interchange and Suffering," 78). In this regard, Stanley's remarks that the quotation "does not serve as a 'proof' for a specific argument" but is a "biblical warrant" which "does function somewhat like a 'proof' since it serves to justify Paul's ministry" (Stanley, "Paul's 'Use' of Scripture," 147) seem contradictory. In any event, we reject his contention that "its link to the preceding verses is so loose that the audience would likely have been puzzled by its appearance" (Stanley, 147).

98. R. E. Watts is correct that "if Paul was knowingly misleading his readers on the meaning of Scripture, he was seriously undermining his own credibility. This is where it seems to me that Stanley's rhetorical model goes awry. It has little appreciation of the centrality of ethics and character to Paul's identity, mission, and message" (R. E. Watts, "In Need of a Second Touch?").

it supports the core speech act by evoking a lifeworld in which Yahweh's people, like Paul and his colleagues, continue to proclaim Yahweh's message with boldness even though they suffer for their speaking. Suffering is not inconsistent with Paul's apostleship; rather, it demonstrates solidarity with Yahweh's faithful, including the psalmist, and Jesus himself.[99]

Successful illocution requires the illocutionary response of understanding. The implied reader makes this response. Paul would have expected some of his audience, particularly those who had a background in the synagogue, to have been able to assume the role of the implied reader at this level. Since "reading and interpreting Paul's letters was an ongoing community process in his churches,"[100] we do not agree with Stanley that Paul was trying to mislead the informed audience. Rather, Paul would have expected the informed group to lead the way in making sure those who had come directly to faith in Christ from paganism had the necessary mutual context to understand Paul's illocutionary intent.

Before we turn to the perlocution, we need to address the possibility that Paul considered the psalm's implied author to be the Messiah, and thus Jesus. A. T. Hanson was the first to argue that "Paul in all probability takes the verse from Ps. 116 as an utterance of the *Messiah*, an utterance of faith in God's salvation. In the context of the psalm the humiliation of the psalmist so emotionally expressed would be taken as referring to the passion."[101] Further, Hanson believes that "'I said in my haste, All men are liars!' is uttered by the pre-existent Messiah to God."[102] He connects Paul to Christ via "the same spirit of faith": "If we go back to the Septuagint and read it with Paul's eyes, there can be only one answer: Paul is claiming the same spirit of faith as Christ."[103] Hays was among the first to adopt Hanson's ar-

---

99. "If Paul is intending to correct any false notion here, it is . . . the belief that afflictions are inconsistent with true apostleship" (Furnish, *II Corinthians*, 286). The "acknowledged weakness, vulnerability, and suffering which characterize his apostolate . . . are interpreted . . . as fully appropriate to the apostolic vocation of preaching 'Jesus Christ crucified'" (Furnish, 287). For R. B. Hays, "the whole passage (2 Cor 4:7–15) is a description of Paul's apostolic ministry and sufferings as an embodiment of the sufferings of Christ" (R. B. Hays, "Christ Prays the Psalms," 108).

100. Abasciano, "Diamonds in the Rough," 171. He contrasts this to "Stanley's highly individualistic approach" (see Abasciano, 169, 172).

101. Hanson, *Studies in Paul's Technique*, 17–18; emphasis added.

102. Hanson, *Studies in Paul's Technique*, 19.

103. Hanson, *Paul's Understanding of Jesus*, 11.

gument.[104] He believes it "almost surely correct, because the whole thrust of the passage depends upon a series of parallels that Paul is drawing between himself and Christ. The verses quoted here say in effect, 'Jesus believed and spoke, and God raised him; therefore, we also believe and speak, knowing that God will raise us too along with him.'"[105] Wagner, who is Hays's former student, also appears to adopt this viewpoint[106] as do Douglas Campbell, Schenck, and Stegman. We discuss the latter arguments below.

According to Douglas Campbell, Paul uses "spirit" pneumatologically. It then follows that "once it has been conceded that the Holy Spirit is identifying Paul with another person, it will be difficult to resist the further implication that this must be Christ; the Spirit is, after all, for Paul the Spirit *of* Christ!"[107] From this, he argues that Paul here takes the Messiah as the "implicit subject of the verb πιστεύω."[108] But even if the "spirit of faith" is taken to be the Holy Spirit,[109] this does not necessarily identify the subject of πιστεύω as Messiah Jesus. Many of Yahweh's faith-filled people, including David, would have been able to make this statement.

Schenck's approach adds the idea that Paul's "belief" is his expectation of a future resurrection of believers. Then, since the OT psalmist "is not speaking of resurrection, only of *deliverance from trial*," Schenck supposes "that Paul is reading Ps 115:1 LXX messianically in reference to Jesus' faith in his own resurrection."[110] For Schenck, "in 4:13, Paul has the same spirit

104. In a work published slightly before Hays's, Hooker tentatively connects "the same faith" in 2 Cor 4 to that of Jesus and thus connects Paul's faith to Jesus's faith (Hooker, "Interchange and Suffering," 79). Many who have followed this line of argument take the quotation in 2 Cor 4:13 to mean Jesus possesses faith or is faithful and thus use it to argue that πίστις Χριστοῦ can be a subjective genitive. We cannot explore this here.

105. R. B. Hays, *Faith of Jesus Christ*, 152n125. He counts Ps 115 LXX among the "messianic psalms" Paul interprets christologically (R. B. Hays, "Christ Prays the Psalms," 108–109). He argues that if modern readers do not find Paul's reading *selbstverständlich*, "it is because we lack the necessary hermeneutical key: that ὁ Χριστός (Rom 15:3, 7) is the true and ultimate speaker of Israel's laments and praises" (R. B. Hays, "Christ Prays the Psalms," 109). Although we cannot fully investigate this claim, Paul's use of Ps 115 LXX in 2 Cor 4 does not substantiate it (see below).

106. "If the speaker of the psalm is understood to be Christ," this quotation becomes an "example of the theme, so prominent in 2 Corinthians, that in his ministry Paul participates in 'the death of Jesus'" (J. R. Wagner, *Heralds of the Good News*, 314n30).

107. D. A. Campbell, "2 Corinthians 4:13," 345.

108. D. A. Campbell, "2 Corinthians 4:13," 353.

109. See n83 above.

110. Schenck, "2 Corinthians," 527, 528. In this regard, we disagree with Young and Ford that the *psalmist's* faith is in the resurrection (Young and Ford, *Meaning and Truth*

of faith that Jesus had, typified in the words of Psalm 115:1 LXX: 'I have faith [that God will raise me from the dead]; I speak this faith.' Paul and his coworkers also have faith [that God will raise them from the dead], and they speak accordingly."[111] But, as we argued earlier, the structure of the LXX psalm makes it unlikely that (expected) deliverance is the content of either the psalmist's belief or speaking.[112]

Although Stegman also considers Paul's reading of Ps 115 LXX messianic,[113] *contra* Schenck he rejects a "principally cognitive understanding of πιστεύω in 4:13" in which the content is "that God raises the dead to life."[114] For Stegman, such an understanding

> fails to recognize that the apostle has been alluding to the story of Jesus and his πίστις since 4:10. And given that Paul offers no indication of changing the subject matter here, I propose that the verb πιστεύω in 4:13 is best translated "be faithful," understood primarily as living in constant fidelity and obedience to God and God's will.[115]

However, in 2 Cor 4:10–12 there is no overt mention of Jesus's πίστις and no discussion of the reason for Jesus's death. Additionally, although Stegman is correct that Paul "makes the daring assertion that his experience of being afflicted, confused, persecuted, and humiliated is somehow

---

in 2 Corinthians, 64).

111. Schenck, "2 Corinthians," 533; brackets original.

112. Schenck's conclusion hinges on the only option for Paul's faith being "rescue from his current mission trials" (Schenck, "2 Corinthians," 527n11; see also 528n15). This presents "faith" too narrowly.

113. Stegman regards "Paul as assuming that these words were spoken by the risen Jesus" (Stegman, "Ἐπίστευσα, διὸ ἐλάλησα," 733n34). And, although Stegman argues that "τὸ πνεῦμα τῆς πίστεως ... ought to be interpreted to mean 'πνεῦμα of *faithfulness*,'" like D. A. Campbell, he believes this reference is to the Holy Spirit (Stegman, 735).

114. Stegman, "Ἐπίστευσα, διὸ ἐλάλησα," 734. By "principally cognitive," Stegman refers to rendering "πιστεύω here as 'believe,' in the sense of having conviction or certainty" (Stegman, 734; see also 733n34, where he contrasts his understanding to Hanson's rendering of ἐπίστευσα as "Jesus believed").

115. Stegman, "Ἐπίστευσα, διὸ ἐλάλησα," 734. Interestingly, although Stegman believes that Paul "was not constrained by the original meaning of the text" (Stegman, 734), he argues that Paul draws on the entire LXX equivalent of Ps 116 MT, i.e., Pss 114 and 115 LXX (Stegman, 733n34; see also 738–39, 745. See also Schenck, "2 Corinthians," 530–32). This is in contrast to Hanson and Hays who, according to Stegman, consider only Ps 115 LXX.

connected with the story of Jesus,"¹¹⁶ that does not mean Paul makes a direct reference to Jesus in every instance.

In summary, the arguments that Paul reads Ps 115 LXX messianically are not compelling. Nor is there evidence for a messianic interpretation of the psalm prior to the writing of this letter,¹¹⁷ and the introductory formula "κατὰ τὸ γεγραμμένον" argues against the idea that Paul initiates a messianic interpretation. Although "Paul uses this precise citation formula nowhere else,"¹¹⁸ it in no way points to Jesus as the author of the Psalm. If Paul were reading Jesus as the subject of πιστεύω, he would more likely introduce the quotation with the formula he uses in Rom 4:18, "κατὰ τὸ εἰρημένον."

To demand exact parallels between the psalmist's situation and Paul's or to postulate that since Paul expected to be resurrected, he must consider the psalmist to be Jesus because Jesus was resurrected both carry co-text too far. There is no indication Paul takes this verse as a Messianic utterance or the psalm as foretelling the Messiah's death and resurrection.

The final step in our analysis is to consider the perlocution of the speech act complex and to determine what transformation of the NT audience is called for and whether Paul reads the OT as an Envisager.

Perlocution and Transformation

The perlocutionary intention and desired perlocutionary effect of an Assertive illocutionary act or speech act complex is that the hearer/reader respond with adherence. The implied reader of the OT source text concurs that the psalmist has acted properly in speaking of his faith and agrees that Yahweh will deliver the believer from any resulting suffering. The Envisaging NT reader of 2 Cor 4:13–14 accepts that Paul's belief impels his speech and that neither his ministry nor his message is negated or compromised by his suffering. Additionally, an Envisaging NT reader adheres to the notions that believers can be confident of Yahweh's protection and that ultimately, they also will be brought into Yahweh's presence with Jesus Christ, who is the means by which they are saved.

Paul clearly reads Ps 115 LXX as an Envisager since the perlocutionary intention of the speech act complex in 2 Corinthians which includes the quotation is in alignment with the perlocutionary intention of the psalm.

---

116. Stegman, "Ἐπίστευσα, διὸ ἐλάλησα," 729.
117. See the section "Intervening Interpretation" above.
118. Furnish, *II Corinthians*, 258; cf. R. P. Martin, *2 Corinthians*, 82.

PART II | CASE STUDIES

Paul evokes the Story of the psalmist—who believes, speaks, suffers, is rescued, and gives thanks—in order to link the Corinthians to the lifeworld of the people of Yahweh, thereby transforming (by realigning or restoring[119]) the attitude of the Corinthians towards Paul's ministry and thus towards his message. The behavior of the Corinthians also is to be transformed; thanksgiving is to be increased to the glory of God (v. 15).[120] This, too, parallels the perlocution of the co-text of the psalmic speech act complex, in which thanks, praise, and worship are offered to Yahweh (see Ps 115:4 LXX, also v. 9 and, especially, v. 8).

With this quotation, then, Paul invites his readers to think as he does about Yahweh, the appropriate relationship a Yahweh-follower is to have with the deity, and what it means to live into one's faith.[121] He creates and/or activates mutual context by evoking the theological Story-lines of Ps 115:1 LXX to encourage his audience also to read as Envisagers, responding with the desired perlocutionary effect of adherence and thereby experiencing a realignment or restoration of their attitude towards Paul's message. Ultimately, for Envisaging readers, their faith in and behavior towards Yahweh and the Lord Jesus Christ is also transformed, and they join Paul in the lifeworld he inhabits.[122]

---

119. For those who have fallen away from faith in Jesus Christ, their current theological position would need to be subverted and their Christian faith re-created or restored.

120. The audience probably is also to take the "speaking" of the psalmist and Paul as a model. It appears in 2 Cor 9:13 that the Corinthian believers are expected, like the psalmist and Paul, to speak of their faith and its object despite the testing which may follow. According to Hughes, "Believing and speaking, or open confession, are in fact two essential aspects of salvation" (Hughes, *Paul's Second Epistle to the Corinthians*, 148, referring also to Rom 10:9–10).

121. The important theological Story-line of coming into or remaining in right relationship with God and Christ is stated firmly in the Directive which arguably forms the peak of this letter segment: "We entreat you on behalf of Christ, be reconciled to God" (2 Cor 5:20b). (N. T. Wright argues convincingly that 2 Cor 5:20–21 "forms the natural climax to the entire argument of the preceding three chapters" [N. T. Wright, "On Becoming the Righteousness of God," 208]). The speech act complex which includes the quotation of Ps 115:1 LXX supports this Directive because the ability of the Corinthians to enter into this state of reconciliation depends on their active acceptance of Paul's message. Throughout the letter Paul defends his apostolic credentials and calls for the Corinthians to "open wide" their hearts to him (2 Cor 6:13)—not to mislead his audience or because he is concerned for his reputation but because he wants them to accept the truth of his message and then to act on it by being reconciled to Yahweh.

122. As Ehrensperger puts it, "The frequent references to the Scriptures in the Pauline letters thus are more than mere proof-texts or ornaments to an argument previously made; they constitute the world in which he lived and thought" (Ehrensperger, *Paul and*

CONCLUSION

As we have applied our methodology to Paul's quotation of Ps 115:1 LXX in 2 Cor 4:13, we have determined it is not "so far removed from the original context as to raise questions about Paul's reliability as an interpreter" nor is it likely that "Paul simply ran across a set of words that sounded like a good 'motto' for his ministry and then copied them down (or memorized them) for later use without regard for their original context."[123] Rather, we have shown that, as Joseph Bonsirven observes with regard to this quotation, "S. Paul reste fidèle au sens général du texte."[124] More specifically, Paul is an Envisaging reader of Ps 115 LXX, who evokes the Story-lines and lifeworld of that psalm to support the desired transformation of the lifeworld of his readers via the intended illocutionary response of understanding and intended perlocutionary responses of beliefs and behaviors that the implied author establishes for the implied reader.[125]

---

the Dynamics of Power, 6).

123. *Contra* Stanley, *Arguing with Scripture*, 100. Nor is this a "power play" or an argument from authority in the sense of attempting to "anticipate and/or close off debate regarding a statement made by a speaker/author in direct speech" (Stanley, 13).

124. J. Bonsirven, *Exégèse rabbinique*, 320, adding "tout au moins tel qu'il le lisait dans la version grecque." Bonsirven does not believe Paul is always faithful to the OT context. He includes the quotation of Ps 68:19 in Eph 4:8 (which we discussed in chapter 5) under the category "Divergences graves."

125. This does not imply, *contra* Witherington, that "*in all cases*, a careful rereading of the Old Testament texts Paul cites or alludes to provides a larger and clearer context in which to understand what he is trying to say" (Witherington, *Paul's Narrative Thought World*, 50; emphasis added). Each quotation must be examined on its own merits.

# 8

Ps 110:1 as Quoted by Various NT Authors

OUR FINAL CASE STUDY is more intricate: the quotation of all or part of Ps 110:1[1] in various NT situations, including by Jesus (as he is quoted in Matt 22:44, Mark 12:36, and Luke 20:42–43), Peter (as he is quoted in Acts 2:34–35), Paul (1 Cor 15:25), and the author of Hebrews (Heb 1:13).[2]

The conclusions of some scholars concerning the relationship of the NT quotations of Ps 110:1 to the OT context put these quotations squarely within the purview of this study. For example, John Goldingay finds that although some verses of this psalm "are applied to Jesus, . . . as a whole it does not fit him, and most of its application to him in the NT requires it to be understood in a way that would not correspond to its meaning in any OT context."[3] More broadly, Hay claims that "apart from their sheer number, the most remarkable feature of early Christian references to Ps 110 is the wide diversity of meanings."[4]

---

1. References to Ps 110 are to Ps 110 MT unless otherwise noted.

2. According to L. C. Allen, Ps 110:1 is the text "most often cited or alluded to in the NT; it appears a score of times" (L. C. Allen, *Psalms 101–150*, 118). Hay lists twenty-three NT quotations/allusions (Hay, *Glory at the Right Hand*, 164–66); Aune finds five quotations and nineteen allusions (Aune, "Christian Prophecy," 404n4). Space precludes a detailed discussion of Rom 8:34, Eph 1:20, Col 3:1, and 1 Pet 3:22, which refer to a seat at the right hand of God but do not directly quote Ps 110:1. We do, however, evaluate Jesus's clear allusion to Ps 110:1 as reported in Matt 26:64, Mark 14:62, and Luke 22:69.

3. Goldingay, *Psalms 90–150*, 292.

4. Hay, *Glory at the Right Hand*, 17. Gourgues also believes "nos passages . . . ne placent

As we use our methodology to evaluate these claims, we consider these specific questions:

1. What does Ps 110:1 contribute to the Story of Yahweh's people? What would it mean to read Ps 110:1 as an Envisager?

2. Since there is little evidence for the pre-Christian interpretation of Ps 110 (it is not, for example, attested at Qumran), what can be said about "messianic expectations" in the first century generally that may help us understand the socio-historical context of the NT quotations of Ps 110:1?

3. Is there any commonality in what the NT speakers/authors mediate to their readers/hearers in their illocutionary and perlocutionary acts? Is there any evidence of development of the OT idea(s)?

4. What would it mean to read these various NT passages as an Envisager? Does evoking the OT Story promote lifeworld/worldview transformation? If so, is there any commonality to the expected perlocutionary response?

We begin by examining the OT text from a speech-act perspective.

PS 110 [109 LXX]

Psalm 110 generally is classified as a royal psalm.[5] "References to 'my Lord' (. . . 110:1), and the kingly diction—'sit at my right hand' (. . . 110:1, 5), 'a footstool for your feet' . . . , and 'scepter' (. . . 110:2)—support a royal psalm

---

pas toujours l'accent sur la même idée et, lorsqu'ils retiennent la même, celle de la droite notamment, ils l'utilisent en des sens divers" (Gourgues, À la droite de Dieu, 212).

5. According to Wendland, royal psalms "speak either of Israel's earthly, human ruler—the LORD's 'anointed (chosen) one'—or of God as the supreme King" (Wendland, *Analyzing the Psalms*, 51). He calls royalty a minor function and lists it under the major functions of petition (lament) and praise (Wendland, 60). Since Ps 110 does not fit into either of these major categories (Wendland, 41, 58), we stop at identifying it as a royal psalm. Bock concisely refutes the arguments against understanding Ps 110 as a royal psalm (see Bock, *Proclamation from Prophecy and Pattern*, 128–29). Also see Bullock for an explanation of why Ps 110 is to be considered a royal psalm even though it does not explicitly mention an anointed person, the king, or David (Bullock, *Encountering the Book of Psalms*, 178–79).

PART II | CASE STUDIES

motif."[6] The structure of Ps 110 is "determined by the oracular introductions of vv 1 and 4."[7] These verses each begin a speech act complex.

The Locution of Ps 110:1–3 [109:1–3 LXX]

The speech act complex that is the psalm's first oracle can be divided into five speech acts: vv. 1, 2a, 2b, 3a, and 3b. The speech acts of this passage for the LXX, NETS, and NRSV are given in Appendix §3 in parallel columns.

Since all the NT authors clearly quote the LXX, we use it to evaluate the illocution and perlocution of the source text. However, because Jesus and Peter may have quoted the Hebrew OT or an Aramaic translation,[8] we briefly discuss two locutionary issues concerning the relationship of the MT and LXX.[9]

The first of these is the rendering in Ps 109:1 LXX of both יהוה and אדני by a form of ὁ κύριος. However, in the psalm, ὁ κύριος and τῷ κυρίῳ μου are distinct personages; the oracle's addressee is not presented as Yahweh or equivalent to Yahweh, i.e., as divine.

---

6. Bateman, *Early Jewish Hermeneutics*, 175. We discuss the metaphors of the "kingly diction" below.

7. L. C. Allen, *Psalms 101–150*, 113. The arguments he presents for a tripartite structure are not convincing.

8. Hay dates Ps 110 LXX to "somewhere between the third and first centuries BCE" and notes it "represents the earliest known interpretation" (Hay, *Glory at the Right Hand*, 21). It may reflect a non-MT Hebrew text (see Jobes and Silva, *Invitation to the Septuagint*, 21).

9. Another issue in v. 1 is the use of εἶπεν for נְאֻם since this bypasses "the special aura of prophetic revelation" נאם has elsewhere in the OT. However, "the OG represents the command to be seated as a divine oracle no less plainly than does the MT" (Hay, *Glory at the Right Hand*, 21). In addition, L. C. Allen believes עד in v. 1 would be better translated as "while" rather than "until" (i.e., ἕως) (L. C. Allen, *Psalms 101–50*, 110n1a, with reference to, among others, Booij, "Psalm cx," 407. See also Clifford, *Psalms 73–150*, 179). Allen finds "until" acceptable "with the understanding that it can mark a relative limit beyond which the activity of the main clause still continues" (L. C. Allen, *Psalms 101–150*, 110n1a). We reject Driver's view of עד in v. 1 as "when" and his understanding that this is "a promise of a seat beside His when he (*sc.* the Messianic king) has won the victory on God's behalf for Israel" (Driver, "Psalm 110," 20*, 19*). Not only is "when" based on an unattested Hebrew form, "I" in v. 1c must be Yahweh. Therefore, Yahweh clearly has a role in the victory (see also vv. 5–6). We agree with Kraus: "With Yahweh's help the king defeats and destroys all his enemies. . . . The decisive factor is not trust in one's potential for waging war, but the invoking of Yahweh, his involvement, and his aid" (Kraus, *Theology of the Psalms*, 120).

The other locutionary issue is that the final two speech acts (vv. 3a and 3b) present serious interpretive challenges in both the MT and LXX. Over fifty years ago, Raymond Jacques Tournay noted that v. 3 "a donné lieu à une foule d'interprétations et de conjectures."[10] Scholars seem no closer to consensus today. Hay, for example, acknowledges the Hebrew is "virtually unintelligible" but believes "the Greek distinctly describes the birth of a divine child."[11] This, however, takes literally language which is very likely metaphoric, given the three metaphors in vv. 1–2. For others, like Ulli Roth, "die LXX-Übersetzung bietet keine messianische Interpretation dieses Verses und des Psalms 110."[12] Since the psalm is not present in the Qumran texts and v. 3 is not quoted in the NT, it cannot be determined how this verse was read in the first century CE.[13] Therefore, we do not consider it in our analysis.

As we have noted, vv. 1–2 contain several metaphors. To bridge our discussion of the locution and illocution, our next move is to unpack these metaphors.

The Metaphors in Ps 110:1–2 [109:1–2 LXX]

The governing metaphor of this speech act complex—the command to be seated at the right hand of Yahweh in v. 1[14]—is more than the offer of a chair or even permission to sit in the royal presence. In the ancient Mediterranean world, the place to the right of a ruler or other important person was a location which indicated the conferring of honor and often also of

---

10. Tournay, "Le Psaume cx," 10, noting that "les mss hébreux ne sont pas d'accord entre eux" and "le texte massorétique est obscur."

11. Hay, *Glory at the Right Hand*, 21. His thought that "the corruption of the present Hebrew text may have resulted from deliberate efforts by scribes to conceal the [messianic] meaning" (Hay, 22) is quite speculative.

12. Roth, *Die Grundparadigmen christlicher Schriftauslegung*, 49. For a discussion of the messianism in Ps 109:3 LXX, see Knibb, "Septuagint and Messianism," and Cordes, "Spricht Ps 109 LXX von einem Messias?"

13. See van der Meer, "Psalm 110," 233–34.

14. "Metaphor" is not an illocutionary category. Nor can metaphoric language be taken literally. "It is difficult to imagine how the king could have literally sat at Yhwh's right hand, on a throne in the temple, and it is in any case unwise to infer some literal, concrete event from a poetic colon in a prophetic oracle in a liturgical text, whose main point is metaphorical" (Goldingay, *Psalms 90–150*, 294). However, although "metaphorical sentences as such can be neither true nor false" (Burkhardt, "Searle on Metaphor," 324), an Assertive which contains a metaphor has truth-value.

PART II | CASE STUDIES

authority. There are literary and pictorial references to monarchs being seated (or sometimes standing) at the right hand of a god in Egyptian, Ugaritic, and Babylonian works.[15] The ancient Greek poets Pindar (c. 522–443 BC) and Callimachus (c. 305–240 BC) speak of Athena and Apollo, respectively, as sitting at the right hand of Zeus.[16] In addition to Ps 110, Ps 80:17 implores Yahweh to "let your hand be upon the one at your right hand, the one whom you made strong for yourself." Other OT usage includes 1 Kgs 2:19 and Ps 45:9, where the king's mother and the queen, respectively, are found at the monarch's (not Yahweh's) right hand.[17]

This metaphor also appears in intertestamental literature. In addition to the king's concubine sitting at his right hand (and removing his crown and slapping him!) in 1 Esd 4:29–30, King Alexander clothes Jonathan in purple and seats him "at his side" in 1 Macc 10:62–63. This is referred to twice as honoring him (1 Macc 10:64, 65) and as a sign that Jonathan was among the king's closest friends as well as "general and governor of the province" (1 Macc 10:65).[18] Since later Jewish works also use this metaphor, it seems clear that the notion of being seated at the right hand of God "would be richly meaningful to contemporary pagans and Jews."[19]

That the use of this metaphor in Ps 110:1 involves not only divine honor but also the conferring of worldly authority and power is made clear in v. 2a, which speaks of "sending out the mighty scepter" and either predicts or proposes earthly rule by the recipient of the oracle as well as victory

---

15. "In the Ugaritic Baal cycle it is recorded that Kothar wa-lasis is seated on a chair at the right hand of the god" (Booij, "Psalm cx," 396n2). An Egyptian pictorial reference shows "Pharaoh Horemheb . . . seated at the right hand of the king's god, Horus" (Keel, *Symbolism of the Biblical World*, 263, fig. 353). See also Hay, *Glory at the Right Hand*, 52–53.

16. Hay, *Glory at the Right Hand*, 53. While no human ruler would have been considered divine in Israel, in other cultural contexts, monarchial divinity may have been presumed (see, e.g., Kraus, *Theology of the Psalms*, 110–11, 113).

17. Only in 1 Kgs 2:19 is there mention that the honored person (the king's mother) is *seated*.

18. L. C. Allen, *Psalms 101–150*, 115, points to this passage as an example of the metaphor although it does not specifically mention the *right* hand. In pagan culture, a similar demonstration of giving honor and potential authority is found in "the pre-Islamic Arabian custom of seating the viceroy of a king at the latter's right (the viceroy took precedence over everyone but the king himself)" (Hay, *Glory at the Right Hand*, 53).

19. Hay, *Glory at the Right Hand*, 58. See Keener for Greek examples of being seated at the right hand as an honor in the Christian era (Keener, *Acts*, 1:948).

in battle. This figurative reference to the rule of the king is followed by a direct reference in the parallel colon (v. 2b).

The second metaphor in v. 1 is of making the enemies of the addressee of the oracle his "footstool." Here, too, "reflection of an ancient Near Eastern cultural pattern is evident: in the El Amarna letters vassals refer to themselves as the footstools of Pharaoh, while a similar promise features in an oracle from Marduk to the Assyrian king Esarhaddon."[20] This situation is also represented in Egyptian iconography. Othmar Keel reproduces two Egyptian illustrations dating to the fifteenth century BCE, each of which shows the figures or heads of nine enemies placed as (or in) a footstool under the feet of the pharaoh or future pharaoh.[21] In another drawing, nine bows, symbolizing the enemies' military capacity, are placed under a pair of feet.[22] The metaphor of serving as a footstool or being placed under the feet indicates total subjection. In the OT, the idea of enemies as/in a footstool is found only in Ps 110. However, the concept of enemies or subjects being placed or falling under the feet of a ruler, ruling nation, or Yahweh is found elsewhere, including 1 Kgs 5:3 and Pss 8:6, 45:5, and 47:3.[23]

Thijs Booij summarizes the symbolism in Ps 110:1-2: "The ruler sitting at YHWH's right hand (representing honour); the enemies laid down as a footstool (submission); the staff, or 'sceptre', stretched out from Zion (dominion)."[24] Taken together, the metaphors in vv. 1 and 2 indicate that a seat at the right hand of Yahweh is "a position of honor in the power structure of God" and that the one seated there "becomes a participant in Yahweh's strength in battle and victory" over that ruler's—and by extension Yahweh's—enemies.[25] There is no doubt, however, "that God is the real

---

20. L. C. Allen, *Psalms 101-150*, 115; cf. Booij, "Psalm cx," 396n3. In the Amarna letters, "the submissive city kings (as, e.g., Ammunira of Berytus) explain: 'A stool for your feet am I'" (Kraus, *Psalms 60-150*, 349).

21. Keel, *Symbolism of the Biblical World*, 253-56, especially figs. 341 and 342. "Nine" is thought to symbolize the totality.

22. Keel, *Symbolism of the Biblical World*, 255, fig. 342.

23. Cf. Booij, "Psalm cx," 396n3; Tournay, "Le Psaume cx," 7; and Clifford, *Psalms 73-150*, 179. These sources also refer to other OT texts, including Josh 10:24, Ps 18:39, and Isa 51:23, which describe submission at or by the feet of a victor or suzerain. The frequent use of this metaphor may explain why many NT quotations merge the language of Ps 8:6 with Ps 110:1. Indeed, "wherever in the NT Ps. 8:4-6 is quoted, it is interpreted in the light of Ps. 110:1" (Ellingworth, *Epistle to the Hebrews*, 151).

24. Booij, "Psalm cx," 397.

25. Kraus, *Psalms 60-150*, 348-49. Booij believes in v. 1 "it is only YHWH who acts" (Booij, "Psalm cx," 396). L. C. Allen also argues that Yahweh promises to vanquish the

PART II | CASE STUDIES

king. David rules not in his own right but as vicegerent and representative, deriving authority from his divine counterpart."[26] Kingship is both an honor and a gift from Yahweh.[27] Thus, "the ultimate goal of the king is to extend the reign of God. The defeat of enemies means the defeat of *evil* enemies in the pursuit of a positive final goal: the realization of the just and peaceful world that the Lord intends."[28] This understanding of the various metaphors helps us explore the illocution.

The Illocution of Ps 110:1 [109:1 LXX][29]

The first speech act is an Assertive which reports the speech of Yahweh.[30] The reported speech contains two embedded speech acts. The first is a Directive (Κάθου ἐκ δεξιῶν μου [1b LXX]),[31] and the second is a Commissive (θῶ τοὺς ἐχθρούς σου ὑποπόδιον τῶν ποδῶν σου [1c LXX]).[32] They are

---

enemies "while the king sat . . . serene and secure" (L. C. Allen, *Psalms 101–150*, 115; cf. Tharel, "Use of Psalm 110:1," 21). However, Booij and Allen agree that vv. 2 and 3 add a different note: In "v. 2 the sovereign is given a more active part. . . . The staff, being stretched forth by YHWH, is nevertheless in the hand of the ruler, who is surrounded by enemies and has to maintain his dominion forcibly" (Booij, "Psalm cx," 397; cf. L. C. Allen, *Psalms 101–150*, 115–16, concerning the role of the royal army).

26. L. C. Allen, *Psalms 101–150*, 115; cf. Keel, *Symbolism of the Biblical World*, 259. Clifford notes that "Davidic kingship was rooted in the kingship of Yahweh. . . . The king represents the god, extending the rule of his divine patron; his enemies are the enemies of the god" (Clifford, *Psalms 73–150*, 177).

27. See, e.g., Booij, "Psalm cx," 396.

28. Clifford, *Psalms 73–150*, 180. Rendtorff expands on this with a look at the co-text: "It is only God himself who gives the king the rule over his enemies and who will execute judgment among the nations (vv. 5–6)" (Rendtorff, "Psalms of David," 62).

29. For the role of Psalm 110 in its psalmic grouping, see B. C. Davis, "Is Psalm 110 a Messianic Psalm?," 168; Clifford, *Psalms 73–150*, 171; and Roth, *Die Grundparadigmen christlicher Schriftauslegung*, 19–32. Kim also considers the relationship of Ps 107 and Pss 111–118 to Pss 108–110 as well as the links between Pss 108, 109, and 110 (Kim, "Speaker and Addressee of Ps 110"). We cannot explore this here.

30. This is probably of the subclass of Ascriptive. See Bach and Harnish, *Linguistic Communication*, 42.

31. This Directive is probably of the subclass of Requestive (see Bach and Harnish, *Linguistic Communication*, 47). If it is considered instead to be of the subclass of Requirement (Bach and Harnish, 47), it would be at a low level of force (i.e., enjoin), since Yahweh is not ordering the hearer to accept power and authority.

32. This Commissive could be a Promise or an Offer. The difference is that "promises are acts of obligating oneself; offers are proposals to obligate oneself" (Bach and Harnish, *Linguistic Communication*, 50). If it is considered that in v. 1b Yahweh's obligation is

connected temporally (ἕως ἄν). Considering the embedded speech acts together gives the reason the Assertive in v. 1 is tellable: "My lord" is being granted honor and authority by Yahweh, along with the promise of victory over his enemies. These are particularly significant words from Yahweh for Yahweh's people, and thus this situation is to be broadly proclaimed and recorded for posterity.

Of the remaining four speech acts in the speech act complex, the second, fourth, and possibly the fifth (vv. 2a, 3a, 3b) are Assertives of the subclass of Predictives[33] which describe how the Commissive in v. 1c is to be fulfilled. The third speech act (v. 2b) is another Commissive, which either occurs contemporaneously with the fulfillment of the Commissive in the oracle or results from its fulfillment.[34]

Since the invitation to be seated at the right hand of Yahweh (the Directive) is the controlling metaphor, the speech act which contains it is the core speech act, and the other speech acts support or enhance its tellability. Here, tellability is enhanced if the Commissive in the embedded speech act complex in v. 1 is read with the Commissive in v. 4 (the immediately following co-text of our speech act complex) so that "forever" (εἰς τὸν αἰῶνα) applies to both. This would mean the Commissive in v. 1 would have no temporal limit, and thus Yahweh's promise to place the enemies of Israel's ruler "under his feet" would cover all subsequent rulers anointed by Yahweh.[35] The hope of the restoration of a Yahweh-anointed ruler would explain why this psalm was preserved in the editing of the Psalter long after the collapse of the Davidic dynasty when Israel had instead become the "footstool" of foreign rulers.[36]

---

unconditional, then this is a Promise. However, this speech act could be considered an Offer if the hearer's action of sitting is a condition for its acceptance. In this case, the expectation is that "my lord" considers this Offer desirable and will gladly and gratefully accept it.

33. For a description of this subclass, see Bach and Harnish, *Linguistic Communication*, 42. Due to the textual difficulties, we do not analyze v. 3 further.

34. Although καταχυρίευε is in the imperative mood, the classification by Waltke and O'Connor as a figure of heterosis seems correct since "with the imperative, heterosis creates a promise or prediction to be fulfilled in the future" (Waltke and O'Connor, *Introduction to Biblical Hebrew Syntax*, 572; see the NIV for this rendering).

35. Relying on "you are a priest forever" from the second oracle (v. 4), Booij claims that "Psalm cx is an assurance of everlasting dominion, made to a ruler on Zion" (Booij, "Psalm cx," 396).

36. "Although the Davidic kingship ceased with the exile," the royal psalms were "preserved in Israel's psalter probably because the Davidic covenant was eternal" (R. E. Watts,

In evaluating the illocution, we next identify the implied author and audience on two interrelated levels: (i) the speaker/issuer and hearer of the oracle and (ii) the reporting speaker/author and audience, i.e., the author and audience of the psalm.³⁷

The Hebrew text identifies the implied author/speaker of the oracle as Yahweh (Hebrew יהוה, translated in the LXX as ὁ κύριος and generally in English as "the Lord").³⁸ Using the socio-historical context of the psalm helps us identify the direct addressee of the oracle. In the Israelite socio-historical context, the invitation to be seated at the right hand of Yahweh would be issued to an earthly ruler—Yahweh's Anointed—upon whom honor and representative authority are being conferred.³⁹ Further, the psalm tells us the direct addressee has enemies, and Yahweh is promising defeat of those foes such that the oracle's recipient will rule in their midst (v. 2). There appears to be no doubt of Yahweh's ability to confer honor and vanquish enemies.⁴⁰

But who is this chosen one, the implied hearer of the oracle? Is it David, the Lord's anointed (as per Pss 18:50, 89:20); a literal "son" of David, e.g., Solomon; or a "messiah" anticipated by the psalmist who has not yet appeared to claim his throne?

Before we attempt to answer this question, we must clarify some terminology. By "messiah," we refer to someone anointed by Yahweh who brings about salvation of any kind, whether or not the term "messiah" is used to describe that person.⁴¹ If the messiah is to bring future salvation, we call that future "eschatological." This does not necessarily refer to the end-times or the end of time.⁴² Rather, "eschatological" can refer to what

---

"Psalms in Mark's Gospel," 27).

37. The NT authors create their own implied authors and audiences. We discuss this below.

38. This often is written as "the LORD." Verse 2 clarifies the speaker's identity since a viceroy's public foes would be the monarch's.

39. Because the oracle speaks of someone chosen, honored, and given authority by Yahweh and for whom Yahweh fights such that the defeat of his foes is assured, it can be considered "messianic" even though the term משיח (χριστός) is not used (see Möller, "Proclaiming the Reign of Christ," 163).

40. Admittedly, this is an argument from silence.

41. For this definition, see de Jonge, "The Use of the Word 'Anointed,'" 132.

42. Following M. F. Bird, we do not conflate messianic expectations and eschatological expectations (see M. F. Bird, *Are You the One?*, 34, 146). Thus we disagree with Juel that overall in the NT "eschatological convictions pervade everything: the prophetic dimensions of the Scriptures are central; the present is understood as the last days and as

Shemaryahu Talmon calls the "the *turn of times*, ... a profound crisis in history marked by tribulations of cosmic dimensions."[43]

To determine the identity of the implied hearer of the oracle, we look at the speech act complex as well as at the broader co-text. First, the direct addressee of the oracle is "my Lord" to the psalmist (v. 1a). Therefore, what we learn about the implied author of the psalm helps us identify the direct addressee of the oracle and vice versa. Another element is the superscription לדוד/Τῷ Δαυιδ. With this, it is clear "daβ der Psalm selbst in eine enge Verbindung mit David als dem israelitischen Idealkönig und legendären Dichter der Psalmen gebracht wird."[44] However, it is not clear how "David" relates to this psalm.[45]

---

a time of fulfilled promises (1 Corinthians 10:11; Acts 2; Matthew 1–2; Luke 1–2; etc.)" (Juel, *Messianic Exegesis*, 57).

43. Talmon, "Concept of *Māšîaḥ* and Messianism," 109. The turn of times is when "the Anointed will come, not at the *end of time*" (Talmon, 109). Thus, "the New Order to be established by the anointed is not otherworldly but rather the realization of a divine plan on earth, the consummation of history in history" (Talmon,112).

Beale offers several summary definitions of eschatology (Beale, *New Testament Biblical Theology*, 112–15), which he sees "not merely as the end of redemptive or cosmic history, or the goal of Israel's hopes, or the goal of the individual saint's hopes, but rather as an 'already-not yet new-creational reign in Christ'" (Beale, 177). This, in turn, refers to "the entire network of ideas that belong to renewal of the whole world, of Israel, and of the individual" (Beale, 178).

44. Roth, *Die Grundparadigmen christlicher Schriftauslegung*, 19. Although Roth points out that there are several options as to "wer mit David überhaupt gemeint ist" (Roth, 19), the superscription indicates Ps 110 takes a monarchical, pre-exilic perspective, and the majority opinion is that it "is a pre-exilic royal psalm, composed for a Davidic monarchy in Jerusalem" (Hay, *Glory at the Right Hand*, 19). Among scholars who "still advocate a post-exilic origin; the favorite theory ... has been one supposing the psalm a piece of Hasmonean propaganda" (Hay, 19). This theory is unlikely, since the Hasmoneans were not Davidides. We discuss this below. Witherington finds it implausible to date Ps 110 to the Maccabean period, "not least because it is found in early psalter collections such as the one at Qumran" (Witherington, *Gospel of Mark*, 131). For a discussion of the time frame of the psalm, see Bateman, "Psalm 110:1," 438–41; and Tharel, "Use of Psalm 110:1," chapter 2. See van der Meer for scholars who defend a pre-exilic context for Ps 110 generally or a Davidic context specifically (van der Meer, "Psalm 110," 227n55).

45. For ל in לדוד, CEV gives "by," and NETS gives "pertaining to." Day argues that "it is impossible to suppose that *ledawid* in these instances is anything but an ascription of authorship" (Day, *Psalms*, 115). However, Goldingay points out that "while *lē* can mean 'of,' it has many other meanings, mostly more common than 'of.' ... In an expression such as 'To the choirmaster. Of David' (Pss, 11 and 14 RSV), 'to' and 'of' both represent *lē*" (Goldingay, *Psalms 1–41*, 27). We do not assume that "of" is the only possible translation or that it denotes authorship.

One alternative is to take David as the direct addressee of the oracle. Then, since David is the psalmist's lord, the psalmist would be a court poet or prophet.[46] This ties into evidence in 1 Sam 24:11 and 2 Sam 15:21 which indicates "royal etiquette" would call for a court poet to address the king as his master or lord.[47] Against this has been raised the argument that David could not "rightly be called a 'priest forever after the order of Melchizedek'" (Ps 110:4).[48] But the "order of Melchizedek" is not the Levitical order. Willem van der Meer gives a number of examples from 2 Samuel and 1 Kings which demonstrate that "in the offices of David and Solomon, a priestly, mediatorial role is present. The king is able to function in this role because he is the head of a theocratic nation."[49] Although this would "not entail that the king becomes a priest in the ordinary sense of that word," the monarchical function of service to Yahweh is similar to the description of Melchizedek as both king of (Jeru)Salem and "priest of God Most High" (Gen 14:18).[50]

---

46. "On the basis of the two divine oracles of vv 1, 4, it is commonly held that it was uttered by a court prophet" (L. C. Allen, *Psalms 101–150*, 111; cf. Kim, "Speaker and Addressee of Ps 110," 16n52). Allen and Bateman both summarize which scholars advocate for the various proposed settings (see L. C. Allen, *Psalms 101–150*, 111–13; and Bateman, "Psalm 110:1," 442–43). A commonly suggested setting is a coronation ritual, but such proposals differ substantially as to the site and the era of the enthronement.

47. See L. C. Allen, *Psalms 101–150*, 115.

48. Aloisi, "Who is David's Lord?," 123.

49. Van der Meer, "Psalm 110," 229; cf. Hay, *Glory at the Right Hand*, 20.

50. Van der Meer, "Psalm 110," 229. On the one hand, this is *contra* Eaton, who believes Ps 110:4 "appoints the king to be God's priest for ever.... There are indications in the historical sources that the role was indeed held by David and his successors, though opposed and obscured in the records by priestly clans after the end of the monarchy" (Eaton, *Psalms*, 385). At the other end of the spectrum is de Fraine, for whom "ni à l'origine, ni dans son développement ultérieur, la royauté israélite n'a entraîné pour le souverain la qualité de prêtre; dès le début, les fonctions 'sacerdotales' étaient clairement distinctes des privilèges du roi-guerrier. Tout en n'étant nullement un 'fonctionnaire du culte', le roi peut être considéré comme investi d'un droit de surveillance concernant le culte" (de Fraine, "Peut-on parler d'un véritable sacerdoce du roi en Israël?," 546–47). However, although David is never identified as a priest, it seems likely that Attridge (referring to 1 Sam 6:12–21; 24:25; 1 Kgs 3:4; 8:1–5, 62; 12:33) is correct that "in the pre-exilic period the high priest was definitely subservient to the king, who could himself exercise priestly functions" (Attridge, *Epistle to the Hebrews*, 97; cf. Beale, *New Testament Biblical Theology*, 72; and Kraus, *Psalms 60–150*, 351). According to Beale, "Solomon is depicted more than any other king, except perhaps David, to be functioning like a priest" (Beale, *New Testament Biblical Theology*, 71).

Another alternative is to consider "of David" in the sense of "by David"—in other words, to hold David to be the (implied) author of the Psalm.⁵¹ But in that case, who is the original addressee of the oracle, that is, who is *David's* lord? The alternatives are either the king under whom David served (Saul) or one of David's heirs.

The psalm's second oracle excludes King Saul from consideration.⁵² Although Saul was promised—and received—victory over his enemies and ruled over Israel (1 Sam 9:15-16, 27; 14:47-48), he was not king in Jerusalem. Further, his downfall came about when he disobeyed Yahweh by *usurping* priestly duties (see 1 Sam 13:9-14). It is therefore unlikely that David would have referred to Saul as "a priest forever according to the order of Melchizedek" (v. 4).⁵³

If David is the psalmist, the other possibility for the hearer of the oracle is a future anointed king or royal "messiah" of Israel whom Yahweh addresses, most likely according to Yahweh's promise in 2 Sam 7:16. There are two options for a messianic interpretation. First, this messiah may be an anointed king of Israel of David's line.⁵⁴ Herbert Bateman argues that "the most viable option is that David spoke the psalm ... to Solomon when David freely handed over his kingship to Solomon (1 Kgs. 1:32-35, 43-45; 1 Chron. 28:1-8, 29:20-25)."⁵⁵ This identification is supported by Benaiah's prayer for Solomon's throne to be even greater than David's in response to David's request that Solomon be crowned king (see 1 Kgs 1:37, 47-48).⁵⁶ This

---

51. See Kim, "Speaker and Addressee of Ps 110," 15n53, for a summary of scholars who hold to this view.

52. Even after being anointed king, "David often referred to King Saul as either 'my lord' ([1 Sam] 24:6, 10; 26:18) or 'my lord the king' (24:8; 26:17, 19)," and "he also referred to Achish of the Philistines as 'my lord the king' (29:8)" (Bateman, "Psalm 110:1," 449). However, Bateman is surely correct to conclude that "neither of these men ... was the recipient of Psalm 110" (Bateman, 449).

53. As Balentine puts it, the addressee of the oracle is "the point of union between God and his people" as both king and priest (Balentine, "Royal Psalms," 57). This is not a description of King Saul.

54. Balentine concludes that "in Ps. 2, and throughout the royal psalms generally, Yahweh's 'anointed one' (*mašia*⊠) should be understood in terms of the earthly Davidic king" (Balentine, "Royal Psalms," 58). Similarly, R. E. Watts argues that "most modern scholars take the addressee to be either David or his royal descendants, possibly at enthronement" (R. E. Watts, "Psalms in Mark's Gospel," 36).

55. Bateman, *Early Jewish Hermeneutics*, 175.

56. Although David is never said to make such a prayer, even in his final charges to Solomon (1 Kgs 2:1-9) and to Israel concerning Solomon's rule (1 Chr 29:1, 19), this prayer is made in David's presence. David also does not refer to Solomon as "my Lord,"

prayer is answered; Yahweh exalts Solomon and bestows on him "such royal majesty as had not been on any king before him in Israel" (1 Chr 29:25).

For this messiah to be a "descendant" of David would not limit the office to Solomon since the Davidic monarchy has no temporal limit: David's house, kingdom, and throne are established forever (עד עולם twice in 2 Sam 7:16). As psalmist, David may consider the oracle addressed to his dynastic line and "prophesy" this.[57]

The second possibility is "that David addressed his messianic Lord, his divine Lord, in a directly prophetic manner," as Derek Kidner and others have argued.[58] But it seems unlikely that a psalm written from a pre-exilic perspective would have leaped history to directly prophesy an eschatological messiah,[59] much less a divine one. David was Yahweh's anointed (see,

---

and David is not listed as among those pledging submission to Solomon when Solomon is acknowledged as king (1 Chr 29:24). But Solomon appears to ascend the throne during David's lifetime (1 Chron 29:22b-24), and his royal splendor surpasses that of his father (1 Chr 29:25); his is the pinnacle of riches and honor (2 Chr 1:12). There is no reason that Waltke's claim that "in Psalm 110:1a David, using distinctively prophetic language, foresees a King greater than himself" could not apply to Solomon (Waltke, "Christ in the Psalms," 38). As Marcus points out, "the 'shoot of Jesse,' the ideal king descended from David in Isa 11:1-16, is not only a military conqueror but also a righteous judge filled with wisdom and understanding—qualities more usually associated with Solomon than with David" (Marcus, *Mark 8-16*, 1120).

57. In 11QPs^a 27:11 David is "considered a prophet who composed the psalms under divine inspiration"; before this, the Chronicler and Nehemiah both give "him the prophetic title 'the Man of God' (2 Chr 8:14; Neh 12:24, 36)" (Dimant, "Use and Interpretation of Mikra," 391n50; cf. Evans, "Praise and Prophecy," 552.

58. According to Kidner, "what is unique" to this psalm "is the royal speaker [David], addressing this more-than-royal person" (Kidner, *Psalms 73-150*, 392). He feels that since the NT presents Jesus as "not only greater than David (Acts 2:34 . . .) but greater than the angels (Heb. 1:13 . . .)," this verse must display "the divine Person of Christ" (Kidner, 393; cf. E. E. Johnson, "Hermeneutical Principles," 431). Others concur. Charlesworth believes the yearning of some Jews "for salvation from their pagan oppressors . . . centered on the future saving acts by a divinely appointed, and anointed, supernatural man: the Messiah" (Charlesworth, "From Messianology to Christology," 3-4). Rydelnik argues that "Psalm 110 does indeed picture the divine Priest-King, now seated at the right hand of God but who will descend from heaven at the end of days to save Israel and extend His rule over all the earth. This is none other than the Messiah" (Rydelnik, *Messianic Hope*, 184; cf. Slusser, "Function of Psalm 110," 14-15). Bateman calls this "the traditional view" (Bateman, "Psalm 110:1," 445, 445n34). See Rydelnik, *Messianic Hope*, 13-33, for a summary of how OT scholarship sees such "messianic prophecy."

59. Some, like Aloisi, find Ps 110 to be direct messianic prophecy (see Aloisi, "Who is David's Lord?," 123) without necessarily involving a divine messiah since "just how much David understood about the nature of the Messiah is difficult to determine" (Aloisi, 119n82). From a slightly different perspective, Roth speaks of "die Prophetie, die nicht

e.g., 1 Sam 16:3, 2 Sam 2:4, Ps 89:20). The Israelites knew others had been anointed previously (e.g., King Saul and various priests) and, based on Yahweh's promises, would have expected David's heirs would be anointed after him.[60]

Linguistic evidence also argues against seeing the oracle as prophecy of a divine messiah. According to Bateman:

> The form "to my lord" (לַאדֹנִי) is never used elsewhere in the Old Testament as a divine reference. Also, none of the 138 forms of "my lord" (אֲדֹנִי) and none of the nine other prefixed forms of "my lord" (מֵאדֹנִי, בַּאדֹנִי, וַאדֹנִי) is a divine reference. . . . Furthermore, when "my lord" (אֲדֹנִי) and 'Lord' (יְהוָה) are used in the same sentence, as in Psalm 110:1, "my lord" (אֲדֹנִי) always refers to an earthly lord.[61]

We agree with Allen that although "one respects the worthy motives of those who seek to restrict the psalm to a messianic intent from the beginning, . . . it hardly accords with the pattern of historical and theological development discernible in the royal psalms in general and with the ancient

---

das Kommen eines Messias, sondern die Ankunft der endzeitlichen Herrschaft Gottes verheißt" (Roth, *Die Grundparadigmen christlicher Schriftauslegung*, 26). We do not find these arguments compelling. However, after the Davidic dynasty appeared to end, it seems likely the psalm was interpreted "eschatologically" in the sense of an expectation of the coming of the turn of times.

60. As did happen (1 Kgs 1:39). As Roberts points out, these "were not prophecies holding out hope for a distant future but oracles that gave expression to political, social, and religious expectations for the reign of a contemporary king just being installed into office" (Roberts, "The Old Testament's Contribution," 42). Here we disagree with J. J. Collins. Although Collins admits that in the OT the term "messiah" does not necessarily refer to an eschatological figure, he applies it only to "a figure who will play an authoritative role in the end time, usually the eschatological king" (J. J. Collins, *Scepter and Star*, 16), and he defines "messianism" as "the expectation of a figure who will act as God's designated agent in the eschatological time" (J. J. Collins, "Messianism and Exegetical Tradition," 129).

61. Bateman, "Psalm 110:1," 448, adding that 94 percent of the 168 forms "refer to earthly lords. The exceptions are when Joshua, Gideon, Daniel, and Zechariah addressed an angelic being as 'my lord'" (Bateman, 448). Aloisi rightly notes that B. C. Davis's claim that the "angelic being" addressed as אדני in Judg 6:13 and Josh 5:14 is later identified as Yahweh does not disprove Bateman's argument. B. C. Davis "has not proven that the OT contains a clear text in which a person knowingly addresses Yahweh as אֲדֹנִי" (Aloisi, "Who is David's Lord?," 118, referring to B. C. Davis, "Is Psalm 110 a Messianic Psalm?," 164). Although Aloisi believes "even if Bateman's distinction holds up, David could very well have used the term אֲדֹנִי with reference to the Messiah" (Aloisi, "Who is David's Lord?," 119), the question remains as to why David would ignore his immediate descendants to prophesy only an eschatological Messiah.

cultural and historical royal references within Ps 110."[62] All in all, the most probable explanation is that a court prophet composed Ps 110 about or "for" David—perhaps "to celebrate David's earlier conquest of Jerusalem and succession to Jebusite kingship (cf. 2 Sam 12:30)."[63] However, it is likely that, beginning with Solomon's coronation, the psalm was used "by succeeding kings in a context of national enthronement and also in any other cultic settings in which the king's relation to Yahweh was celebrated."[64] "Like the other royal psalms, Ps 110 became in the postexilic canonical Psalter a witness to the restoration of the dynasty, guaranteed by God's 'forever,' and so a witness to Israel's messianic hope."[65] This explains its attribution to David in the Synoptic Gospels and in Acts 2.[66]

In any event, in all these cases, the use in the psalm of the metaphors of sitting at the right hand and enemies as a footstool indicates that honor and authority/power have been or are to be conferred on a recipient who will rule over Yahweh's people and whose enemies will be vanquished with Yahweh's help. The implied audience, no matter what the situational particulars, understands these aspects of the illocution. The implied audience also knows who Yahweh is, what Yahweh's nature is like, and what Yahweh can do. More specifically, the implied reader understands that Yahweh has promised to anoint a ruler for Israel whose enemies will be defeated and

---

62. L. C. Allen, *Psalms 101–150*, 113. For Cordes, "gut möglich ist es, dass sich auch der Übersetzer unter dem von JHWH gezeugten χύριος einen Messias vorgestellt hat. Aber eine dahingehende interpretatorische Tendenz im Sinne einer bewussten theologischen Exegese des Vorlagentextes lässt sich aus dem Text von Ps 109 LXX selbst nicht ablesen" (Cordes, "Spricht Ps 109 LXX von einem Messias?," 260).

63. L. C. Allen, *Psalms 101–150*, 113. See also Goldingay, *Psalms 90–150*, 291.

64. L. C. Allen, *Psalms 101–150*, 113, adding that "the divine oracles of vv 1 and 4 certainly appear to belong to such a context [enthronement], but the psalm as a whole may not intend to issue them but to simply echo them (cf. 2 Sam 3:18; 5:2)."

65. L. C. Allen, *Psalms 101–150*, 118. Kim believes Ps 110 has become an "eschatological psalm in its final form in the context of the psalter" (Kim, "Speaker and Addressee of Ps 110," 15; see also 18n60).

66. Kim points out that "the Synoptic Gospels and Acts clearly describe David as the speaker in Ps 110 (Mark 12:36; Matt 22:43-44; Luke 20:42-44; Acts 2:34-35)" (Kim, "Speaker and Addressee of Ps 110," 17). It is also possible David preserved for posterity something originally spoken about him (see, e.g., Bateman "Psalm 110:1," 445, 443n27). Bock offers another alternative: "Could it reflect that the prophet was regarded as acting as David's mouthpiece in declaring the authority of the king as his successor into his covenant? . . . David would be seen as the real speaker in the cultic context in the hope that this king will fulfil the Davidic covenant" (Bock, *Proclamation from Prophecy and Pattern*, 129).

will become subject to his rule. Ps 110:1 speaks to the protection, assistance, and deliverance which Yahweh provides; the implied audience expects that as a result of the work of Yahweh, "my lord" will come to rule over his foes.[67]

In order to read as an Analyst (a reader who understands the illocutionary act), empirical readers must either activate these aspects of mutual context or add this Story-line to the mutual context they share with the implied author. We wrap up our discussion of Ps 110:1 with an evaluation of the impact on lifeworld, worldview, and theology of reading the OT speech act complex as an Envisager.

The Perlocution of Ps 110:1 [109:1 LXX]

The embedded oracle contains a Directive and a Commissive illocutionary act. For a Commissive illocutionary act, the related perlocution is "that H believe S intends to fulfil his obligation to do A."[68] With regard to the Commissive in the oracle, the intended perlocutionary effect/response is that the listeners believe Yahweh has the capacity and the intention to give the direct addressee dominion over his enemies. For a Directive illocutionary act, the intended perlocution is "that H (intend to) do A."[69] Here, the intended perlocutionary effect is that the direct addressee accept the honor and anointing Yahweh offers.

Within the psalm, v. 1 is an Assertive illocutionary act, for which the related perlocution is "that H believe that P."[70] The psalmist's audience is called to believe that this report is true, i.e., that Yahweh has offered the addressee of the oracle honor, authority, and power to rule and that Yahweh can and will place the enemies of that ruler in subjection. The remaining speech acts of this speech act complex describe how this is to come about (v. 2a) and the ultimate result (v. 2b).

By the time of the NT, when the Davidic dynasty had not ruled Israel in centuries, an Envisaging reader of the Psalm takes a position of trust that the promises of the oracle continue past their fulfillment in David and his pre-exilic heirs. An Envisaging reader looks to the future and "forever" fulfillment of these promises. Depending on the situation of each empirical

---

67. According to van der Meer, שׁב לימיני emphasizes that v. 1 speaks to "the protection which God provides" (van der Meer, "Psalm 110," 224).
68. Bach and Harnish, *Linguistic Communication*, 81.
69. Bach and Harnish, *Linguistic Communication*, 81.
70. Bach and Harnish, *Linguistic Communication*, 81.

PART II | CASE STUDIES

hearer/reader, to respond with the intended perlocutionary effect (the response of the implied reader), an Envisaging reader must transform (realign or subvert/re-create) their understanding of Yahweh and these promises. This transformation of the Envisager's belief system—and the actions that flow from it—is linked to Story, lifeworld/worldview, and theology.

A SUMMARY OF THE CONTRIBUTION OF PS 110:1 TO STORY, LIFEWORLD, AND THEOLOGY

In terms of the basic theological questions and the role of this speech act complex in Story, Ps 110 speaks to the question of how Yahweh relates to the world, and, in particular, the role of the monarch in relationship to Yahweh as well as to the world. The speech acts later quoted contribute to Story the information that Yahweh has made temporally unlimited promises regarding the honor and authority to be given to a ruler of Yahweh's people and that Yahweh will place that ruler's (and by extension, the people's) enemies in submission. The Envisaging reader expects that Yahweh will fulfill these promises, and the lifeworld and worldview of such a reader incorporates these Story-lines.

POST-EXILIC INTERPRETATION OF PS 110

Although there is no evidence to support the claim of those who believe Ps 110:1 was direct messianic prophecy from its inception, it is possible that it was interpreted that way once the Davidic succession had collapsed.[71] But there is scant evidence for intervening interpretations of Ps 110 and even less evidence of any interpretation involving an eschatological messiah.[72]

---

71. Balentine believes that "by the time of Jesus it is likely that Psalm 2 and probably Psalm 110 had already come to be understood as messianic, that is as pointing to the king who would come in the future to rule as Yahweh's anointed son" (Balentine, "Royal Psalms," 61; cf. Marcus, *Mark 8–16*, 846; and Marcus, *Way of the Lord*, 132–37). For Hengel, "Ps 8 und 110, schon in Jerusalem von der Urgemeinde als 'messianische Hymnen' gesungen wurden, wobei sie sich gegenseitig interpretierten und zugleich einen entscheidenden Einfluß auf die Entstehung der frühen Christologie ausübten" (Hengel, "'Setze dich zu meiner Rechten!,'" 146).

72. Messianic references to Ps 110 have been seen in the OT books of Daniel and Zechariah. For the idea that Dan 7 refers to Ps 110:1, see Hay, *Glory at the Right Hand*, 26; Rydelnik *Messianic Hope*, 182; and R. E. Watts, "Psalms in Mark's Gospel," 38. Rydelnik believes that both the book of Daniel and the book of Zechariah provide "a clear

PS 110:1 AS QUOTED BY VARIOUS NT AUTHORS

Perhaps the most telling absence is that no part of Ps 110 is found in any form among the Dead Sea Scrolls.[73] Overall, we concur with Hans-Joachim Kraus that "no messianic interpretation of Psalm 110 in Jewish circles can

---

messianic hope by relying on the words and images contained in Ps 110. Plainly, these later writers understood Ps 110 to refer to the Messiah of Israel" (Rydelnik, *Messianic Hope*, 183). But we do not find any of these arguments compelling. Rather, we would agree with J. J. Collins that the Son of Man in Daniel "is not a Davidic messiah in any conventional sense" (J. J. Collins, *Scepter and Star*, 205).

Hay and others have found messianic references to Ps 110 in 1 Maccabees, the Similitudes of Enoch (1 Enoch 37–71), Testament of Job, Assumption of Moses, Jubilees, Testament of Levi, 11QMelchizedek, the writings of Rabbi Akiba, and also in later Jewish witnesses. For these arguments, see Hay, *Glory at the Right Hand*, 22–33. For arguments concerning the interpretation of Ps 110 in 1 Enoch 37–71, see also M. F. Bird, *Are You the One?*, 93–94. For Testament of Job, see also Keener, *Acts*, 1:961; and Bateman, *Early Jewish Hermeneutics*, 181. For 11QMelchizedek, see also Witherington, *Gospel of Mark*, 333; Bateman, *Early Jewish Hermeneutics*, 181; VanderKam, *Dead Sea Scrolls and the Bible*, 47; and Eskola, *Messiah and the Throne*, 130. For counter-arguments concerning the possible use in 1 Maccabees, see Tharel, "Use of Psalm 110:1," 29, 29n20; de Lang, "Psalm 110," 43, 43n1; and Roth, *Die Grundparadigmen christlicher Schriftauslegung*, 51. For counter-arguments concerning the possible use in 1 Enoch, see Longenecker, *Biblical Exegesis*, 157n50. For counter-arguments concerning Testament of Job, see Hengel, "'Setze dich zu meiner Rechten!,'" 180; and Evans, *Ancient Texts*, 42. For counter-arguments concerning Testament of Levi, see de Jonge, *Jewish Eschatology*, 234; and Knibb, "Septuagint and Messianism," 13. Concerning 11QMelchizedek, Hay admits that it "never plainly alludes to either the psalm or Gen 14.18–20" (Hay, *Glory at the Right Hand*, 27).

In general, Jobes and Silva have pointed out that "in the study of the history of the messianic idea, one must be able to identify texts that were understood in this way by the Jews before the time of Jesus. This is not always easy or straightforward to do, because most of the extant manuscripts have been preserved by the Christian tradition" (Jobes and Silva, *Invitation to the Septuagint*, 300; cf. Evans, "Prophecy and Polemic," 189n75; and Heard, "New Testament Background," 24). With regard to the rabbis, Rese believes that a messianic interpretation of Ps 110:1 cannot be proven before AD 260 (Rese, *Alttestamentliche Motive*, 62n84). Attridge concludes correctly that, in general, "in Jewish tradition attestations of a messianic interpretation of the text [Ps 110 (109):1] are weak" (Attridge, *Epistle to the Hebrews*, 61). We do not find any interpretive traditions of Ps 110 that are clearly pre-Christian.

73. According to Flint, Ps 110 is one of twenty-four canonical psalms "missing" from the forty Psalms scrolls and related manuscripts (such as the pesharim) found among the Dead Sea Scrolls (Flint, "Psalms and Psalters," 234; cf. Kraus, *Theology of the Psalms*, 186; and Hay, *Glory at the Right Hand*, 27). Flint believes the missing psalms were originally included but "are now lost due to the fragmentary state of most of the scrolls" (Flint, *Dead Sea Psalms Scrolls*, 48). Flint restores "Ps 110 after 109, mainly on the basis of its Davidic superscription" since "computerized reconstruction shows the sequence 109–110 followed by 113–118 in cols. iv–vi [of 11QPs^a] to be very plausible on the basis of spacing" (Flint, 191).

be documented."⁷⁴ However, absent any consideration of Ps 110, there were messianic expectations in Judaism at the turn of the millennium. Since this issue is important to our analysis of the NT use of Ps 110:1, we examine it briefly below.⁷⁵

MESSIANIC EXPECTATIONS IN THE FIRST CENTURY

Interest in messianism remained "virtually dormant from the early fifth to the late second century BCE."⁷⁶ Messianic expectation experienced a resurgence in the first century BCE,⁷⁷ although it was far from uniform.⁷⁸ One prominent source for the expectation of a Davidic messiah is Pss. Sol. 17 and 18, two of a collection of eighteen psalms critical of the Hasmonean rulers.⁷⁹ In the introduction to his critical edition of the Greek text,

---

74. Kraus, *Theology of the Psalms*, 186. Hay attributes to Strack and Billerbeck the unsupportable conclusion that "messianic interpretation was the norm for rabbis of the first century" (Hay, *Glory at the Right Hand*, 29); Aune relies on Hay to make a similar argument (Aune, "Christian Prophecy," 409). But Hay himself claims only that "it seems fair to suppose that in the NT era a messianic interpretation of Ps 110 was current in Judaism, although we cannot know how widely it was accepted" and that "Jews shortly before and during the period of Christian origins applied the psalm variously, sometimes to a future messiah, sometimes to the heavenly vindication of a righteous sufferer (T Job), perhaps sometimes to a reigning Hasmonean king or supernatural being (the son of man, the heavenly Melchizedek)" (Hay, *Glory at the Right Hand*, 30, 161).

75. For a helpful list of some of the studies of messianism in the intertestamental period and Second Temple Judaism, see M. F. Bird, *Are You the One?*, 31n1.

76. J. J. Collins, *Scepter and Star*, 51. See also J. J. Collins, "Messianism and Exegetical Tradition," 133; and Oegema, "Messianic Expectations," 56. Knibb adds that "the Apocrypha and Pseudepigrapha and the Scrolls provide strong evidence for messianic belief in the first century before the Common Era, but much less substantial evidence for such belief in the preceding period" (Knibb, "Septuagint and Messianism," 15).

77. Charlesworth credits the resurgence to "the degeneration in the Hasmonean dynasty and the claim of the final ruling Hasmoneans, especially Alexander Jannaeus, to be 'the king,' and . . . the loss of the land promised as Israel's inheritance to the gentile and idolatrous nation Rome" (Charlesworth, "From Messianology to Christology," 35; cf. Oegema, "Messianic Expectations," 56). Similarly, Broer believes "dürfte dann durch den Zusammenbruch der Hasmonäerdynastie . . . die Hoffnung auf Erneuerung der Davidsdynastie bestärkt worden sein" (Broer, "Versuch zur Christologie," 1255).

78. For Keener, "there was no single interpretation of messiahship in the first century, but at the heart of most messianic expectation was an ultimate Davidic ruler associated with the eschatological restoration of Israel" (Keener, *Acts*, 1:964).

79. "For the period before the Common Era, Psalms of Solomon 17 and 18, from

Robert Wright calls Ps. Sol. 17 "an extended messianic hymn describing the anticipated victory and reign of the expected redeeming king, the anointed Son of David."[80] The king, the Lord Messiah (or Lord's Messiah, Ps. Sol. 17:32),[81] "is to lead the pious in a rebellion against the occupying forces, in the expulsion of foreign influences, and in the displacement of the corrupt administrations of state and temple. He is to establish an independent and holy Jewish theocratic state to which foreign nations would be subordinate."[82] To accomplish this victory, Yahweh will undergird the Davidic king with strength (Ps. Sol. 17:22), and the king will continue to rely on Yahweh during his reign (Ps. Sol. 17:33–34, 37–39). As with Ps 110, in the Psalms of Solomon, the authority of the human king is derivative,

---

the middle of the first century, provide the main evidence in the Pseudepigrapha for the belief in a Davidic messiah" (Knibb, "Septuagint and Messianism," 11). J. J. Collins believes that although the Psalms of Solomon were written about fifteen years after the end of the Hasmonean dynasty, the psalmist remembered Hasmonean rule vividly and judged it illegitimate in part because the later Hasmoneans usurped the Davidic throne (J. J. Collins, *Scepter and Star*, 56). For the dating of the Psalms of Solomon, see R. B. Wright, "Introduction," 6–7; and Evans, *Ancient Texts*, 58.

80. R. B. Wright, "Introduction," 1. Charlesworth considers the Psalms of Solomon (along with the Similitudes of Enoch) to be "the earliest explicit use of the *terminus technicus*—'*Messiah*' or 'Christ'" (Charlesworth, "From Messianology to Christology," 24; see Charlesworth, "Messianology in the Biblical Pseudepigrapha," 40, for his argument that "*1 Enoch* 37–71 antedates the Palestinian Jesus Movement"). In addition, Ps. Sol. 17:23 explicitly states the Messiah is to be the "son of David," which, according to Witherington, is the first known use of this precise phrase (Witherington, *Gospel of Mark*, 331). Thus, Davies's idea that Pss. Sol. 17 and 18 may already present "the term Son of David as a standard messianic title" (Davies, "Jewish Sources," 500) outstrips the available evidence. By the time of the NT writings, however, "the Anointed One or Messiah = *Christos* is the expected eschatological king from the line of David" (Marcus, *Mark 8–16*, 1105; cf. J. J. Collins, *Scepter and Star*, 52).

81. The choice between these readings is not material to our analysis (cf. R. B. Wright, "Introduction," 48–49; Keener, *Acts*, 1:960; and the Rahlfs-Hanhart LXX).

82. R. B. Wright, "Introduction," 1. As Broer points out, "der irdische Charakter dieses Königstums ist schließlich auch in dem Stück aus PsSal 17, das ja vom Davidssohn und Messias spricht, deutlich" (Broer, "Versuch zur Christologie," 1255; cf. Stein, *Mark*, 213). Although de Jonge agrees the king expected in Ps. Sol. 17 "is a national figure using political means and even military power," he finds him "not a typical warrior-king, striving for the mastery of the world; the deliverance of Israel is only a means towards a greater goal, the triumph of God's righteousness and power as manifested in His Torah, which will then be obeyed by Israel and by the nations" (de Jonge, "Use of the Word 'Anointed,'" 136).

PART II | CASE STUDIES

that is, "the king-Messiah rules in the messianic kingdom, with authority and power given him by God."[83] It is Yahweh who is the true king.[84]

Not all messianic expectations involved a ruler or only a ruler. "The Hebrew word משיח ... means simply 'anointed'. While it refers to a royal figure some thirty times in the Hebrew Bible, it can also refer to other figures, most notably the anointed High Priest."[85] The expectation of a coming leadership pair—king and high priest—is reflected in Zechariah 4:14 and in some Qumran documents.[86]

Although not every Qumran document that speaks of a messianic ruler refers specifically to Davidic descent,[87] a number of Qumran documents do speak of a Davidic "messiah" or "anointed" one. 4QPBlessing 1:34 (4QpGen=4Q252–254a) appears to speak of the coming of "the Messiah of righteousness, the Shoot of David" to whom and to whose seed "has been

---

83. Chester, "Jewish Messianic Expectations," 28. Keener does not provide any support for his theory that "the *Psalms of Solomon* ... probably is interpreting Ps 110:1, since the pseudepigraphic psalm goes on to identify the Messiah's king as the 'Lord himself' (κύριος αὐτός, 17:46)" (Keener, *Acts*, 1:960).

84. Charlesworth points out that in the Psalms of Solomon, it is not the Messiah, but God, who "is clearly the actor" and that Ps. Sol. 17 "is close to the Old Testament emphasis that God is King" (Charlesworth, "Messianology in the Biblical Pseudepigrapha," 31).

85. J. J. Collins, *Scepter and Star*, 16. Starcky finds that, after the Exile, "on considéra que toute mission divine supposait une onction" (Starcky, "Les quatre étapes du messianism," 481).

86. "The prominence of the priesthood was more enduring than that of the Davidic line in the Second Temple period. . . . For most of the postexilic period, with exceptions in the times of Ezra and Nehemiah, the High Priest was sole leader in Judah" (J. J. Collins, *Scepter and Star*, 36). But that does not mean Horsley is correct that "there was little interest in a Messiah, Davidic or otherwise, . . . in the diverse Palestinian Jewish literature of late Second Temple times" (Horsley, "'Messianic' Figures and Movements," 295). Rather, "by the second century B.C. the idea of an ideal king who would come as 'anointed prince' (Dan. 9:25) began to lay the foundation for the messianic expectations which would emerge full blown in the New Testament" (Balentine, "Royal Psalms," 61).

87. For example, in the two-Messiah scheme of 1QS (Rule of the Community), the "Messiah of Israel is nowhere said to be Davidic" (Schiffman, "Messianic Figures and Ideas," 20). Furthermore, in both 1QS and 1QSa (Rule of the Congregation), "the priest is the more important" of the two messiahs (de Jonge, "Use of the Word 'Anointed,'" 138). With regard to 4QAhA (=4Q451), Starcky concurs: "Pour notre auteur comme pour celui de la *Règle de la Congrégation*, le messie d'Aaron sera le messie principal" (Starcky, "Les quatre étapes du messianism," 492). "The division between priestly and political functions and their allotment to two figures may have been a critical reaction to the uniting of the Highpriesthood and the Kingdom by the Hasmonaeans" (Lichtenberger, "Messianic Expectations," 13).

given the Covenant of Kingship over his people for eternal generations."[88] A clearer reference is found in 4QFlor (4Q174), where the single messiah is a Davidic king.[89] Other texts which use metaphors such as "shoot," "branch," or "horn" of David to refer to a Davidic messiah include 4QpIsa[a] (4Q161),[90] which is a commentary or *pesher*, and the Rule of War (4Q285). Overall, Mark Strauss believes the "various Cave 4 documents suggest an *increase in royal-Davidic expectation* in the sect's later years (*c.* 4 BC to AD 68)."[91]

James Dunn helpfully puts most of this (and more) together, averring that the hoped-for Davidic or royal messiah is

> so designated explicitly in the Psalms of Solomon 17 (see esp. 17:32; cf. 18:57), and *Shemoneh 'Esreh* 14, and almost certainly

88. See Chester, "Jewish Messianic Expectations," 23. Evans translates "Shoot" as "Branch" (Evans, *Ancient Texts*, 106). Bateman links the "'covenant of royalty' in 4QpGen[a] and 'covenant of kings' in Sirach 47:11" since both "emphasize the dynastic permanence of Yahweh's covenant with David" (Bateman, *Early Jewish Hermeneutics*, 161). However, Charlesworth refers to 4QPBlessing as an "obscure reference" (Charlesworth, "From Messianology to Christology," 25).

89. See Charlesworth, "From Messianology to Christology," 26. According to Chester, 4QFlor 11 refers to the future salvific work of the "Shoot of David" (Chester, "Jewish Messianic Expectations," 23; cf. Schiffman, "Messianic Figures and Ideas," 125), and Bateman argues that 4QFlor "applies 2 Samuel to a Davidic heir yet to come" (Bateman, *Early Jewish Hermeneutics*, 159). Since "the common rabbinic epithet, 'son of David,' has not been found at Qumran," Abegg and Evans find that "only the reference in 4Q174 is indisputably messianic. In this passage not only is the 'son' of 2 Sam 7:14 identified as the 'Branch of David,' this figure is understood to be the fulfillment of the prophecy of Amos 9:11 (cf. 4Q174 1-3 i 12)" (Abegg and Evans, "Messianic Passages," 199; cf. Witherington, *Gospel of Mark*, 331).

90. According to Eskola, "In 4Q161 Isa 11:1-5 is quoted, followed by an interpretation. The idea of a throne is introduced when the power of the Davidic Messiah is described (Frags. 8-10, col. III, 18-21, Vermes): "[Interpreted, this concerns the Branch] of David who shall arise at the end [of days]. . . . God will uphold him with [the spirit of might, and will give him] a throne of glory and a crown of [holiness]. . . . [He will put a sceptre] in his hand and he shall rule over all the [nations]" (Eskola, *Messiah and the Throne*, 85; see also 132, 342). Evans believes "the interpretation of Isa 10:34—11:5 in 4Q161 frgs. 7-10 iii coheres with the prophecy of 4Q285, in which the Messiah is expected to defeat Rome" (Evans, *Ancient Texts*, 147). However, Charlesworth accurately calls the "reference to the Branch of David which shall arise at the end of days" in 4Q161 "frustratingly brief" (Charlesworth, "From Messianology to Christology," 25).

91. Strauss, *Davidic Messiah in Luke-Acts*, 43. Charlesworth's conclusion that "statistically we must admit that messianology was not a major concern of this [Qumran] community, at least not in its early history" (Charlesworth, "From Messianology to Christology," 25), is based only on the number of times the noun "Messiah" is used and overlooks the metaphoric references of the Cave 4 documents. For a list of messianic terms (some disputed), see Evans, "Are the 'Son' Texts at Qumran 'Messianic'?," 135-36.

in view in the DSS's designation of the "messiah of Israel" (1QSa 2.12, 14, 20; also 1QS 9.11; cf. CD 12.23f.; 14.19; 19.10; 20.1). This more specific language is clearly part of a richer strain influenced both by other "messiah" references with eschatological overtones (1Sam 2:10; Pss 2:2, 89:51, 132:17; Dan 9:25–26); and by specific promises regarding the Davidic dynasty—David's son/God's son (2Sam 7:12–4; 4QFlor 1.10–13), the royal "branch" (Jer 23:5 and 33:15; 4QPat 3–4 and 4QFlor 1.11), and the Davidic "prince" (Ezek 34:24 and 37:25; CD 7.20, 1QSb 5.20, 1QM 5.1, 4Q161); see also Isa 11:1–2; Hag 2:23; Zech 3:8, 4, 6:12; Sir 47:11, 22; 1Mac 2:57. We may conclude that these passages must have nurtured a fairly vigorous and sustained hope of a royal messiah within several at least of the various subgroups of Israel at the time of Jesus, and that that hope was probably fairly widespread at a popular level (such being the symbolic power of kingship in most societies then and since).[92]

John Collins sums this up well: The Messiah "is presumably a human figure, although he is endowed with the spirit of the Lord. He is expected to re-establish a dynasty, rather than rule forever himself.... But the most basic and widespread expectation in this period was for a royal, Davidic, messiah, who would restore the kingdom of Israel!"[93]

Nowhere in Dunn's comprehensive summary of messianic texts is there mention of Ps 110.[94] Ps 110 did not meet the needs or expectations of any pre-Christian Jewish group. The Hasmoneans, who had ancestral priestly prerogatives and non-Davidic kingly pretensions, would have shied away from Ps 110 because of its ties to David. Jewish groups who rejected Hasmonean kingship would have avoided a text that suggested the kingship and priesthood might be combined in one individual. One such group would have been the Qumran community, for whom the psalm's heralding of one individual as both king and Melchizedekian priest would not

---

92. Dunn, "Messianic Ideas," 367. Dunn's reference is to a royal, not a *divine*, messiah. See also Bateman, who believes "the conceptual sense of Yahweh's covenant to David as a perpetual covenant for David's descendants is clearly observed in early Jewish literature (4QFlor 1:1–13; 4QpGen[a] 5:1–7; Sir. 47:11, 22; *Pss. Sol.* 17:4, 21)" (Bateman, *Early Jewish Hermeneutics,* 163; see also 203). For J. J. Collins, "the Dead Sea Scrolls provide evidence of the messianic interpretation of several biblical texts which were also taken as messianic prophecies in other strands of Judaism" (J. J. Collins, "Messianism and Exegetical Tradition," 132). Examples are Isa 11:1–5, Num 24, Gen 49, and 2 Sam 7.

93. J. J. Collins, "Messianism and Exegetical Tradition," 132.

94. Neither is Ps 110 included in M. F. Bird's compilation of "Old Testament Texts and Messianic Interpretations" (see M. F. Bird, *Are You the One?*, 47).

have been compatible with the "Two Messiah" scheme.[95] Additionally, the availability of Ps 2 to support renewed interest in the coming of a Davidic messiah may have minimized interest in Ps 110 in the first century BCE.[96] Thus, although it may be true that "there is nothing in the psalm which . . . Jews could not have predicated of the messiah,"[97] there is no evidence that any group did so. To draw conclusions about a messianic interpretation of Ps 110 in first-century Judaism is at best speculative.

Our next step is to determine what of the Story to which Ps 110 contributes is mediated by the implied NT speakers and authors to their implied audiences. Because the NT speakers/authors themselves may contribute to the interpretive history of Ps 110:1, we present the NT quotations of this verse in roughly the order of their occurrence.[98] Chronologically, the first speaker is Jesus.

---

95. For R. E. Watts, "it might be these two factors—sitting at God's right hand and the Melchizedekian priest-king connection—that explain the relative absence of this text in intertestamental literature" (R. E. Watts, "Psalms in Mark's Gospel," 37).

96. Hay believes "Christians of the earliest period neglected it [Ps 110] . . . because they knew that its meaning (and form) were disputed and because they could find other scriptural texts to support ideas of Jesus's divine sonship (notably Ps 2.7; 2 Sam 7.14)" (Hay, *Glory at the Right Hand*, 22).

97. Hay, *Glory at the Right Hand*, 30. Similarly, although Aloisi is correct that "nothing in the text of the psalm prohibits identifying this king-priest as the Messiah" (Aloisi, "Who is David's Lord?," 122), no evidence indicates the king-priest was so identified. Aloisi's contention that "a directly messianic interpretation of Psalm 110:1 seems the most viable position" (Aloisi, 122) is based on the fact that Jesus and the NT authors take the psalm as messianic. But, given the paucity of evidence concerning any pre-Christian use of Ps 110, we believe Jesus may have been the first to highlight a messianic interpretation of the Psalm. See pp. 197–205 below for further discussion.

98. We assume the Stories of Jesus and of the Church's founding at Pentecost were transmitted orally before being committed to writing in the Synoptic Gospels and Acts, respectively, and thus formed part of the mutual context of other NT authors. See R. B. Hays for the idea that although Paul is the first to document a christological reading of Ps 110:1 (in 1 Cor 15:25–27), it is likely "he is appealing to an already established tradition" (R. B. Hays, *Echoes of Scripture*, 84).

PART II | CASE STUDIES

PS 110:1 AS QUOTED BY JESUS AND REPORTED IN THE SYNOPTIC GOSPELS[99]

As reported in Matt 22:44, Mark 12:36 and Luke 20:42–43, Jesus quoted the entirety of Ps 110:1 as part of a teaching exchange.[100]

The Locution

We show NA[27] and the NRSV translation of the speech act complexes from each Synoptic Gospel in parallel columns in Appendix §4.[101] In Luke, the speech act complex is composed of three speech acts: (i) Jesus's opening question concerning what the scribes say about the identity of the Messiah, (ii) the quotation of Ps 110:1, and (iii) Jesus's final question concerning the identity of the Messiah as both David's son and David's Lord. Mark's Gospel has an additional concluding speech act describing the crowd's reaction. Matthew adds an introductory interchange between Jesus and a group of Pharisees which Jesus initiates by posing a question to the Pharisees concerning the sonship of the Messiah. The Pharisees' response that the Messiah is the son of David makes explicit what Mark and Luke imply in their presentation of Jesus's opening question. In each Gospel, the quotation follows the form of Ps 109:1 LXX closely,[102] and Jesus's final question

---

99. Although for convenience we refer to the authors of the Synoptic Gospels as Matthew, Mark, and Luke, it is not important for our purposes to assert that people with those names were the empirical authors or to adduce historical details about the empirical authors from other writings.

100. Nolland presents the grounds for rejecting this as an episode of the historical Jesus along with the main views of its original function (Nolland, *Luke 18:35—24:53*, 970–71). We follow Roth in attributing this episode to Jesus (Roth, *Die Grundparadigmen christlicher Schriftauslegung*, 57–58; cf. M. F. Bird, *Are You the One?*, 131; and Bock, "Blasphemy," 98).

101. Each gospel has different teaching before this speech event. Afterwards, Mark and Luke present the episode of the poor widow's gift, while Matthew lists a series of "woes" against the Pharisees. Therefore, although to broaden each speech act complex would give a Directive speech act as the climax ("Watch out for the teachers of the law" in Mark 12:38; Luke 20:46a; Matt 23:3a), it would complicate our analysis unduly. So we limit our speech act complexes to the verses which include the quotation.

102. All three quotations omit "ὁ" before the first "κύριος," and Matthew and Mark use "ὑποκάτω" instead of the LXX "ὑποπόδιον," which Luke retains. Matthew and Mark appear to be influenced here by "the association between Ps. cx. 1 and Ps. viii. 7" (Loader, "Christ at the Right Hand," 210n1).

runs along the lines of "if David calls him [the Messiah] Lord, how can he be his son?"

The Illocution

In each Gospel, Jesus is the implied speaker of the episode.[103] And in each case, the first "Lord" of the quoted oracle is Yahweh, and the identity of the second "Lord" (the implied hearer of the oracle) is the subject of Jesus's initial question, i.e., the Messiah.

Discerning the implied audience is more complex. In Mark's Gospel, Jesus is teaching in the Temple (12:35a),[104] where his interlocutors have been, variously, οἱ ἀρχιερεῖς καὶ οἱ γραμματεῖς καὶ οἱ πρεσβύτεροι (11:27), τινας τῶν Φαρισαίων καὶ τῶν Ἡρῳδιανῶν (12:13), Σαδδουκαῖοι (12:18), and εἷς τῶν γραμματέων (12:28). It is not clear whether any of these are the direct addressees of Jesus's question in v. 35 or whether he is now speaking to πολὺς ὄχλος (v. 37), as is the case beginning with v. 38.[105]

In Luke's Gospel, Jesus addresses the *Davidssohnfrage* πρὸς αὐτούς (20:41). The previously referenced plural audiences are scribes (vv. 39–40), Sadducees (vv. 27–34), and the scribes and chief priests (vv. 19–26), but it seems unlikely that Jesus would direct "How can they say?" to these groups. Rather it seems that λέγουσιν (v. 41) refers to the scribes and chief priests while Jesus's question is addressed to the people (τὸν λαόν) he is teaching (Luke 20:1, 9).[106] This would explain why Jesus finds it necessary to tell his audience that David said this in the Book of Psalms (v. 42)—the scribes,

---

103. This is a double-level quotation (the NT authors quote Jesus quoting Ps 109:1 LXX). Thus, we are interested in the implied author and audience at both the episode and the discourse levels.

104. Jesus remains in the temple until Mark 13:1a (see Moloney, *Gospel of Mark*, 229). It may be significant that Jesus comes closer in this episode "to revealing his identity in public" than he has earlier and also "not incidental that he does so in the temple, which is to say in the place where people come to encounter their God and his truth and redemption" (Witherington, *Gospel of Mark*, 332; cf. R. E. Watts, "Psalms in Mark's Gospel," 44–45).

105. Mark 12:35 begins καὶ ἀποκριθείς, but the question to which Jesus is responding is not given.

106. J. B. Green makes a similar point (J. B. Green, *Gospel of Luke*, 723). Nolland points out that "most likely, . . . we should think of address to the People" but v. 43, in which Jesus addresses the disciples in the presence of the crowd, "raises the possibility of address to the disciples in the hearing of the People" (Nolland, *Luke 18:35—24:53*, 972).

chief priests, and Sadducees would have been expected to know these basics about the quoted verses.

In Matthew's Gospel, the direct addressees are Pharisees, with a group of Jewish overhearers or side participants (the disciples and the crowd, 23:1) also present. Here also, as overhearers/side participants, these groups are to be considered in evaluating the intended illocutionary and perlocutionary effects of this speech act complex.

In each Gospel, the first illocutionary act of the speech act complex is a question, which in Mark and Luke can be rephrased as a negative Assertive:[107] "The scribes cannot say (λέγουσιν) that the Messiah is (merely) David's son/the son of David" (Mark 12:35, Luke 20:41).[108] More details are given in Matthew's account. There Jesus begins by asking the Pharisees whose son is the Messiah (Matt 22:41). When they answer, "The son of David," Jesus builds on their answer to ask, "How is it then that David by the Spirit calls him Lord . . . ?"

In each case, the apparent expectation of the scribes and Pharisees was that the messiah was to be a descendant ("son") of David, who, with Yahweh's help, would restore a powerful, independent kingdom of Israel on earth. This aligns with the Psalms of Solomon and the Qumran writings which refer to a Davidic messiah as well as with the metaphoric OT references to Yahweh raising "up for David a righteous Branch" (Jer 23:5; see also Jer 33:15; Isa 11:1; Zech 3:8, 6:12).[109] Jesus's question signals that this existing scribal/Pharisaic interpretation of Scripture is going to be challenged in some way.[110]

---

107. G. H. Guthrie points out that many rhetorical questions are semantically equivalent to "propositions," i.e., Assertives (G. H. Guthrie, *Structure of Hebrews*, 62).

108. In Mark, Jesus asks, "How can the scribes say that the Messiah is the son of David? (Mark 12:35). In Luke, Jesus asks, "How can they say that the Messiah is David's son?" (Luke 20:41). The Assertive would be different if the Greek πῶς is translated as "Why?" as per the NIV.

109. "In view of prophecies such as these, the scribal habit of referring to the Messiah as 'son of David' seems reasonable" (Evans, *Mark 8:27—16:20*, 272). Juel considers "the view of the scribes that 'the Christ is David's son' may be a shorthand substitution for the actual citation of a passage like 2Sam 7:12–14" (Juel, "Origin of Mark's Christology," 454). See M. F. Bird, *Are You the One?*, 104–7, for a discussion of how Jesus seeing himself as king of God's kingdom is to be understood messianically.

110. Evans points out that "on the face of it, this is a curious position [for Jesus] to adopt" (Evans, *Mark 8:27—16:20*, 272). For him, this supports the authenticity of Mark 12:35-37 (Evans, 275).

PS 110:1 AS QUOTED BY VARIOUS NT AUTHORS

In all three Gospels, Jesus follows his question by quoting the oracle from Ps 110:1 as the speech of David. This report is an Assertive. As it is framed in the various Gospels, different aspects of mutual context are created/activated. For example, Luke's direct addressee, Theophilus, whether an actual person or a way to address Gentile "God-lovers," had received "instruction" concerning Jesus, of whom he was a follower (see Luke 1:1–4), but he may have been less familiar with the Story of Yahweh and Yahweh's Anointed.[111] This would explain why Luke includes the information that Jesus tells the audience that David said this in the Book of Psalms (Luke 20:42). As Jews, Matthew's audience would have been aware of the presumed connection of the Psalms to David and the Jewish expectations of a messiah who would ascend David's throne. Mark's audience also was "familiar with both the gospel traditions and the Judaism of the first century."[112] However, both Mark 12:35 and Matt 22:43 report that Jesus tells his audience that David spoke "in" or "by" (ἐν) the Holy Spirit. This is apparently a reminder of David's prophetic role.[113]

The framings of this episode indicate that a connection between messianic expectations and Ps 110 may not have existed prior to this quotation by Jesus. Although Hay points out that "the universal opinion of early Christians that the psalm is messianic is readily explained if Jews of that period commonly took that view,"[114] there is no evidence any first-century Jews did so. That some background about the Psalm is given in each Gospel also argues against Donald Juel's contention that "Jesus' question presumes his learned audience knows that Ps 110:1 refers to the Messiah;

---

111. Based on other ancient prefaces, Nolland suggests Theophilus is an individual, although "a symbolic significance for the name cannot be entirely ruled out" (Nolland, *Luke 1—9:20*, 10). Mallen, however, believes Luke writes more broadly to an audience of "Hellenistic Jewish Christians and/or Hellenistic Gentile Christians" who have been "associated with the Jewish synagogue" (Mallen, *Reading and Transformation of Isaiah*, 163). If not the direct addressees, such a group would likely be overhearers.

112. Stein, *Mark*, 10. He believes "the original audience of Mark consisted primarily of gentile Christians," possibly God-fearers, "but this cannot be proven" (Stein, 10). In any case, "the intended audience would have some detailed knowledge of Jewish scripture" (Ahearne-Kroll, *Psalms of Lament*, 28).

113. "The tradition of David's being inspired and prophetic reaches back to the ancient Scriptures themselves" (Evans, *Mark 8:27—16:20*, 273, with reference to 2 Sam 23:2; 11QPsᵃ 27:2–4, 11). Menken equates "speaking by the Spirit" to David speaking "as a prophet" as in Acts 2:30 (Menken, "Psalms in Matthew's Gospel," 74). See the discussion below of Acts 2.

114. Hay, *Glory at the Right Hand*, 30.

that interpretation does not have to be argued."[115] Rather, it appears Jesus *creates*—rather than simply activating—mutual context concerning Ps 110, using the psalm's Story-lines to point to a new kind of messiah.[116] It is significant that all the implied authors include Jesus's quotation of the entirety of Ps 109:1 LXX, thus making it clear that David's "Lord" is both the one given honor and authority via a seat at the right hand of Yahweh[117] and "the one linked to God's decisive intervention" against the enemies.[118]

115. Juel, "Origin of Mark's Christology," 455.

116. As Nolland points out, "There is no good evidence of a messianic understanding of the psalm prior to Jesus" (Nolland, *Luke 18:35—24:53*, 973; cf. Witherington, *Gospel of Mark*, 131n138; Dodd, *According to the Scriptures*, 110; N. T. Wright, *Jesus and the Victory of God*, 508, 508n116; and Moyise, *Later New Testament Writings*, 146. Moyise makes a good argument for Jesus as the originator of this speech event: "Had this dialogue been invented by the early Church, one might have expected Jesus' identification with the figure addressed in the psalm to be more explicit" (Moyise, *Jesus and Scripture*, 109).

117. On the basis that "in all other NT citations of this verse the emphasis lies on the second or third part of the line," Johansson objects to an "interpretation that the citation speaks of Yahweh designating one to rule" (Johansson, "*Kyrios* in the Gospel of Mark," 116n61; cf. Stein, *Mark*, 570). But the quotation of the entire verse by all three implied authors negates this argument. Furthermore, "Mark's readers have already been introduced" to the honor of the seat ἐκ δεξιῶν by "James and John's ill-timed request in 10:35-40" (Evans, *Mark 8:27—16:20*, 273; cf. Matt 20:20-21), and this Story-line of Ps 110:1 is alluded to again at Jesus's trial (see below).

118. Nolland, *Luke 18:35—24:53*, 971. As R. E. Watts points out, "If the significance of messianic identity was the only issue in question the first strophe of Ps. 110:1 would have sufficed" (R. E. Watts, "Psalms in Mark's Gospel," 40; cf. Marcus, *Way of the Lord*, 134). Although the identity of the enemies remains vague, Witherington's suggestion that "the motif of combat and victory may allude to Jesus' verbal victories over his scribal foes" (Witherington, *Gospel of Mark*, 333-34) seems quite tame. Marcus's thoughts regarding Mark 8:29-30 seem relevant here. He points out that both Jesus and Peter have accepted that Jesus is the Messiah; "the point at issue is exactly how his messianic victory over the forces of evil will be accomplished. For Peter, steeped in traditional versions of Davidic messiahship, the struggle anticipated is one in which victory will be accomplished through a military assault on flesh-and-blood enemies (cf. the Qumran War Scroll). . . . For Jesus, however, the messianic victory will in the first instance be a cosmic one over supernatural foes (cf. 1:24; 3:23-27), and it will be achieved not by a conventional battle but by death and resurrection" (Marcus, *Mark 8-16*, 614). This is *contra* Ahearne-Kroll, who believes that Mark denies "the epithet 'Son of David' for the Messiah" and thereby also "denies the association of the Messiah with the earthly, bellicose characteristics most likely evoked by this title. . . . In this case, the earthly, militaristic images evoked by the 'Son of David' are downplayed and denied, but the royal imagery is still upheld by the quotation of Ps 110:1" (Ahearne-Kroll, *Psalms of Lament*, 164).

With regard to the subjection of enemies, Matt 22:44 and Mark 12:36 conflate Pss 110:1c and 8:6b. These psalms are also intertwined in 1 Cor 15:25, Eph 1:20-22, and Heb 2:5-9. See Koester, *Hebrews*, 204; Hay, *Glory at the Right Hand*, 35; and Hengel, who argues that

Jesus's final speech act is also a question: "How can he (the Messiah) be his (David's) son if David calls him 'Lord'?" This question also can be rephrased as an Assertive: Since David calls the Messiah "Lord," the Messiah cannot (merely) be David's son.[119]

Given the broader co-text, Jesus's question cannot be taken to imply that the Messiah was not "Son of David."[120] And, although Jesus makes no explicit messianic claim here, the evolution of the narrative supports the notion that Jesus's audience and the implied audiences of the Gospels would have considered the *Davidssohnfrage* to apply to *Jesus's* own identity as both Son of David and Messiah.[121]

All the implied authors of the Gospels have already presented Jesus as "the son of David."[122] In Matthew, this happens in the very first verse.

"lediglich die schriftgelehrte Akribie des Hebräerbriefs vermeidet jede Zitatenkontamination zwischen Ps 110 und Ps 8" (Hengel, "'Setze dich zu meiner Rechten!,'" 147).

119. While "the most natural reading of the concluding question of Mark 12:37 is that it expects a negative answer" (Marcus, *Way of the Lord,* 152), the co-text makes it clear that the situation is not so simple.

120. *Contra* Shaw, who believes Jesus "denies the Davidic descent of the Messiah (12.35–37)" (Shaw, *Cost of Authority,* 225; see also 191, 218); Moloney, who contends "David cannot possibly be the father of the Messiah because . . . a person cannot be 'father' of his 'lord'" (Moloney, *Gospel of Mark,* 243; see also 243n148); and Bock, who argues that for David to call his own descendant his Lord would have been "a very unusual designation in a patriarchal culture" (Bock, *Proclamation from Prophecy and Pattern,* 183), we agree it is "highly unlikely" Jesus "is questioning the popular assumption that the Christ would be a son of David" (R. E. Watts, "Psalms in Mark's Gospel," 39; cf. Evans, "Praise and Prophecy," 563n28). Since the Synopticists "show no embarrassment in combining this episode with an affirmation of Davidic descent," we must "leave the possibility open that from the beginning no denial of Davidic descent was intended" (Nolland, *Luke 18:35—24:53,* 971). Furthermore, "the scribal habit of referring to the Messiah as the 'son of David'" does not necessarily imply "he is in some sense subordinate or inferior to David" (Evans, "Praise and Prophecy," 563). For Moyise, "all that is required is the recognition that a descendant of David (the Messiah) will be greater than David, though one should not underestimate the size of that claim" (Moyise, *Jesus and Scripture,* 109).

121. Stein makes the reasonable argument that "it would be unlikely that the early church, which took for granted that Jesus the Messiah was the Son of David, would create an account that appears to question this. The Davidic lineage of Jesus and the Messiah does not seem to have been an issue in the Jewish-Christian debates or within the Christian community" (Stein, *Mark,* 568).

122. Nowhere in Mark's gospel is "there a suggestion that Jesus is not the 'Son of David'" (Juel, "Origin of Mark's Christology," 454; cf. Stein, *Mark,* 569). Additionally, "Luke's repeated emphasis on Jesus' Davidic descent (Lk. 1,27. 32. 69; 2,4; 3,31) rules out the possibility that the question is meant to deny the messiah's Davidic origin" (Strauss, *Davidic Messiah in Luke-Acts,* 317; see also 197–98).

PART II | CASE STUDIES

Similarly, in Luke, the angel tells Mary that her child will receive τὸν θρόνον Δαυὶδ τοῦ πατρὸς αὐτοῦ (Luke 1:32; see also 1:69, 2:4). Jesus is addressed as "Son of David" by a blind man or men earlier in each Gospel (Mark 10:46–48; Luke 18:38–39; Matt 9:27, 20:30–31).[123] In each case, a crowd hears Jesus called "Son of David" and is aware that Jesus does not challenge this title. In Matthew, Jesus's miraculous healing of a man who is blind and mute prompts the crowd to query, "Can this be the Son of David?" (Matt 12:22–23).[124] Later, as Jesus rides into Jerusalem, the crowd shouts "Hosanna to the Son of David!" (Matt 21:9; cf. Mark 11:9–10 where the crowd also refers to "the coming kingdom of our father David").[125] Thus, since Jesus never rejects the title "Son of David," it seems likely that at the episode level his disciples and most, if not all, of the rest of his audience would have

---

123. Since the gospels relate these episodes in the same order, this appears to represent their chronology. Mark and Luke place this title for Jesus in the mouth of a blind man begging near Jericho (Mark 10:46–48, Luke 18:38–39) who persistently requests mercy from the "Son of David." Stein points out that in Mark 10:46, "the wording of the address, 'Son of David, Jesus,' places the title in the emphatic position. This . . . indicates that Mark wants to emphasize that Jesus is indeed the Son of David" (Stein, *Mark*, 495; see also 497, 570–72). In both Gospels, the newly healed blind man follows Jesus, which for Ahearne-Kroll gives the reader "every confidence that Bartimaeus is a reliable character, and so his identification of Jesus as 'Son of David' should be taken seriously" (Ahearne-Kroll, *Psalms of Lament*, 143, referring to Mark 10:52; the blind man is not named in Luke). Ahearne-Kroll makes this interesting connection: "By constructing the story of the healing of the blind Bartimaeus in such a way as to combine the title 'Son of David' with the healing of a reliable character, he stresses the tradition of healing that is associated with Solomon as the Son of David" (Ahearne-Kroll, 144; see n124).

Matthew reports two incidents in which Jesus heals blind men who appeal to the "Son of David" (Matt 9:27, 20:30–31). In the first, the blind men disobey Jesus's injunction to not tell anyone about their healing. Perhaps the news they spread (Matt 9:31) included that he did not reject the title "Son of David."

124. Evans believes "rumors that Jesus was some sort of 'son of David' probably arose from his ministry of healing and exorcism. The association of 'Solomon, son of David' with healing and exorcism is attested in the *Testament of Solomon,* which dates to the end of the first century C. E." (Evans, *Mark 8:27—16:20,* 275). But this does not fully account for the references to Jesus as son/Son of David in Matt 1 and Luke 2.

125. In the parallel account in Luke 19, there is no "Hosanna!" and no mention of David. Jesus is promised "the throne of his father David" in Luke 1:32 as part of the annunciation to Mary (see n128), and Jesus's genealogy includes "of David" (Luke 3:31; cf. Matt. 1:6). Moreover, Davies is wrong that "Son of David" never occurs in Luke; it appears in the story of the blind man (Luke 18:38, 39). However, "of all New Testament writers it is Matthew who most emphasizes that Jesus is of Davidic ancestry" (Davies, "Jewish Sources," 500). Even a Gentile woman cries out to Jesus as "Lord, Son of David" in Matt 15:22.

understood that Jesus considered himself the "Son of David," whether or not they were willing to accord him that title.

The implied authors have already made it clear that Jesus also is the Messiah.[126] Matthew and Mark refer to Ἰησοῦ Χριστοῦ in their opening verses.[127] In Luke, Jesus is named χριστός and also called σωτήρ and κύριος in 2:11 by the angel announcing his birth to the Bethlehem shepherds.[128] Luke refers to the adult Jesus as χριστός in 4:41. Additionally, all the implied authors have presented the episode in which Jesus asks his disciples, "But who do you say that I am?" (Matt 16:15, Mark 8:29a, Luke 9:20). When Peter replies, "You are the Messiah [ὁ χριστός]" (Mark 8:29; cf. Matt 16:16, Luke 9:20),[129] Jesus does not reject the title (see especially Matt 16:17). Although at the point of the *Davidssohnfrage*, Jesus has made no explicit messianic claims, at the episode level, the disciples would have believed Jesus considered himself the Messiah.[130] And if they disobeyed Jesus's injunction to keep the messianic secret (Matt 16:20, Mark 8:30, Luke 9:21),[131] others may have also heard this news.

Some argue "Psalm 110 is invoked to make the point that Jesus is not the Davidic messiah, that he stands for a different messianic hope."[132] But

---

126. For Juel, the "major focus" of Christian "interpretations of Israel's Scriptures ... was Jesus, the crucified and risen Messiah" (Juel, *Messianic Exegesis*, 1). M. F. Bird gives a convincing demonstration of the weaknesses inherent in the various arguments denying Jesus's messianic self-understanding (M. F. Bird, *Are You the One?*, chapter 3).

127. Many ancient sources add υἱοῦ θεοῦ in Mark 1:1. With regard to Mark, M. F. Bird believes that "the whole context of Jesus's entry [into Jerusalem]—precursors, content, sequel, result—all point in the direction of a messianic claim" (M. F. Bird, *Are You the One?*, 126). As "precursors," M. F. Bird includes the *Davidssohnfrage* and also Jesus's earlier action in the Temple (Mark 11:15–17). As Donahue and Harrington point out, "From the opening of the gospel, readers know that *Jesus* is the 'Messiah.' What awaits full disclosure is *the kind of* Messiah Jesus is" (Donahue and Harrington, *Gospel of Mark*, 29).

128. Luke's birth narrative emphasizes that Jesus is no ordinary child (see 1:32–33, 35, 43; 2:29, 32).

129. Luke adds "of God," and Matthew adds "the son of the living God."

130. In Matt 12:42 and Luke 11:31, Jesus has also made the self-reference as "someone [something] greater than Solomon." N. T. Wright finds that "for Jesus to compare himself with Solomon, to the latter's disadvantage, was to stake a definite messianic claim" (N. T. Wright, *Jesus and the Victory of God*, 535).

131. With regard to Mark, M. F. Bird believes Jesus responds to Peter's confession with an injunction to secrecy because Jesus is moving "along the thread of a different messianic story, one related to the enigmatic 'Son of Man'" (M. F. Bird, *Are You the One?*, 120). We discuss this in the following section.

132. Hamerton-Kelly, "Sacred Violence," 477. Moyise also finds that in Mark 12:35–37

since the *Davidssohnfrage* activates the already established mutual context of Jesus's identity as Son of David *and* as Messiah, it is more likely that Jesus instead is subtly informing his audience that Davidic messiahship is not going to be what the religious experts were expecting. Jesus's messiahship is "more than the traditional expectations of the Davidic messiah";[133] the Messiah is "more than" the heir to the Davidic monarchy. Via the quotation of Ps 110:1 and its metaphors, Jesus signals to his audience that what was expected of the Messiah, that is, that he would occupy David's earthly throne, did not correspond to the full reality of Yahweh's Messiah. As David's Lord (κυρίῳ μου), the Messiah is more than David's biological son or descendant.[134] He is David's "Lord"; his honor and authority and even his kingdom are in some way greater than David's.[135]

"there is no attempt to identify Jesus as the 'Lord' of the Psalm" (Moyise, *Later New Testament Writings*, 86).

133. Strauss, *Davidic Messiah in Luke-Acts*, 30; cf. J. B. Green, *Gospel of Luke*, 724; Bock, *Proclamation from Prophecy and Pattern*, 132; M. F. Bird, *Are You the One?*, 107; and Broer, "Versuch zur Christologie," 1254. This is substantively different from the claim that "the Jesus known to us from the New Testament simply does not fit the profile of the Davidic Messiah which was espoused by many Jews of his time" (Charlesworth, "Introduction," 6). As Thiselton cogently argues, "It was important that an understanding of Jesus, seen in his words and in his completed work, should govern interpretations of conventional 'messianic' language, rather than that ready-made assumptions about the meaning of such language should govern an understanding of Jesus" (Thiselton, *New Horizons in Hermeneutics*, 287).

134. "The challenge to this normal understanding of the Son of David (cf. Ps. Sol. 17.21) in [Mark] 12:35-37 is not that this is an incorrect understanding of Jesus Christ, but that it is an inadequate one. . . . The NT understanding of the person and work of Jesus does not deny that he is the Son of David (Matt. 1:1, 17, 20; 9:27; 12:23; 15:22; Luke 1:27, 32, 69; 2:4, 11; Acts 13:22-23; Rom. 1:3; 2 Tim. 2:8; Rev. 5:5; 22:16). It points out that he is this and more" (Stein, *Mark*, 495; cf. R. E. Watts, "Psalms in Mark's Gospel," 39; Marcus, *Mark 8-16*, 848; and Marcus, *Way of the Lord*, 145). In Luke also, "there is something bigger here than can be contained in merely Davidic categories" (Nolland, *Luke 18:35—24:53*, 973). Witherington explains it well: "Is Jesus here repudiating the Davidic origins of Messiah, as some have suggested? This seems unlikely, since elsewhere he doesn't repudiate the title Son of David, but he may well have repudiated certain popular early Jewish notions about the Davidic Messiah, for instance, that he would simply be a normal, though God-empowered, human being like David himself. It is best to say that Jesus is repudiating the adequacy, not the accuracy, of assessing the Messiah by means of his Davidic descent. The point is that in Jesus' view the Messiah is more than, not other than, Son of David" (Witherington, *Gospel of Mark*, 333; see also 52n150).

135. "Unless it was [*sic*] true, it would be peculiar to refer to one's own son as greater than oneself" (Donahue and Harrington, *Gospel of Mark*, 360) since "normal conventions would have the son showing honor to his father rather than vice versa" (J. B. Green, *Gospel of Luke*, 724; cf. Hagner, *Matthew 14-28*, 651). Thus, Jesus must be "more than

The tellability of this speech act complex stems from its contradiction of the beliefs/expectations of the legal experts (either present or referred to) and of those who rely on their expertise (the crowds). The quotation itself is tellable because it sheds new light on the relationship between David, David's heirs, and the Messiah. And, by presenting his thought that the coming Messiah would not be what was expected in the form of a question, Jesus promotes involvement in his listeners.[136]

Each Gospel ends the speech act complex differently. Like his introduction, Luke's ending is the briefest; he concludes with Jesus's question (Luke 20:44) and gives no indication of the response of the audience. Mark comments that "the large crowd was listening to him with delight" (Mark 12:37b). This may be the crowd's appreciation of Jesus's ability to confound the legal experts, rather than an affirmation of Jesus's message. In Matthew, the audience disengages. Jesus's audience was not able to answer (οὐδεὶς ἐδύνατο ἀποκριθῆναι) the question, "nor from that day did anyone dare to ask him any more questions" (Matt 22:46).[137] The implication is that the direct addressees are either unwilling to be put in a position of feeling ignorant by asking further questions or so uncomfortable with the direction Jesus's thoughts are taking that they are unwilling to pursue this topic.[138]

The second option seems quite likely. The Jewish leaders (and the crowds)

> could have answered Jesus' question a number of different ways. They could have denied that the passage had anything to do with the Messiah, but they did not. If they had understood "my Lord" as a reference to David or Solomon, the Jewish leaders could have explained that the primary or perhaps exclusive referent of "my

---

David's son and more than the messiah of Jewish expectations" (Donahue and Harrington, *Gospel of Mark*, 360).

136. This goes beyond what Amador suggests is common in the NT: "The pronouncements are legitimated strictly by appeal to the assumed authority of Jesus himself" (Amador, *Academic Constraints in Rhetorical Criticism*, 147).

137. "Anyone" apparently did not include the disciples, since they ask Jesus theological questions in Matt 24:3 and again in 26:8. In Mark and Luke, the comment that "they no longer dared to ask him another question" (Luke 20:40; cf. Mark 12:34) concludes the episode prior to the *Davidssohnfrage*.

138. The religious authorities' silence may also hearken back to their fear of the people, which each gospel has recently highlighted (Matt 21:23-27, Mark 11:27-33, Luke 20:1-8).

lord" was a historical king, and therefore resolved the dilemma. But they did not.[139]

Although Aloisi believes "their silence conceded Jesus' point,"[140] it seems as plausible that the Jewish leaders among the direct addressees were unwilling to enter into any further discussion of the Messiah that might bring into the conversation the priestly references of Ps 110's second oracle.

In any event, what "more than Messiah" means is left undefined by Jesus and the implied authors.[141] Not only is the son/Lord question left unanswered, Jesus's role/identity remains implicit. The *Davidssohnfrage* is "a provocative remark designed to open up the question of the nature of the hoped-for ultimate intervention of God in the affairs of his People"—a question which cannot "be separated from the question of Jesus' own relationship to the fulfillment of the hoped-for kingdom of God."[142] At the end of this episode, these questions remain unresolved.[143] The *Davidssohnfrage*

---

139. Aloisi, "Who is David's Lord?," 120-21; cf. E. E. Johnson, "Hermeneutical Principles," 432-33. However, the contention that "Jesus and the Jewish leaders agreed that Psalm 110:1 was a direct prophecy about the Messiah" (Aloisi, "Who is David's Lord?," 121; cf. E. E. Johnson, "Hermeneutical Principles," 433) goes too far.

140. Aloisi, "Who is David's Lord?," 121. Similarly, Kistemaker contends Jesus gave "the correct interpretation and application of the psalm, which the Pharisees were unable to refute" (Kistemaker, "Psalm 110," 141; cf. Nolland, *Gospel of Matthew*, 917. However, Jesus's "interpretation and application" are at best implicit; it is unclear whether the Pharisees were unable to respond to Jesus or simply chose not to.

141. "Jesus provides no immediate resolution of the enigma he poses" (J. B. Green, *Gospel of Luke*, 724; cf. M. F. Bird, *Are You the One?*, 132; and Witherington, *Gospel of Mark*, 333). Nor do the implied authors of the gospels draw any explicit conclusions. However, according to Witherington, "the implication . . . seems to be that the scribes' notion of Messiah is far too mundane. He is a much greater figure than the original David, not merely a chip off the old block. Indeed, he is a transcendent figure, exercising lordship over even David" (Witherington, 333).

142. Nolland, *Luke 18:35—24:53*, 972. As Keener points out, "Given the environment in which Jesus ministered, he had to know that his teachings about the kingdom and some of his actions would lead to speculation about his messianic character" (Keener, *Acts*, 1:968).

143. Thus, it is premature to conclude that "the point of Jesus' speech is evident. The messiah . . . must be a heavenly ruler who shall also be David's Lord, not his son and subordinate" (Eskola, *Messiah and the Throne*, 180). The same is true for E. E. Johnson's assertion regarding Mark 12:35-37 that Jesus's "interpretation of Psalm 110:1 establishes 'my lord' as a reference by David to Christ as *deity*" (E. E. Johnson, "Hermeneutical Principles," 432; emphasis added; cf. Keener, *Acts*, 1:962, regarding Luke; and Hagner, *Matthew 14-28*, 651, regarding Matthew). *Contra* the claim that "'Lord' (*kyrios*)" was "a title that at least in Jewish circles placed him on a level with the 'Lord' who is God"

is not a complete teaching; rather, with it Jesus initiates a transformation that continues to unfold during his trial and is subsequently moved forward by other NT authors. The Analytic reader understands both the questions which are being raised and what challenges to the existing interpretation of Story are posed by those questions. An Analytic reader also understands that the resolution of this issue remains in the future.

The Perlocution

The intended perlocution is a disruption of the beliefs of the implied audiences (both Jesus's audiences and the implied readers of the Gospels) concerning the identity of the Messiah. Jesus's questions, which do not cast doubt on a messianic hope, make it plain that the Messiah is not to be as expected, that is, the Messiah is to be more than an earthly king who would assume David's throne.

The implied hearers at the episode level of each Gospel would be aware that a key element of the religious belief system was now in flux. A transformation of Story, lifeworld, and theology has been initiated, although not completed, and mutual context is altered. The same is true at the discourse level. The implied readers of the Gospels would have understood this speech act complex to intend the transformation of the existing

---

(Donahue and Harrington, *Gospel of Mark*, 361; cf. Marcus, *Mark 8–16*, 850), "there is no basis for speaking of a 'divine predicate' in connection with the use of 'lord' in the pericope" (Nolland, *Luke 18:35—24:53*, 971). Even Brawley's more restrained use of "exalted" to describe the messiah outpaces the development of Story to this point (Brawley, *Text to Text*, 86). It is possible, however, that Jesus's divine sonship may be alluded to. The argument that "the emphatic placement of αὐτοῦ in [Mark] 12:37b . . . implies that Jesus is the son of someone other than David," and that "the logical candidate is God" (Marcus, *Way of the Lord*, 141; cf. Evans, "Praise and Prophecy," 564; and Broer, "Versuch zur Christologie," 1258) would apply also to Luke's Gospel. But along with numerous other scholars (see n120 and n134 above), we reject Marcus's implication that this denies Jesus's Davidic sonship.

Unfortunately, we do not have space to explore here Johansson's thoughts about the relevance of the quotation of the Shema (Deut 6:4) in Mark 12:29 to the relationship between the *Davidssohnfrage* and Jewish monotheism (Johansson, "*Kyrios* in the Gospel of Mark," 118–19). We do note that "in Mark's eyes, . . . the picture of the figure enthroned at God's right hand does not refute the statement that God is one" (Marcus, *Way of the Lord*, 145). Nor can we investigate Donahue and Harrington's interesting contention that "in the Roman empire *kyrios* was also used as a title for the emperor. And so for early Christians to proclaim Jesus as 'Lord' could be taken to suggest that the emperor is not" (Donahue and Harrington, *Gospel of Mark*, 361).

PART II | CASE STUDIES

understanding of the Story of Israel's coming messiah. In each Gospel, this speech act complex prepares the way for further lifeworld/worldview transformation. This is therefore a critical point in the transformation of the Story of God's work among God's people and in creation through Jesus Christ. The Envisaging empirical reader prepares to continue to be transformed as Story and theology evolve.[144]

THE "SON OF MAN" SEATED AT THE RIGHT HAND OF GOD

The *Davidssohnfrage* episode is not complete in itself. Whether "Jesus' concluding question implies an answer to the problem he poses,"[145] the "solution" continues to develop in subsequent events, beginning with Jesus's speech before the Sanhedrin (Matt 26:64, Mark 14:62, Luke 22:69). In each Gospel, a religious authority (in Matthew and Mark, the high priest; in Luke, the Sanhedrin) asks Jesus whether he is the Messiah, and Jesus's response includes an obviously tellable Assertive (a Predictive)[146] that his audience will see him, i.e., the "Son of Man," seated at the right hand of (the) power

---

144. The same options are available to modern readers. Although not the original addressees, by choosing to read, they become side participants and can be Envisaging readers.

145. Juel, "Origin of Mark's Christology," 455, referring to Mark's gospel.

146. This is not a promise, since promises are "acts of obligating oneself" (Bach and Harnish, *Linguistic Communication*, 50). That the Assertive is tellable can be seen in the reaction of the hearers, who charge blasphemy, condemn Jesus as deserving death, have him beaten, and turn him over to the Roman authorities. It therefore is odd that Moloney does not include Mark 14:62 among the "significant turning points in the story" (Moloney, *Gospel of Mark*, 16).

(τῆς δυνάμεως).¹⁴⁷ Although not a marked quotation, the Gospel authors no doubt intend their "readers to see Psalm 110 in Jesus' response."¹⁴⁸

To describe "the Christ" in the query concerning Jesus's identity, Matthew and Luke append "Son of God," and Mark includes "Son of the Blessed One" (Matt 26:63; Luke 22:67, 70; Mark 14:61).¹⁴⁹ Earlier in each Gospel, Jesus is identified as Son of God by the narrator (Mark 1:1, Luke 3:38), an angel (Luke 1:35), the devil (Matt 4:3, 6; Luke 4:3, 9), and certain demons (Matt 8:29; Mark 3:11; Luke 4:41, 8:28). But, except for Matt 14:43 and 16:16, this is the first time Jesus is named "Son of God" by the religious authorities or so names himself. However, *contra* Marcus and Witherington, the title "Son of God" does not necessarily imply Jesus's divinity.¹⁵⁰ Wither-

---

147. Luke 22:69 adds τοῦ θεοῦ to τῆς δυνάμεως, making the source of honor and messiahship explicit. A. Y Collins's argument that Jesus did not identify himself as the Son of Man but rather understood the one like a son of man "as a heavenly being, perhaps an angel, and associated his own teaching and activity with that being" (A. Y. Collins, "Influence of Daniel," 105) is not compelling. Nor is Shaw's contention that "in referring to the Son of Man, Jesus is . . . outrageously introducing himself at God's right hand. If it was a reference to the prophecy in Daniel (7.13), it would only be a platitude of Jewish expectation. What makes it blasphemy is precisely its self-reference" (Shaw, *Cost of Authority*, 197). Not only has the Son of Man language already appeared in all three gospels, Jesus has already at least implicitly "introduced himself at God's right hand" in the *Davidssohnfrage*.

148. Geddert, "Use of Psalms," 116, with regard to Mark. M. F. Bird notes that the OT "formed the interpretive grid through which the story of Jesus's passion was interpreted, rather than comprising the creative pool from which the story was created" (M. F. Bird, *Are You the One?*, 75).

149. The wording differs in each case. Because "the trial scenes are regarded as historically dubious and loaded with Christian theology, and Jesus's reply to Caiaphas is markedly different in all four Gospels . . . the historicity of the scene in Mark 14:61-64 is disputed" (M. F. Bird, *Are You the One?*, 136). See M. F. Bird, 137-40, for arguments in favor of the authenticity of the passage. One of the most telling is that it is Jesus's opponents who raise the issue of Jesus's messiahship at his trial (see J. J. Collins, *Scepter and Star*, 204).

150. Marcus contends that in Mark 14:62, where "the title 'Son of God' is brought into close connection with Ps. 110:1, . . . the title is thus seen as implying commensurability with God," and Mark thereby implies Jesus's "participation in the divine majesty" (Marcus, *Way of the Lord*, 143, 144). Although Marcus does admit that "Mark stops short of taking such stories to their logical conclusion and calling Jesus God" (Marcus, 145), both he and Bullock feel that the declaration of Jesus as God is the "logical deduction" (Bullock, *Encountering the Book of Psalms*, 185). D. A. Brueggemann goes further in arguing that "anyone actually claiming to be called 'lord' (*kyrios*) with 'right hand' status in the heavenly throne room could fairly be claiming divinity" (D. A. Brueggemann, "Evangelists and Psalms," 268). All of these overreach. Similarly, although Tasker is correct that "Jesus seems to be saying in effect 'I am not the kind of Messiah that you suppose Me to

ington himself points out that "one source for messianic thinking about Messiah as God's Son was Ps. 2, perhaps coupled with 2 Sam. 7:14," and these "texts do not really imply the divinity of the person in question."[151]

Matthew and Mark add that the Son of Man will be seen coming "on" (Matt: ἐπί) or "with" (Mark: μετά) the clouds of heaven.[152] "Coming with

be, . . . but nevertheless I *am* the Messiah,'" we disagree with his conclusion that Jesus is claiming, "This exaltation will be the prelude to My coming as the divine Judge in the role depicted by Daniel" (Tasker, *Gospel According to St. Matthew*, 254; cf. Witherington, *Gospel of Mark*, 384).

We also do not find compelling Gathercole's argument that as early as the *Davidssohnfrage* episodes, "the clear implication . . . is that Jesus is not so much son of David as Son of God. . . . The principal reason for this is that just as the Jesus of the Gospels supplies Ps. 110.1 as support for the idea that the Messiah cannot be David's son—and therefore can lay claim to being Son of God—so also Ps. 110.3 *and* 4 would have been understood by the readers of the Gospels in much the same way and would have been taken to imply the preexistence of the Messiah" (Gathercole, *Preexistent Son*, 236; see also 294). As we have noted, Ps 110:3 [109:3 LXX] is not quoted in the NT, and there is no way to know how this verse was read in the first century CE. Gathercole bases his assumption that Ps 109:3 LXX is in view in the quotation of the prior two verses on the argument that "since the Psalms were sung as part of Jewish worship, they would most likely be known as wholes: the first line cited in the Gospels would be very likely to suggest the rest of this short Psalm" (Gathercole, 238). But, if Jesus or the Gospel authors had intended to evoke v. 3, there would have been no reason not to include it in their quotations.

Rather, although "to be 'Son of God' is an exalted status and relationship to God experienced by the messiah (cf. at [Luke] 3:22; 1:26-38), . . . the words should be taken as no more than a synonym for 'messiah'" (Nolland, *Luke 18:35—24:53*, 1111, referring to Luke 22:70). This is supported by Knohl, who looks at several pre-Christian examples and concludes that in those cases "the claim to be the 'son of God' . . . was a political tool for supporting a ruler in his struggle with his enemies" (Knohl, "Religion and Politics in Psalm 2," 726; cf. J. J. Collins, for whom a messianic reading of the "Son of God" text [4Q246] would present "the Davidic/royal messiah . . . as a warrior to subdue the Gentiles" [J. J. Collins, "Jesus, Messianism and the Dead Sea Scrolls," 111]). This is highly reminiscent of what is said of "my lord" in Ps 109:1c-2b LXX.

Hurtado helpfully points out that in "*biblical and Jewish traditions . . .* divine sonship did not necessarily connote divinity. In these traditions divine sonship language was applied to the divinely chosen king, the devout, righteous individual, and to Israel collectively, particularly in the Second Temple period; in these cases divine sonship connoted *special favor and relationship with God*" (Hurtado, *Lord Jesus Christ*, 22).

151. Witherington, *Gospel of Mark*, 384; cf. J. J. Collins, "Jesus, Messianism and the Dead Sea Scrolls, 110-11.

152. Although Luke does not use "clouds" language here (which Moyise, *Jesus and Scripture*, 64, feels "makes the link with Daniel 7:13 much less explicit," all three Synoptics have previously referred to the Son of Man coming in the clouds (Matt 24:30 [ἐπί]; Mark 13:26 and Luke 21:27 [ἐν]). Whether there is christological significance to ἐπί vs. μετά is debated (see Goldingay, *Daniel*, 2002], 171; and Bock, "Blasphemy," 76). However, since the "preposition עם, 'with,' is variously rendered" in the versions of Dan 7:13 and "the OG

the clouds of heaven" is a clear link to Dan 7:13 and the presentation of "one like a son of man" before the Ancient of Days.[153] Although we cannot undertake a full evaluation of Dan 7:13, we note that a connection between the Son of Man and the Messiah has already been placed into mutual context in all three Gospels via Peter's reference to Jesus as the Messiah and Jesus's subsequent self-reference as the Son of Man (Matt 16:13–16, Mark 8:29–38, Luke 9:18–21).[154] And in Matt 24:30 and Mark 13:26, Jesus alludes to Dan 7:13 to contrast the Son of Man with false messiahs.[155] Whether this comparison was initiated by Jesus is uncertain.[156] In any event, as was the

has the 'one like a son of man' come *on* rather than *with* the clouds" (J. J. Collins, *Daniel*, 311, 8), it seems likely the gospels simply reflect different Greek readings of the OT. In any event, it is unwarranted to say that "since elsewhere it is only God who travels on the clouds . . . the Son of Man is portrayed as a divine being as he approaches the Ancient of Days' throne" (Beale, *New Testament Biblical Theology*, 192; cf. Witherington, *Gospel of Mark*, 385). Nor is Donahue and Harrington's argument compelling that the description of "this figure . . . as being 'like' a human being suggests that it is something else—most likely an angel, probably Michael (see Dan 12:1)" (Donahue and Harrington, *Gospel of Mark*, 374, where they do see that "in the Markan context, . . . the Son of Man is Jesus"). We agree with Ahearne-Kroll that "the one like a son of man is not God, but he receives the authority to reign in the same way as God reigns" (Ahearne-Kroll, *Psalms of Lament*, 165n81).

153. It is not clear whether "the figure is ascending or descending or moving horizontally" (J. J. Collins, *Daniel*, 311; cf. Marcus, *Mark 8–16*, 1008). *Contra* Goldingay, it cannot be determined that "the humanlike figure . . . comes unequivocally from heaven" (Goldingay, *Daniel*, 190). We know only that the one like a son of man, now certainly Jesus (see Donahue and Harrington, *Gospel of Mark*, 27), ends up in Yahweh's presence.

154. Witherington suggests "the interesting prospect that Jesus, who repeatedly identified himself as the Son of Man, read his own destiny out of some of the stories in Daniel" (Witherington, *Gospel of Mark*, 269).

155. Luke 21:27 contains a similar allusion to Dan 7:13 without the contrast between false messiahs and the true messiah. Bock's argument that Luke removes the reference to Dan 7 in Luke 22 in order to "stress the present session of Jesus, not to the exclusion of the parousia, but as a guarantee of it (Luke 21.27; Acts 1.9–11; 3.19–21)" (Bock, *Proclamation from Prophecy and Pattern*, 142) is not compelling.

156. Some argue for a first-century messianic interpretation of "Son of Man" (see, e.g., Marcus, *Mark 8–16*, 1007; and A. Y. Collins, "Influence of Daniel," 96). M. F. Bird argues that "the son of man figure of Dan. 7 . . . was occasionally interpreted as messianic in pockets of pre-Christian Judaism, and Jesus's employment of the phrase taps into this background" (M. F. Bird, *Are You the One?*, 84; see also his chapter 4). Pennington believes "Second Temple Judaism was already reading this text [Dan 7:13] messianically (e.g., *1 Enoch*; *4 Ezra*; 4Q246 2.1–10; 4Q174, 4Q252)" and that it thus "was easy for early Christianity to do the same, applied to the person of Jesus" (Pennington, "Refractions of Daniel," 72).

We find the counter-arguments more compelling. According to Goldingay, "the

case earlier in each Gospel with regard to the quotation from Ps 110:1 as it connected the Son of David to the "more than" Messiah, in both Matthew's and Mark's gospels it is Jesus who links the one exalted to God's right hand (Ps 110:1), the Son of Man coming on/in the clouds (Dan 7:13), and the Messiah.[157] As also was true earlier, Jesus's self-definition as the "Son of Man" qualifies Davidic messianism but does not necessarily supersede it.[158]

Jesus's audience's understanding of his identity is enhanced through this episode, and the meaning of "Messiah" is clarified for the implied readers of the Gospels. That the high priest takes Jesus's words as blasphemy indicates that with "the quoted material from Dan 7:13 and the allusion to Ps 110:2," Jesus is portrayed as "more than the Messiah as a merely human agent."[159] In Jesus's claim to be Son of Man and in his acclaim as Son of

grounds for identifying the humanlike figure as the Davidic anointed are circumstantial" (Goldingay, *Daniel*, 169). Aune points out that "in pre-Christian Judaism there was no concept of 'the Son of man' as an eschatological heavenly redeemer figure. The Jewish and Christian texts which use the Son of man designation in a titular sense all date from the last half of the first century C. E." (Aune, "Christian Prophecy," 410; cf. Hurtado, *Lord Jesus Christ*, 19). For Hengel, "leider wissen wir nichts über die Auslegung von Ps 110 und Dan 7 in Qumran" (Hengel, "'Setze dich zu meiner Rechten!,'" 160). Attridge finds "the only clear case of the Jewish use of the title Son of Man for God's eschatological agent is the parable section of Enoch.... It remains problematic whether these passages, which are probably to be dated in the first century CE, provide any evidence for the background of the NT use of the title" (Attridge, *Epistle to the Hebrews*, 73n45). Thus, J. J. Collins's finding that "the two earliest Jewish interpretations of Daniel 7 are found in the *Similitudes of Enoch* and *4 Ezra* 13" (J. J. Collins, *Scepter and Star*, 188) is not strong evidence, and his conclusion that "the Son of God text [4Q246] suggests that the messianic interpretation of Daniel 7 had begun already in the Hasmonean period" (J. J. Collins, 188; cf. M. F. Bird, *Are You the One?*, 91) is speculative. Rather, Stein's conclusion that "the title 'Son of Man' was almost certainly not a popular 'messianic' title in first-century Judaism" (Stein, *Mark*, 49) appears correct.

157. M. F. Bird believes Jesus may have originated the linking of these texts (M. F. Bird, *Are You the One?*, 139; cf. Evans, *Mark 8:27—16:20*, 451). Whether Jesus's prediction refers to the exaltation or the second coming is debated. For the former, see Aune, "Christian Prophecy," 422. For the latter, see J. J. Collins, *Daniel*, 307; and Bock, *Proclamation from Prophecy and Pattern*, 141-42. We adopt Eskola's position that these themes may be related since it is "logical to conclude that a heavenly dominion of Christ was considered as a necessary premise for an idea of parousia" (Eskola, *Messiah and the Throne*, 281).

158. For this, see Evans, *Mark 8:27—16:20*, 274. Whether the one like a son of man in Daniel is a symbol for or representative of faithful Israel is much debated (see, e.g., Marcus, *Way of the Lord*, 169, 171; Beale, *New Testament Biblical Theology*, 193; and Koester, *Hebrews*, 215), but our analysis is consistent with either understanding.

159. Hagner, *Matthew 14–28*, 800. For the idea that "the word δυνάμεως, 'Power,'" in Mark 14:62 may have been "suggested by LXX Ps 109:2," see Evans, *Mark 8:27—16:20*,

God, the implied audiences on both levels see a clearer picture of what his "more than" messiahship looks like.¹⁶⁰ Combining the metaphors from Ps 110 and Dan 7 both activates in mutual context and emphasizes the honor and authority given to the Messiah, Jesus.

The perlocutionary intent of the allusions to the core metaphor of Ps 110:1 and to Dan 7:13 is that the belief system of the Envisaging hearers/readers be transformed to understand the nature of the messiahship of Jesus, i.e., that he is the climactic and ultimate fulfillment of Yahweh's promises to David and the people of Israel.¹⁶¹ In turn, this modifies the Story of the people of God and their lifeworld/worldview and theology. We see some results of this plus further development of Jesus's identity as we move to Luke's report of Peter's quotation of Ps 110:1 in Acts 2.¹⁶²

---

452. For the idea that Jesus is accusing his opponents "of being Yahweh's enemies," see R. E. Watts, "Psalms in Mark's Gospel," 41; and R. E. Watts, "Lord's House and David's Lord," 320.

160. *Contra* Nolland, who finds that "Jesus has stopped short of directly claiming to be the Son of Man who is to be exalted to royal dignity in heaven" (Nolland, *Luke 18:35—24:53*, 1110; cf. Nolland, *Gospel of Matthew*, 1132), we believe Jesus's words do have that import. Nolland himself agrees Jesus's "words are more than suggestive of this possibility" [Nolland, *Luke 18:35—24:53*, 1110]). R. E. Watts points out that in "his first public affirmation of messianic identity (Mark 14:62), Jesus' second reference to Ps. 110:1 reaffirms his divinely mandated status as the Davidic heir who shares in God's rule" (R. E. Watts, "Lord's House and David's Lord," 320). This is not the same, however, as calling Jesus "divine" (see n150).

161. Although it is not clear that Matthew's or Mark's implied audience had familiarity with the co-text of Dan 7:13, Dan 7:14 is highly reminiscent of the first oracle of Ps 110 in that the one like a son of man receives from Yahweh the honor and privilege of a ruler. "The humanlike figure comes in order to be invested as king (v 14).... He is, then, a symbol for some entity given authority by God" (Goldingay, *Daniel*, 168; *contra* Roth, *Die Grundparadigmen christlicher Schriftauslegung*, 58). Marcus agrees that "although the phrase 'sitting at the right hand' in 14:62 is most directly an allusion to Ps. 110:1, it is also consonant with the picture in Dan. 7:13-14 of the humanlike figure being presented to the Ancient of Days and made his co-regent" (Marcus, *Way of the Lord*, 165). For Witherington, "the roles assigned to the Son of Man in Dan. 7:13-14 are in fact royal roles—he will have dominion, glory, and kingship. In other words, Mark does not see Son of Man terminology as an alternative to royal phrases being used of Jesus, but as another way of putting the point about Jesus' kingship" (Witherington, *Gospel of Mark*, 51). In addition to "enthronement with God," M. F. Bird finds a second possible link in that "both Ps. 110 and Dan. 7 have to do with the subjugation of enemies" (M. F. Bird, *Are You the One?*, 138). Furthermore, Dan 7:14 makes it clear that the dominion of this ruler is everlasting (שלטן עלם/ἐξουσία αἰώνιος), a conclusion that is also reached by reading together the two oracles of Ps 110 (see pp. 176-185 above).

162. Although A. Y. Collins correctly considers Mark 14:62 to be "the climax of the theme of Jesus' identity" in Mark (A. Y. Collins, "Influence of Daniel," 98; cf. Hengel,

PART II | CASE STUDIES

PS 110:1 AS QUOTED BY PETER AND REPORTED IN ACTS 2:34-35

In Acts 2:34-35, Luke reports that Peter quoted the entirety of Ps 110:1 in his Pentecost speech (a speech event). Some scholars call this "simple Scripture proof"[163] or "a prophetic promise fulfilled,"[164] but we find this quotation to be a key element of the transformation of Story as it pertains to Jesus's messiahship.

The Locution

We present NA[27] and the NRSV of Acts 2:33-36 in Appendix §5, splitting this speech act complex into four Assertives.[165] The quotation in the third speech act, vv. 34b-35, reproduces Ps 109:1 LXX verbatim.[166] It is introduced by λέγει δὲ αὐτός, where "he" is clearly David.

In the first speech act (v. 33), Peter introduces Jesus's exaltation. Whether Jesus has been exalted "to" or "by" God's right hand is not clear. Either seems possible. "To" would cohere with the metaphor presented in v. 34b; "by" would mean that Peter was giving additional details as to how God raised Jesus, which is the subject of v. 24.[167] That different metaphors about "the right hand" can exist in close proximity is demonstrated by

---

"'Setze dich zu meiner Rechten!,'" 151), Jesus's identity continues to be developed in post-resurrection events (see below).

163. Bock attributes the former classification to Martin Rese (Bock, *Proclamation from Prophecy and Pattern*, 186; with reference to Rese, *Alttestamentliche Motive*, 62. See also Bock, 40). Similarly, according to Doble, in Acts 2:16-36, Peter is "portrayed quarrying scriptural material" in order "to prove that 'Jesus is the Christ'" (Doble, "Psalms in Luke-Acts," 88).

164. Bock, *Proclamation from Prophecy and Pattern*, 186, where he adds that "again, Jesus is proclaimed through prophecy."

165. Turner refers to the assertions of 2:33-36 as "climactic" (Turner, *Power from on High*, 267). Although one could argue this speech act complex begins with v. 29, it is more logical to include vv. 29-32 with the preceding speech act complex since it is in v. 33 that Peter turns to Jesus's exaltation. However, we do include elements of the entire speech event in our analysis.

166. Some LXX manuscripts omit ὁ before κύριος.

167. Conzelmann's argument that "despite Ps 118 (117):16 and *Odes Sol.* 25.9, τῇ δεξιᾷ should be understood as local ('to the right hand') rather than instrumental (cf. vss 30-36; 5:31; *Odes Sol.* 8.21)" (Conzelmann, *Acts of the Apostles*, 21) actually provides good reasons to consider v. 33 as *instrumental*. The latter argument is also made by Bruce, *Acts of the Apostles*, 126; and D. J. Williams, *Acts*, 53.

Ps 110:1, 5 and is also seen in Acts 2:25, where Peter quotes Ps 15:8 LXX concerning God being at David's right hand, and in Acts 2:34b, where the exalted one is seated at God's right hand.[168]

The Illocution

At the episode level, Peter is the implied speaker of the Pentecost speech (Acts 2:14–40). His implied audience is devout Jews in Jerusalem for Pentecost who have witnessed either the coming of the Holy Spirit or its aftermath and are confused or doubting (Acts 2:1–13). The implied author of Acts is the implied author of Luke. In Acts, as for Luke's Gospel, the implied audience is the Greek "Theophilus."[169]

According to Luke, Peter's speech includes multiple quotations from and allusions to the OT.[170] For these Assertives to be tellable at both the level of Peter's Jewish audience and Luke's presumably predominantly Gentile Christian audience, both Peter's use of these OT quotations and allusions and Luke's relating of this episode must either create or activate mutual context about Jesus. We consider both the episode and discourse levels below, beginning with the episode level.

---

168. As Keener points out, "Since one can hardly be at another's right hand and have that person at one's own right hand (unless each faces the other, not the usual arrangement of thrones), the language of the 'right hand' is metaphor in both psalms (Pss 16:8, 11; 110:1, 5)" (Keener, *Acts*, 1:947). His idea that the "right hand" language of Acts 2:25 (Ps 16:8) is linked by *gezerah shevah* with Acts 2:34 (Ps 110:1) seems unlikely since different metaphors are used in the two verses. However, there may be an implicit connection between Acts 2:34 (Ps 110:1) and the "right hand" language in the unquoted portion of Ps 16:11 (see, e.g., Keener, 1:944–45).

169. See p. 197 and n111 above. If Luke's Gentile Christian audience had been "God fearers," as the name Theophilus implies, it is likely they would have been familiar with the Psalms. Certainly, if they had previously read Luke's gospel, they would have encountered Ps 110.

170. Juel believes that "the speech . . . represents a developed, sophisticated midrashic argument that cannot be classified as early or typical" (Juel, *Messianic Exegesis*, 147), and Hurtado reminds us that "we have to be very careful about reading the narratives without taking account of the author's own literary purposes, and we should not take the speeches as records of what was said by the characters to whom they are attributed" (Hurtado, *Lord Jesus Christ*, 177). However, although Luke included the Pentecost speech in his narrative for a purpose, that does not mean that he invented that speech and attributed it to Peter. In any event, the implied audience for Peter's speech is different from Luke's own implied audience.

PART II | CASE STUDIES

Because this speech act complex occurs near the end of the speech event, it is helpful to set it within the context of Peter's argument. At the beginning of Peter's speech, there is a lengthy quotation from Joel which ends with the words "Then everyone who calls on the name of the Lord shall be saved" (Acts 2:21, quoting Joel 3:5 LXX). In Acts 2:25a, Peter introduces a quotation from Ps 15:8–11 LXX[171] with the claim that David spoke these words concerning Jesus, who has been raised by God and freed from death (see vv. 22–24).[172] Then in v. 31, Peter again attributes Ps 15:10 LXX to David as prophecy of the resurrection of the Messiah.[173] Since there is no evidence that Ps 15:10 LXX was considered "messianic" in or by the first century,[174] it appears this interpretation originated with Jesus's original followers and possibly with Peter himself.

---

171. See chapter 4 for an analysis of Paul's quotations of Ps 15 LXX, Ps 2, and Isa 55 in Acts 13.

172. In Ps 15 LXX, the psalmist (from the superscription, possibly David) speaks of his rescue from difficulty (vv. 5–6) and of his confidence that his life will be long and prosperous thanks to Yahweh's protection. Eaton notes that "a common interpretation is that the reference here is to deliverance from a current danger; he [the psalmist] is not to die on this occasion. This would suit the usual trend of Old Testament thought" (Eaton, *Psalms*, 98).

173. Much has been written about the relationship between Ps 16 [15 LXX] and the resurrection of the Messiah. Schenck's conclusion that "Acts 2:25–31 understands similar words in Psalm 16 (15:8–11 LXX) as Jesus' confidence that God would raise him from the dead" (Schenck, "2 Corinthians," 531) outstrips Peter's claim, which concerns David's knowledge, not Jesus's. Bock finds significant the substitution in v. 31 of ἡ σάρξ αὐτοῦ (used in Ps 15:9 LXX and Acts 2:26b for resting in hope) for τὸν ὅσιόν σου (used in Ps 15:10 LXX and Acts 2:27b in connection with avoidance of decay). But his conclusion that "the substitution guarantees that the point of the passage is not mere spiritual translation, bodily preservation, or terminal illness, but bodily resurrection" (Bock, *Proclamation from Prophecy and Pattern*, 178) is too strong. Other scholars distinguish between τὴν ψυχήν μου in Acts 2:27a (Ps 15:10a LXX) and τὸν ὅσιόν σου in Acts 2:27b (Ps 15:10b LXX). For example, Polhill believes that "'Holy One' could apply to David as the anointed king, but for Peter it was even more appropriate as a designation for Christ" (Polhill, *Acts*, 113; cf. Marshall, *Acts of the Apostles*, 76). See Moessner, "Two Lords 'at the Right Hand,'" 221n7, for a list of scholars who believe Acts 2:27b=Ps 15:10b foretells Jesus's resurrection. We consider instead that, although in Acts 2 the Psalm is "attributed to David who is understood to have a prophetic role" (Koester, *Hebrews*, 177), Litwak is correct that this does not mean David made a "straightforward prophecy of the Messiah rising from the dead" (Litwak, *Echoes of Scripture*, 179). We also reject Eskola's thought that "Psalm 16 was perfectly suitable for the purposes of the writer, since there the exaltation terminology was connected with the idea of resurrection" (Eskola, *Messiah and the Throne*, 163). There is no explicit "exaltation terminology" in Ps 16, and Ps 16:11c is not quoted in Acts 2.

174. See D. J. Williams, *Acts*, 52. This does not, however, require considering Ps

Acts 2:30 is another key element of the speech event. In it, Peter claims that David's prophetic gift allowed him to understand that God's promise to seat a descendant on his (David's) throne (an allusion to Ps 132:11–12)[175] would have fulfillment beyond David's immediate successors. Thus, not only does Ps 15 LXX describe David's own situation,[176] it would also be applicable to those of his line who, according to Yahweh's promise, would also receive Yahweh's anointing.[177] This promise culminates in Messiah Jesus, for whom what was said about David in a particular situation—that he would not then be given over to the grave and would not experience decay—is true *eternally*.[178]

15:8–11 LXX to be either "some obscure text which Christians allegedly mined from the Scriptures in order to find proof for the resurrection or . . . a text which simply makes one point, namely that Messiah's resurrection was already foretold by David, or both" (Moessner, "*Two* Lords 'at the Right Hand,'" 221).

175. In Ps 132:11–12, Yahweh's dynastic promise concerns the succession to David's throne, not Yahweh's. However, "the idea that the throne is ultimately God's is certainly correct" (Strauss, *Davidic Messiah in Luke-Acts*, 138).

176. *Contra* Moyise, who sees Luke's argument to be "that David could not have been speaking about himself but was speaking as a prophet" (Moyise, *Later New Testament Writings*, 19), David knew he was anointed and loved by Yahweh. He also knew he would die (see, e.g., Ps 39:13). Furthermore, to say that "David did not ascend into heaven, so he could not have been speaking of himself" as exalted to God's right hand (Polhill, *Acts*, 115; cf. Bruce, *Acts of the Apostles*, 124, 127) misses the point that the seat at God's right hand is a metaphor of being granted authority and power. As Gourgues points out, "la session à la droite n'entre pas dans la catégorie des événements historiques observables mais constitue plutôt l'expression métaphorique d'une réalité théologique" (Gourgues, *À la droite de Dieu*, 202).

177. Hebrew thought "saw a close link between individuals and their descendants. The Greek [of Acts 2:30] expresses this concept quite graphically with the phrase 'from the fruit of his loins' ('one of his descendants,' NIV)" (Polhill, *Acts*, 114). *Contra* Polhill, *Acts*, 114; Aloisi, "Who is David's Lord?," 122; and Keener, *Acts*, 1:951, rather than speaking only of *one* descendant, i.e., Messiah Jesus, David's words about Yahweh's protection would apply to *all* his successors. D. J. Williams argues "it was of a line of kings that the psalmist wrote and not of any one king in particular, as [Ps 132] verse 12 clearly shows" (D. J. Williams, *Acts*, 52). Rendtorff points out that in Ps 132 (alluded to in Acts 2:30), the "transition from David to his successors and back again shows the focus to be . . . that the name David represents the Davidic dynasty through the centuries" (Rendtorff, "Psalms of David," 63). However, if, as Marshall proposes, Ps 132 was "understood in the same way" as 4QFlor, which "clearly interprets 2 Samuel 7:10–16 as a reference to the Messiah," Peter and his hearers may have "shared a belief that the passages about David's descendants included a reference to the Messiah in particular" (Marshall, *Acts of the Apostles*, 77).

178. "Through Jesus God fulfilled his promise to David of a kingdom without end" (Doble, "Psalms in Luke-Acts," 117). See also Moyise, *Later New Testament Writings*, 16.

PART II | CASE STUDIES

It is this dynastic promise to David, plus the affirmation of Jesus's resurrection (vv. 24, 32), that permits the conclusion in v. 33 that Jesus has been exalted to the right hand of God,[179] from which position Jesus pours out the Holy Spirit (v. 33c).[180] To support this point, Peter quotes all of Ps 109:1 LXX in vv. 34b–35, evoking with regard to Jesus the Story of one who received the honor, authority, and power represented by a seat at Yahweh's right hand. In v. 34a, Peter leads into this quotation by re-stating a point he made in v. 29: οὐ γὰρ Δαυὶδ ἀνέβη εἰς τοὺς οὐρανούς, thus continuing the comparison between David and Jesus that he began in v. 25.[181] Peter is contrasting David's burial and eventual decay with Jesus's ascension (reported in Acts 1:9)[182] and exaltation (vv. 33a and 34b).

Although Ps 110 may not have been understood messianically prior to the *Davidssohnfrage*, there Jesus implicitly identified the Messiah with David's Lord. After Jesus's resurrection and ascension, the disciples, NT authors, and early Christians would have had no doubt that Jesus's earlier reference was to himself.[183] In Acts 2:36, Peter makes this identification explicit: Jesus is "both Lord and Messiah" (καὶ κύριον . . . καὶ Χριστόν).[184]

---

179. For this, see, e.g., Turner, *Power from on High*, 275.

180. We agree with Eskola against Hay that the theme of Peter's speech is "the work of the exalted Christ" rather than "'the vindication implied by his exaltation'" (Eskola, *Messiah and the Throne*, 173n49, quoting Hay, *Glory at the Right Hand*, 72). As Bock points out, "The point of the passage is that Jesus is now doing the work of the Father while being seated at his side. Jesus now acts for the Father with his power and authority. He is the mediating dispenser of the Spirit" (Bock, *Proclamation from Prophecy and Pattern*, 183).

181. As Jesus did in the Synoptics, Peter clearly connects Ps 110 and David. Some consider the comparison to include the suffering and vindication of Jesus and David. Creach finds that "in Acts 2, Peter appeals to the suffering of David in the Psalms and to God's vindication of David to explain the suffering and resurrection of Jesus" (Creach, "Destiny of the Righteous," 60–61; cf. Litwak, *Echoes of Scripture*, 179). But even if one uses the co-text of the psalm to make an argument about the suffering of Jesus, it is clear (*contra* Creach and perhaps also Moessner) that Jesus's passion is not the focal issue of Peter's speech.

182. The ascension account in Acts 1:9 "appears to be a reflection of Dan. 7:10, 13–14" (Beale, *New Testament Biblical Theology*, 246), although Luke does not allude to the Daniel passage in his gospel.

183. This explains the otherwise abrupt reference to Χριστός in Acts 2:31. As Moessner points out, "it is curious that Peter uses the term 'the Messiah' since χριστός occurs neither in Psalm 15 nor in his speech thus far. In fact, Acts 2:31a is the first use of χριστός in the book of Acts" (Moessner, "*Two Lords 'at the Right Hand*,'" 228).

184. In chapter 7, we saw another example of the importance to the early church of the confession "Jesus is Lord." Some find Jesus's lordship more important than his messiahship. For example, Bock speaks of a "christology which moves from Messiah-Servant

Furthermore, Jesus is the *eternal* Messiah and Lord.[185] "In Acts, Ps 110:1 becomes part of an argument according to which God's promise to David of a 'seed' to sit on his throne *forever* (2 Sam 7:12-14, Ps 89:3-4) is fulfilled only with the installation of the risen Christ in heaven."[186] As is true for David and others to whom the metaphors of Ps 110:1 would apply,[187] Jesus

---

to Lord" (Bock, *Proclamation from Prophecy and Pattern*, 268; cf. M. F. Bird, *Are You the One?*, 150; and Donahue and Harrington, *Gospel of Mark*, 27, who believe the title "Lord" is superior to both "Messiah/Christ" and "Son of David"). We agree instead with Strauss that "in three key texts expressing Jesus' salvation-historical significance (Lk. 2.11; Acts 2.36; 10.36) κύριος appears together with χριστός, suggesting that the two titles are complementary (in these contexts); together they express the *status and authority* of Jesus" (Strauss, *Davidic Messiah in Luke-Acts*, 27, where he adds that "Luke uses 'Lord' *primarily* as an expression of Jesus' *authority*"). Further, "in Acts 2.36 'Christ' and 'Lord' stand parallel to one another, suggesting they are integrally related in the context of Jesus' exaltation glory. One is not subordinated to the other" (Strauss, 30).

We cannot take up here the timing of Jesus being "made . . . both Lord and Messiah" beyond noting that the angels announcing Jesus's birth inform the shepherds ὅτι ἐτέχθη ὑμῖν σήμερον σωτὴρ ὅς ἐστιν χριστὸς κύριος (Luke 2:11). This argues against the idea that Jesus became Messiah only at his resurrection and also makes adoptionism unlikely (see Eskola, *Messiah and the Throne*, 160-76; and Kraus, *Theology of the Psalms*, 187, for a presentation of some of these arguments). Conzelmann correctly notes that "for Luke Jesus was certainly Messiah during his lifetime ([Acts] 10:38; Luke 4:18), and he makes no essential distinction between κύριος and χριστός" (Conzelmann, *Acts of the Apostles*, 21). This negates Loader's theory that Acts 2, where "Jesus is made Lord at the exaltation," is a more primitive use of Ps 110:1 and that Mark 12:35ff. "is the product of *later* christological reflection" since in it "Jesus is Lord already on earth" (Loader, "Christ at the Right Hand," 215; emphasis added). We also disagree with Juel's conclusion that "it is as the enthroned 'Lord' that Jesus is Son of David" (Juel, "Origin of Mark's Christology," 455). Jesus was called "Son of David" during his incarnation.

Nor can we address the question of when Jesus's reign began or will begin. Strauss, for example, believes that "Jesus begins his messianic reign already at his exaltation-enthronement" (Strauss, *Davidic Messiah in Luke-Acts*, 264; cf. Keener, *Acts*, 1:956) while Hay argues that "in a major way Luke seems to imply that Jesus' kingdom will begin only with the parousia (22.29-30; Acts 1.6-7)" (Hay, *Glory at the Right Hand*, 71). The former argument seems more plausible.

185. See, e.g., Strauss, *Davidic Messiah in Luke-Acts*, 317. Moessner believes the psalms alluded to in 2:30 all "characterize David as the Lord's anointed whose offspring will 'sit upon his throne' *'forever'*" (Moessner, "*Two* Lords 'at the Right Hand,'" 228; emphasis added).

186. Juel, "Origin of Mark's Christology," 455; emphasis added. Also see Strauss, *Davidic Messiah in Luke-Acts*, 65; and Bateman, *Early Jewish Hermeneutics*, 234. As noted above, the allusion to Ps 132 in v. 30 evokes Yahweh's promise of an eternal dynasty.

187. Kraus is incorrect in saying that "David was not the one who carried out the striking command to sit at God's right hand and to reign there" (Kraus, *Theology of the Psalms*, 187). As Israel's king, David was granted the honor and authority of the

PART II | CASE STUDIES

reigns over the earth. However, unlike an earthly monarch, Jesus does not reign only from or over the earth. He both reigns *from* heaven and *over* heaven;[188] "exalted to the right hand of God," Jesus has "poured out" God's Spirit (v. 33c, a link to the quotations of Joel 3:1, 2 LXX in vv. 17 and 18).[189] And he does so eternally in his own person rather than dynastically.

"The remarkable statement in 2.33,"[190] in which the authority of the exalted Jesus is shown to surpass that of Israel's earthly kings, furthers the resolution of the "more than messiah" tension.[191] We expand on this below in discussing the perlocution.

---

metaphoric seat at the right hand of God. And David was exalted (2 Sam 33:49, 23:1), as was Solomon (1 Chr 29:25). Nor are we convinced the identification of Jesus as David's Lord in Acts 2 means "the dialogue in the psalm is between God and Jesus" (Moyise, *Later New Testament Writings*, 18), although Jesus would be included in the dialogue as David's descendant.

188. See, e.g., Matt 28:18. "For Jesus to take David's throne *in heaven* . . . redefines the traditional Jewish expectation of Davidic rule" (Keener, *Acts*, 1:954; cf. Bock, *Proclamation from Prophecy and Pattern*, 155; and Strauss, *Davidic Messiah in Luke-Acts*, 30). "In essence Acts 2.33 answers to the hopes of Lk. 1.32-33, and . . . the kingdom of God comes in greater than hitherto experienced power and presence in Israel through Jesus' attainment of the eternal throne of David to rule over Jacob" (Turner, *Power from on High*, 268). At Pentecost, "the throne and power Jesus is given . . . transcend even the expectations of the infancy narratives" since "Jesus now fully enters the promise to David, sits on the throne at God's right hand, and receives Lordship over the Spirit" (Turner, 296, 306).

189. Strauss notes that there is also a link "to the words of Jesus in Lk. 24.49 and Acts 1.4, where the pouring out of the Spirit is likewise referred to as the 'promise of the Father' (ἐπαγγελία τοῦ πατρός)" (Strauss, *Davidic Messiah in Luke-Acts*, 141). Turner makes the important point that "it is doubtful whether in a Jewish context a human figure exalted to God's right hand would readily be 'called on' for salvation in the way implied by the association of baptism 'in the name of Jesus Christ' with Joel 3.5 [2.32]. The presupposition which allows this surprising claim is to be found in [Acts] 2.33b, c; the one exalted at God's right hand has 'received the promise of the Holy Spirit' from the Father, and himself (in God's own place, cf. 2.17b, c) '*pours out this which you see and hear*'" (Turner, *Power from on High*, 276; cf. Bock, *Proclamation from Prophecy and Pattern*, 183-85). We discuss this further below.

190. Turner, *Power from on High*, 267.

191. Although for Strauss, the "'more than messiah' . . . tension is resolved in Acts when Jesus is openly declared to be Lord (Acts 2.36; 10.43)" (Strauss, *Davidic Messiah in Luke-Acts*, 28; see also 18, 317; cf. Doble, "Psalms in Luke-Acts," 88; and Moyise, *Later New Testament Writings*, 18), we believe critical elements in resolving the tension are (i) the dynastic promise referred to in Acts 2:30 and (ii) Jesus pouring out the Holy Spirit in Acts 2:33, i.e., the demonstration that Jesus reigns over heaven. Whether Pao is correct that "lordship of the risen Jesus" is a theme "developed throughout the New Exodus program" (Pao, *Acts and the Isaianic New Exodus*, 212) cannot be explored here. We do note that Mallen, who finds "the outpouring of the Spirit at Pentecost in Acts 2" to be "a

The Perlocution

Building on the "more than" connections Jesus made between "messiah," "David's son," and "Lord" as reported in the Synoptic Gospels, Peter combines quotations from or allusions to Joel 2 and Pss 16, 132, and 110 to paint a more detailed picture of "this Jesus, whom you crucified" (Acts 2:36; see also 2:23). Peter's Story includes the synthesis of messiahship and lordship already implied by Jesus in the *Davidssohnfrage*. This mutual context is activated and strengthened by a quotation of Ps 110:1, a verse Jesus quoted and alluded to earlier.

Taken with Jesus's Predictive Assertive in the Synoptic passion narratives,[192] Peter's quotation of Ps 110:1 in Acts 2 focuses on the unparalleled honor, power, and authority that inures to the exalted Jesus. In his exaltation, as well as in his messiahship and lordship (v. 36), Jesus is seen to be "more than" the expectation of his Jewish contemporaries. Peter calls his audience not only to understand this but to live into the lifeworld where the exalted Jesus rules on earth and in heaven forever.

In the Directive in 2:38, Peter tells his empirical audience what he wants them to *do*: "Repent and be baptized, every one of you, in the name of Jesus Christ for the forgiveness of your sins." The Envisaging audience will do the same. Envisaging readers will incorporate the information contained in the Assertives of this speech act complex into their theological worldview and will respond positively to the Directive to "repent and be baptized" and move into or establish themselves more firmly in a lifeworld in which the exalted Jesus is eternally Messiah and Lord.

Clearly, Peter's use of Ps 110:1 incorporates Jesus's intervening interpretation as revealed by the *Davidssohnfrage* and the passion narrative as well as the subsequent events of Jesus's death, resurrection, and exaltation.[193] But does this justify a claim that Peter's naming Jesus "Lord" in 2:36

---

key event ... interpreted through reference to Joel 3.1–5 LXX and the Davidic psalms" (Mallen, *Reading and Transformation of Isaiah*, 62), makes no mention of Isaiah. Moyise adds that "Luke's primary source for understanding Jesus is the Psalms" (Moyise, *Later New Testament Writings*, 22; cf. Moyise, 39; and Doble, "Psalms in Luke-Acts," 104, 117).

192. See pp. 206–207 above.

193. For Tharel, "Peter's understanding of the psalm's language is more complete than the psalmist's because Peter has witnessed the advent of Christ. Peter's interpretation of the psalm, however, is not inconsistent with the psalm's original meaning. Jesus is the ultimate Davidic king and the recipient of God's promise" (Tharel, "Use of Psalm 110:1," 84).

is an explicit ascription of divinity?[194] Not in and of itself. The title "Lord" comes from Ps 110:1, in which the authority of the ruler is derivative.[195] And if Peter quoted, as seems likely, the Hebrew psalm, then "the first word translated 'Lord' is YHWH, the name of God, and the second word is 'aḏôn which can be used of human lords and masters."[196] From this, Marshall concludes that in vv. 34-35 "it is simply the attribute of lordship which is given to Jesus; he is not equated with Yahweh."[197]

But if one considers the Pentecost speech as a whole at the episode level and within in its literary context at the discourse level, there is other evidence which points to Jesus's "more than" messiahship encompassing his divinity. Most immediately, as Craig Keener points out, Jesus "is the one who pours out the Spirit (2:33; Luke 3:16), a divine role (Acts 2:17)."[198]

---

194. Dunn provides a helpful summary of scholarship on this question in "ΚΥΡΙΟΣ in Acts." He does not mention Bock, who finds "Lord" to be a "title which shows Jesus in his task and person to be equal with God" (Bock, *Proclamation from Prophecy and Pattern*, 184; cf. Eskola, *Messiah and the Throne*, 172).

195. Yahweh effects Jesus's resurrection (v. 32), exalts Jesus to/by His right hand and gives Jesus the Holy Spirit (v. 33), invites Jesus to sit at His right hand (vv. 34-35), and "makes" Jesus both Lord and Christ/Messiah (καὶ κύριον αὐτὸν καὶ χριστὸν ἐποίησεν ὁ θεός, v. 36). Brawley concludes that "the Lucan appropriation of scripture is primarily theocentric" (Brawley, *Text to Text*, 59). Dunn believes Ps 110:1 "made clear the relationship of the two lordships: . . . the lordship of Jesus was a derivative lordship, but as derived from the Lord God it was in effect an expression of God's lordship" (Dunn, "ΚΥΡΙΟΣ in Acts," 252-53). Further, that "Luke clearly thought of both God and Jesus as κύριος . . . does not mean that he thought of them as two equal κύριοι, or casually mixed them up, or saw them in some sophisticated pretrinitarian way as expressions of the one θεός καὶ κύριος" (Dunn, 252).

196. Marshall, *Acts of the Apostles*, 79.

197. Marshall, *Acts of the Apostles*, 80; see also 25. Turner points out that O'Neill also denies that the earliest Aramaic speaking community would have acknowledged Jesus "as 'Lord' . . . in its transcendent sense" (Turner, *Power from on High*, 278, 278n28). According to O'Neill, "the Aramaic-speaking Church read the O.T. in Hebrew and would be fully aware of the distinction in Psalm 110 between 'the Lord' . . . and 'my Lord'" (O'Neill, *Theology of Acts*, 130). O'Neill concludes that "at this stage there are no indications that there was any confusion between the two Lords, or any attempt to claim divinity for Jesus because he was called Lord (O'Neill, 131). However, Turner notes correctly that "it is not clear that אדני need necessarily mean *less* than יהוה, and if the earliest community had other reasons for using God-talk of Jesus it would have read the two titles as equivalents" (Turner, *Power from on High*, 278n28). Hurtado concurs that "*Adonay* was widely used as a reverential oral substitute for *Yahweh* by Hebrew-speaking readers of the Bible" (Hurtado, *Lord Jesus Christ*, 183).

198. Keener, *Acts*, 1:502; cf. Bock, *Proclamation from Prophecy and Pattern*, 184. Gathercole believes that the giving of the Spirit "presupposes divine identity" (Gathercole,

Additionally, the prophet Joel's words concerning salvation for those who call on the name of the Lord (Yahweh in the original context) are applied to Jesus.[199] Jesus is now presented as the "Lord upon whose name one must call for salvation, even as Joel envisaged one would call on God's name."[200]

At the discourse level, Luke develops Jesus's divine identity further as Acts progresses. Notable examples include 5:31, which may echo Ps 110:1, and where, like 2:38, "God offers Israel and others forgiveness . . . in Jesus's name"[201]; 7:55–56, which clearly alludes to Ps 110:1; and 8:16 and 19:5, where "it is in his [Jesus's] name that those turning to God must be baptized."[202] Extremely significant is Acts 10:36. Although in the OT only

---

Preexistent Son, 73). More emphatically, Turner argues that *"there is simply NO analogy for an exalted human* (or any other creature) *becoming so integrated with God that such a person may be said to 'commission' God's Spirit, and through that to extend that exalted person's own 'presence' and activity to people on earth.* For the Jew, such relationship to, and activity in or through, the Spirit appears to be necessarily, inalienably, and so distinctively, *God's*" (Turner, "Spirit of Christ," 423). Keener contrasts this to Dunn's thought that "Luke presents Jesus only as 'a plenipotentiary representative of God'" (Keener, *Acts*, 1:923, quoting Dunn, *Acts of the Apostles*, 29, although Dunn does not use the word "only" and does say that "'the Lord' should presumably be understood as the exalted Jesus" [Dunn, 29; see also 30–31]; cf. Strauss, *Davidic Messiah in Luke-Acts*, 144).

199. For Bock, "Jesus now mediates God's salvation as a 'co-regent'" (Bock *Proclamation from Prophecy and Pattern*, 264).

200. Turner, *Power from on High*, 267; see also 273. Hurtado adds that "it is surely remarkable enough to identify 'the great and notable day of the Lord' as the future coming of Jesus (2:20, citing Joel 2:31 [3:4 Heb.]), for in the Old Testament 'the day of the Lord' consistently refers to a time of God's own special action of deliverance or judgment. . . . It is, however, an absolutely more stunning move still for early Christians to have taken the biblical expression that means the cultic worship of God, to 'call upon the name of the Lord [*Yahweh*],' as referring also to cultic acclamation/invocation of Jesus (Acts 2:21, citing Joel 2:32 [3:5 Heb.])" (Hurtado, *Lord Jesus Christ*, 181; cf. Bock, *Proclamation from Prophecy and Pattern*, 184).

Hurtado makes the interesting point that "the crucial line from Joel cited in the Acts account of Peter's speech (Acts 2:21), 'Everyone who calls upon the name of the Lord shall be saved,' is also cited . . . by Paul in Romans 10:13, in a context . . . that indicates that Paul means the biblical phrase to refer to the ritual act of 'confessing [*homologeō*]' the Lord *Jesus* (10:9). . . . This ritual use of Jesus' name reflects an explicit identification of Jesus as an appropriate recipient of such cultic devotion" (Hurtado, *Lord Jesus Christ*, 198). We cannot explore here how the events of Pentecost, the writing of Romans, and the writing of Acts are related.

201. Keener, *Acts*, 1:502; cf. Bock, *Proclamation from Prophecy and Pattern*, 184.

202. Keener, *Acts*, 1:502, where he also gives numerous other examples from other parts of Acts which point to Luke's affirming Jesus's divine nature. The injunction to be baptized in Jesus's name is found in Acts 2:38.

PART II | CASE STUDIES

Yahweh is referred to as "the Lord of all the earth,"[203] in 10:36, Jesus reigns over both heaven and earth and is πάντων κύριος—"*everything* is now under his control."[204]

Another distinction between the episode and discourse levels concerns the implied reader. At the episode level, Peter's implied readers are Jews (see, e.g., Acts 2:14, 22, 29, and 36).[205] At the discourse level, Luke recounts the events of Pentecost to an implied audience who are Greek and presumably Gentile. For such an implied audience, terms like "everyone" (πᾶς ὅς, 2:21; ὅσους, 2:39) and "all who are far away" (πᾶσιν τοῖς εἰς μακράν, 2:39) indicate that the OT promises of God as they are fulfilled by the "more than" Messiah, Jesus, were intended for the Gentiles as well as the Jews.[206]

As a result of hearing/reading this speech event, and especially the climactic speech act complex that includes the quotation from Ps 110:1, our understanding of Jesus's "more than" messiahship has evolved. At the episode level, the derived authority of the exalted Jesus—eternally reigning over both earth and heaven at the right hand of God—is presented as greater than that of any earthly monarch. To the exalted Jesus also belong certain prerogatives of divinity, namely the forgiveness of sins, the gifting of the Holy Spirit, and the power to save. Moreover, at the discourse level, this episode promotes a fuller understanding both of Jesus's divine identity

---

203. References to אדון כל הארץ appear in Jos 3:11, 13; Ps 97:5; Mic 4:13; and Zech 4:14.

204. Pao, *Acts and the Isaianic New Exodus*, 210n83; emphasis added. Although Pao believes the quotation from Ps 109 LXX at the end of the Pentecost speech indicates "the resurrection and exaltation of Jesus are understood as his enthronement as Lord of all" (Pao, 210), in Acts 10:36 it is made explicit that Jesus is πάντων κύριος. Strauss makes the comparison to David: "While Jesus is indeed David's son and the heir to his throne, his universal dominion and authority far exceeds that of David. He is *Lord of all* (Acts 10.36)" (Strauss, *Davidic Messiah in Luke-Acts*, 317).

205. Peter addresses ἄνδρες Ἰουδαῖοι in 2:14, ἄνδρες Ἰσραηλῖται in 2:22, ἄνδρες ἀδελφοί in 2:29, and refers to οἶκος Ἰσραήλ in 2:36.

206. Moyise points out that "with Peter's speeches in Acts 2 and 3, the issue is not so much about the difference between the Greek and Hebrew texts but the different contexts: Peter is preaching to Jews in Jerusalem, and Luke is writing to Gentiles like Theophilus. . . . The issue . . . is more a debate about what Luke wanted Theophilus to deduce from these speeches. Did he want him to assume that Peter and James would have meant the same thing that he, as a Gentile, would have understood by these texts? Or was he expecting a little more sophistication; that texts that were ambiguous when quoted in Jerusalem have become clear now that the gospel has been preached to the Gentiles?" (Moyise, *Later New Testament Writings*, 11–12; cf. Litwak, *Echoes of Scripture*, 159, who attributes the prominence given to the Gentiles in Acts 2 to *Peter's* reading of Joel 3).

and of the inclusion of the Gentiles in the divine promises. Thus, at both the episode and discourse levels, in adhering to these Assertives, the empirical audience transforms its theology, Story, and lifeworld/worldview.

Peter's quotation of Ps 110:1 includes its final clause concerning the submission of all things under the feet, perhaps to warn his listeners of the perils of being numbered among Jesus's enemies.[207] Although Acts 2:40 also may refer to Jesus's enemies, this metaphor is more fully developed in 1 Cor 15, where Paul refers to Ps 110:1c.

PS 110:1 AS QUOTED IN 1 COR 15:25[208]

The Locution

A comparison of 1 Cor 15:25 and Ps 109:1c LXX appears in Appendix §6, where double underlining shows matching words and single underlining indicates the same word in different forms.[209] There are no significant locutionary issues.[210] Appendix §7 presents the speech act complex (1 Cor

---

207. *Contra* Mack's contention that "reasons why Jews would have wanted to repent and be forgiven are not evident" (Mack, *Rhetoric and the New Testament*, 91).

208. First Corinthians is an undisputed Pauline letter and is generally dated about 55 CE—earlier than Ephesians, Colossians, or Hebrews. Although Koch points out that, if one assumes Ps 109:1 LXX is quoted in 1 Cor 15:25 (which he does not), "es läge dann hier die früheste Verwendung dieses später häufig zitierten Textes vor" (Koch, *Die Schrift als Zeuge*, 19). Although this letter may have been written before the Synoptic Gospels and Acts, we believe oral accounts of earlier events (later recorded in the Synoptic Gospels and Acts) were part of the mutual context of Paul and those he taught.

Although we follow NA^{27} in treating Ps 110:1 in 1 Cor 15:25 as a quotation, others do not. For this, see Hay, *Glory at the Right Hand*, 36; and Stanley, *Paul and the Language of Scripture*, 206n85. Koch argues quite forcefully that "liegt in 1 Kor 15,25 überhaupt kein Zitat von Ψ 109,1b (und erst recht nicht von V 1a) vor" (Koch, *Die Schrift als Zeuge*, 244). He adds that "ein Zitat von Ψ 109,1b kann man hier nur annehmen, wenn man voraussetzt, daβ Ψ 109,1 insgesamt ein im Urchristentum derart bekanntes Schriftwort war, daβ Paulus dessen Kenntnis bei seinen Lesern als selbstverständlich voraussetzen konnte" (Koch, 19). However, the assumption he rejects is not unreasonable, given the use of Ps 110:1 by Jesus and in Peter's Pentecost speech. In any event, Paul "expects his audience to recognize the scriptural authority of 1 Cor 15:25, whether considered as a quotation or an allusion to Ps 110:1" (Heil, *Rhetorical Role of Scripture*, 206n4; see also 207 for details of Paul's adaptation).

209. Both texts contain the verb τίθημι and references to enemies (ἐχθρός) and feet (πούς). In 1 Cor 15:25, the enemies are put under the feet (ὑπὸ τοὺς πόδας) rather than made a footstool (LXX ὑποπόδιον).

210. Fee points out that in v. 28a "most MSS have a καί following τότε (=even the Son

15:24-28) divided into seven speech acts, with NA[27] and the NRSV in parallel columns.

The Illocution

"Messiah/Christ Jesus" appears eight times in 1 Cor 1:1-10. So, from the outset, it is clear the belief that Jesus is the Messiah forms part of the mutual context the implied author shares with the implied readers.[211] By chapter 15, we know that the empirical audience is fractured (1:10-11, 3:3, 10:18), spiritually immature, and immoral (3:2; 5:1, 11; 11:29-30), as well as arrogant (4:18, 5:2). The Corinthians are in danger of being diverted from the good news Paul has taught them of Messiah Jesus, in whom they have been sanctified (1:2). The goals of the implied author are for the readers to become united (καταρτίζω, 1:10) and blameless (ἀνέγκλητος, 1:8).

This speech act complex consists of a series of Assertives and is part of a speech event which includes all or most of 1 Cor 15.[212] The topic of the speech event is victory over death; this speech act complex addresses what happens at "the end." Many Corinthians held a Greek worldview of life after death without a resurrection of the dead (15:1-58), and thus "they failed to comprehend how an earthly body that is physical and perishable could be made suitable for a heavenly realm that is spiritual and imperishable."[213] Since the bodily resurrection of Messiah Jesus and of believers is a central

---

himself)" (Fee, *First Epistle to the Corinthians*, 746n2). The addition of καί does not alter the basic meaning of the verse.

211. J. J. Collins pithily puts it this way: "Jesus is called *Christos*, anointed, the Greek equivalent of messiah, 270 times in the Pauline corpus. If this is not ample testimony that Paul regarded Jesus as messiah, then words have no meaning" (J. J. Collins, *Scepter and Star*, 2). Of course, this does not answer the question of *how* Paul understood the term "messiah" in connection with Jesus.

212. First Corinthians 15 is one of the four speech events introduced by 1 Cor 7:1 which together comprise the last part of the letter body. Whether Paul's summary of the gospel message in 1 Cor 15:1-11 is a separate (fifth) speech event does not bear on our discussion.

213. Garland, "1 Corinthians," 106. According to Amador, Wire uses Paul's rhetoric to reconstruct the theological position of the Corinthians: "They reject the emphasis upon the future resurrection of the dead, stressing instead the experience of the living resurrection in the life of the believer through participation in the dying and rising of christ [sic] in baptism" (Amador, *Academic Constraints in Rhetorical Criticism*, 230, with reference to Wire, *Corinthian Women Prophets*, 167-68).

concept in Paul's lifeworld and theology, Paul addresses this misconception in order to restore or maintain correct belief in his readers.[214]

A crucial step in determining the illocution is to identify the referents of the various third person masculine singular pronouns in the first two speech acts, vv. 24 and 25. The opening event is the destruction or overthrow of all earthly institutions, following which is "the end" when "he," i.e., the Messiah, hands the kingdom over to God the Father (v. 24a). In light of Ps 110, the "he" who has accomplished the destruction (v. 24b) is God the Father since, according to the psalm, Yahweh vanquishes the enemies. In v. 25a, the "he" who reigns is the Messiah.[215] The enemies (also described in v. 24) are the Messiah's, and they are to be put under the Messiah's feet. The "he" in v. 25b who puts the enemies under the Messiah's feet is God the Father, the agent of subjection.[216] The Messiah's reign will last until that happens. Via this metaphor of subjection under the feet, Paul

---

214. "There is no suggestion that Paul is here addressing cultured scoffers outside the Christian community, as Acts represents him doing at Athens. The criticism is coming from the faithful themselves, from those who have been baptized, and the implication of this is very destructive of those accounts of the earliest Christian churches which see them as resurrection creations. Here is a very early community in which certainly some elements felt able to repudiate resurrection while expecting to retain a Christian identity" (Shaw, *Cost of Authority*, 95).

215. Thiselton reminds us that in 1 Cor 15 "Christ remains God's *righteous* agent of salvation" (Thiselton, *First Epistle to the Corinthians*, 1228).

216. Fee is among those who argue that Christ is the subject of θῇ in v. 25. He bases his argument on two factors: (i) the "natural antecedent is the subject of the preceding 'he must reign,' referring to Christ," and (ii) this verse serves to explain v. 24 "where Christ is the subject of the clause 'when he destroys all dominion, etc.'" (Fee, *First Epistle to the Corinthians*, 755; see also 754n40, 756; cf. Thiselton, *First Epistle to the Corinthians*, 1234). Neither argument is compelling. First, Christ is not the subject of "he has destroyed" in v. 24. The "natural" antecedent of καταργήσῃ is the immediately preceding noun phrase, τῷ θεῷ καὶ πατρί. Second, it is more logical that the actor be the same as in the first-person Commissive reported in the psalm verse quoted, i.e., Yahweh, especially since v. 25 uses the same verbiage (τίθημι, ἐχθρός, and ὑπὸ τοὺς πόδας [ὑποπόδιον]) as Ps 110:1c. Fee acknowledges that many scholars favor the position that God is the subject of "until he has put" in 1 Cor 15:25b (Fee, *First Epistle to the Corinthians*, 755n49). Two of these are Hengel, "'Setze dich zu meiner Rechten!,'" 144; and Heil, *Rhetorical Role of Scripture*, 207n8. In turn, Heil follows Holleman, who argues that "there is a change of subjects, from Jesus to God, between verses 25a (δεῖ βασιλεύειν) and 25b (θῇ), where Paul quotes or refers to Ps. 110 (109):1" on the basis of v. 28 in which "the Son will subject himself to 'the one who put all things in subjection under him.' The 'one who put all things in subjection' (τῷ ὑποτάξαντι) can only be God. Since God is the subject in verse 28, he must also be the subject of the same action described in verse 27 (ὑπέταξεν, ὑποτάξαντος) and 25b (θῇ)" (Holleman, *Resurrection and Parousia*, 59, 59n4).

evokes a Story-line of Ps 110:1—that Yahweh has promised victory over the enemies of the one invited to sit at Yahweh's right hand, i.e., the one who reigns (see Ps 110:2). As in Ps 110, where "although the king is the actual ruler, it is God who exercises his power through the king," in this segment of 1 Corinthians "the same idea is expressed: Jesus is the one who reigns, but God acts through Jesus."[217] Paul uses the Commissive from the oracle reported in the psalm—the fate Yahweh promises for the enemies of Yahweh's Anointed—as the centerpiece of his argument.

The third speech act, v. 26, repeats the key ideas of destruction/overthrow (καταργέω) and enemies (ἐχθρός) and adds to tellability the important information that the last enemy to suffer destruction is death. In the final verses of the speech act complex, vv. 27–28, the masculine singular third person pronouns all have as referent the Messiah—"he" who is reigning and the one to whom the enemies are being made subject. Both references to "the one who put all things in subjection" (vv. 27b, 28a) are to God the Father.

The last four speech acts are connected to the first three by the repetition of ὑπὸ τοὺς πόδας in vv. 25 and 27a. Additionally, a form of ὑποτάσσω appears six times in vv. 27–28; subjection is heavily emphasized in these speech acts via repetition.[218] Since ὑπὸ τοὺς πόδας and ὑποτάσσω also appear in Ps 8 LXX, many consider v. 27a to refer to Ps 8:6, where it is clear that God the Father is the agent of subjection, although there is no direct mention of enemies.[219] The climactic conclusion of this speech act complex is v.

---

217. De Lang, "Psalm 110," 45n5.

218. The verb in vv. 24 and 26 is καταργέω (I destroy, put down, make powerless) rather than ὑποτάσσω (I put under, subject) which appears in vv. 27–28. For Lambrecht, "the verb καταργέω, here in vv. 26 and 24 with the meaning 'to destroy', would seem to be the typically Pauline word. The other two verbs 'to put (under his feet)' (v. 25) and 'to subject' (vv. 27–28) are given by the psalms, and by themselves they do not point to destruction" (Lambrecht, "Paul's Christological Use of Scripture," 519n24, italics omitted). But "destroy" in the sense of "causing something to no longer exist" (BDAG, s.v. "καταργέω" §3) may not be the lexical meaning of this word in vv. 24 and 26. Rather, καταργέω may have its sense of "to cause someth. to lose its power or effectiveness, . . . make powerless" (BDAG, s.v. "καταργέω" §2). Lambrecht himself speaks of Christ handing "over the kingdom to God after having *overthrown* all inimical powers" (Lambrecht, "Paul's Christological Use of Scripture," 505; emphasis added). This would cohere with ὑπὸ τοὺς πόδας in vv. 25 and 27 and ὑποτάσσω in the later verses.

219. See, e.g., Koch, *Die Schrift als Zeuge*, 13, 13n11. For B. L. Tanner, the connection between Pss 8 and 110 "further solidifies the claim of kingship for Christ, tying the 'adam' of Psalm 8 with the royal motif of Psalm 110" (B. L. Tanner, *Book of Psalms*, 64). H. H. D. Williams points out that when Pss 110:1 and 8:7 "are considered together, they provide

28b: ἦ ὁ θεὸς πάντα ἐν πᾶσιν (v. 28b).²²⁰ This speech act complex is tellable because if Paul's audience denies the resurrection of believers, they deny the ability of God to subject *all* things, including death, to the "more than" Messiah. In that case, God would not be all in all.²²¹

It is clear the Story evoked here by the quotation of Ps 110 includes aspects of the Jesus-event. First Corinthians 15 assumes as mutual context the Story of the resurrection, ascension, exaltation, and eternal reign of Christ; this mutual context is activated by the quotation. In 1 Cor 15, "every ruler and every authority and power" (v. 24), including death (v. 26) will be subjected to Jesus, ὁ υἱός (v. 28) and Χριστός (v. 23). This expanded role and authority are those equated with the Messiah's eternal reign in and over heaven as this has evolved in events later reported by the Synoptics and Acts.²²² The Analytic reader understands this.

The Perlocution

The desired perlocutionary effect of an Assertive is adherence. In this case, adherence takes the form of realigning lifeworld around the reaffirmation of truths Paul previously taught (see 1 Cor 15:12). In broad terms, the quotation supports what Paul has taught concerning Yahweh's nature and character and Yahweh's relationship to Yahweh's people and the world. Envisaging readers reaffirm the validity of Paul's earlier teaching and reorient

---

a double grounding for the total reign of Christ over every ruler, power and authority" (H. H. D. Williams, "Psalms in 1 and 2 Corinthians," 171). In addition, since "his feet" in Ps 8:4 refers to the feet of "the son of man" (NASB) and because in 1 Cor 15, "all things" are to be subjected to Christ the Son (vv. 27 and 28), this passage links the Son and the Son of Man.

220. This argument is not subordinationist. Rather, "Paul is pointing out that *God is responsible for that subjection [of all things] through Christ*" (Fee, *First Epistle to the Corinthians*, 759). "As in 3:22–23 and 11:3, the language of the subordination of the Son to the Father is functional, referring to his 'work' of redemption, not ontological, referring to his being as such" (Fee, 760).

221. See Garland, "1 Corinthians," 106. Thiselton points out that "the emphasis lies in πάντα" (Thiselton, *First Epistle to the Corinthians*, 1236).

222. Chester argues convincingly that "the fact that Paul can assume his allusions to a citation of Ps. 110.1 will be understood in both Corinth and Rome suggests that the underlying tradition goes back very early, probably to the Jerusalem community" (Chester, *Messiah and Exaltation*, 37). R. B. Hays also finds in 1 Cor 15:25–27 "further evidence for an established pre-Pauline tradition of messianic psalm interpretation" (R. B. Hays, "Christ Prays the Psalms," 109).

their worldview/lifeworld around the truths of the resurrection of believers, the subjection of all things—including death—to the Messiah, and Yahweh as "all in all."

One or both of the metaphors of Ps 110:1 concerning the seat at Yahweh's right hand and the subjection of enemies under the feet are found elsewhere in the NT.[223] However, their use in Hebrews can be considered their fullest development. We center our discussion on the explicit quotation in Heb 1:13.

PS 110:1 AS QUOTED IN HEB 1:13

The Locution

Hebrews 1:4 begins a speech event which extends through 2:18.[224] Immediately after introducing the topic of the relationship of God's Son to the angels, the author launches into a series of seven OT (LXX) quotations,[225] five of which come from five different Psalms.[226] Psalm 109:1b–c LXX is

---

223. The metaphor of being seated at Yahweh's right hand is found in Rom 8:34, Eph 1:20–21, Col 3:1, and 1 Pet. 3:22. Of these, only Eph 1:22 also alludes to the second metaphor—the placing of all things under the feet in submission. See B. L. Tanner, *Book of Psalms*, 64–65, for a discussion of Eph 1.

For D. A. Campbell, Satan's future subjection under the feet of Christians in Rom 16:20 "echoes both 1 Corinthians 15:25–27 and underlying messianic readings of Psalms 8 and 110 (8:6 and 110:1)" (D. A. Campbell, "Echo of Scripture in Paul," 384). However, "the inclusion of Ps. 8 among the messianic texts of the OT is disputed" (Gheorghita, *Role of the Septuagint*, 143–44). Koch confirms "eine messianische Auslegung von Ps 8 ist in der jüdischen Lit. bislang überhaupt nicht nachgewiesen" (Koch, *Die Schrift als Zeuge*, 245; cf. Gheorghita, *Role of the Septuagint*, 144). The messianic reading of Ps 8 in Hebrews (see de Villiers, "Reflections on Creation and Humankind," 80) was likely developed by the early church.

224. These boundaries approximate G. H. Guthrie's first "main movement" (1:5—2:18), which he titles "The Position of the Son in Relation to the Angels" (G. H. Guthrie, *Structure of Hebrews*, 116).

225. "The writer of Hebrews has a remarkable knowledge of the LXX and used it exclusively" (Lane, *Hebrews 1–8*, lxxi; cf. Ellingworth, *Epistle to the Hebrews*, 27). The quotations in this series are introduced with a form of λέγω, i.e., "as the direct speaking of God" (Lane, *Hebrews 1–8*, cxvii), which is the most common introduction in Hebrews. This reduces the likelihood of it being a "traditional collection" (*contra* Attridge, *Epistle to the Hebrews*, 24). For an overview of various suggestions for the hermeneutic behind the OT quotations in Hebrews, see Motyer, "Psalm Quotations of Hebrews 1," 3–22; and Docherty, *Use of the Old Testament*, 61–82.

226. For the reliance of the implied author of Hebrews on the Psalms for his

quoted verbatim in Heb 1:13. The speech act complex which includes this quotation is Heb 1:13–14, both verses of which are speech acts. Appendix §8 presents NA[27] and the NRSV for this passage, divided into the two speech acts. There are no major issues of locution.

The Illocution

To identify the implied author and audience, we look to the clues found in Hebrews. From the reference to God having spoken τοῖς πατράσιν ἐν τοῖς προφήταις (1:1), we learn the implied author is someone who acknowledges the value of Jewish tradition, and especially prophecy.[227] Similarly, the implied reader has "a detailed knowledge of the OT" and "assumes on the part of his audience a deep familiarity with their [sic] contents."[228] In v. 2a, we learn that God has spoken to us (ἡμῖν) through the son (ἐν υἱῷ); thus, the implied author is a follower of Jesus Christ, as is the implied audience. Further, the identification of Jesus as Son (of God, v. 5) is part of the mutual context of the implied author and implied audience (2:9). In 2:1 the author states his purpose for writing: So "we" (ἡμᾶς) do not drift away from what we have heard.[229] "What we have heard" includes the quotations in 1:5–13, which are part of how God has previously spoken through the prophets (1:1).

The empirical audience is experiencing "loss of confidence in the viability of their convictions. They display lack of interest in the message of

---

christology, see Kistemaker, *Psalm Citations*, 12; Lane, *Hebrews 1–8*, cxvi; and Longenecker, *Biblical Exegesis*, 149. Ellingworth calls attention to the "curious fact that, of the quotations for which divine authority is specifically claimed, all but one (Je. 31[LXX 38]:33f.=Heb. 10:16f.) are from the Psalms, and none from the Torah" (Ellingworth, *Epistle to the Hebrews*, 38–39). However, Eskola's notion that Hebrews "appears to be really a commentary on Psalm 110" is without warrant (Eskola, *Messiah and the Throne*, 258; cf. Jordaan and Nel, "From Priest-King to King-Priest," 230–31, 240). Eskola, *Messiah and the Throne*, 258n26; Jordaan and Nel, "From Priest-King to King-Priest," 229; Ellingworth, *Epistle to the Hebrews*, 90, 130; and Attridge, *Epistle to the Hebrews*, 23n188, 46n138, all attribute the idea that Hebrews is a commentary/midrash on Ps 110 to G. Buchanan's 1972 volume in the Anchor Bible commentary series.

227. Although the title *Hebrews* suggests the implied author is writing to Jews, Ellingworth makes a strong case for a mixed community of readers from Jewish and Gentile backgrounds (Ellingworth, *Epistle to the Hebrews*, 25).

228. Lane, *Hebrews 1–8*, cxv. As we noted in chapter 7, presumably more informed empirical readers mediated their knowledge to their less-informed counterparts.

229. This is reiterated throughout the remainder of the book (see Hebrews chapters 3, 4, 5, 6, 10, and 12).

PART II | CASE STUDIES

salvation they had embraced (2:1–4), which formerly had given them a sense of identity as the new covenant people of God. The writer implies that they are no longer listening to the voice of God in Scripture and preaching (2:1; 3:7b—4:13, 5:11; 12:25)."[230] Both as a group and individually, the readers have need of this message of exhortation (13:22).[231]

That both speech acts of this speech act complex (Hebrews 1:13–14) are Assertives is seen when we transpose them:

(v. 13) God has not said to any angel, "Sit at my right hand until I make your enemies a footstool for your feet."

(v. 14) All angels are spirits in the divine service, sent to serve those who are to inherit salvation.

Taking the negative Assertive in v. 13 with the positive Assertive in v. 14 brackets the role of angels in the divine economy. Angels are not rulers—heavenly or earthly—but rather servants of Yahweh who minister to "those who are to inherit salvation" (1:14) in part by bringing messages (2:2).[232]

The transposition of v. 13 makes it clear that although Yahweh has not said what is quoted from Ps 110 to an *angel*, Yahweh has said it to *someone*.[233] From the co-text and especially the introductory verses, it appears it was said to the Son, through whom "in these last days he [God] has spoken to us" (1:2a).[234] Since the verb in v. 13 appears in the perfect (εἴρηκεν), there

---

230. Lane, *Hebrews 1–8*, lxi. Apparently "the listeners had not actually fallen away, since the author can assume that they still affirmed basic Christian beliefs. For example, he does not try to convince the listeners that Jesus died and was exalted to God's right hand, but assumes that they will grant these points as the basis for his argument (1:1–4)" (Koester, *Hebrews*, 71).

231. "For listeners who remain committed to God and Christ, Hebrews . . . maintains the values they already hold. For those tending to drift away from the faith, Hebrews . . . seeks to dissuade them from apostasy and move them toward a clearer faith commitment" (Koester, *Hebrews*, 82).

232. J. J. Collins points out that "angels are never anointed" (J. J. Collins, "Jesus, Messianism and the Dead Sea Scrolls," 115).

233. This is also true of the quotations in Heb 1:5, which are introduced by the same phrase. Ellingworth believes "the author of Hebrews assumes that his readers would respond to the rhetorical question: 'to which of the angels did God ever say . . . ?' with the answer: 'to no angel, but to the one whom the psalmist calls "my Lord."' . . . It now emerges that his main interest in this chapter is not negatively to demote angels in his readers' eyes, but positively to reaffirm and strengthen their existing faith in the one who is now exalted to sit at God's right hand" (Ellingworth, *Epistle to the Hebrews*, 130).

234. *Contra* Docherty, this does not imply that for the author of Hebrews "the words of scripture are to be assumed to be literally true—there really is conversation in heaven between the exalted Jesus and God, for example" (Docherty, *Use of the Old Testament*,

is an emphasis on the present consequences of what Yahweh previously spoke.²³⁵ The speech act complex (vv. 13-14) is christological since it clarifies what is true about Jesus as compared to the angels.²³⁶

However, this does not mean "the invitation to be enthroned at God's right hand was addressed to the Son alone."²³⁷ Verse 13 may refer to Yahweh's offer to David and his descendants to be seated at Yahweh's right hand.²³⁸ In that case, the quotation is a reminder that no angel has been offered this position of honor and authority. Under this scenario, "to which of the angels did God ever say" in v. 13, which parallels the similar phrase in v. 5, introduces a new argument consisting of 1:13-14 and 2:5b-9.²³⁹ This argument explains the relationship between the angels and David and the kings of his line, a line which culminates in the incarnate Christ.

The Assertive in v. 13 is thus tellable as the introduction to an argument concerning Jesus's non-subordination to the angels even during his earthly existence. It serves as the link between the current position of

---

181).

235. "The perfect emphasizes a decisive event in the Son's life which has continuing ramifications. We might even say that the climax of the catena occurs with Psalm 110:1b which speaks of the Son's present situation as well as the Son's future expectations" (Bateman, *Early Jewish Hermeneutics*, 233; cf. Attridge, *Epistle to the Hebrews*, 61).

236. Although Ἰησοῦς and χριστός do not appear until 2:9 and 3:6, respectively, according to Longenecker, all six OT passages quoted in Heb 1:5-13 "are interpreted christologically as referring to Jesus" (Longenecker, *Biblical Exegesis*, 156). When Motyer classifies Ps 109:1 LXX in Heb 1:13 as "certainly understood as messianic," he is referring to "the early church," since he agrees that "the evidence that this was read messianically in Judaism is very slight" and that "it may well be that its prominent use in the New Testament derives from Jesus himself (Mk. 12:35-37 *par.*)" (Motyer, "Psalm Quotations of Hebrews 1," 16).

237. *Contra* Lane, *Hebrews 1-8*, 45.

238. The seating of the Son at God's right hand (Heb 1:3) may not be the only such seating referred to by v. 13 since vv. 13-14 have no explicit reference to the Son, lord, messiah, Last Days, etc. Regarding v. 1:5b, Ellingworth finds it "not surprising that God's promise to David should have been understood as extending beyond Solomon to an ideal king of Davidic descent, known as the Messiah" (Ellingworth, *Epistle to the Hebrews*, 115).

239. For G. H. Guthrie, 1:5 and 1:13 form an *inclusio* (G. H. Guthrie, *Structure of Hebrews*, 77; cf. Bateman, *Early Jewish Hermeneutics*, 241). But since only the phrase "to which of the angels has God ever said" is repeated and the content of God's speech in the two verses is quite different, Guthrie's Parallel Introductions category seems as likely (see G. H. Guthrie, *Structure of Hebrews*, 104). Gourgues believes "1:3 lance un développement qui vient aboutir en 1:13, lequel, après en avoir récapitulé les éléments majeurs, relance à son tour un nouveau développement" in 2:5 (Gourgues, *À la droite de Dieu*, 94; cf. Lane, *Hebrews 1-8*, 45).

Messiah Jesus "at the right hand of the Majesty on high" (1:3) and his status during his incarnation (2:9). Although in his earthly incarnation, Jesus was made "lower than" the angels and even submitted to death (2:7, 9),[240] his incarnation was not only temporary but was designed to serve "the descendants of Abraham" (2:16) rather than angels.[241]

This reading makes better sense of Heb 1:14, which tells us angels are not the rulers but rather the servants of humanity, i.e., "those who are to inherit salvation." In contrast "to the Son, who is invited to share the divine presence and splendor, angels are sent forth on a mission of assistance to those who find themselves oppressed and confused in a hostile world."[242] Angels serve humanity, including the incarnate Christ. Thus, for the Messiah, being "lower than the angels" is not a matter of subjection to them.[243] Ultimately, "all things"—presumably including angels—are "put in subjection under his feet" (Heb 2:8 NASB quoting Ps 8:6).[244] Both the world to

---

240. For this, see, e.g., Lane, *Hebrews 1-8*, 46. Although we cannot explore in detail what being "made lower" might mean, Koester believes the author of Hebrews correlates being made lower "with Christ's suffering and death" (Koester, *Hebrews*, 217, referring to Heb 5:7, 12:2, and 13:12; cf. Moyise, *Later New Testament Writings*, 89). If this is the case, Heb 2:9 makes it clear that "Jesus' suffering is not incompatible with his glory and honor" (McCann, *Theological Introduction to the Book of Psalms*, 63).

241. According to Gheorghita, most commentators choose "the temporal sense" rather than that of degree because of "the adverbial particle νῦν" in 2:8 (Gheorghita, *Role of the Septuagint*, 106; cf. Lane, *Hebrews 1-8*, 43; and Koester, *Hebrews*, 34, 116).

242. Lane, *Hebrews 1-8*, 32. "In Hebrews 1:7 angels serve the Davidic king, and in Hebrews 1:14 that service involves serving the saints. . . . Thus, while waiting for the future consummation of the Son's rule, angels serve the Son by serving the subjects of the Son" (Bateman, *Early Jewish Hermeneutics*, 235; cf. Attridge, *Epistle to the Hebrews*, 62). For Ellingworth, also, "better sense is made of the verse as a whole . . . if it is paraphrased as follows: 'All these angels, as we have been showing from scripture, are subordinate to God and therefore to Christ as Son. They live to worship God in heaven, and serve him by being sent . . . on earthly missions for the benefit of those to whom God is to give salvation'" (Ellingworth, *Epistle to the Hebrews*, 133). Heb 1:14 marks "the beginning of a change from (a) the sharp contrast between angels and the Son, which dominated 1:5-13, to (b) a more positive assessment of the subordinate role of angels, suggested in 1:14 and developed in 2:2" (Ellingworth, 134). Note that there is "no indication of any enmity" between Christ and the angels (Attridge, *Epistle to the Hebrews*, 62). The enemy over whom Jesus has victory is "the one who has the power of death" (Heb 2:14).

243. *Contra* Attridge, *Epistle to the Hebrews*, 69.

244. We use NASB here because the NRSV takes "man" (Ps 8:4 MT: אנוש; Ps 8:5 LXX: ἄνθρωπος) as "human beings" and translates the possessive pronoun in Ps 8:6 as plural, i.e., "their feet," which is misleading (for this, see Moyise, *Later New Testament Writings*, 88). Interestingly, Wallis notes a parallel between Heb 1 and 2 and 1 Cor 15:25-27: "The thought of Psalm 110:1 is advanced first and then confirmed by the climactic parallel

come and this world are subjected not to angels, but to the "more than" Messiah—Jesus.

The quotation from Ps 110:1 evokes for the implied reader the Story-lines of Yahweh giving the Anointed the honor and authority of a seat at Yahweh's right hand and of Yahweh's active engagement in subjecting the enemies to the rule of the eternal Messiah.[245] These Story-lines have been refracted through the lens of the Jesus-event; only Jesus is now referred to as Messiah.

How does this speech act complex fit into the illocution of the speech event? William Lane argues that in Hebrews "argumentation serves exhortation. . . . The primary function of exhortation is to motivate the community to appropriate action."[246] Using our terminology, we conclude that the Assertives in 1:5–14 support the Directive in 2:1 to "pay greater attention to what we have heard, so that we do not drift away from it."[247] The Assertives in 2:2–4 also support this Directive. The return to exposition in 2:5, also an Assertive, looks back to 1:13 (and 1:3), thus linking the citations in 1:5–13 with those in 2:6–13 and creating discourse cohesion.

---

from Psalm 8" (Wallis, "Use of Psalms 8 and 110," 27; see also 29).

245. For Loader, Heb 1:3 and 1:13 "are clearly associated with present rule" (Loader, "Christ at the Right Hand," 205). This dovetails with the presentations in Acts 2 and 1 Cor 15. "Many scholars . . . believe . . . ἕως ἄν here indicates a period extending indefinitely beyond the action of the main verb; that is, that the Son will continue to 'sit' even after his enemies have been defeated" (Ellingworth, *Epistle to the Hebrews*, 131). This mirrors our earlier discussion of עד/ἕως in the psalm (see n9). As with the other quotations of Ps 110:1 we have analyzed, here also "to sit at God's right hand is therefore to share his power without limitation, though always with the subordination implied in the fact that it is God who gives, and the Son who receives, this supreme status" (Ellingworth, 103).

246. Lane, *Hebrews 1–8*, c, adding that "Hebrews was written to arouse, urge, encourage, and exhort those addressed to maintain their Christian confession and to dissuade them from a course of action that the writer believed would be catastrophic. He calls them to fidelity and obedience and seeks to prepare them for suffering."

247. According to Westfall, "1:5–14 is marked as support material by the γάρ (for) and contains supportive quotations, and it has correspondingly lower prominence than the surrounding co-text. However, . . . the passage is contoured by a marked perfect for the speaking verb (εἴρηκεν in v. 13) and the marked use of rhetorical questions (vv. 5, 13, 14) which places a moderate emphasis on the partial summary in 1:14 at the end of the list" (Westfall, *Discourse Analysis*, 97).

PART II | CASE STUDIES

The Perlocution

Overall, the desired perlocutionary effect of the opening chapters of Hebrews is that the audience complete the action called for by the Directive in 2:1; this will lead to transformation of the current behavior of the community.

The speech act complex which contains the quotation (1:13–14) is composed of Assertives recounting things that God has "said"; it therefore presents elements of the content of what "we have heard." The desired perlocutionary effect of an Assertive is that the audience respond not only with understanding but with adherence. In order to obey the Directive, Envisaging readers must adhere to the Assertives presented in connection with the Directive, including those of the speech act complex in 1:13–14. Specifically, they will reaffirm their belief that the Son not only rules over the angels at the present time but was not subject to them during his incarnation. If they have abandoned that belief, they will revert to it. The Story told by Ps 110:1, and specifically Yahweh's granting honor and authority to Yahweh's Anointed by offering a seat at the right hand (an honor not granted to any angel), thus becomes an important part of the theological argument for the role of the Son, Messiah Jesus, as compared to the angels.

"A Priest Forever"

Although we cannot explore the use of Ps 110:4 in Hebrews in detail, we want to highlight its contribution to Story, theology, and lifeworld/worldview. It is in the opening verses of Hebrews that the reader learns that when God's Son "had made purification for sins, he sat down at the right hand of the Majesty on high" (1:3c). Some see an allusion to Ps 110:1b in the second clause.[248] Not to be overlooked, however, is that the Son "made purification for sins" (1:3c) points to the priestly nature of Jesus's messiahship.[249] In addition to 1:3c, allusions to Ps 110:1 and 4 are found in Heb 8:1 and 10:12–13.[250] These passages, taken with other quotations of and allusions

---

248. See, e.g., Hay, *Glory at the Right Hand*, 164. Hebrews follows the wording of Ps 109:1 LXX (ἐκ δεξιῶν) only in 1:13, perhaps because it is an explicit quotation. Elsewhere, "the right hand" is expressed by ἐν δεξιᾷ. Whether the author uses a hymn in 1:3 (see Koester, *Hebrews*, 178–79) is not material to our argument.

249. For this, see Attridge, *Epistle to the Hebrews*, 95.

250. In Heb 10:12–13, the thought that the Messiah has offered a "single sacrifice for sins" (v. 12) is linked to Ps 110:1 via two allusions to the final two clauses of that verse.

to Ps 110:1 and 4,²⁵¹ triumphally present Jesus, the Son and Messiah, as not only the exalted Lord of all but also the eternal high priest and once-for-all sacrifice.

Radu Gheorghita rightly calls the development of "Christ as the High Priest, one of the theological *tours de force* of the epistle."²⁵² But he is not entirely correct that it was the author of Hebrews who "combined into one person the twofold office of the Messiah, the Son who was made the High Priest."²⁵³ Although Hebrews is the only NT book to quote or allude to Ps 110:4, there is evidence of a priestly function for Messiah Jesus in the co-texts of both of our other non-Synoptic examples of the use of Ps 110:1 (Acts 2:21, 38–39; 1 Cor 15:3, 17).²⁵⁴

However, as we said in our discussion of the *Davidssohnfrage*, the unwillingness of Jesus's audience to engage with him concerning Ps 110 may have been due to their discomfort with the priestly references in the second oracle. Since only Hebrews makes explicit use of Ps 110:4, it is possible that "the connection with Psalm 110:4 was invented by the author of Hebrews."²⁵⁵ In developing explicitly a theological connection that may

---

251. Ps 110:1 is also alluded to in Heb 12:2. There are three other direct quotations (5:6; 7:15–17, 21) of Ps 110:4 and seven allusions (5:10; 6:20; 7:3, 8, 11, 24–25, 28) (Hay, *Glory at the Right Hand*, 165–66).

252. Gheorghita, *Role of the Septuagint*, 145.

253. Gheorghita, *Role of the Septuagint*, 14. In the Document of Damascus, "les deux 'messies d'Aaron et d'Israël' sont devenus l'unique 'messie d'Aaron et d'Israël.' . . . Un passage tiré de la partie législative de D nous assure que le Messie sera bien le futur grand prêtre, car c'est lui qui 'expiera (*ykpr*) leurs fautes'" (Starcky, "Les quatre étapes du messianism," 495–96).

254. Cf. Rom 8:34, which refers to the intercession of the exalted Christ and where the metaphor of a seat at the right hand is also found. If the author of Hebrews was familiar with Romans, that author is developing an existing connection (as per de Lang, "Psalm 110," 47; and *contra* Loader, "Christ at the Right Hand," 206; Westfall, *Discourse Analysis*, 105; and Koester, *Hebrews*, 22). M. F. Bird points to a merger of the "royal and redemptive roles of Jesus" as early as Mark 8:27—9:1 (M. F. Bird, *Are You the One?*, 144). R. E. Watts looks back further—to Mark's opening sentence—to connect Jesus with the Temple as "Lord of the house" (R. E. Watts, "Lord's House and David's Lord," 320). But this does not necessarily mean "the image of Christ as a heavenly High Priest was traditional within the early Christian community addressed by Hebrews" (Attridge, *Epistle to the Hebrews*, 102; see also 26, 103).

255. De Lang, "Psalm 110," 48, calls this "probable." This is *contra* Hengel, for whom "aufgrund der Verwandtschaft von Rö 8,34 mit verschiedenen Hebräer-Texten scheint es mir wahrscheinlich zu sein, daß die Verbindung von Ps 110,1 und 4 nicht erst auf den Verfasser dieses relativ späten Briefes zurückgeht, sondern schon wesentlich älter ist und bereits Paulus vertraut war" (Hengel, "'Setze dich zu meiner Rechten!,'" 130).

have been only implicit previously, the author of Hebrews uses Ps 110:1 and 4 in a manner congruent with their original co-texts.[256]

CONCLUSION

Hatina suggests this query: "If the story world serves as the point of departure, what then is the cohesive feature within the story to which the quotations and allusions contribute?"[257] Asking this question helps summarize our analyses of these quotations of Ps 110:1 by various NT speakers/authors. First, the metaphor well-known in the ancient world of being invited to sit at the right hand of the deity, i.e., an offer of honor and authority, is either explicitly referred to or obviously part of the mutual context of all the quotations. Additionally, all the quotations explicitly reproduce Yahweh's offer to subject the enemies as a footstool/under the feet. Both metaphors are part of the Story evoked with each quotation.

By quoting Ps 110:1 and evoking these OT Story-lines, the implied NT speakers/authors, as Envisagers, activate or create mutual context to guide their hearers/readers in realigning or subverting/re-creating their understanding of Yahweh and Yahweh's relationships with Yahweh's people.[258] However, the NT speakers/authors do not simply retell the OT Story. Story evolves. The *Davidssohnfrage*, Jesus's allusion at his trial to the metaphor of the seat at the right hand, and the events of his crucifixion, resurrection, and ascension all become part of mutual context and Story for other NT speakers/authors.[259] In addition, the events of Pentecost, including the

---

256. Ellingworth calls "the author's general theological position . . . the opposite of atomistic exposition" (Ellingworth, *Epistle to the Hebrews*, 41; see also 109, 147–48). Gheorghita adds that "current opinion now swings more towards admitting that the Author quotes from the OT with full awareness of the texts' original contexts, evidenced in the way the quotations frequently align themselves with ideas from the passage in which they originate" (Gheorghita, *Role of the Septuagint*, 57). For him, "it seems extremely likely that . . . the context itself played a significant role in shaping the use of the quotations" (Gheorghita, 69).

257. Hatina, *In Search of a Context*, 3.

258. As Dodd argues with regard to Pss 2, 8, and 110, "I believe reflection will show that the development of meaning is a living growth within the given environment, and that the doctrines associated with these passages by New Testament writers gain in depth and significance when we have regard to the original, historical intention of the psalms they cite" (Dodd, *According to the Scriptures*, 133).

259. Hengel is correct that the "unsagbar kühne und zugleich anstößige Schritt" of placing the ignominiously-executed Jesus "in die Throngemeinschaft mit Gott nach Ps

content of Peter's speech, are or become part of the mutual context of the implied author and audience of Acts 2, 1 Cor 15 and Heb 1–2.[260]

From Jesus's first use in the *Davidssohnfrage*, the quotation of Ps 110:1 reveals Jesus as "more than" messiah and helps shed light on what it means to say that Jesus is Son of David, Messiah, Lord, and Son of God.[261] And, at Pentecost and after, Ps 110:1 is a critical text in witnessing to and describing Jesus's exaltation, providing a deeper understanding of his "more than" messiahship.[262]

Envisaging hearers/readers of the NT are those who realign or subvert/recreate their theological perspective and Story according to the perlocutionary intentions of the various implied NT speakers/authors. Considering the totality of these quoting texts, the implied reader understands that Messiah Jesus is seated in the position of power and authority at the right hand of God, where his enemies are being put under his feet. Jesus "pours out" the Spirit, forgives sins, and is to be called on for salvation. All things, including angels and the ultimate enemy, death, are subject to him. Ultimately Envisaging readers come to live in the lifeworld established by the recontextualized Story of the people of God, in which Messiah Jesus reigns eternally over all things of earth and heaven.

110,1" must be grounded "in Lehre und Verhalten Jesus selbst" (Hengel, "'Setze dich zu meiner Rechten!,'" 177).

260. Koester believes "many similarities between Hebrews and the Pauline writings may result from each writer's reliance on a common pool of early Christian ideas," including "the use of Ps 110:1 as a principal witness to Christ's exaltation" (Koester, *Hebrews*, 56; cf. Attridge, "Psalms in Hebrews," 197).

261. In Hebrews, references to Ps 110:4 speak to priestly elements of Jesus's messiahship.

262. We disagree with Attridge's claim that the "use" of Ps 110 in the *Davidssohnfrage* accounts is different from its "use" in Acts 2, Rom 8, 1 Cor 15, Eph 1, and Col 3 (Attridge, "Psalms in Hebrews," 198, 198n4).

9

Conclusion

THE DEVELOPMENT AND USE OF THIS METHODOLOGY

IN THE FIRST PART of our study, we created a model to explore how OT quotation serves as a transformational call to live into the lifeworld of the people of God and adopt the corresponding worldview. Rejecting both the idea that either the quoted or quoting author "controls" the other and the claim that quoting is necessarily manipulative, we adopted a hermeneutics of author-reader cooperation through the medium of the text.

Our first step was to evaluate the proposed functions of quotation. Making the determination that quotation can evoke tradition led us to explore the relationship between the source and receptor contexts of a quotation and the interaction between author and reader generally. We developed the concept of "Story" (narrative plus non-narrative textual tradition) as our link between quotation and lifeworld/worldview transformation. The theological positions (basic questions and answers) of the elements of textual tradition evoked via quotation we term its "Story-lines."

Transformation of lifeworld/worldview and Story is necessary in response to tension, such as the reinforcement or interposition of a Story via quotation. When Story is evoked and mutual context is created and/or activated, transformation is in view. Adapting communication theorist Walter Fisher's categorization of the functions of stories, we consider transformation to be one of two basic types, either realignment or subversion/re-creation.

Finally, we created an "action model" of communicative interaction based in Speech Act Theory. The inclusion of not only illocution but also perlocution (in each case, both acts and effects) in our action model allows us to delineate three reader roles: the locutionary role of "Independent," the illocutionary role of "Analyst," and the perlocutionary role of "Envisager." Our study focuses on the Envisager, a reader who not only understands the illocutionary act but also responds with the perlocutionary effect (belief and/or action) of the implied reader which corresponds to the perlocutionary act of the implied author. The intended perlocutionary response of the implied reader points to the implied author's desired future transformation of Story, theology, and lifeworld/worldview. By including perlocution, incorporating the construct of the implied author/reader, and considering Envisagers as distinct from Analysts, our action model holds the author, reader, and text in creative tension, providing a bridge across the chasm between meaning as authorial intention versus reader response. Only at the perlocutionary level is communicative interaction fully successful, i.e., only then does an empirical reader move beyond understanding to adherence and transformation.

In quoting, the Envisaging NT speaker/author, who is a reader of the source text, evokes the theological Story-lines of the OT Story and/or an intervening interpretive tradition in order to give guidance and direction to the potentially Envisaging empirical NT audience. Via quotation and through the implied author and reader, the NT author calls for a response of belief and/or action which is intended to realign or subvert/re-create the current Story and the related theological lifeworld/worldview of the empirical NT audience. Using our action model, we can evaluate what theological elements of Story (tradition) are evoked by a quotation, what lifeworld/worldview transformation is in view, and whether the NT speaker/author reads as an Envisager.

In our first case study, Paul's quotation of Ps 115:1a LXX in 2 Cor 4:13, we concluded that Paul evokes the Story of the psalmist, who believes, speaks, suffers, is rescued, and gives thanks, in order to link the Corinthians to the lifeworld of the people of Yahweh and encourage a transformation of his readers' beliefs and behaviors. Via the illocutionary and perlocutionary responses of the implied reader, an Envisaging NT reader adheres to the idea that Paul's faith impels his speech and that neither his ministry nor his message is compromised by his suffering. Rather, Paul's suffering demonstrates solidarity with Messiah Jesus and the truth of his message.

Additionally, Paul's Envisaging readers adhere to the notion that all believers can be confident of Yahweh's protection, and that ultimately, all will be brought into Yahweh's presence with Messiah Jesus. Not only what they know but what they do is to be transformed; thanksgiving is to be increased to the glory of God. Envisaging readers join Paul—himself an Envisaging reader—in the lifeworld he inhabits.

In our second case study, we examined some purportedly divergent uses of Ps 110:1 by NT authors, applying our methodology to see what transformation of belief or action is in view in each instance. The metaphor of being invited to sit at the right hand of the deity, i.e., an offer of honor and authority, is explicitly referred to in five of the six quotations we examined.[1] Additionally, all six quotations explicitly reproduce Yahweh's guarantee of victory via the subjection of the enemies as a footstool for or under the feet.[2] Thus, one or both of these elements are part of the evoked Story in every instance.

In terms of the theological import, from Jesus's first use in the *Davidssohnfrage*, the quotation of Ps 110:1 substantiates and develops Jesus's "more than" messiahship. Jesus's speech at his trial, which has roots in the *Davidssohnfrage*, is part of the mutual context—along with Jesus's crucifixion, resurrection, ascension, and exaltation—when Peter evokes the Story at Pentecost. And Peter's Pentecost speech becomes part of mutual context for the implied author and audience of Acts 2, 1 Cor 15, and Heb 1–2.

Although the quotation is used in a variety of settings, each NT speaker/author appears to read the OT text as an Envisager. That does not mean that by quoting Ps 110:1, they simply retell the OT Story. The Story of the people of God now encompasses the events of the life, death, resurrection, and exaltation of Messiah Jesus.

LOOKING AHEAD

As Booth laments, "since everything is in one way or another related to everything else, . . . to write a book at all—any book—one must rule out

---

1. If we include the allusions in the accounts of Jesus's trial, the count rises to eight out of nine. This aspect of Ps 110:1 is part of the mutual context of 1 Cor 15:25 but is not referred to explicitly.

2. The allusions in the trial narratives do not reproduce this element.

almost everything that is potentially interesting."³ We have only scratched the surface of exploring NT quotation of the OT with our methodology.⁴ Investigation of other OT quotations would be profitable. There may also be value in modifying the methodology to investigate allusion or even echo.⁵ Other interesting studies would be of quotations used ironically or in parody or punning or in which the NT author appears to read the OT as an Independent.⁶

Additionally, because our methodology involves evoking Story to call readers to the transformation necessary to inhabit a lifeworld, an interesting topic to explore would be how evoking Story helps form and sustain identity.⁷ For the NT, this would involve investigating both how individuals become and grow as followers of Jesus and how the identity of the NT communities as the people of Yahweh is established. A natural follow-on to this would be how ethical standards are established and sustained.⁸ Of additional interest might be the relaxing of our implied assumption of the equality of participants to add to our model the consideration of what Pratt calls "affective relations, power relations, and the question of shared goals."⁹

3. Booth, *Rhetoric of Fiction,* 404.

4. We have not, for example, considered any quotations from Johannine literature. Given the exchange between Beale (*John's Use of the Old Testament* and "Questions of Authorial Intent") and Moyise ("Intertextuality and the Study of the Old Testament in the New"), our methodology might be of value there.

5. For allusion and echo, see R. B. Hays, *Echoes of Scripture.* The construct of the implied author/reader obviates Wilk's concern that "one can only assume a communicative function of scriptural connections on the basis of explicitly marked citations" (Wilk, "Paul as User, Interpreter, and Reader," 85).

6. An example would be to explore whether Fitzmyer's four classes ("Literal or Historical," "Modernized Texts," "Accommodated Texts" [that is, "wrested from its original context or modified somehow to suit the new situation"], and "Eschatological") capture meaningful distinctions (see Fitzmyer, "Use of Explicit Old Testament Quotations," 305–30; quote is from p. 316). Other fruitful explorations would be the examples in Moyise, "Does Paul Respect the Context?" and "How Does Paul Read Scripture?"

7. We saw in chapter 4 that many scholars (including Keesmaat, R. E. Watts, Pao, Horrell, J. B. Green, and Crites) tie tradition/story to social identity. See also R. B. Hays, *Faith of Jesus Christ,* 221. M. F. Bird concludes that "the messianic Christology . . . of the early church was the central means through which it related its own claims to be the people of God in *continuity with* and as the *climax to* Israel's sacred traditions" (M. F. Bird, *Are You the One?,* 151).

8. R. B. Hays points out that "some contemporary ethicists have emphasized the importance of stories as the medium through which character is formed and values are sustained" (R. B. Hays, *Faith of Jesus Christ,* 221).

9. Pratt, "Ideology and Speech-Act Theory," 67.

Thus, the model we have developed here, which uses Speech Act Theory—notably perlocution—to link quotation as the evoking of Story (textual tradition) to lifeworld/worldview transformation, may provide additional opportunities to gain insights into the purposes of NT authors and readers in communicative interaction.

Appendix

The Speech Act Complexes of Pss 115:1–3 and 109:1 LXX and Their Quoting NT Texts

1. A Comparison of Ps 115:1–3 LXX and the NETS Translation

LXX	NETS
¹ Ἀλληλουια.	Hallelouia
1aʼἘπίστευσα,	I believed,
1b διὸ ἐλάλησα·	and so I spoke;
1c ἐγὼ δὲ ἐταπεινώθην σφόδρα.	but I was brought very low.
² ἐγὼ εἶπα ἐν τῇ ἐκστάσει μου Πᾶς ἄνθρωπος ψεύστης.[1]	I said in my alarm, "Every person is a liar."
³ τί ἀνταποδώσω τῷ κυρίῳ περὶ πάντων, ὧν ἀνταπέδωκέν μοι;	What shall I return to the Lord for all he returned to me?

---

1. Ps 115:2 LXX contains a direct self-quotation (introduced by the Greek verb λέγω rather than the verb λαλέω as in 1b). As a result, we consider it one speech act.

APPENDIX

2. The Quotation of Ps 115:1 LXX in 2 Cor 4:13-14 (NA[27] and NRSV)

NA[27] [italics omitted]	NRSV
¹³ᵃ Ἔχοντες δὲ τὸ αὐτὸ πνεῦμα τῆς πίστεως κατὰ τὸ γεγραμμένον· ἐπίστευσα διὸ ἐλάλησα,	But just as we have the same spirit of faith that is in accordance with scripture — "I believed, and so I spoke"
¹³ᵇ καὶ ἡμεῖς πιστεύομεν,	we also believe,
¹³ᶜ διὸ καὶ λαλοῦμεν,	and so we speak,
¹⁴ εἰδότες ὅτι ὁ ἐγείρας τὸν κύριον Ἰησοῦν καὶ ἡμᾶς σὺν Ἰησοῦ ἐγερεῖ καὶ παραστήσει σὺν ὑμῖν.	because we know that the one who raised the Lord Jesus will raise us also with Jesus, and will bring us with you into his presence.

3. A Comparison of Ps 109:1-3 LXX and the NETS and NRSV Translations

LXX	NETS	NRSV
¹ Τῷ Δαυιδ ψαλμός. Εἶπεν ὁ κύριος τῷ κυρίῳ μου Κάθου ἐκ δεξιῶν μου, ἕως ἂν θῶ τοὺς ἐχθρούς σου ὑποπόδιον τῶν ποδῶν σου.	Pertaining to Dauid. A Psalm. The Lord said to my lord, "Sit at my right hand until I make your enemies a footstool for your feet."	Of David. A Psalm. The LORD says to my lord, "Sit at my right hand until I make your enemies your footstool."
²ᵃ ῥάβδον δυνάμεώς σου ἐξαποστελεῖ κύριος ἐκ Σιων,	The Lord will send out from Sion your powerful rod.	The LORD sends out from Zion your mighty scepter.
²ᵇ καὶ κατακυρίευε ἐν μέσῳ τῶν ἐχθρῶν σου.	So have dominion in the midst of your enemies.	Rule in the midst of your foes.
³ᵃ μετὰ σοῦ ἡ ἀρχὴ ἐν ἡμέρᾳ τῆς δυνάμεώς σου ἐν ταῖς λαμπρότησιν τῶν ἁγίων·	Rule is yours on the day of your power among the splendor of the holy ones.	Your people will offer themselves willingly on the day you lead your forces on the holy mountains.
³ᵇ ἐκ γαστρὸς πρὸ ἑωσφόρου ἐξεγέννησά σε.	From the womb, before the morning star, I brought you forth.	From the womb of the morning, like dew, your youth will come to you.

APPENDIX

4. The Synoptic Texts of the *Davidssohnfrage* (NA²⁷ and NRSV)
[all italics omitted from the text of NA²⁷]

Matt 22:41–45		Mark 12:35–37		Luke 20:41–44	
⁴¹ Συνηγμένων δὲ τῶν Φαρισαίων ἐπηρώτησεν αὐτοὺς ὁ Ἰησοῦς ⁴²ᵃλέγων· τί ὑμῖν δοκεῖ περὶ τοῦ χριστοῦ; τίνος υἱός ἐστιν;	Now while the Pharisees were gathered together, Jesus asked them this question: "What do you think of the Messiah? Whose son is he?"	³⁵ Καὶ ἀποκριθεὶς ὁ Ἰησοῦς ἔλεγεν διδάσκων ἐν τῷ ἱερῷ· πῶς λέγουσιν οἱ γραμματεῖς ὅτι ὁ χριστὸς υἱὸς Δαυίδ ἐστιν;	While Jesus was teaching in the temple, he said, "How can the scribes say that the Messiah is the son of David?	⁴¹ Εἶπεν δὲ πρὸς αὐτούς· πῶς λέγουσιν τὸν χριστὸν εἶναι Δαυὶδ υἱόν;	Then he said to them, "How can they say that the Messiah is David's son?
⁴²ᵇ λέγουσιν αὐτῷ· τοῦ Δαυίδ.	They said to him, "The son of David."				
⁴³ λέγει αὐτοῖς· πῶς οὖν Δαυὶδ ἐν πνεύματι καλεῖ αὐτὸν κύριον λέγων· ⁴⁴εἶπεν κύριος τῷ κυρίῳ μου· κάθου ἐκ δεξιῶν μου, ἕως ἂν θῶ τοὺς ἐχθρούς σου ὑποκάτω τῶν ποδῶν σου;	He said to them, "How is it then that David by the Spirit calls him Lord, saying, 'The Lord said to my Lord, "Sit at my right hand, until I put your enemies under your feet"'?	³⁶ αὐτὸς Δαυὶδ εἶπεν ἐν τῷ πνεύματι τῷ ἁγίῳ· εἶπεν κύριος τῷ κυρίῳ μου· κάθου ἐκ δεξιῶν μου, ἕως ἂν θῶ τοὺς ἐχθρούς σου ὑποκάτω τῶν ποδῶν σου.	David himself, by the Holy Spirit, declared, 'The Lord said to my Lord, "Sit at my right hand, until I put your enemies under your feet."'	⁴² αὐτὸς γὰρ Δαυὶδ λέγει ἐν βίβλῳ ψαλμῶν· εἶπεν κύριος τῷ κυρίῳ μου· κάθου ἐκ δεξιῶν μου, ⁴³ἕως ἂν θῶ τοὺς ἐχθρούς σου ὑποπόδιον τῶν ποδῶν σου.	For David himself says in the book of Psalms, 'The Lord said to my Lord, "Sit at my right hand, until I make your enemies your footstool."'
⁴⁵ εἰ οὖν Δαυὶδ καλεῖ αὐτὸν κύριον, πῶς υἱὸς αὐτοῦ ἐστιν;	If David thus calls him Lord, how can he be his son?"	³⁷ᵃ αὐτὸς Δαυὶδ λέγει αὐτὸν κύριον, καὶ πόθεν αὐτοῦ ἐστιν υἱός;	David himself calls him Lord; so how can he be his son?"	⁴⁴ Δαυὶδ οὖν κύριον αὐτὸν καλεῖ, καὶ πῶς αὐτοῦ υἱός ἐστιν;	David thus calls him Lord; so how can he be his son?"

APPENDIX

Matt 22:41-45		Mark 12:35-37		Luke 20:41-44	
⁴⁶ καὶ οὐδεὶς ἐδύνατο ἀποκριθῆναι αὐτῷ λόγον οὐδὲ ἐτόλμησέν τις ἀπ' ἐκείνης τῆς ἡμέρας ἐπερωτῆσαι αὐτὸν οὐκέτι.	No one was able to give him an answer, nor from that day did anyone dare to ask him any more questions.	³⁷ᵇ καὶ [ὁ] πολὺς ὄχλος ἤκουεν αὐτοῦ ἡδέως.	And the large crowd was listening to him with delight.		

5. The Quotation of Ps 110:1 in Peter's Pentecost Speech

Acts 2:33-36 (NA²⁷) [italics omitted]	Acts 2:33-36 (NRSV)
³³ τῇ δεξιᾷ οὖν τοῦ θεοῦ ὑψωθείς, τήν τε ἐπαγγελίαν τοῦ πνεύματος τοῦ ἁγίου λαβὼν παρὰ τοῦ πατρός, ἐξέχεεν τοῦτο ὃ ὑμεῖς [καὶ] βλέπετε καὶ ἀκούετε.	[Peter said,] "Being therefore exalted at [by} the right hand of God, and having received from the Father the promise of the Holy Spirit, he has poured out this that you both see and hear.
³⁴ᵃ οὐ γὰρ Δαυὶδ ἀνέβη εἰς τοὺς οὐρανούς,	For David did not ascend into the heavens,
³⁴ᵇ λέγει δὲ αὐτός· εἶπεν [ὁ] κύριος τῷ κυρίῳ μου· κάθου ἐκ δεξιῶν μου, ³⁵ἕως ἂν θῶ τοὺς ἐχθρούς σου ὑποπόδιον τῶν ποδῶν σου.	but he himself says, 'The Lord said to my Lord, "Sit at my right hand, until I make your enemies your footstool."'
³⁶ ἀσφαλῶς οὖν γινωσκέτω πᾶς οἶκος Ἰσραὴλ ὅτι καὶ κύριον αὐτὸν καὶ Χριστὸν ἐποίησεν ὁ θεός, τοῦτον τὸν Ἰησοῦν ὃν ὑμεῖς ἐσταυρώσατε.	Therefore let the entire house of Israel know with certainty that God has made him both Lord and Messiah, this Jesus whom you crucified."

APPENDIX

6. A Comparison of Ps 110:1c [109:1c LXX] and 1 Cor 15:25b[2]

Ps 109:1c LXX [italics omitted]	1 Cor 15:25b (NA[27]) [italics omitted]
... ἕως ἂν θῶ τοὺς ἐχθρούς σου ὑποπόδιον τῶν ποδῶν σου.	... ἄχρι οὗ θῇ πάντας τοὺς ἐχθροὺς ὑπὸ τοὺς πόδας αὐτοῦ.

7. The Quotation of Ps 110:1 [109:1c LXX] in 1 Cor 15:24–28

NA[27] [italics omitted]	NRSV
[24] εἶτα τὸ τέλος, ὅταν παραδιδῷ τὴν βασιλείαν τῷ θεῷ καὶ πατρί, ὅταν καταργήσῃ πᾶσαν ἀρχὴν καὶ πᾶσαν ἐξουσίαν καὶ δύναμιν.	Then comes the end, when he hands over the kingdom to God the Father, after he has destroyed every ruler and every authority and power.
[25] δεῖ γὰρ αὐτὸν βασιλεύειν ἄχρι οὗ θῇ πάντας τοὺς ἐχθροὺς ὑπὸ τοὺς πόδας αὐτοῦ.	For he must reign until he has put all his enemies under his feet
[26] ἔσχατος ἐχθρὸς καταργεῖται ὁ θάνατος·	The last enemy to be destroyed is death
[27a] πάντα γὰρ ὑπέταξεν ὑπὸ τοὺς πόδας αὐτοῦ.	For "God has put all things in subjection under his feet."
[27b] ὅταν δὲ εἴπῃ ὅτι πάντα ὑποτέτακται, δῆλον ὅτι ἐκτὸς τοῦ ὑποτάξαντος αὐτῷ τὰ πάντα.	But when it says, "All things are put in subjection," it is plain that this does not include the one who put all things in subjection under him.
[28a] ὅταν δὲ ὑποταγῇ αὐτῷ τὰ πάντα, τότε [καὶ] αὐτὸς ὁ υἱὸς ὑποταγήσεται τῷ ὑποτάξαντι αὐτῷ τὰ πάντα,	When all things are subjected to him, then the Son himself will also be subjected to the one who put all things in subjection under him,
[28b] ἵνα ᾖ ὁ θεὸς [τὰ] πάντα ἐν πᾶσιν.	so that God may be all in all.

2. The double underlined words are identical in each text; the single underlined words are different forms of the same word.

APPENDIX

8. The Quotation of Ps 110:1b–c [109:1b–c LXX] in Heb 1:13–14

NA²⁷ [italics omitted]	NRSV
¹³ πρὸς τίνα δὲ τῶν ἀγγέλων εἴρηκέν ποτε· κάθου ἐκ δεξιῶν μου, ἕως ἂν θῶ τοὺς ἐχθρούς σου ὑποπόδιον τῶν ποδῶν σου;	But to which of the angels has he [God] ever said, "Sit at my right hand until I make your enemies a footstool for your feet"?
¹⁴ οὐχὶ πάντες εἰσὶν λειτουργικὰ πνεύματα εἰς διακονίαν ἀποστελλόμενα διὰ τοὺς μέλλοντας κληρονομεῖν σωτηρίαν;	Are not all angels spirits in the divine service, sent to serve for the sake of those who are to inherit salvation?

Bibliography

Abasciano, Brian J. "Diamonds in the Rough: A Reply to Christopher Stanley Concerning the Reader Competency of Paul's Original Audiences." *NovT* 49 (2007) 153–83.
Abegg, Martin G., and Craig A. Evans. "Messianic Passages in the Dead Sea Scrolls." In *Qumran-Messianism: Studies on the Messianic Expectations in the Dead Sea Scrolls*, edited by James H. Charlesworth et al., 191–203. Tübingen: Mohr Siebeck, 1998.
Adams, Edward. "Paul's Story of God and Creation: The Story of How God Fulfils His Purposes in Creation." In *Narrative Dynamics in Paul: A Critical Assessment*, edited by Bruce W. Longenecker, 19–43. Louisville: Westminster John Knox, 2002.
Ahearne-Kroll, Stephen P. *The Psalms of Lament in Mark's Passion: Jesus' Davidic Suffering*. SNTSMS 142. Cambridge: Cambridge University Press, 2007.
Akmajian, Adrian, et al. *Linguistics: An Introduction to Language and Communication*. 5th ed. Cambridge: MIT Press, 2001.
Alkier, Stefan. "Intertextuality and the Semiotics of Biblical Texts." In *Reading the Bible Intertextually*, edited by Richard B. Hays et al., 3–21. Waco: Baylor University Press, 2009.
———. "New Testament Studies on the Basis of Categorical Semiotics." In *Reading the Bible Intertextually*, edited by Richard B. Hays et al., 223–48. Waco: Baylor University Press, 2009.
Allen, Graham. *Intertextuality*. New Critical Idiom. London: Routledge, 2000.
Allen, Leslie C. *Psalms 101–150, Revised*. WBC 21. Nashville: Nelson, 2002.
Aloisi, John. "Who Is David's Lord? Another Look at Psalm 110:1." *Detroit Baptist Seminary Journal* 10 (2005) 103–23.
Alston, William P. *Illocutionary Acts and Sentence Meaning*. Ithaca: Cornell University Press, 2000.
Alter, Robert. *The Art of Biblical Narrative*. New York: Basic Books, 1981.
Amador, J. David Hester. *Academic Constraints in Rhetorical Criticism of the New Testament: An Introduction to a Rhetoric of Power*. JSNTSup 174. Sheffield: Sheffield Academic, 1999.
Anderson, A. A. "Psalms." In *It is Written: Scripture Citing Scripture; Essays in Honour of Barnabas Lindars, SSF*, edited by D. A. Carson and H. G. M. Williamson, 56–66. 1988. Reprint, Cambridge: Cambridge University Press, 2008.
Attridge, Harold W. *The Epistle to the Hebrews: A Commentary on the Epistle to the Hebrews*. Hermeneia. Philadelphia: Fortress, 1989.
———. "The Psalms in Hebrews." In *The Psalms in the New Testament*, edited by Steve Moyise and Maarten J. J. Menken, 197–212. NTSI. London: T. & T. Clark, 2004.

Auffret, Pierre. "'Je marcherai à la face de Yahvé': Étude structurelle du Psaume 116." *Nouvelle Revue Théologique* 106 (1984) 383–96.
Aune, David E. "Christian Prophecy and the Messianic Status of Jesus." In *The Messiah: Developments in Earliest Judaism and Christianity*, edited by James H. Charlesworth, 404–22. Minneapolis: Fortress, 1992.
Austin, J. L. *How To Do Things with Words*. 2nd ed. Edited by J. O. Urmson and Marina Sbisà. Cambridge: Harvard University Press, 1975.
———. *Philosophical Papers*. 2nd ed. Edited by J. O. Urmson and G. J. Warnock. Galaxy Books 312. Oxford: Clarendon, 1970.
Bach, Kent. "Pragmatics and the Philosophy of Language." In *The Handbook of Pragmatics*, edited by Laurence R. Horn and Gregory Ward, 463–87. Blackwell Handbooks in Linguistics 16. Malden, MA: Blackwell, 2004.
Bach, Kent, and Robert M. Harnish. *Linguistic Communication and Speech Acts*. Cambridge: MIT Press, 1979.
Bakhtin, M. M. "The Problem of Speech Genres." In *Speech Genres and Other Late Essays*, edited by Caryl Emerson and Michael Holquist, 60–102. Translated by Vern W. McGee. University of Texas Press Slavic Series 8. Austin: University of Texas Press, 1986.
Balentine, Samuel E. "The Royal Psalms and the New Testament: From 'messiah' to 'Messiah.'" *Theological Educator* 29 (1984) 56–62.
Bar-Hillel, Yehoshua. "Communication and Argumentation in Pragmatic Languages." In *Linguaggi nella società e nella tecnicà*, 269–84. Milan: Edizioni di Comunità, 1970.
Barker, Kit. "Speech Act Theory, Dual Authorship, and Canonical Hermeneutics: Making Sense of *Sensus Plenior*." *Journal of Theological Interpretation* 3 (2009) 227–39.
Barnett, Paul. *The Second Epistle to the Corinthians*. NICNT. Grand Rapids: Eerdmans, 1997.
Barr, James. *The Concept of Biblical Theology: An Old Testament Perspective*. Minneapolis: Fortress, 1999.
Barrett, C. K. *A Commentary on the Second Epistle to the Corinthians*. New York: Harper & Row, 1973.
Barthes, Roland. *Image, Music, Text*. Translated by Stephen Heath. New York: Hill & Wang, 1977.
Bateman, Herbert W., IV. *Early Jewish Hermeneutics and Hebrews 1:5–13: The Impact of Early Jewish Exegesis on the Interpretation of a Significant New Testament Passage*. American University Studies, Series 7: Theology and Religion 193. New York: Lang, 1997.
———. "Psalm 110:1 and the New Testament." *BSac* 149 (1992) 438–53.
Beal, Timothy K. "Ideology and Intertextuality: Surplus of Meaning and Controlling the Means of Production." In *Reading between Texts: Intertextuality and the Hebrew Bible*, edited by Danna Nolan Fewell, 27–39. Louisville: Westminster John Knox, 1992.
Beale, G. K. *John's Use of the Old Testament in Revelation*. JSNTSup 166. Sheffield: Sheffield Academic, 1998.
———. *A New Testament Biblical Theology: The Unfolding of the Old Testament in the New*. Grand Rapids: Baker Academic, 2011.
———. "Questions of Authorial Intent, Epistemology, and Presuppositions and Their Bearing on the Study of the Old Testament in the New: A Rejoinder to Steve Moyise." *Irish Biblical Studies* 21 (1999) 152–80.

———. Review of *Acts and the Isaianic New Exodus*, by David W. Pao. *Trinity Journal* n.s. 25 (2004) 93–101.

Beaumont, Daniel. "The Modality of Narrative: A Critique of Some Recent Views of Narrative in Theology." *JAAR* 65 (1997) 125–39.

Becker, Eve-Marie. *Letter Hermeneutics in 2 Corinthians: Studies in Literarkritik and Communication History*. Translated by Helen S. Heron. JSNTSup 279. London: T. & T. Clark, 2004.

BeDuhn, Jason David. "The Historical Assessment of Speech Acts: Clarifications of Austin and Skinner for the Study of Religions." *Method & Theory in the Study of Religion* 14 (2002) 84–113.

Beker, J. Christiaan. "Echoes and Intertextuality: On the Role of Scripture in Paul's Theology." In *Paul and the Scriptures of Israel*, edited by Craig A. Evans and James A. Sanders, 64–69. JSNTSup 83. SSEJC 1. Sheffield: JSOT Press, 1993.

Berkley, Timothy W. *From a Broken Covenant to Circumcision of the Heart: Pauline Intertextual Exegesis in Romans 2:17–29*. SBLDS 175. Atlanta: Society of Biblical Literature, 2000.

Bierwisch, Manfred. "Semantic Structure and Illocutionary Force." In *Speech Act Theory and Pragmatics*, edited by John R. Searle et al., 1–35. Synthese Language Library. Dordrecht: Reidel, 1980.

Binder, Donald D. *Into the Temple Courts: The Place of the Synagogues in the Second Temple Period*. SBLDS 169. Atlanta: Society of Biblical Literature, 1999.

Bird, Graham H. "Relevance Theory and Speech Acts." In *Foundations of Speech Act Theory: Philosophical and Linguistic Perspectives*, edited by Savas L. Tsohatzidis, 292–311. London: Routledge, 1994.

Bird, Michael F. *Are You the One Who Is to Come?: The Historical Jesus and the Messianic Question*. Grand Rapids: Baker Academic, 2009.

Black, Max. "Austin on Performatives." *Philosophy* 38 (1963) 217–26.

———. "Meaning and Intention: An Examination of Grice's Views." *NLH* 4 (1973) 257–79.

Bock, Darrell L. "Blasphemy and the Jewish Examination of Jesus." *Bulletin for Biblical Research* 17 (2007) 53–114.

———. "Evangelicals and the Use of the Old Testament in the New, Part 1." In *Rightly Divided: Readings in Biblical Hermeneutics*, edited by Roy B. Zuck, 206–17. Grand Rapids: Kregel, 1996.

———. *Proclamation from Prophecy and Pattern: Lucan Old Testament Christology*. JSNTSup 12. Sheffield: JSOT Press, 1987.

Bonsirven, Joseph. *Exégèse rabbinique et exégèse paulinienne*. Bibliothèque de Théologie Historique. Paris: Beauchesne, 1938.

Booij, Th. "Psalm cx: 'Rule in the Midst of Your Foes!'" *Vetus Testamentum* 41 (1991) 396–407.

———. "Psalm 116,10–11: The Account of an Inner Crisis." *Bib* 76 (1995) 388–95.

Booth, Wayne C. *The Rhetoric of Fiction*. 2nd ed. Chicago: University of Chicago Press, 1983.

———. *A Rhetoric of Irony*. Chicago: University of Chicago Press, 1974.

Botha, J. Eugene. *Jesus and the Samaritan Woman: A Speech Act Reading of John 4:1–42*. NovTSup 65. Leiden: Brill, 1991.

Boyarin, Daniel. "Old Wine in New Bottles: Intertextuality and Midrash." *PT* 8 (1987) 539–56.

BIBLIOGRAPHY

Brawley, Robert L. *Text to Text Pours Forth Speech: Voices of Scripture in Luke–Acts.* ISBL. Bloomington: Indiana University Press, 1995.

Brendel, Elke, et al. *Understanding Quotation.* Mouton Series in Pragmatics 7. Berlin: de Gruyter Mouton, 2011.

Briggs, Richard S. "Speech-Act Theory." In *DTIB*, 763–66.

———. *Words in Action: Speech Act Theory and Biblical Interpretation: Toward a Hermeneutic of Self-Involvement.* Edinburgh: T. & T. Clark, 2001.

Broer, Ingo. "Versuch zur Christologie des ersten Evangeliums." In vol. 2 of *The Four Gospels, 1992: Festschrift Frans Neirynck*, edited by F. van Segbroeck et al., 1251–82. BETL 100. Leuven: Leuven University Press, 1992.

Brown, Gillian, and George Yule. *Discourse Analysis.* Cambridge Textbooks in Linguistics. Cambridge: Cambridge University Press, 1983.

Brown, Jeannine K. "Exodus in Matthew's Gospel." In *Exodus in the New Testament*, edited by Seth M. Ehorn, 31–47. LNTS 663. London: T. & T. Clark, 2022.

———. "Genesis in Matthew's Gospel." In *Genesis in the New Testament*, edited by Maarten J. J. Menken and Steve Moyise, 42–59. LNTS 466. London: T. & T. Clark, 2012.

———. "Metalepsis." In *Exploring Intertextuality: Diverse Strategies for New Testament Interpretations of Texts*, edited by B. J. Oropeza and Steve Moyise, 29–41. Eugene, OR: Cascade Books, 2016.

———. *Scripture as Communication: Introducing Biblical Hermeneutics.* 1st ed. Grand Rapids: Baker Academic, 2007.

———. *Scripture as Communication: Introducing Biblical Hermeneutics.* 2nd ed. Grand Rapids: Baker Academic, 2021.

Brown, William P. *Seeing the Psalms: A Theology of Metaphor.* Louisville: Westminster John Knox, 2002.

Bruce, F. F. *The Acts of the Apostles: The Greek Text with Introduction and Commentary.* 3rd ed. Grand Rapids: Eerdmans, 1990.

Brueggemann, Dale A. "The Evangelists and the Psalms." In *Interpreting the Psalms: Issues and Approaches*, edited by David Firth and Philip S. Johnston, 263–78. Downers Grove, IL: IVP Academic, 2005.

Brueggemann, Walter. *Israel's Praise: Doxology vs Idolatry and Ideology.* Philadelphia: Fortress, 1988.

———. *The Message of the Psalms: A Theological Commentary.* Minneapolis: Augsburg, 1984.

Bullock, C. Hassell. *Encountering the Book of Psalms: A Literary and Theological Introduction.* Encountering Biblical Studies. Grand Rapids: Baker Academic, 2001.

Burke, Kenneth. *A Rhetoric of Motives.* New York: Prentice-Hall, 1950.

Burkhardt, Armin. "Searle on Metaphor." In *Speech Acts, Meaning and Intentions: Critical Approaches to the Philosophy of John R. Searle*, edited by Armin Burkhardt, 303–35. Foundations of Communication and Cognition. Berlin: de Gruyter, 1990.

———. "Speech Act Theory—The Decline of a Paradigm." In *Speech Acts, Meaning and Intentions: Critical Approaches to the Philosophy of John R. Searle*, edited by Armin Burkhardt, 91–128. Foundations of Communication and Cognition. Berlin: de Gruyter, 1990.

Callow, Kathleen. *Man and Message: A Guide to Meaning-Based Text Analysis.* Lanham, MD: University Press of America, 1998.

Callow, Kathleen, and John C. Callow. "Text as Purposive Communication: A Meaning-based Analysis." In *Discourse Description: Diverse Linguistic Analyses of a Fund-*

Raising Text, edited by William C. Mann and Sandra A. Thompson, 5–37. Pragmatics and Beyond n.s. 16. Amsterdam: Benjamins, 1992.

Campbell, Douglas A. "2 Corinthians 4:13: Evidence in Paul That Christ Believes." *JBL* 128 (2009) 337–56.

———. "An Echo of Scripture in Paul, and Its Implications." In *The Word Leaps the Gap: Essays on Scripture and Theology in Honor of Richard B. Hays*, edited by J. Ross Wagner et al., 367–91. Grand Rapids: Eerdmans, 2008.

Campbell, Paul Newell. "A Rhetorical View of Locutionary, Illocutionary, and Perlocutionary Acts." *QJS* 59 (1973) 284–96.

Campbell, William S. "The Contribution of Traditions to Paul's Theology: A Response to C. J. Roetzel." In *1 & 2 Corinthians*, edited by David M. Hay, 234–54. Vol. 2 of *Pauline Theology*. SBLSymS 22. Minneapolis: Fortress, 1993.

Cappelen, Herman, and Ernie Lepore. "Quotation." *The Stanford Encyclopedia of Philosophy (Spring 2012 Edition)*. http://plato.stanford.edu/archives/spr2012/entries/quotation.

———. "Varieties of Quotation." *Mind* n.s. 106 (1997) 429–50.

———. "Varieties of Quotation Revisited." *Belgian Journal of Linguistics* 17 (2003) 51–75.

Carassa, Antonella, and Marco Colombetti. "Joint Meaning." *JPrag* 41 (2009) 1837–54.

Castelli, Elizabeth A. *Imitating Paul: A Discourse of Power*. Literary Currents in Biblical Interpretation. Louisville: Westminster John Knox, 1991.

Charlesworth, James H. "From Messianology to Christology: Problems and Prospects." In *The Messiah: Developments in Earliest Judaism and Christianity*, edited by James H. Charlesworth, 3–35. Minneapolis: Fortress, 1992.

———. "Introduction: Messianic Ideas in Early Judaism." In *Qumran-Messianism: Studies on the Messianic Expectations in the Dead Sea Scrolls*, edited by James H. Charlesworth et al., 1–8. Tübingen: Mohr Siebeck, 1998.

———. "Messianology in the Biblical Pseudepigrapha." In *Qumran-Messianism: Studies on the Messianic Expectations in the Dead Sea Scrolls*, edited by James H. Charlesworth et al., 21–52. Tübingen: Mohr Siebeck, 1998.

Chatman, Seymour. *Coming to Terms: The Rhetoric of Narrative in Fiction and Film*. Ithaca: Cornell University Press, 1990.

———. *Story and Discourse: Narrative Structure in Fiction and Film*. Ithaca: Cornell University Press, 1978.

Chazon, Esther G. "The Use of the Bible as a Key to Meaning in Psalms from Qumran." In *Emanuel: Studies in Hebrew Bible, Septuagint, and Dead Sea Scrolls in Honor of Emanuel Tov*, edited by Shalom M. Paul et al., 85–96. VTSup 94. Leiden: Brill, 2003.

Chester, Andrew. "Jewish Messianic Expectations and Mediatorial Figures and Pauline Christology." In *Paulus und das antike Judentum*, edited by Martin Hengel and Ulrich Heckel, 17–89. WUNT 1/58. Tübingen: Mohr Siebeck, 1991.

———. *Messiah and Exaltation: Jewish Messianic and Visionary Traditions and New Testament Christology*. WUNT 1/207. Tübingen: Mohr Siebeck, 2007.

Ciampa, Roy E. "Scriptural Language and Ideas." In *As It is Written: Studying Paul's Use of Scripture*, edited by Stanley E. Porter and Christopher D. Stanley, 41–57. SBLSymS 50. Atlanta: Society of Biblical Literature, 2008.

Clark, David. "Beyond Inerrancy: Speech Acts and an Evangelical View of Scripture." In *For Faith and Clarity: Philosophical Contributions to Christian Theology*, edited by James K. Beilby, 113–31. Grand Rapids: Baker Academic, 2006.

Clark, Herbert H. *Using Language*. Cambridge: Cambridge University Press, 1996.

Clark, Herbert H., and Richard J. Gerrig. "Quotations as Demonstrations." *Language* 66 (1990) 764–805.
Clayton, Jay. "The Alphabet of Suffering: Effie Deans, Tess Durbeyfield, Martha Ray, and Hetty Sorrel." In *Influence and Intertextuality in Literary History*, edited by Jay Clayton and Eric Rothstein, 37–60. Madison: University of Wisconsin Press, 1991.
Clayton, Jay, and Eric Rothstein. "Figures in the Corpus: Theories of Influence and Intertextuality." In *Influence and Intertextuality in Literary History*, edited by Jay Clayton and Eric Rothstein, 3–36. Madison: University of Wisconsin Press, 1991.
Clayton, Jay, and Eric Rothstein, eds. *Influence and Intertextuality in Literary History*. Madison: University of Wisconsin Press, 1991.
Clifford, Richard J. *Psalms 73–150*. Abingdon Old Testament Commentaries. Nashville: Abingdon, 2003.
Cohen, Philip R., and C. Raymond Perrault. "Elements of a Plan-Based Theory of Speech Acts." *Cognitive Science* 3 (1979) 177–212.
Cohen, Ted. "Illocutions and Perlocutions." *Foundations of Language* 9 (1973) 492–503.
Collins, Adela Yarbro. "The Influence of Daniel on the New Testament." In *Daniel: A Commentary on the Book of Daniel*, by John J. Collins, 90–112. Hermeneia. Minneapolis: Fortress, 1993.
Collins, John J. *Daniel: A Commentary on the Book of Daniel*. Hermeneia. Minneapolis: Fortress, 1993.
———. "Jesus, Messianism and the Dead Sea Scrolls." In *Qumran-Messianism: Studies on the Messianic Expectations in the Dead Sea Scrolls*, edited by James H. Charlesworth et al., 100–119. Tübingen: Mohr Siebeck, 1998.
———. "Messianism and Exegetical Tradition: The Evidence of the LXX Pentateuch." In *The Septuagint and Messianism*, edited by Michael A. Knibb, 129–49. BETL 195. Leuven: Peeters, 2006.
———. *The Scepter and the Star: Messianism in Light of the Dead Sea Scrolls*. 2nd ed. Grand Rapids: Eerdmans, 2010.
Connor-Linton, Jeff. "A Sociolinguistic Model of Successful Speech Act Construction." In *Pragmatics at Issue*, edited by Jef Verschueren, 93–112. Vol. 1 of *Selected Papers of the International Pragmatics Conference, Antwerp, August 17–22, 1987*. Pragmatics & Beyond n.s. 6:1. Amsterdam: Benjamins, 1991.
Constant, Pierre. "Le Psaume 118 et son emploi christologique dans Luc et Actes: Une étude exégétique, littéraire et herméneutique." PhD diss., Trinity International University, 2001.
Conzelmann, Hans. *Acts of the Apostles: A Commentary on the Acts of the Apostles*. Translated by James Limburg et al. Edited by Eldon Jay Epp. Hermeneia. Philadelphia: Fortress, 1987.
Cordes, Ariane. "Spricht Ps 109 LXX von einem Messias oder nicht?" In *The Septuagint and Messianism*, edited by Michael A. Knibb, 253–60. BETL 195. Leuven: Peeters, 2006.
Cotterell, Peter. "Sociolinguistics and Biblical Interpretation." *Vox Evangelica* 16 (1986) 61–76.
Cotterell, Peter, and Max Turner. *Linguistics and Biblical Interpretation*. Downers Grove, IL: InterVarsity, 1989.
Crafton, Jeffrey A. "The Dancing of an Attitude: Burkean Rhetorical Criticism and the Biblical Interpreter." In *Rhetoric and the New Testament: Essays from the 1992*

Heidelberg Conference, edited by Stanley E. Porter and Thomas H. Olbricht, 429–42. JSNTSup 90. Sheffield: JSOT Press, 1993.

Cranfield, C. E. B. "A Study of St Mark 1.9–11." *SJT* 8 (1955) 53–63.

Creach, Jerome F. D. "The Destiny of the Righteous and the Theology of the Psalms." In *Soundings in the Theology of Psalms: Perspectives and Methods in Contemporary Scholarship*, edited by Rolf A. Jacobson, 49–61. Minneapolis: Fortress, 2011.

Crites, Stephen. "The Narrative Quality of Experience." *JAAR* 39 (1971) 291–311.

Dahood, Mitchell. "Two Pauline Quotations from the Old Testament." *CBQ* 17 (1955) 19–24.

Davies, W. D. "The Jewish Sources of Matthew's Messianism." In *The Messiah: Developments in Earliest Judaism and Christianity*, edited by James H. Charlesworth, 494–511. Minneapolis: Fortress, 1992.

Davis, Barry C. "Is Psalm 110 a Messianic Psalm?" *BSac* 157 (2000) 160–73.

Davis, Steven. "Perlocutions." In *Speech Act Theory and Pragmatics*, edited by John R. Searle et al., 37–55. Synthese Language Library. Dordrecht: Reidel, 1980.

Day, J. *Psalms*. 1999. Reprint, T&T Clark Study Guides. London: T. & T. Clark, 2003.

Dijk, Teun A. van. *Text and Context: Explorations in the Semantics and Pragmatics of Discourse*. LLL 21. London: Longman, 1977.

Dimant, Devorah. "Use and Interpretation of Mikra in the Apocrypha and Pseudepigrapha." In *Mikra: Text, Translation, Reading and Interpretation of the Hebrew Bible in Ancient Judaism and Early Christianity*, edited by Martin Jan Mulder, 379–419. Vol. 1 of *The Literature of the Jewish People in the Period of the Second Temple and the Talmud*. CRINT. Philadelphia: Fortress, 1988.

Doble, Peter. "The Psalms in Luke-Acts." In *The Psalms in the New Testament*, edited by Steve Moyise and Maarten J. J. Menken, 83–117. NTSI. London: T. & T. Clark, 2004.

―――. "Something Greater than Solomon: An Approach to Stephen's Speech." In *The Old Testament in the New Testament: Essays in Honour of J. L. North*, edited by Steve Moyise, 181–207. JSNTSup 189. Sheffield: Sheffield Academic, 2000.

Docherty, Susan E. *The Use of the Old Testament in Hebrews: A Case Study in Early Jewish Bible Interpretation*. WUNT 2/260. Tübingen: Mohr Siebeck, 2009.

Dodd, C. H. *According to the Scriptures: The Sub-Structure of New Testament Theology*. London: Nisbet, 1952.

Dodewaard, J. A. E. van. "La force évocatrice de la citation: Mise en lumière en prenant pour base l'Évangile de S. Matthieu." *Bib* 36 (1955) 482–91.

Dominicy, Marc, and Nathalie Franken. "Speech Acts and Relevance Theory." In *Essays in Speech Act Theory*, edited by Daniel Vanderveken and Susumu Kubo, 263–83. Pragmatics & Beyond n.s. 77. Amsterdam: Benjamins, 2002.

Donahue, John R., and Daniel J. Harrington. *The Gospel of Mark*. SP 2. Collegeville, MN: Liturgical, 2002.

Driver, G. R. "Psalm 110: Its Form, Meaning and Purpose." In *Studies in the Bible Presented to M. H. Segal*, edited by J. M. Grintz and J. Liver, 17*–31*. Publications of the Israel Society for Biblical Research 17. Jerusalem: Kiryat Sepher, 1964.

Dunn, James D. G. *The Acts of the Apostles*. Valley Forge, PA: Trinity Press International, 1996.

―――. "ΚΥΡΙΟΣ in Acts." In *Christology*, 241–53. Vol. 1 of *The Christ and the Spirit: Collected Essays of James D. G. Dunn*. Grand Rapids: Eerdmans, 1998.

———. "Messianic Ideas and Their Influence on the Jesus of History." In *The Messiah: Developments in Earliest Judaism and Christianity*, edited by James H. Charlesworth, 365–81. Minneapolis: Fortress, 1992.

Eaton, John. *The Psalms: A Historical and Spiritual Commentary with an Introduction and New Translation*. London: T. & T. Clark, 2003.

Eco, Umberto. "Between Author and Text." In *Interpretation and Overinterpretation*, by Umberto Eco, 67–88. Edited by Stefan Collini. Cambridge: Cambridge University Press, 1992.

———. *The Limits of Interpretation*. Advances in Semiotics. Bloomington: Indiana University Press, 1990.

———. *The Role of the Reader: Explorations in the Semiotics of Texts*. Advances in Semiotics. First Midland Book ed. Bloomington: Indiana University Press, 1984.

Eemeren, Frans H. van, and Rob Grootendorst. *Speech Acts in Argumentative Discussions: A Theoretical Model for the Analysis of Discussions Directed towards Solving Conflicts of Opinion*. Studies of Argumentation in Pragmatics and Discourse Analysis. Dordrecht: Foris, 1984.

———. "The Study of Argumentation from a Speech Act Perspective." In *Pragmatics at Issue*, edited by Jef Verschueren, 151–70. Vol. 1 of *Selected Papers of the International Pragmatics Conference, Antwerp, August 17–22, 1987*. Pragmatics & Beyond n.s. 6:1. Amsterdam: Benjamins, 1991.

Ehrensperger, Kathy. "Paul and the Authority of Scripture: A Feminist Perception." In *As It is Written: Studying Paul's Use of Scripture*, edited by Stanley E. Porter and Christopher D. Stanley, 291–319. SBLSymS 50. Atlanta: Society of Biblical Literature, 2008.

———. *Paul and the Dynamics of Power: Communication and Interaction in the Early Christ-Movement*. LNTS 325. London: T. & T. Clark, 2007.

Ellingworth, Paul. *The Epistle to the Hebrews: A Commentary on the Greek Text*. NIGTC. Grand Rapids: Eerdmans, 1993.

Elliott, Mark A. *The Survivors of Israel: A Reconsideration of the Theology of Pre-Christian Judaism*. Grand Rapids: Eerdmans, 2000.

Ellis, E. Earle. *Paul's Use of the Old Testament*. 1981. Reprint, Eugene, OR: Wipf and Stock, 2003.

Eskola, Timo. *Messiah and the Throne: Jewish Merkabah Mysticism and Early Christian Exaltation Discourse*. WUNT 2/142. Tübingen: Mohr Siebeck, 2001.

Evans, Craig A. *Ancient Texts for New Testament Studies: A Guide to the Background Literature*. Peabody, MA: Hendrickson, 2005.

———. "Are the 'Son' Texts at Qumran 'Messianic'?: Reflections on 4Q369 and Related Scrolls." In *Qumran-Messianism: Studies on the Messianic Expectations in the Dead Sea Scrolls*, edited by James H. Charlesworth et al., 135–53. Tübingen: Mohr Siebeck, 1998.

———. "The Beginning of the Good News in the Gospel of Mark." In *Hearing the Old Testament in the New Testament*, edited by Stanley E. Porter, 83–103. Grand Rapids: Eerdmans, 2006.

———. "The Function of the Old Testament in the New." In *Introducing New Testament Interpretation*, edited by Scot McKnight, 163–93. GNTE 1. Grand Rapids: Baker, 1989.

———. "Listening for Echoes of Interpreted Scripture." In *Paul and the Scriptures of Israel*, edited by Craig A. Evans and James A. Sanders, 47–51. JSNTSup 83. SSEJC 1. Sheffield: JSOT Press, 1993.

———. *Mark 8:27—16:20*. WBC 34B. Nashville: Nelson, 2001.

———. "Praise and Prophecy in the Psalter and in the New Testament." In *The Book of Psalms: Composition and Reception*, edited by Peter W. Flint and Patrick D. Miller, Jr., 551–79. VTSup 99. FIOTL 4. Leiden: Brill, 2005.

———. "Prophecy and Polemic: Jews in Luke's Scriptural Apologetic." In *Luke and Scripture: The Function of Sacred Tradition in Luke-Acts*, edited by Craig. A. Evans and James A. Sanders, 171–211. Minneapolis: Fortress, 1993.

Fee, Gordon D. *The First Epistle to the Corinthians*. NICNT. Grand Rapids: Eerdmans, 1987.

———. "Toward a Theology of 1 Corinthians." In *1 & 2 Corinthians*, edited by David M. Hay, 37–58. Vol. 2 of *Pauline Theology*. SBLSymS 22. Minneapolis: Fortress, 1993.

Ferrera, Alessandro. "Pragmatics." In *Dimensions of Discourse*, edited by Teun A. van Dijk, 137–57. Vol. 2 of *Handbook of Discourse Analysis*. London: Academic Press, 1985.

Fish, Stanley. *Is There a Text in This Class? The Authority of Interpretive Communities*. Cambridge: Harvard University Press, 1980.

Fishbane, Michael. *Biblical Interpretation in Ancient Israel*. Oxford: Clarendon, 1985.

———. "Torah and Tradition." In *Tradition and Theology in the Old Testament*, edited by Douglas A. Knight, 275–300. Philadelphia: Fortress, 1977.

Fisher, Walter R. *Human Communication as Narration: Toward a Philosophy of Reason, Value, and Action*. Paperback ed. Studies in Rhetoric/Communication. Columbia: University of South Carolina Press, 1989.

Fitzmyer, Joseph A. "The Use of Explicit Old Testament Quotations in Qumran Literature and in the New Testament." *NTS* 7 (1960—1961) 297–333.

Flesher, Paul Virgil McCracken. "Palestinian Synagogues before 70 C.E.: A Review of the Evidence." In vol. 1 of *Ancient Synagogues: Historical Analysis and Archaeological Discovery*, edited by Dan Urman and Paul V. M. Flesher, 27–39. Studia Post Biblica 47:1. Leiden: Brill, 1995.

Flint, Peter W. *The Dead Sea Psalms Scrolls and the Book of Psalms*. Studies on the Texts of the Desert of Judah 17. Leiden: Brill, 1997.

———. "Psalms and Psalters in the Dead Sea Scrolls." In *Scripture and the Scrolls*, 233–72. Vol. 1 of *The Bible and the Dead Sea Scrolls: The Second Princeton Symposium of Judaism and Christian Origins*, edited by James H. Charlesworth. Waco: Baylor University Press, 2006.

Fowler, Roger. *Linguistic Criticism*. 2nd ed. OPUS. Oxford: Oxford University Press, 1996.

———. *Linguistics and the Novel*. The New Accent Series. London: Routledge, 2003.

Fraine, Jean de. "Peut-on parler d'un véritable sacerdoce du roi en Israël?" In vol. 1 of *Sacra Pagina: Miscellanea Biblica Congressus Internationalis Catholici de Re Biblica*, edited by J. Coppens et al., 537–47. BETL 12. Gembloux: Duculot, 1959.

Frey, Lawrence R., et al. *Investigating Communication: An Introduction to Research Methods*. Englewood Cliffs, NJ: Prentice Hall, 1991.

Friedman, Susan Stanford. "Weavings: Intertextuality and the (Re)Birth of the Author." In *Influence and Intertextuality in Literary History*, edited by Jay Clayton and Eric Rothstein, 146–80. Madison: University of Wisconsin Press, 1991.

Fuhrmann, Justin M. "The Use of Psalm 118:22–23 in the Parable of the Wicked Tenants." *Proceedings: Eastern Great Lakes and Midwest Biblical Societies* 27 (2007) 67–81.

Funk, Robert W. *The Poetics of Biblical Narrative*. Foundations and Facets. Sonoma, CA: Polebridge, 1988.
Furnish, Victor Paul. *II Corinthians: Translated with Introduction, Notes and Commentary*. AB 32A. Garden City, NY: Doubleday, 1984.
Gadamer, Hans-Georg. *Truth and Method*. Rev. ed. Translation revised by J. Weinsheimer and D. G. Marshall. Continuum Impacts. London: Continuum, 2004.
Gaines, Robert N. "Doing by Saying: Toward a Theory of Perlocution." *QJS* 65 (1979) 207–17.
Garland, David E. "1 Corinthians." In *Theological Interpretation of the New Testament: A Book-by-Book Survey*, edited by Kevin J. Vanhoozer, 97–107. Grand Rapids: Baker Academic, 2008.
Gathercole, Simon J. *The Preexistent Son: Recovering the Christologies of Matthew, Mark, and Luke*. Grand Rapids: Eerdmans, 2006.
Geddert, Timothy J. "The Use of Psalms in Mark." *Baptistic Theologies* 1 (2009) 109–124.
Georgi, Dieter. *The Opponents of Paul in Second Corinthians*. Philadelphia: Fortress, 1986.
Gese, Hartmut. "Tradition and Biblical Theology." In *Tradition and Theology in the Old Testament*, edited by Douglas A. Knight, 301–26. Philadelphia: Fortress, 1977.
Gheorghita, Radu. *The Role of the Septuagint in Hebrews: An Investigation of its Influence with Special Consideration to the Use of Hab 2:3–4 in Heb 10:37–38*. WUNT 2/160. Tübingen: Mohr Siebeck, 2003.
Gilfillan Upton, Bridget. *Hearing Mark's Endings: Listening to Ancient Popular Texts through Speech Act Theory*. BibInt 79. Leiden: Brill, 2006.
Gillingham, Sue. "From Liturgy to Prophecy: The Use of Psalmody in Second Temple Judaism." *CBQ* 64 (2002) 470–89.
Goldingay, John. "Biblical Narrative and Systematic Theology." In *Between Two Horizons: Spanning New Testament Studies and Systematic Theology*, edited by Joel B. Green and Max Turner, *Between Two Horizons*, 123–42. Grand Rapids: Eerdmans, 2000.
———. *Daniel*. WBC 30. Dallas: Word Books, 2002.
———. *Psalms 1–41*. Vol. 1 of *Psalms*. BCOTWP. Grand Rapids: Baker Academic, 2006.
———. *Psalms 90–150*. Vol. 3 of *Psalms*. BCOTWP. Grand Rapids: Baker Academic, 2008.
Gourgues, Michel. *À la droite de Dieu: Résurrection de Jésus et actualisation du Psaume 110:1 dans le Nouveau Testament*. Études bibliques. Paris: Gabalda, 1978.
Grabbe, Lester L. "Synagogues in Pre–70 Palestine: A Re-assessment." In vol. 1 of *Ancient Synagogues: Historical Analysis and Archaeological Discovery*, edited by Dan Urman and Paul V. M. Flesher, 17–26. Studia Post Biblica 47:1. Leiden: Brill, 1995.
Grant, C. K. "Pragmatic Implication." *Philosophy* 33 (1958) 303–24.
Grant, Jamie A. "Interpreting the Psalms." In *Interpreting the Psalms: Issues and Approaches*, edited by David Firth and Philip S. Johnston, 101–18. Downers Grove, IL: IVP Academic, 2005.
Green, Joel B. "Context." In *DTIB*, 130–33.
———. *The Gospel of Luke*. NICNT. Grand Rapids: Eerdmans, 1997.
———. "Practicing the Gospel in a Post-Critical World: The Promise of Theological Exegesis." *JETS* 47 (2004) 387–97.
———. "Scripture and Theology: Failed Experiments, Fresh Perspectives." *Interpretation* 56 (2002) 5–20.
Green, William Scott. "Doing the Text's Work for It: Richard Hays on Paul's Use of Scripture." In *Paul and the Scriptures of Israel*, edited by Craig A. Evans and James A. Sanders, 58–63. JSNTSup 83. SSEJC 1. Sheffield: JSOT Press, 1993.

Greene, Thomas M. *The Light in Troy: Imitation and Discovery in Renaissance Poetry.* Elizabethan Club Series. New Haven: Yale University Press, 1982.
Grey, Jacqueline. "Acts of the Spirit: Ezekiel 37 in the Light of Contemporary Speech-Act Theory." *Journal of Biblical and Pneumatological Research* 1 (2009) 69–82.
Grice, H. Paul. *Studies in the Way of Words.* Cambridge: Harvard University Press, 1989.
Griffin, Em. *A First Look at Communication Theory.* 3rd ed. New York: McGraw-Hill, 1997.
Gu, Yueguo. "The Impasse of Perlocution." *JPrag* 20 (1993) 405–32.
Gunkel, Hermann. *Introduction to Psalms: The Genres of the Religious Lyric of Israel.* Completed by Joachim Begrich. Translated by James D. Nogalski. Mercer Library of Biblical Studies. Macon, GA: Mercer University Press, 1998.
Guthrie, George H. "Discourse Analysis." In *Interpreting the New Testament: Essays on Methods and Issues,* edited by David Alan Black and David S. Dockery, 253–71. Nashville: Broadman & Holman, 2001.
———. *The Structure of Hebrews: A Text-Linguistic Analysis.* First paperback ed. BSL. Grand Rapids: Baker Books, 1998.
Guthrie, Harvey H., Jr. *Israel's Sacred Songs: A Study of Dominant Themes.* New York: Seabury, 1966.
Habermas, Jürgen. *Lifeworld and System: A Critique of Functionalist Reason.* Vol. 2 of *The Theory of Communicative Action.* Translated by Thomas McCarthy. Boston: Beacon, 1987.
———. *On the Pragmatics of Communication.* Edited by Maeve Cooke. Cambridge: MIT Press, 1998.
———. *Reason and the Rationalization of Society.* Vol. 1 of *The Theory of Communicative Action.* Translated by Thomas McCarthy. Boston: Beacon, 1984.
Hagner, Donald A. *Matthew 14–28.* WBC 33B. Dallas: Word, 1995.
Halliday, M. A. K. *Language as Social Semiotic: The Social Interpretation of Language and Meaning.* Baltimore: University Park Press, 1978.
Hamerton-Kelly, Robert G. "Sacred Violence and the Messiah: The Markan Passion Narrative as a Redefinition of Messianology." In *The Messiah: Developments in Earliest Judaism and Christianity,* edited by James H. Charlesworth, 461–93. Minneapolis: Fortress, 1992.
Hanson, Anthony Tyrrell. *Paul's Understanding of Jesus: Invention or Interpretation?* Hull, UK: University of Hull Publications, 1963.
———. *Studies in Paul's Technique and Theology.* Grand Rapids: Eerdmans, 1974.
Harnish, Robert M. "Speech Acts and Intentionality." In *Speech Acts, Meaning and Intentions: Critical Approaches to the Philosophy of John R. Searle,* edited by Armin Burkhardt, 169–93. Foundations of Communication and Cognition. Berlin: de Gruyter, 1990.
Harrelson, Walter. "Life, Faith, and the Emergence of Tradition." In *Tradition and Theology in the Old Testament,* edited by Douglas A. Knight, 11–30. Philadelphia: Fortress, 1977.
Harris, Murray J. *The Second Epistle to the Corinthians: A Commentary on the Greek Text.* NIGTC. Grand Rapids: Eerdmans, 2005.
Hartman, L. "Scriptural Exegesis in the Gospel of St. Matthew and the Problem of Communication." In *L'Évangile selon Matthieu: Rédaction et théologie,* edited by M. Didier, 131–52. BETL 29. Gembloux: Duculot, 1972.

Hartt, Julian. "Theological Investments in Story: Some Comments on Recent Developments and Some Proposals." In *Why Narrative? Readings in Narrative Theology*, edited by Stanley Hauerwas and L. Gregory Jones, 279–92. Grand Rapids: Eerdmans, 1989.

Hatch, Evelyn. *Discourse and Language Education*. Cambridge Language Teaching Library. Cambridge: Cambridge University Press, 1992.

Hatina, Thomas R. *In Search of a Context: The Function of Scripture in Mark's Narrative*. JSNTSup 232. Studies in Scripture in Early Judaism and Christianity 8. London: Sheffield Academic, 2002.

———. "Intertextuality and Historical Criticism in New Testament Studies: Is There a Relationship?" *BibInt* 7 (1999) 28–43.

Hauerwas, Stanley, and David Burrell. "From System to Story: An Alternative Pattern for Rationality in Ethics." In *Why Narrative? Readings in Narrative Theology*, edited by Stanley Hauerwas and L. Gregory Jones, 158–90. Grand Rapids: Eerdmans, 1989.

Hay, David M. *Glory at the Right Hand: Psalm 110 in Early Christianity*. 1973. Reprint, SBLMS 18. Atlanta: Society of Biblical Literature, 1989.

———. "The Shaping of Theology in 2 Corinthians: Convictions, Doubts, and Warrants." In *1 & 2 Corinthians*, edited by David M. Hay, 135–55. Vol. 2 of *Pauline Theology*. SBLSymS 22. Minneapolis: Fortress, 1993.

Hays, Christopher B. "Echoes of the Ancient Near East? Intertextuality and the Comparative Study of the Old Testament." In *The Word Leaps the Gap: Essays on Scripture and Theology in Honor of Richard B. Hays*, edited by J. Ross Wagner et al., 20–43. Grand Rapids: Eerdmans, 2008.

Hays, Richard B. "Christ Prays the Psalms: Israel's Psalter as Matrix of Early Christianity." In *The Conversion of the Imagination: Paul as Interpreter of Israel's Scripture*, 101–18. Grand Rapids: Eerdmans, 2005.

———. *Echoes of Scripture in the Gospels*. Waco: Baylor University Press, 2016.

———. *Echoes of Scripture in the Letters of Paul*. New Haven: Yale University Press, 1989.

———. "*Echoes of Scripture in the Letters of Paul*: Abstract." In *Paul and the Scriptures of Israel*, edited by Craig A. Evans and James A. Sanders, 42–46. JSNTSup 83. SSEJC 1. Sheffield: JSOT Press, 1993.

———. *The Faith of Jesus Christ: The Narrative Substructure of Galatians 3:1—4:11*. 2nd ed. Biblical Resource Series. Grand Rapids: Eerdmans, 2002.

———. "The Liberation of Israel in Luke-Acts: Intertextual Narration as Countercultural Practice." In *Reading the Bible Intertextually*, edited by Richard B. Hays et al., 101–18. Waco: Baylor University Press, 2009.

———. "On the Rebound: A Response to Critiques of *Echoes of Scripture in the Letters of Paul*." In *Paul and the Scriptures of Israel*, edited by Craig A. Evans and James A. Sanders, 70–96. JSNTSup 83. SSEJC 1. Sheffield: JSOT Press, 1993.

———. "Salvation by Trust? Reading the Bible Faithfully." *Christian Century* 114 (1997) 218–23.

Hays, Richard B., and Joel B. Green. "The Use of the Old Testament by New Testament Writers." In *Hearing the New Testament: Strategies for Interpretation*, edited by Joel B. Green, 122–39. 2nd ed. Grand Rapids: Eerdmans, 2010.

Heard, Warren. "New Testament Background." In *Introducing New Testament Interpretation*, edited by Scot McKnight, 21–51. GNTE 1. Grand Rapids: Baker, 1989.

Heil, John Paul. *The Rhetorical Role of Scripture in 1 Corinthians*. SBLMS 15. Atlanta: Society of Biblical Literature, 2005.

Heimerdinger, Jean-Marc. *Topic, Focus and Foreground in Ancient Hebrew Narratives.* JSOTSup 259. Sheffield: Sheffield Academic, 1999.
Hengel, Martin. "'Setze dich zu meiner Rechten!' Die Inthronisation Christi zur Rechten Gottes und Psalm 110,1." In *Le Trône de Dieu,* edited by Marc Philonenko, 108–94. WUNT 1/69. Tübingen: Mohr, 1993.
Hirsch, E. D., Jr. "Meaning and Significance Reinterpreted." *Critical Inquiry* 11 (1984) 202–25.
———. *Validity in Interpretation.* New Haven: Yale University Press, 1967.
Holleman, Joost. *Resurrection and Parousia: A Traditio-Historical Study of Paul's Eschatology in 1 Corinthians 15.* NovTSup 84. Leiden: Brill, 1996.
Hooker, Morna D. "Beyond the Things that are Written? St. Paul's Use of Scripture." *NTS* 27 (1981) 295–309.
———. "Interchange and Suffering." In *Suffering and Martyrdom in the New Testament: Studies Presented to G. M. Styler by the Cambridge New Testament Seminar,* edited by William Horbury and Brian McNeil, 70–83. Cambridge: Cambridge University Press, 1981.
Horrell, David G. "The Significance of 'Paul's Story': Paul's Narratives or Narrative Substructure?" In *Narrative Dynamics in Paul: A Critical Assessment,* edited by Bruce W. Longenecker, 157–71. Louisville: Westminster John Knox, 2002.
Horsley, Richard A. "'Messianic' Figures and Movements in First-Century Palestine." In *The Messiah: Developments in Earliest Judaism and Christianity,* edited by James H. Charlesworth, 276–95. Minneapolis: Fortress, 1992.
Houston, Walter. "What Did the Prophets Think They Were Doing? Speech Acts and Prophetic Discourse in the Old Testament." *BibInt* 1 (1993) 167–88.
Howard, David M., Jr. "The Psalms and Current Study." In *Interpreting the Psalms: Issues and Approaches,* edited by David Firth and Philip S. Johnston, 23–40. Downers Grove, IL: IVP Academic, 2005.
Huang, Yan. *Pragmatics.* Oxford Textbooks in Linguistics. Oxford: Oxford University Press, 2007.
Hübner, Hans. "Intertextualität—die hermeneutische Strategie des Paulus." *Theologische Literaturzeitung* 116 (1991) 881–97.
Hughes, Philip Edgcumbe. *Paul's Second Epistle to the Corinthians: The English Text with Introduction, Exposition and Notes.* NICNT. Grand Rapids: Eerdmans, 1962.
Hurtado, Larry W. *Lord Jesus Christ: Devotion to Jesus in Earliest Christianity.* Grand Rapids: Eerdmans, 2003.
Iersel, Bas van. "The Sun, Moon, and Stars of Mark 13,24–25 in Greco-Roman Reading." *Bib* 77 (1996) 84–92.
Irsigler, Hubert. "Psalm-Rede als Handlungs-, Wirk- und Aussageprozeß: Sprechaktanalyse und Psalmeninterpretation am Beispiel von Psalm 13." In *Neue Wege der Psalmenforschung: Für Walter Beyerlin,* edited by Klaus Seybold and Erich Zenger, 63–104. 2nd ed. Herders biblische Studien 1. Freiburg im Breisgau: Herder, 1995.
Iser, Wolfgang. *The Act of Reading: A Theory of Aesthetic Response.* Baltimore: Johns Hopkins University Press, 1978.
———. *The Implied Reader: Patterns of Communication in Prose Fiction from Bunyan to Beckett.* Johns Hopkins Paperbacks ed. Baltimore: Johns Hopkins University Press, 1978.

Jakobson, Roman. "Concluding Statement: Linguistics and Poetics." In *Style in Language*, edited by Thomas A. Sebeok, 350–77. First MIT Press Paperback ed. Cambridge: MIT Press, 1960.
Jeremias, Joachim. *New Testament Theology: The Proclamation of Jesus*. Translated by John Bowden. New York: Scribner, 1971.
———. "παῖς θεοῦ." In *TDNT* 5:654–717.
Jobes, Karen H., and Moisés Silva. *Invitation to the Septuagint*. Grand Rapids: Baker Academic, 2000.
Johansson, Daniel. "*Kyrios* in the Gospel of Mark." *JSNT* 33 (2010) 101–24.
Johnson, David H. Review of *Isaiah's New Exodus in Mark*, by Rikki E. Watts. *Didaskalia* 13 (2002) 106–8.
Johnson, Elliott E. "Hermeneutical Principles and the Interpretation of Psalm 110." *BSac* 149 (1992) 428–37.
Johnson, Luke Timothy. "Imagining the World Scripture Imagines." *ModTh* 14 (1998) 165–80.
———. Review of *The New Testament and the People of God*, by Nicholas Thomas Wright. *JBL* 113 (1994) 536–38.
Johnson, Michael, and Ernie Lepore. "Misrepresenting Misrepresentation." In *Understanding Quotation*, edited by Elke Brendel et al., 231–48. Mouton Series in Pragmatics 7. Berlin: de Gruyter Mouton, 2011.
Jonge, M. de. *Jewish Eschatology, Early Christian Christology and the Testaments of the Twelve Patriarchs*. NovTSup 63. Leiden: Brill, 1991.
———. "The Use of the Word 'Anointed' in the Time of Jesus." *NovT* 8 (1966) 132–48.
Jordaan, Gert J. C., and Pieter Nel. "From Priest-King to King-Priest: Psalm 110 and the Basic Structure of Hebrews." In *Psalms and Hebrews: Studies in Reception*, edited by Dirk J. Human and Gert Jacobus Steyn, 229–40. T&T Clark Library of Biblical Studies. New York: T. & T. Clark, 2010.
Juel, Donald H. *Messianic Exegesis: Christological Interpretation of the Old Testament in Early Christianity*. Library of Early Christianity. Philadelphia: Fortress, 1988.
———. "The Origin of Mark's Christology." In *The Messiah: Developments in Earliest Judaism and Christianity*, edited by James H. Charlesworth, 449–60. Minneapolis: Fortress, 1992.
Kapelrud, Arvid S. "Tradition and Worship: The Role of the Cult in Tradition Formation and Transmission." In *Tradition and Theology in the Old Testament*, edited by Douglas A. Knight, 101–24. Philadelphia: Fortress, 1977.
Keel, Othmar. *The Symbolism of the Biblical World: Ancient Near Eastern Iconography and the Book of Psalms*. Translated by Timothy J. Hallett. 1978. Reprint, Winona Lake, IN: Eisenbrauns, 1997.
Keener, Craig S. *Acts: An Exegetical Commentary*. Vol. 1. Grand Rapids: Baker, 2012.
Keesmaat, Sylvia C. *Paul and His Story: (Re)Interpreting the Exodus Tradition*. JSNTSup 181. Sheffield: Sheffield Academic, 1999.
Kennedy, George A. *New Testament Interpretation through Rhetorical Criticism*. Studies in Religion. Chapel Hill: University of North Carolina Press, 1984.
Kidner, Derek. *Psalms 73–150: A Commentary on Books III–V of the Psalms*. Tyndale Old Testament Commentaries. Leicester, UK: Inter-Varsity, 1973.
Kim, Jinkyu. "The Speaker and the Addressee of Ps 110 in its Literary Context." Paper presented at the Annual Meeting of the Evangelical Theological Society, Baltimore, MD, November 2013.

Kistemaker, Simon J. "Psalm 110 in the Epistle to the Hebrews." In *The Hope Fulfilled: Essays in Honor of O. Palmer Robertson*, edited by Robert L. Penny, 138–49. Phillipsburg, NJ: P & R Publishing, 2008.

———. *The Psalm Citations in the Epistle to the Hebrews*. Amsterdam: Van Soest, 1961.

Kleinknecht, Karl Theodor. *Der leidende Gerechtfertigte: Die alttestamentlich-jüdische Tradition vom "leidenden Gerechten" und ihre Rezeption bei Paulus*. WUNT 2/13. Tübingen: Mohr, 1984.

Knibb, Michael A. "The Septuagint and Messianism: Problems and Issues." In *The Septuagint and Messianism*, edited by Michael A. Knibb, 3–19. BETL 195. Leuven: Peeters, 2006.

Knight, Douglas A. "Introduction: Tradition and Theology." In *Tradition and Theology in the Old Testament*, edited by Douglas A. Knight, 1–8. Philadelphia: Fortress, 1977.

———. "Revelation through Tradition." In *Tradition and Theology in the Old Testament*, edited by Douglas A. Knight, 143–80. Philadelphia: Fortress, 1977.

Knohl, Israel. "Religion and Politics in Psalm 2." In *Emanuel: Studies in Hebrew Bible, Septuagint, and Dead Sea Scrolls in Honor of Emanuel Tov*, edited by Shalom M. Paul et al., 725–27. VTSup 94. Leiden: Brill, 2003.

Koch, Dietrich-Alex. *Die Schrift als Zeuge des Evangeliums: Untersuchungen zur Verwendung und zum Verständnis der Schrift bei Paulus*. Beiträge zur historischen Theologie 69. Tübingen: Mohr, 1986.

Koester, Craig R. *Hebrews: A New Translation with Introduction and Commentary*. 2001. Reprint, AB 36. New Haven: Yale University Press, 2010.

Kraftchick, Steven. J. "Death in Us, Life in You: The Apostolic Medium." In *1 & 2 Corinthians*, edited by David M. Hay, 156–81. Vol. 2 of *Pauline Theology*. SBLSymS 22. Minneapolis: Fortress, 1993.

Kraus, Hans-Joachim. *Psalms 60–150: A Commentary*. Translated by Hilton C. Oswald. Continental Commentaries. Minneapolis: Augsburg, 1989.

———. *Theology of the Psalms*. Translated by Keith Crim. Con-tinental Commentaries. Minneapolis: Fortress, 1992.

Kruse, Colin G. *The Second Epistle of Paul to the Corinthians: An Introduction and Commentary*. 1987. Reprint, TNTC. Grand Rapids: Eerdmans, 1994.

Kurzon, Dennis. "The Speech Act Status of Incitement: Perlocutionary Acts Revisited." *JPrag* 29 (1998) 571–96.

Lambrecht, Jan. "Paul's Christological Use of Scripture in I Cor. 15.20–28." *NTS* 28 (1982) 502–27.

———. *Second Corinthians*. SP 8. Collegeville, MN: Liturgical, 1999.

Lane, William L. *Hebrews 1–8*. WBC 47A. Dallas: Word Books, 1991.

Lane-Mercier, Gillian. "Quotation as a Discursive Strategy." *Kodikas/Code* 14 (1991) 199–214.

Lang, Marijke H. de. "Psalm 110 in the New Testament." *Melita Theologica* 59 (2008) 43–50.

Lanser, Susan Snaider. "(Feminist) Criticism in the Garden: Inferring Genesis 2–3." *Semeia* 41 (1988) 67–84.

———. *The Narrative Act: Point of View in Prose Fiction*. Princeton: Princeton University Press, 1981.

Lee, Max J., and B. J. Oropeza, eds. *Practicing Intertextuality: Ancient Jewish and Greco-Roman Exegetical Techniques in the New Testament*. Eugene, OR: Cascade Books, 2021.

Lee, Patricia. "Perlocution and Illocution." *Journal of English Linguistics* 8 (1974) 32–40.

Leech, Geoffrey N. *Principles of Pragmatics*. LLL 30. London: Longman, 1983.

Levine, Lee I. *The Ancient Synagogue: The First Thousand Years*. New Haven: Yale University Press, 2000.

Lichtenberger, Hermann. "Messianic Expectations and Messianic Figures During the Second Temple Period." In *Qumran-Messianism: Studies on the Messianic Expectations in the Dead Sea Scrolls*, edited by James H. Charlesworth et al., 9–20. Tübingen: Mohr Siebeck, 1998.

Lincicum, David. Review of *Arguing with Scripture: The Rhetoric of Quotations in the Letters of Paul*, by Christopher D. Stanley. *JETS* 49 (2006) 429–31.

Lindars, Barnabas. *New Testament Apologetic: The Doctrinal Significance of the Old Testament Quotations*. Philadelphia: Westminster, 1961.

Lindbeck, George. "Scripture, Consensus, and Community." In *Biblical Interpretation in Crisis: The Ratzinger Conference on Bible and Church*, edited by Richard John Neuhaus, 74–101. Encounter Series 9. Grand Rapids: Eerdmans, 1989.

Litwak, Kenneth Duncan. *Echoes of Scripture in Luke-Acts: Telling the History of God's People Intertextually*. JSNTSup 282. London: T. & T. Clark, 2005.

Loader, W. R. G. "Christ at the Right Hand—Ps. cx. 1 in the New Testament." *NTS* 24 (1978) 199–217.

Lonergan, Bernard J. F. *Method in Theology*. Seabury Paperback ed. Seabury Library of Contemporary Theology. London: Seabury, 1979.

Longacre, Robert E. *The Grammar of Discourse*. 2nd ed. Topics in Language and Linguistics. New York: Plenum, 1996.

Longenecker, Richard N. *Biblical Exegesis in the Apostolic Period*. 2nd ed. Grand Rapids: Eerdmans 1999.

Loughlin, Gerard. *Telling God's Story: Bible, Church and Narrative Theology*. Cambridge: Cambridge University Press, 1996.

Louw, Johannes P. "Discourse Analysis and the Greek New Testament." *Bible Translator* 24 (1973) 101–18.

Luge, Elisabeth. "Perlokutionäre Effekte." *Zeitschrift für germanistische Linguistik* 19 (1991) 71–86.

Luttikhuisen, Gerard. "Intertextual References in Readers' Responses to the Apocryphon of John." In *Intertextuality in Biblical Writings: Essays in Honour of Bas van Iersel*, edited by Sipke Draisma, 117–26. Kampen: Kok, 1989.

MacIntyre, Alasdair. "The Virtues, the Unity of a Human Life, and the Concept of a Tradition." In *Why Narrative? Readings in Narrative Theology*, edited by Stanley Hauerwas and L. Gregory Jones, 89–110. Grand Rapids: Eerdmans, 1989.

Mack, Burton L. *Rhetoric and the New Testament*. Guides to Biblical Scholarship, New Testament Series. Minneapolis: Fortress, 1992.

Maher, Michael. "The Psalms in Jewish Worship." *Proceedings of the Irish Biblical Association* 17 (1994) 9–36.

Mallen, Peter. *The Reading and Transformation of Isaiah in Luke-Acts*. LNTS 367. London: T. & T. Clark, 2008.

Marcu, Daniel. "Perlocutions: The Achilles' Heel of Speech Act Theory." *JPrag* 32 (2000) 1719–41.

Marcus, Joel. *Mark 8–16: A New Translation with Introduction and Commentary*. AB 27. New Haven: Yale University Press, 2009.

———. *The Way of the Lord: Christological Exegesis of the Old Testament in the Gospel of Mark*. London: T. & T. Clark, 2004.

Marshall, I. Howard. *The Acts of the Apostles: An Introduction and Commentary.* 1980. Reprint, TNTC. Grand Rapids: Eerdmans, 2001.
Martin, Dale. B. Review of *Echoes of Scripture in the Letters of Paul*, by Richard B. Hays. *ModTh* 7 (1991) 291–92.
Martin, Ralph P. *2 Corinthians*. WBC 40. Waco: Word, 1986.
Mays, James L. "The Centre of the Psalms." In *Language, Theology, and the Bible: Essays in Honour of James Barr*, edited by Samuel E. Balentine and John Barton, 231–46. Oxford: Clarendon, 1994.
McCann, J. Clinton, Jr. *A Theological Introduction to the Book of Psalms: The Psalms as Torah*. Nashville: Abingdon, 1993.
McKinnon, James W. "On the Question of Psalmody in the Ancient Synagogue." *Early Music History* 6 (1986) 159–91.
Mead, Richard T. "A Dissenting Opinion about Respect for Context in Old Testament Quotations." *NTS* 10 (1964) 279–89.
Meer, Willem van der. "Psalm 110: A Psalm of Rehabilitation?" In *The Structural Analysis of Biblical and Canaanite Poetry*, edited by Willem van der Meer and Johannes C. de Moor, 207–34. JSOTSup 74. Sheffield: JSOT Press, 1988.
Menken, Maarten J. J. "The Psalms in Matthew's Gospel." In *The Psalms in the New Testament*, edited by Steve Moyise and Maarten J. J. Menken, 61–82. NTSI. London: T. & T. Clark, 2004.
Meyer, Ben F. *Critical Realism and the New Testament*. Princeton Theological Monograph Series 17. Allison Park, PA: Pickwick Publications, 1989.
———. *Reality and Illusion in New Testament Scholarship: A Primer in Critical Realist Hermeneutics*. Collegeville, MN: Liturgical, 1994.
Meyers, Robert B., and Karen Hopkins. "A Speech-Act Theory Bibliography." *Centrum* 5 (1977) 73–108.
Miller, Patrick D. *The Way of the Lord: Essays in Old Testament Theology*. Grand Rapids: Eerdmans, 2007.
Moessner, David P. "'Two Lords 'at the Right Hand'? The Psalms and an Intertextual Reading of Peter's Pentecost Speech (Acts 2:14–36)." In *Literary Studies in Luke-Acts: Essays in Honor of Joseph B. Tyson*, edited by Richard P. Thompson and Thomas E. Phillips, 215–32. Macon, GA: Mercer University Press, 1998.
Möller, Karl. "Proclaiming the Reign of Christ, the Lord: The Psalms in the New Testament." In *Praying by the Book: Reading the Psalms*, edited by Craig Bartholomew and Andrew West, 147–81. Carlisle, UK: Paternoster, 2001.
———. "Reading, Singing and Praying the Law: An Exploration of the Performative, Self-Involving, Commissive Language of Psalm 101." In *Reading the Law: Studies in Honour of Gordon J. Wenham*, edited by J. G. McConville and Karl Möller, 111–37. Library of Hebrew Bible/Old Testament Studies 461. New York: T. & T. Clark, 2007.
Moloney, Francis J. *The Gospel of Mark: A Commentary*. Grand Rapids: Baker Academic, 2002.
Morawski, Stefan. "The Basic Functions of Quotation." In *Sign, Language, Culture*, edited by A. J. Greimas et al., 690–705. Janua Linguarum 1/1. The Hague: Mouton, 1970.
Moritz, Thorsten. "Critical but Real: Reflecting on N. T. Wright's *Tools for the Task*." In *Renewing Biblical Interpretation*, edited by Craig Bartholomew et al., 172–97. Scripture and Hermeneutics Series 1. Grand Rapids: Zondervan, 2000.
———. *A Profound Mystery: The Use of the Old Testament in Ephesians*. NovTSup 85. Leiden: Brill, 1996.

BIBLIOGRAPHY

———. "Scripture and Theological Exegesis." In *The Sacred Text: Excavating the Texts, Exploring the Interpretations, and Engaging the Theologies of the Christian Scriptures*, edited by Michael Bird and Michael Pahl, 119–40. Gorgias Précis Portfolios 7. Piscataway, NJ: Gorgias Press, 2010.

Motsch, Wolfgang, and Renate Pasch. "Illokutive Handlungen." In *Satz, Text, sprachliche Handlung*, edited by Wolfgang Motsch, 11–79. Studia Grammatica 25. Berlin: Akademie, 1987.

Motyer, Stephen. "The Psalm Quotations of Hebrews 1: A Hermeneutic-Free Zone?" *Tyndale Bulletin* 50 (1999) 3–22.

Mowinckel, Sigmund. *The Psalms in Israel's Worship*. Translated by D. R. Ap-Thomas. 2 vols. New York: Abingdon, 1962.

Moyise, Steve. "Does the NT Quote the OT Out Of Context?" *Anvil* 11 (1994) 133–43.

———. "Does Paul Respect the Context of His Quotations?" In *Paul and Scripture: Extending the Conversation*, edited by Christopher D. Stanley, 97–114. ECL 9. Atlanta: Society of Biblical Literature, 2012.

———. *Evoking Scripture: Seeing the Old Testament in the New*. London: T. & T. Clark, 2008.

———. "How Does Paul Read Scripture?" In *Thematic Studies*, edited by Craig A. Evans and H. Daniel Zacharias, 184–96. Vol. 1 of *Early Christian Literature and Intertextuality*. SSEJC 14. LNTS 391. London: T&T Clark, 2009.

———. "Intertextuality and Biblical Studies: A Review." *VE* 23 (2002) 418–31.

———. "Intertextuality and Historical Approaches to the Use of Scripture in the New Testament." *VE* 26 (2005) 447–58.

———. "Intertextuality and the Study of the Old Testament in the New Testament." In *The Old Testament in the New Testament: Essays in Honour of J. L. North*, edited by Steve Moyise, 14–41. JSNTSup 189. Sheffield: Sheffield Academic, 2000.

———. *Jesus and Scripture: Studying the New Testament Use of the Old Testament*. Grand Rapids: Baker Academic, 2011.

———. "Latency and Respect for Context: A Response to Mitchell Kim." In *Paul and Scripture: Extending the Conversation*, edited by Christopher D. Stanley, 131–39. ECL 9. Atlanta: Society of Biblical Literature, 2012.

———. *The Later New Testament Writings and Scripture: The Old Testament in Acts, Hebrews, the Catholic Epistles and Revelation*. Grand Rapids: Baker Academic, 2012.

———. *The Old Testament in the New: An Introduction*. Continuum Biblical Studies Series. London: Continuum, 2001.

———. *Paul and Scripture: Studying the New Testament Use of the Old Testament*. Grand Rapids: Baker Academic, 2010.

———. "Quotations." In *As It is Written: Studying Paul's Use of Scripture*, edited by Stanley E. Porter and Christopher D. Stanley, 15–28. SBLSymS 50. Atlanta: Society of Biblical Literature, 2008.

———. "The Use of Analogy in Biblical Studies." *Anvil* 18 (2001) 33–42.

Murphy-O'Connor, Jerome. "Faith and Resurrection in 2 Cor 4:13–14." *RB* 95 (1988) 543–50.

———. *The Theology of the Second Letter to the Corinthians*. New Testament Theology. Cambridge: Cambridge University Press, 1991.

Naugle, David K. *Worldview: The History of a Concept*. Grand Rapids: Eerdmans, 2002.

Neufeld, Dietmar. *Reconceiving Texts as Speech Acts: An Analysis of 1 John*. BibInt 7. Leiden: Brill, 1994.

Nolland, John. *The Gospel of Matthew: A Commentary on the Greek Text*. NIGTC. Grand Rapids: Eerdmans, 2005.
———. *Luke 1—9:20*. WBC 35A. Dallas: Word, 1989.
———. *Luke 18:35—24:53*. WBC 35C. Dallas: Word, 1993.
Oegema, Gerbern S. "Messianic Expectations in the Qumran Writings: Theses on their Development." In *Qumran-Messianism: Studies on the Messianic Expectations in the Dead Sea Scrolls*, edited by James H. Charlesworth et al., 53–82. Tübingen: Mohr Siebeck, 1998.
Ohmann, Richard. "Speech, Literature, and the Space Between." *NLH* 4 (1972) 47–63.
Olthuis, James H. "On Worldviews." *Christian Scholar's Review* 14 (1985) 153–64.
O'Neill, J. C. *The Theology of Acts in Its Historical Setting*. London: SPCK, 1961.
Oropeza, B. J., and Steve Moyise, eds. *Exploring Intertextuality: Diverse Strategies for New Testament Interpretation of Texts*. Eugene, OR: Cascade Books, 2016.
Osborne, Grant R. *The Hermeneutical Spiral: A Comprehensive Introduction to Biblical Interpretation*. 2nd ed. Downers Grove, IL: IVP Academic, 2006.
Pao, David W. *Acts and the Isaianic New Exodus*. 2000. Reprint, BSL. Grand Rapids: Baker Academic, 2002.
Patrick, Dale, and Allen Scult. *Rhetoric and Biblical Interpretation*. JSOTSup 82. Bible and Literature Series 26. Sheffield: Almond, 1990.
Patte, Daniel. "Speech Act Theory and Biblical Exegesis." *Semeia* 41 (1988) 85–102.
Paul, Ian. "The Use of the Old Testament in Revelation 12." In *The Old Testament in the New Testament: Essays in Honour of J. L. North*, edited by Steve Moyise, 256–76. JSNTSup 189. Sheffield: Sheffield Academic, 2000.
Pennington, Jonathan T. "Refractions of Daniel in the Gospel of Matthew." In *Thematic Studies*, edited by Craig A. Evans and H. Daniel Zacharias, 65–86. Vol. 1 of *Early Christian Literature and Intertextuality*. SSEJC 14. LNTS 391. London: T. & T. Clark, 2009.
Perelman, Chaïm, and L. Olbrechts-Tyteca. *The New Rhetoric: A Treatise on Argumentation*. Translated by John Wilkinson and Purcell Weaver. Notre Dame, IN: University of Notre Dame Press, 1969.
Perrin, Nicholas. "Dialogic Conceptions of Language and the Problem of Biblical Unity." In *Biblical Theology: Retrospect and Prospect*, edited by Scott J. Hafemann, 212–224. Downers Grove, IL: IVP Academic, 2002.
Petrey, Sandy. *Speech Acts and Literary Theory*. New York: Routledge, 1990.
Pfister, Manfred. "Konzepte der Intertextualität." In *Intertextualität: Formen, Funktionen, anglistische Fallstudien*, edited by Ulrich Broich and Manfred Pfister, 1–30. Konzepte der Sprach- und Literaturwissenschaft 35. Tübingen: Niemeyer, 1985.
Plett, Heinrich F. "Intertextualities." In *Intertextuality*, edited by Heinrich F. Plett, 3–29. Research in Text Theory. Berlin: de Gruyter, 1991.
———. "Sprachliche Konstituenten einer intertextuellen Poetik." In *Intertextualität: Formen, Funktionen, anglistische Fallstudien*, edited by Ulrich Broich and Manfred Pfister, 78–98. Konzepte der Sprach- und Literaturwissenschaft 35. Tübingen: Niemeyer, 1985
Polhill, John B. *Acts*. NAC 26. Nashville: Broadman, 1992.
Polk, Timothy. *The Prophetic Persona: Jeremiah and the Language of the Self*. JSOTSup 32. Sheffield: JSOT Press, 1984.

Porter, Stanley E. "Greek Grammar and Syntax." In *The Face of New Testament Studies: A Survey of Recent Research*, edited by Scot McKnight and Grant R. Osborne, 76–103. Grand Rapids: Baker Academic, 2004.

Poythress, Vern Sheridan. "Canon and Speech Act: Limitations in Speech-Act Theory, with Implications for a Putative Theory of Canonical Speech Acts." *Westminster Theological Journal* 70 (2008) 337–54.

Pratt, Mary Louise. "Ideology and Speech-Act Theory." *PT* 7 (1986) 59–72.

———. *Towards a Speech Act Theory of Literary Discourse*. Midland Books 264. Bloomington: Indiana University Press, 1977.

Price, Stuart. *Communication Studies*. Harlow, UK: Longman, 1996.

Prinsloo, W. S. "Psalm 116: Disconnected Text or Symmetrical Whole?" *Bib* 74 (1993) 71–82.

Punt, Jeremy. "Paul and Postcolonial Hermeneutics: Marginality and/in Early Biblical Interpretation." In *As It is Written: Studying Paul's Use of Scripture*, edited by Stanley E. Porter and Christopher D. Stanley, 261–90. SBLSymS 50. Atlanta: Society of Biblical Literature, 2008.

Rabinowitz, Louis I. "The Psalms in Jewish Liturgy." *Historia Judaica* 6 (1944) 109–22.

Rajan, Tilottama. "Intertextuality and the Subject of Reading/Writing." In *Influence and Intertextuality in Literary History*, edited by Jay Clayton and Eric Rothstein, 61–74. Madison: University of Wisconsin Press, 1991.

Récanati, François. "Content, Mode, and Self-Reference." In *John Searle's Philosophy of Language: Force, Meaning, and Mind*, edited by Savas L. Tsohatzidis, 49–63. Cambridge: Cambridge University Press, 2007.

———. "Open Quotation." *Mind* n.s. 110 (2001) 637–87.

Reed, Jeffrey T. "Modern Linguistics and the New Testament: A Basic Guide to Theory, Terminology, and Literature." In *Approaches to New Testament Study*, edited by Stanley E. Porter and David Tombs, 222–65. JSNTSup 120. Sheffield: Sheffield Academic, 1995.

Rees, M. A. van. "The Adequacy of Speech Act Theory for Explaining Conversational Phenomena: A Response to Some Conversation Analytical Critics." *JPrag* 17 (1992) 31–47.

Reich, Wendelin. "The Cooperative Nature of Communicative Acts." *JPrag* 43 (2011) 1349–65.

Rendtorff, Rolf. "The Psalms of David: David in the Psalms." In *The Book of Psalms: Composition and Reception*, edited by Peter W. Flint and Patrick D. Miller, Jr., 53–64. VTSup 99. FIOTL 4. Leiden: Brill, 2005.

Rese, Martin. *Alttestamentliche Motive in der Christologie des Lukas*. Studien zum Neuen Testament 1. Gütersloh: Mohn, 1969.

Ricoeur, Paul. *Figuring the Sacred: Religion, Narrative, and Imagination*. Translated by David Pellauer. Edited by Mark I. Wallace. Minneapolis: Fortress, 1995.

———. "The Hermeneutical Function of Distanciation." In *Hermeneutics and the Human Sciences: Essays on Language, Action and Interpretation*, 131–44. Translated and edited by John B. Thompson. Cambridge: Cambridge University Press, 1981.

———. *Interpretation Theory: Discourse and the Surplus of Meaning*. Fort Worth: Texas Christian University Press, 1976.

———. "Metaphor and the Central Problem of Hermeneutics." In *Hermeneutics and the Human Sciences: Essays on Language, Action and Interpretation*, 165–81. Translated and edited by John B. Thompson. Cambridge: Cambridge University Press, 1981.

———. "The Model of the Text: Meaningful Action Considered as Text." In *Hermeneutics and the Human Sciences: Essays on Language, Action and Interpretation*, 197–221. Translated and edited by John B. Thompson. Cambridge: Cambridge University Press, 1981.

———. "Phenomenology and Hermeneutics." In *Hermeneutics and the Human Sciences: Essays on Language, Action and Interpretation*, 101–28. Translated and edited by John B. Thompson. Cambridge: Cambridge University Press, 1981.

———. "A Response by Paul Ricoeur." In *Hermeneutics and the Human Sciences: Essays on Language, Action and Interpretation*, 32–40. Translated and edited by John B. Thompson. Cambridge: Cambridge University Press, 1981.

———. "What Is a Text? Explanation and Understanding." In *Hermeneutics and the Human Sciences: Essays on Language, Action and Interpretation*, 145–64. Translated and edited by John B. Thompson. Cambridge: Cambridge University Press, 1981.

Roberts, J. J. M. "The Old Testament's Contribution to Messianic Expectations." In *The Messiah: Developments in Earliest Judaism and Christianity*, edited by James H. Charlesworth, 39–51. Minneapolis: Fortress, 1992.

Rolf, Eckard. "On the Concept of Action in Illocutionary Logic." In *Speech Acts, Meaning and Intentions: Critical Approaches to the Philosophy of John R. Searle*, edited by Armin Burkhardt, 147–65. Foundations of Communication and Cognition. Berlin: de Gruyter, 1990.

———. "Perlokutionäre Akte und perlokutionäre Effekte." In *Sprache erkennen und verstehen*, edited by Klaus Detering et al., 262–71. Vol. 2 of *Akten des 16. Linguistischen Kolloquiums, Kiel, 1981*. Linguistische Arbeiten 119. Tübingen: Niemeyer, 1982.

Rorty, Richard. "The Pragmatist's Progress." In *Interpretation and Overinterpretation*, by Umberto Eco, 89–108. Edited by Stefan Collini. Cambridge: Cambridge University Press, 1992.

Roth, Ulli. *Die Grundparadigmen christlicher Schriftauslegung—im Spiegel der Auslegungsgeschichte von Psalm 110*. Berlin: LIT, 2010.

Rydelnik, Michael. *The Messianic Hope: Is the Hebrew Bible Really Messianic?* NAC Studies in Bible & Theology. Nashville: B&H Academic, 2010.

Sanborn, Scott F. Review of *Arguing with Scripture: The Rhetoric of Quotations in the Letters of Paul*, by Christopher D. Stanley. *Kerux* 23 (2008) 74–81.

Sanders, E. P. *Judaism: Practice and Belief, 63 BCE—66 CE*. Philadelphia: Trinity, 1992.

Sanders, James A. *The Psalms Scroll of Qumrân Cave 11 (11Qps^a)*. DJD 4. Oxford: Clarendon, 1965.

Savran, George W. *Telling and Retelling: Quotation in Biblical Narrative*. ISBL. Bloomington: Indiana University Press, 1988.

Sbisà, Marina. "Speech Acts in Context." *Language & Communication* 22 (2002) 421–36.

Schenck, Kenneth. "2 Corinthians and the Πίστις Χριστοῦ Debate." *CBQ* 70 (2008) 524–37.

Schiffman, Lawrence H. "Foreword: The Ancient Synagogue and the History of Judaism." In *Sacred Realm: The Emergence of the Synagogue in the Ancient World*, edited by S. Fine, xxvii–xxix. New York: Oxford University Press, 1996.

———. "Messianic Figures and Ideas in the Qumran Scrolls." In *The Messiah: Developments in Earliest Judaism and Christianity*, edited by James H. Charlesworth, 116–29. Minneapolis: Fortress, 1992.

Schneider, Michael. "How Does God Act? Intertextual Readings of I Corinthians 10." In *Reading the Bible Intertextually*, edited by Richard B. Hays et al., 35–52. Waco: Baylor University Press, 2009.
Schutz, Alfred, and Thomas Luckmann. *The Structures of the Life-World*. 2 vols. Vol. 1 translated by Richard M. Zaner and H. Tristram Engelhardt, Jr. Vol. 2 translated by Richard M. Zaner and David J. Parent. Northwestern University Studies in Phenomenology and Existential Philosophy. Evanston: Northwestern University Press, 1973, 1989.
Scott, Ian W. *Implicit Epistemology in the Letters of Paul: Story, Experience & the Spirit*. WUNT 2/205. Tübingen: Mohr Siebeck, 2006.
Scott, James M. "'For as Many as Are of Works of the Law Are under a Curse' (Galatians 3.10)." In *Paul and the Scriptures of Israel*, edited by Craig A. Evans and James A. Sanders, 187–221. JSNTSup 83. SSEJC 1. Sheffield: JSOT Press, 1993.
Searle, John R. "Austin on Locutionary and Illocutionary Acts." In *Essays on J. L. Austin*, by I. Berlin et al., 141–59. Oxford: Clarendon, 1973.
———. *Expression and Meaning: Studies in the Theory of Speech Acts*. Paperback ed. Cambridge: Cambridge University Press, 1985.
———. *Intentionality: An Essay in the Philosophy of Mind*. Cambridge Paperback Library. Cambridge: Cambridge University Press, 1983.
———. "Intentionality and Method." *Journal of Philosophy* 78 (1981) 720–33.
———. "Literary Theory and Its Discontents." *NLH* 25 (1994) 637–67.
———. *Speech Acts: An Essay in the Philosophy of Language*. Cambridge: Cambridge University Press, 1969.
———. "What Is Language: Some Preliminary Remarks." In *John Searle's Philosophy of Language: Force, Meaning, and Mind*, edited by Savas L. Tsohatzidis, 15–45. Cambridge: Cambridge University Press, 2007.
———. "What Is a Speech Act?" In *Philosophy in America*, edited by Max Black, 221–39. Muirhead Library of Philosophy. Ithaca: Cornell University Press, 1965.
Searle, John R., and Daniel Vanderveken. *Foundations of Illocutionary Logic*. Cambridge: Cambridge University Press, 1985.
Shaw, Graham. *The Cost of Authority: Manipulation and Freedom in the New Testament*. Philadelphia: Fortress, 1983.
Sherwood, Yvonne. *The Prostitute and the Prophet: Hosea's Marriage in Literary-Theoretical Perspective*. JSOTSup 212. Gender, Culture, Theory 2. Sheffield: Sheffield Academic, 1996.
Shires, Henry M. *Finding the Old Testament in the New*. Philadelphia: Westminster, 1974.
Skehan, Patrick W., et al. "Psalms." In *Psalms to Chronicles*, by Eugene Ulrich et al., 7–170. Vol. 11 of *Qumran Cave 4*. DJD 16. Oxford: Clarendon, 2000.
Skinner, Quentin. "Conventions and the Understanding of Speech Acts." *Philosophical Quarterly* 20 (1970) 118–38.
———. "Meaning and Understanding in the History of Ideas." *History and Theory* 8 (1969) 3–53.
———. "Motives, Intentions and the Interpretation of Texts." *NLH* 3 (1972) 393–408.
———. "A Reply to My Critics." In *Meaning and Context: Quentin Skinner and his Critics*, edited by James Tully, 231–88. Princeton: Princeton University Press, 1988.
Slusser, Wayne T. "The Function of Psalm 110 in the Argument of Hebrews: An Examination of the Uses of Psalm 110 Found in the Priesthood Section of Hebrews (4:14—10:18)."

(2005) 1–47. https://www.yumpu.com/en/document/view/28580303/the-function-of-psalm-110-in-the-argument-of-hebrews.
Smith, J. A. "The Ancient Synagogue, the Early Church and Singing." *Music & Letters* 65 (1984) 1–16.
Snodgrass, Klyne. "Reading to Hear: A Hermeneutics of Hearing." *Horizons in Biblical Theology* 24 (2002) 1–32.
Sperber, Dan, and Deirdre Wilson. *Relevance: Communication and Cognition.* 2nd ed. Oxford: Blackwell, 1995.
Stalnaker, Robert C. "Assertion." In *Pragmatics*, edited by Peter Cole, 315–32. Syntax and Semantics 9. New York: Academic Press, 1978.
Stanley, Christopher D. *Arguing with Scripture: The Rhetoric of Quotations in the Letters of Paul.* New York: T. & T. Clark, 2004.
———. *Paul and the Language of Scripture: Citation Technique in the Pauline Epistles and Contemporary Literature.* SNTSMS 69. Cambridge: Cambridge University Press, 1992.
———. "Paul's 'Use' of Scripture: Why the Audience Matters." In *As It is Written: Studying Paul's Use of Scripture*, edited by Stanley E. Porter and Christopher D. Stanley, 125–55. SBLSymS 50. Atlanta: Society of Biblical Literature, 2008.
———. "'Pearls before Swine': Did Paul's Audiences Understand His Biblical Quotations?" *NovT* 41 (1999) 124–44.
———. Review of *Heralds of the Good News: Isaiah and Paul "In Concert" in the Letter to the Romans*, by J. Ross Wagner. *JBL* 124 (2005) 778–82.
Starcky, J. "Les quatre étapes du messianism à Qumran." *RB* 70 (1963) 481–504.
Stegman, Thomas D. "'Ἐπίστευσα, διὸ ἐλάλησα (2 Corinthians 4:13): Paul's Christological Reading of Psalm 115:1a LXX." *CBQ* 69 (2007) 725–45.
Stein, Robert H. *Mark.* Baker Exegetical Commentary on the New Testament. Grand Rapids: Baker Academic, 2008.
Steiner, George. "'Critic'/'Reader.'" *NLH* 10 (1979) 423–52.
Steinmann, Martin, Jr. "Perlocutionary Acts and the Interpretation of Literature." *Centrum* 3 (1975) 112–16.
———. "Speech-Act Theory and Writing." In *What Writers Know: The Language, Process, and Structure of Written Discourse*, edited by Martin Nystrand, 291–323. New York: Academic Press, 1982.
Sternberg, Meir. *The Poetics of Biblical Narrative: Ideological Literature and the Drama of Reading.* First Midland Book ed. ISBL. Bloomington: Indiana University Press, 1987.
———. "Proteus in Quotation-Land: Mimesis and the Forms of Reported Discourse." *PT* 3 (1982) 107–56.
Still, Judith, and Michael Worton. "Introduction." In *Intertextuality: Theories and Practices*, edited by Michael Worton and Judith Still, 1–44. Manchester: Manchester University Press, 1990.
Strack, Hermann L., and Paul Billerbeck. *Kommentar zum Neuen Testament aus Talmud und Midrasch.* 6 vols. Munich: Beck, 1922–1961.
Strauss, Mark L. *The Davidic Messiah in Luke-Acts: The Promise and its Fulfillment in Lukan Christology.* JSNTSup 110. Sheffield: Sheffield Academic, 1995.
Strom, Mark. *Reframing Paul: Conversations in Grace and Community.* Downers Grove, IL: InterVarsity, 2000.
Stroup, George W. *The Promise of Narrative Theology: Recovering the Gospel in the Church.* Atlanta: John Knox, 1981.

BIBLIOGRAPHY

Stuhlmacher, Peter. *Historical Criticism and Theological Interpretation of Scripture: Towards a Hermeneutics of Consent*. Translated by Roy A. Harrisville. 1977. Reprint, Eugene, OR: Wipf & Stock, 2003.

Swanson, Dwight D. "Qumran and the Psalms." In *Interpreting the Psalms: Issues and Approaches*, edited by David Firth and Philip S. Johnston, 247–61. Downers Grove, IL: IVP Academic, 2005.

Swartley, Willard M. *Israel's Scripture Traditions and the Synoptic Gospels: Story Shaping Story*. Peabody, MA: Hendrickson, 1994.

Talmon, S. "The Concept of *Māšiaḥ* and Messianism in Early Judaism." In *The Messiah: Developments in Earliest Judaism and Christianity*, edited by James H. Charlesworth, 79–115. Minneapolis: Fortress, 1992.

Tannen, Deborah. *Talking Voices: Repetition, Dialogue, and Imagery in Conversational Discourse*. 2nd ed. Studies in Interactional Sociolinguistics 25. Cambridge: Cambridge University Press, 2007.

———. "What's in a Frame? Surface Evidence for Underlying Expectations." In *Framing in Discourse*, edited by Deborah Tannen, 14–56. New York: Oxford University Press, 1993.

Tanner, Beth LaNeel. *The Book of Psalms Through the Lens of Intertextuality*. Studies in Biblical Literature 26. New York: Lang, 2001.

Tanner, Cullen. "Climbing the Lampstand-Witness-Trees: Revelation's Use of Zechariah 4 in Light of Speech Act Theory." *Journal of Pentecostal Theology* 20 (2011) 81–92.

Tasker, R. V. G. *The Gospel According to St. Matthew: An Introduction and Commentary*. TNTC. Grand Rapids: Eerdmans, 1961.

Tate, Marvin E. *Psalms 51–100*. WBC 20. Dallas: Word, 1990.

Terrien, Samuel. *The Psalms: Strophic Structure and Theological Commentary*. Eerdmans Critical Commentary. Grand Rapids: Eerdmans, 2003.

Tharel, Nathan C. "The Use of Psalm 110:1 in Acts 2:34–35." ThM diss., Dallas Theological Seminary, 2008.

Thiselton, Anthony C. "Communicative Interaction and Promise in Interdisciplinary, Biblical, and Theological Hermeneutics." In *The Promise of Hermeneutics*, by Roger Lundin et al., 133–239. Grand Rapids: Eerdmans, 1999.

———. *The First Epistle to the Corinthians: A Commentary on the Greek Text*. NIGTC. Grand Rapids: Eerdmans, 2000.

———. *New Horizons in Hermeneutics: The Theory and Practice of Transforming Biblical Reading*. Grand Rapids: Zondervan, 1992.

———. "Reader-Response Hermeneutics, Action Models, and the Parables of Jesus." In *The Responsibility of Hermeneutics*, by Roger Lundin et al., 79–113. Grand Rapids: Eerdmans, 1985.

Thrall, Margaret. E. *Introduction and Commentary on II Corinthians I-VII*. Vol. 1 of *A Critical and Exegetical Commentary on the Second Epistle to the Corinthians*. International Critical Commentary. Edinburgh: T. & T. Clark, 1994.

Tilley, Terrence W. *The Evils of Theodicy*. Washington, DC: Georgetown University Press, 1991.

Tournay, Raymond Jacques. "Le Psaume cx." *RB* 67 (1960) 5–41.

———. *Seeing and Hearing God with the Psalms: The Prophetic Liturgy of the Second Temple in Jerusalem*. Translated by J. Edward Crowley. JSOTSup 118. Sheffield: JSOT Press, 1991.

Tov, Emanuel. "The Septuagint." In *Mikra: Text, Translation, Reading and Interpretation of the Hebrew Bible in Ancient Judaism and Early Christianity*, edited by Martin Jan Mulder, 161–88. Vol. 1 of *The Literature of the Jewish People in the Period of the Second Temple and the Talmud*. CRINT 2. Philadelphia: Fortress, 1988.

Tovey, Derek. *Narrative Art and Act in the Fourth Gospel*. JSNTSup 151. Sheffield: Sheffield Academic, 1997.

Tsohatzidis, Savas L. "The Gap between Speech Acts and Mental States." In *Foundations of Speech Act Theory: Philosophical and Linguistic Perspectives*, edited by Savas L. Tsohatzidis, 220–33. London: Routledge, 1994.

Turner, Max. "Historical Criticism and Theological Hermeneutics of the New Testament." In *Between Two Horizons: Spanning New Testament Studies and Systematic Theology*, edited by Joel B. Green and Max Turner, *Between Two Horizons*, 44–70. Grand Rapids: Eerdmans, 2000.

———. *Power from on High: The Spirit in Israel's Restoration and Witness in Luke-Acts*. Journal of Pentecostal Theology Supplement Series 9. Sheffield: Sheffield Academic, 1996.

———. "The Spirit of Christ and 'Divine' Christology." In *Jesus of Nazareth: Lord and Christ: Essays on the Historical Jesus and New Testament Christology*, edited by Joel B. Green and Max Turner, 413–36. Grand Rapids: Eerdmans, 1994.

VanderKam, James C. *The Dead Sea Scrolls and the Bible*. Grand Rapids: Eerdmans, 2012.

Vanderveken, Daniel. *Meaning and Speech Acts*. Vol. 1 of *Principles of Language Use*. Cambridge: Cambridge University Press, 1990.

———. "Universal Grammar and Speech Act Theory." In *Essays in Speech Act Theory*, edited by Daniel Vanderveken and Susumu Kubo, 25–62. Pragmatics & Beyond n.s. 77. Amsterdam: Benjamins, 2002.

Vanhoozer, Kevin J. "Discourse on Matter: Hermeneutics and the 'Miracle' of Understanding." In *Hermeneutics at the Crossroads* edited by Kevin J. Vanhoozer et al., 3–34. ISPR. Bloomington: Indiana University Press, 2006.

———. *First Theology: God, Scripture & Hermeneutics*. Downers Grove, IL: IVP Academic, 2002.

———. "From Speech Acts to Scripture Acts: The Covenant of Discourse and the Discourse of the Covenant." In *After Pentecost: Language and Biblical Interpretation*, edited by Craig Bartholomew et al., 1–49. Scripture and Hermeneutics Series 2. Grand Rapids: Zondervan, 2001.

———. "Imprisoned or Free? Text, Status, and Theological Interpretation in the Master/Slave Discourse of Philemon." In *Reading Scripture with the Church: Toward a Hermeneutic for Theological Interpretation,* by A. K. M. Adam et al., 51–93. Grand Rapids: Baker Academic, 2006.

———. *Is There a Meaning in This Text?: The Bible, the Reader, and the Morality of Literary Knowledge*. Grand Rapids: Zondervan, 1998.

———. "The Reader in New Testament Interpretation." In *Hearing the New Testament: Strategies for Interpretation*, edited by Joel B. Green, 259–88. 2nd ed. Grand Rapids: Eerdmans, 2010.

Verschueren, Jef. "Lexical Decomposition, Perlocutions, and Meaning Postulates." *PiL* 8 (1975) 347–64.

Villiers, Gerda de. "Reflections on Creation and Humankind in Psalm 8, the Septuagint and Hebrews." In *Psalms and Hebrews: Studies in Reception*, edited by Dirk J. Human and Gert Jacobus Steyn, 69–82. T&T Clark Library of Biblical Studies. New York: T. & T. Clark, 2010.

Völzing, Paul-Ludwig "Gebrauchstexte, Linguistik und perlokutive Akte." In *Gebrauchsliteratur: Methodische Überlegungen und Beispielanalysen*, edited by Ludwig Fischer et al., 99–113. Stuttgart: Metzler, 1976.

Vorster, J. N. "Toward an Interactional Model for the Analysis of Letters." *Neotestamentica* 24 (1990) 107–30.

Wagner, Andreas. "Der Lobaufruf im israelitischen Hymnus als indirekter Sprechakt." In *Studien zur hebräischen Grammatik*, edited by Andreas Wagner, 143–54. Orbis Biblicus et Orientalis 156. Freiburg: Universitätsverlag, 1997.

———. "Die Stellung der Sprachakttheorie in Hebraistik und Exegese." In *Congress Volume: Basel 2001*, edited by André Lemaire, 55–83. VTSup 92. Leiden: Brill, 2002.

Wagner, J. Ross. *Heralds of the Good News: Isaiah and Paul "In Concert" in the Letter to the Romans*. NovTSup 101. Leiden: Brill, 2002.

———. "Psalm 118 in Luke–Acts: Tracing a Narrative Thread." In *Early Christian Interpretation of the Scriptures of Israel: Investigations and Proposals*, edited by Craig A. Evans and James A. Sanders, 154–78. JSNTSup 148. SSEJC 5. Sheffield: Sheffield Academic, 1997.

Walhout, Clarence. "Narrative Hermeneutics." In *The Promise of Hermeneutics*, by Roger Lundin et al., 65–131. Grand Rapids: Eerdmans, 1999.

———. "Texts and Actions." In *The Responsibility of Hermeneutics*, by Roger Lundin et al., 31–77. Grand Rapids: Eerdmans, 1985.

Wallace, Daniel B. *Greek Grammar Beyond the Basics: An Exegetical Syntax of the New Testament*. Grand Rapids: Zondervan, 1996.

Wallis, Wilber B. "The Use of Psalms 8 and 110 in I Corinthians 15:25–27 and Hebrews 1 and 2." *JETS* 15 (1972) 25–29.

Waltke, Bruce K. "Christ in the Psalms." In *The Hope Fulfilled: Essays in Honor of O. Palmer Robertson*, edited by Robert L. Penny, 26–46. Phillipsburg, NJ: P & R, 2008.

Waltke, Bruce K., and M. O'Connor. *An Introduction to Biblical Hebrew Syntax*. Winona Lake, IN: Eisenbrauns, 1990.

Ward, Timothy. *Word and Supplement: Speech Acts, Biblical Texts, and the Sufficiency of Scripture*. Oxford: Oxford University Press, 2002.

Watson, Francis. *Paul and the Hermeneutics of Faith*. London: T. & T. Clark, 2004.

———. *Text and Truth: Redefining Biblical Theology*. Grand Rapids: Eerdmans, 1997.

Watts, James W. *Psalm and Story: Inset Hymns in Hebrew Narrative*. JSOTSup 139. Sheffield: JSOT Press, 1992.

Watts, Rikki E. "In Need of a Second Touch? Why Paul's Readers Are Not Pigs on Legs: A Rejoinder to Chris Stanley's 'Pearls before Swine' and Other Related Works." Paper presented at the Annual Meeting of the Society of Biblical Literature, New Orleans, LA, November, 2009.

———. *Isaiah's New Exodus in Mark*. Rev. ed. 1997. Reprint, BSL. Grand Rapids: Baker Academic, 2000.

———. "The Lord's House and David's Lord: The Psalms and Mark's Perspective on Jesus and the Temple." *BibInt* 15 (2007) 307–22.

———. "The Psalms in Mark's Gospel." In *The Psalms in the New Testament*, edited by Steve Moyise and Maarten J. J. Menken, 25–45. NTSI. London: T. & T. Clark, 2004.

———. Review of *Acts and the Isaianic New Exodus*, by David W. Pao. *Journal of Theological Studies* n.s. 55 (2004) 258–61.

Weiser, Artur. *The Psalms: A Commentary*. Translated by Herbert Hartwell. Old Testament Library. Philadelphia: Westminster, 1962.
Wendland, Ernst R. *Analyzing the Psalms: With Exercises for Bible Students and Translators*. 2nd ed. Dallas: SIL International, 2002.
———. "Continuity and Discontinuity in Hebrew Poetic Design: Patterns and Points of Significance in the Structure and Setting of Psalm 30." In *Discourse Perspectives on Hebrew Poetry in the Scriptures*, edited by Ernst R. Wendland, 28–66. UBS Monograph Series 7. Reading, UK: United Bible Societies, 1994.
Westermann, Claus. *Praise and Lament in the Psalms*. Translated by Keith R. Krim and Richard N. Soulen. Atlanta: John Knox, 1981.
Westfall, Cynthia Long. *A Discourse Analysis of the Letter to the Hebrews: The Relationship between Form and Meaning*. LNTS 297. London: T. & T. Clark, 2005.
White, Hugh C. "Introduction: Speech Act Theory and Literary Criticism." *Semeia* 41 (1988) 1–24.
Whitlock, Jonathan M. Review of *Paul and His Story: (Re)Interpreting the Exodus Tradition*, by Sylvia C. Keesmaat. *Review of Biblical Literature* (2001). https://www.sblcentral.org/API/Reviews/444_351.pdf.
Wicker, Brian. *The Story-Shaped World: Fiction and Metaphysics: Some Variations on a Theme*. Notre Dame, IN: University of Notre Dame Press, 1975.
Wierzbicka, Anna. "The Semantics of Direct and Indirect Discourse." *PiL* 7 (1974) 267–307.
Wilk, Florian. "Paul as User, Interpreter, and Reader of the Book of Isaiah." In *Reading the Bible Intertextually*, edited by Richard B. Hays et al., 83–99. Waco: Baylor University Press, 2009.
———. Review of *Heralds of the Good News: Isaiah and Paul "In Concert" in the Letter to the Romans*, by J. Ross Wagner. *Theologische Literaturzeitung* 130 (2005) 49–51.
Williams, David John. *Acts*. New International Biblical Commentary 5. Peabody, MA: Hendrickson, 1990.
Williams, H. H. Drake, III. "The Psalms in 1 and 2 Corinthians." In *The Psalms in the New Testament*, edited by Steve Moyise and Maarten J. J. Menken, 163–80. NTSI. London: T. & T. Clark, 2004.
Wilson, Deirdre, and Dan Sperber. "Relevance Theory." In *The Handbook of Pragmatics*, edited by Laurence R. Horn and Gregory Ward, 607–32. Blackwell Handbooks in Linguistics 16. Malden, MA: Blackwell, 2004.
Wimsatt, W. K. Jr., and Monroe C. Beardsley. "The Intentional Fallacy." In *The Verbal Icon: Studies in the Meaning of Poetry*, by W. K. Wimsatt, Jr., 3–18. University Paperback ed. London: Methuen, 1970.
Wire, Antoinette Clark. *The Corinthian Women Prophets: A Reconstruction through Paul's Rhetoric*. Minneapolis: Fortress, 1990.
Witherington, Ben, III. *Conflict and Community in Corinth: A Socio-Rhetorical Commentary on 1 and 2 Corinthians*. Grand Rapids: Eerdmans, 1995.
———. *The Gospel of Mark: A Socio-Rhetorical Commentary*. Grand Rapids: Eerdmans, 2001.
———. *Paul's Narrative Thought World: The Tapestry of Tragedy and Triumph*. Louisville: Westminster John Knox, 1994.
Wolterstorff, Nicholas. *Art in Action: Toward a Christian Aesthetic*. Grand Rapids: Eerdmans, 1980.

———. *Divine Discourse: Philosophical Reflections on the Claim that God Speaks.* Cambridge: Cambridge University Press, 1995.

———. "Resuscitating the Author." In *Hermeneutics at the Crossroads,* edited by Kevin J. Vanhoozer et al., 35–50. ISPR. Bloomington: Indiana University Press, 2006.

———. *Works and Worlds of Art.* Clarendon Library of Logic and Philosophy. Oxford: Clarendon, 1980.

Wright, N. T. "Faith, Virtue, Justification, and the Journey to Freedom." In *The Word Leaps the Gap: Essays on Scripture and Theology in Honor of Richard B. Hays,* edited by J. Ross Wagner et al., 472–97. Grand Rapids: Eerdmans, 2008.

———. *Jesus and the Victory of God.* Christian Origins and the Question of God 2. Minneapolis: Fortress, 1996.

———. *The New Testament and the People of God.* Christian Origins and the Question of God 1. Minneapolis: Fortress, 1992.

———. "On Becoming the Righteousness of God: 2 Corinthians 5:21." In *1 & 2 Corinthians,* edited by David M. Hay, 200–208. Vol. 2 of *Pauline Theology.* SBLSymS 22. Minneapolis: Fortress, 1993.

Wright, Robert B. "Introduction." In *The Psalms of Solomon: A Critical Edition of the Greek Text,* edited by Robert B. Wright, 1–13. Jewish and Christian Texts in Context and Related Studies 1. New York: T. & T. Clark, 2007.

Wunderlich, Dieter. "Methodological Remarks on Speech Act Theory." In *Speech Act Theory and Pragmatics,* edited by John R. Searle et al., 291–312. Synthese Language Library. Dordrecht: Reidel, 1980.

Young, Frances, and David F. Ford. *Meaning and Truth in 2 Corinthians.* Biblical Foundations in Theology. Grand Rapids: Eerdmans, 1988.

Yule, George. *Pragmatics.* Oxford Introductions to Language Study. Oxford: Oxford University Press, 1996.

www.ingramcontent.com/pod-product-compliance
Lightning Source LLC
Chambersburg PA
CBHW061433300426
44114CB00014B/1663